Land, Lust &
Gun Smoke

LAND, LUST & GUN SMOKE

A SOCIAL HISTORY OF GAME SHOOTS IN IRELAND

PETER BACON

The
History
Press
Ireland

For my grandchildren Emily-Kate and Oliver, that they may experience in their lifetimes the joy of the countryside I have enjoyed in mine

First published 2012

The History Press Ireland
119 Lower Baggot Street
Dublin 2
Ireland
www.thehistorypress.ie

British Library Cataloguing in Publication Data.
A catalogue record for this book is available from the British Library.

ISBN 978 1 84588 717 9

Typesetting and origination by The History Press

CONTENTS

ACKNOWLEDGEMENTS

I would like to begin with thanks to shooting companions Adrian Bourke and Michael Lennon for awakening an interest in the social life and shooting histories of 'Big Houses' in Ireland. However, it would not have been possible to write this book without the most generous co-operation of the many people who provided me with access to Game Books, Game Registers and Game Records in their possession relating to their families' shooting histories. In this regard I wish to acknowledge my debt of gratitude to Mary-Rose Barrington-Manuel, Alexander Bayly, Edward Bayly, Dominic Berridge, Patrick Bradish, Viscount Brookeborough, the Hon. Garech de Brun, Hugh Cobbe, Charles Cooper, Edward Cooper, Fiach Dowling and family, Countess of Dunraven and Mount Earl, Christine Fiske, Tom Fiske, Ivor and Susan Fitzpatrick, Col. Sir Robert and Lady Sheelagh Goff, Lord Anthony Hamilton, the Marquess of Hamilton, John and Radine Hamilton, Caroline Hamilton, Brendan Hanrahan, Brigadier Francis Henn, CBE, Charlie Hernon, Henry Horsman, Jack Kelly, Michael May, Dr Willie Irwin, Ben Jellett, John Jobson, Susan Kellett, Beatrice Macdonald, the Earl of Meath, Drummond Nelson, James and Sylvia O'Connor and James O'Connor Jnr, Donal and Durcan O'Hara, Alexander Robert (Sandy) and Roderick Perceval, Susan Quinn-Jones, Paul Smithwick, George H. Stacpoole, Patrick Stacpoole, Andrew Stainer, Donald Walshe, Hugh and Grainne Weir, Paul Wood, and Richard Wood-Martin.

In relation to the reclamation and shooting history of Wexford harbour, including its land ownership, I wish to acknowledge the assistance of members of the Bent family and especially Declan Bent, Mayler Collotton, Larry Duggan Snr and Larry Duggan Jnr, Ger Foley, Tom Hassett, Brian Murphy, Philip Stafford, Alyn Walsh, and Stanley Warren.

The following individuals provided me with information, contacts, leads or insights into the history of particular families or shooting relationships, for which I am grateful and of which I hope I have made good use: Simon Ashe, John Byrne, Thomas Crozier, Martin Crozier, Prof. Terence Dooley, Nigel Everett, Rodney Freeburn, George Gossip, Bridie Heffernan, Julian Jameson, Des Lally, Joe MacGowan, John MacTernan, Paddy Melvin, Harry Nash, Pat Power, Nicholas Prins, Michael Purser, Tim Robinson, Niall Rochford, Dr Sean Ryan, Dr David Trotmann, Edward Walsh, SC, Nicky Wright.

I would like to thank the following individuals and the organisations which they represent for the information and assistance provided to me in the course of the research: Vincent Flannelly, Irish Red Grouse Association; Dolores Gaffney, Kilkenny Castle; Michael Lynch, Archivist, Kerry Library, County Galway; Mike Maguire, Granary Library, Limerick; Gavin McMahon and colleagues of the Public Records Office of Northern Ireland; Collete O'Daly and Glenn Dunne of the National Library of Ireland; Patricia O'Hare, Muckross House Library; Fr

Mark Tierney and Fr Brian Murphy, Glenstal Abbey; Walter Phelan, curator, Irish Fly-Fishing and Game Shooting Museum, Attanagh, County Laois; Larry Taaffe of the National Woodcock Association of Ireland. I am grateful also to historian Dr Brian Casey for reading and providing comments on an earlier draft.

To anyone I have unwittingly omitted I apologise.

The majority of text quotations are acknowledged in the corresponding endnotes. In addition, grateful acknowledgement is made for permission to reproduce from the publishers involved.

I would like to thank my shooting companions at the North Slob Shooting Syndicate, the Shelton Abbey Shooting Syndicate, and those with whom I have shared many days shooting in the west of Ireland, for their unflinching camaraderie, ground-levelling wit and outright scepticism!

Finally, but by no means least, to Jacqueline for the support and encouragement she has offered during this and many other projects undertaken in the past thirty-five or so years, and for her companionship in the field.

PHOTOGRAPHIC ACKNOWLEDGEMENTS

I wish to record my gratitude to Ger Lawlor, Principal, Ger Lawlor Photography, for his contribution to this book through his skill and dedication to achieving the best-quality images, often from tired and faded originals. In addition, I wish to record the following credits:

Simon Ashe: 058 Ballynahinch Castle. Tarquin Blake: 074 Lough Cutra Castle. Eyre and Spottiswoode (Publishers): 010 Woodcock, Philip Rickman; 089 The Pheasant, Philip Rickman. Patricia Cooper: 044 Markree Castle. David Davison, The Irish Picture Library: 014 Lord Ardilaun at work; 016 The Royal Party at the Lunch Pavilion; 020 Lord Ardilaun with beaters; 021 Gamekeeper with game stick, Ashford Castle. Getty Images: 009 Women shooting at Mount Juilliet, County Kilkenny. Colonel Sir Robert and Lady Sheelagh Goff: 092 Michael Branigan, Gamekeeper, Powerscourt, Charles Gray, RHA (1808-1892). Tatiana Hamilton: 061 Baronscourt, County Tyrone. Lissadell Collection: 045 Lissadell House. Joe MacGowan, Sligo Heritage: 052 Classiebawn. Office of Public Works, Kilkenny Castle: 001 Mixing it – Members of the Irish Aristocracy at a royal shoot at Sandringham, *c.* 1904. Valerie O'Sullivan: 082 Glenstal Abbey, County Limerick. The Trustees of Muckross House (Killarney) Ltd: 086 Muckross House. The Board of the National Library of Ireland: 071 Returning to Clonbrock House after a morning's Grouse shooting. Clonbrock Collection: 072 Shooting party hosted by Dillons, Clonbrock. Clonbrock Collection, 073 Beaters at Castlegar, Clonbrock Collection. David Waters, Woodland Gallery and author of *Archibald Thorburn: Artist and Illustrator, The Prints and Proofs, 1889-1934*: 011 *Snipe in the Reeds*, Archibald Thorburn; 012 *Spring Grouse* (detail); 090 *Grey Partridge*, Archibald Thorburn; 094 *Unapproachable Geese*, Archibald Thorburn; 096 *Wigeon and Teal*, Archibald Thorburn; 097 *Lapwing and Golden Plover*, 1903, Archibald Thorburn. PRONI: 046 Sir Robert Gore-Booth's Game Book, 1840; 047 Sir Henry Gore-Booth with Woodcock Bag; 048 Lissadell Game Book: Ringing recovery record, 049 Sir Mark Beresford Russell Sturgis (1884-1949) and Revd Flethcher Sheridan Le Fanu (1860-1939) at Lissadell; 050 Shooting party, Lissadell: From left: Brian Gore-Booth (1912-1940), Gabrielle Gore-Booth (1918-1973), Unknown, Angus Gore-Booth (1920-1996), Hugh Gore-Booth (1910-1943) – in a bomber jacket; unknown; Rosaleen Gore-Booth (1914-1991), Unknown, The Keeper; 051 A bag of Barnacle Geese: Angus Gore-Booth (1920-1996), with the keeper on his right; 053 Wilfrid William Ashley, 1st Baron Mount Temple (1867-1939) at Lissadell House.

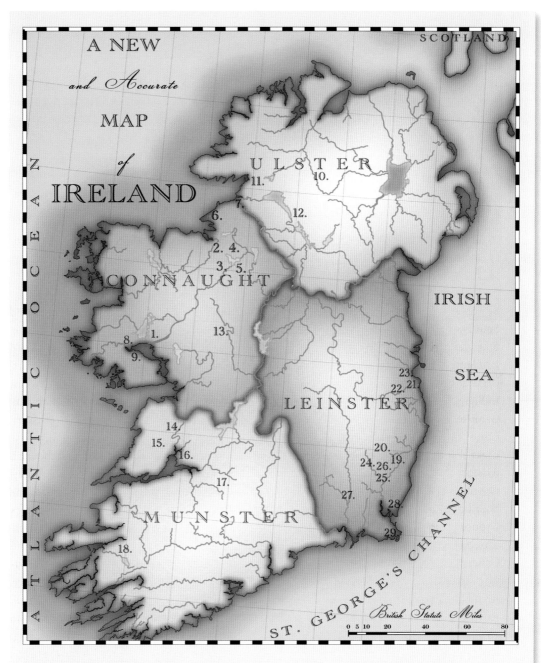

A NEW and Accurate MAP of IRELAND

ATLANTIC OCEAN

SCOTLAND

ULSTER

CONNAUGHT

LEINSTER

MUNSTER

IRISH SEA

ST. GEORGE'S CHANNEL

British Statute Miles
0 5 10 20 40 60 80

Map showing the location of estates mentioned in the book.

1 The Ashford Estate, Cong, Co. Galway
2 Annaghmore Manor House & Coopershill, Colloney, Co. Sligo
3 Temple House, Ballymore, Co. Sligo
4 Hazelwood House, Hazelwood, Co. Sligo
5 Markree Castle, Callooney, Co. Sligo
6 Lissadell, Drumclif. Co. Sligo
7 Classiebawn Castle, Mullaghmore, Co. Sligo
8 Ballynahinch Castle, Ballynahinch, Co. Galway
9 Screebe Lodge, Screebe, Co. Galway
10 Baronscourt, Newtonsteward, Co. Tyrone
11 Brown Hall, Ballintra, Co. Donegal
12 Colebrooke Park, Colebrooke, Co. Fermanagh
13 Castlegar, Ahascragh, Co. Galway
14 Lough Cutra Castle, Gort, Co. Galway
15 Eden Vale, Ennis, Co. Clare

16 Dromoland, Newmarket-on-Fergus, Co. Clare
17 Glenstal Abbey, Murroe, Co. Limerick
18 Muckross Abbey, Killarney, Co. Kerry
   (Inc. Estate of the Earl of Kenmare)
19 Glenart, Woodenbridge, Co. Wicklow
20 Ballinacor, Rathdrum, Co. Wicklow
21 Kilruddery, Bray, Co. Wicklow
22 Lough Bray, Glencree & Luggala, Roundwood, Co. Wicklow
23 Glenasmole Lodge & Glencullen, Co. Dublin
24 Ballyarthur, Woodenbridge, Co. Wicklow
25 Shelton Abbey, Avoca, Co. Wicklow
26 Castle Howard, Avoca, Co. Wicklow
27 Coollattin, Shillelagh, Co. Wicklow
28 North Sloblands, Co. Wexford
29 South Sloblands, Co. Wexford

Contact Details of Shoots

Annaghmore Manor House, Collooney,
County Sligo
Durcan O'Hara

Temple House, Ballymote, County Sligo
www.templehouse.ie
Roderick Perceval

Markree Castle, Collooney, County Sligo
www.markreecastle.ie
Charles Cooper

Ballynahinch Castle, Ballynahinch, County
Galway
www.ballynahinch-castle.com
Simon Ashe

Screebe Lodge, Screebe, County Galway
www.Screebe.com
Paul Wood

Baronscourt, Newtownstewart, County
Tyrone
www.barons-court.com
Marquess of Hamilton

Brown Hall, Ballintra, County Donegal
John Hamilton

Colebrooke Park, Brookeborough, County
Fermanagh
www.colebrooke.info

Lough Cutra Castle, Gort, County Galway
www.Loughcutra.com
Don Walshe

Dromoland Castle, Newmarket on Fergus,
County Clare
www.dromoland.ie
Don Walshe

Ballinacor, Rathdrum, County Wicklow
Sir Robert Goff

Kilruddery Bray, County Wicklow
www.kilruddery.com
Earl of Meath

Ballyarthur, Woodenbridge, County Wicklow
Alex Bayly

Shelton Abbey, Avoca, County Wicklow
Harry Nash

Castle Howard, Avoca, County Wicklow
Gerry Merrick

Coollattin, Shillelagh, County Wicklow
Fiach Dowling

North Slob, Curracloe, County Wexford
Tom Fiske

South Slob, County Wexford
Turlough Coffey

Foreword by Edward Guinness, 4ᵀᴴ Earl of Iveagh

It's not often that you get asked to foreword a treasure!

Herein unearthed is a much overlooked element of Ireland in evidence since early in the nineteenth century. Written by one of our country's leading game-sports enthusiasts, *Land, Lust and Gun Smoke* brings the many diverse elements of shooting together, following a huge effort of painstaking research. The author's passion for shooting makes these pages come alive, and the attention to detail afforded to individual shoots places the reader in as close proximity to the participants as can be, so much so that you can almost smell the gunpowder as you turn these pages.

It is ground-breaking for the island of Ireland to have the records of so many a leading shoot distilled as one and intertwined with such loving care. *Land, Lust and Gun Smoke*'s illustrations, photographs and assembled vignettes not only create a beautiful work in their own right; the illustrations bring a feast of the eyes as much as these recreational pursuits bring a feast to our tables.

The author's authoritative knowledge is uniquely placed to interpret that of a bygone age, clearly linking the past with that of the present. Many thanks must go to Peter Bacon for putting together this seminal work and to all those custodians of private and public collections who have granted access to a treasure trove of material. It must be said that the background network of the Countryside Alliance in Ireland has proven invaluable to the project, and each copy of this book contributes to this very worthwhile charity.

There's no doubt that *Land, Lust and Gun Smoke* will contribute significantly to our society's understanding of shooting, past and present, and thus to the preservation of a proud and notable tradition in our rural areas, nurturing a social network, reconnecting people with their land, keeping our rural communities alive and their livelihoods reassured.

Lord Iveagh,
Elveden

INTRODUCTION

A number of factors influenced me to sit down and write this book. Perhaps the most important one came about in May 2010, when, sitting on a boat on Lough Mask, County Mayo on a bad 'mayfly' fishing day, a close friend pointed across to the shore to tell me, 'That's where the record shoot for Woodcock was established many years ago and still holds to the present day.' I can recall clearly the questions that came into my mind. When exactly was that? Who was there? Where had they come from? What did they do afterwards? And most importantly *what was it like to be there*? These questions became mixed with others that have held something of a fascination for me for many years. Every year, when Wigeon and other migratory species of duck and the evocative White-fronted geese return to the North Slob in County Wexford, with an annual rhythm predictable to within days, I have reflected on the changes in life and in the world around me since the previous time their distinctive calls enlivened the autumn dawns. And yet the Slobs are not a natural phenomenon; they are the result of reclamations that were made only a century and a half ago. A controversial, pioneering and bold investment in its day gave rise to a unique wetlands habitat that has been managed to support shooting in a sustainable way. In this way, it has come to be an internationally important wintering ground for many species of wintering wildfowl – especially the Greenland White-fronted goose – to the present day. Development, shooting and other conservation interests can be friends, and here is a great example, the story behind which, I believe, is worth telling and recording. This raises the broader issue of what has been referred to as a:

> … strange, paradoxical relationship between shooting game birds and the conservation or stewardship of diverse and beautiful natural habitat. It must be equally difficult to comprehend the possibility of someone enjoying shooting while at the same time having a great love and intimate knowledge of nature and wildlife in general … Gradually we are becoming aware, but only little by little, that by our actions we have been unnecessarily upsetting the natural rhythms and harmony by which this oasis in the universe has been governed for so long – and for very good reasons. Perhaps this painful and growing awareness will lead to a re-discovery of the importance of 'stewardship' of the land, by which it is understood that each generation has a duty to pass on some piece of countryside in a better condition, if possible, than it was originally found, rather than exploit it entirely for our own advantage.[1]

Lack of connectivity between everyday life and nature, in my opinion, has been the key factor behind the 'upsetting of those natural rhythms'; urbanisation has made that connectivity difficult to maintain. A consequence has been misunderstanding of game shooting and field sports generally and worse, prejudice, that shooting game birds is 'wrong'. However, there is truth also in the view that a 'rediscovery' is underway of the importance of living sustainably with nature; the new appreciation of seasonal and locally produced foods, the proliferation of country markets, including in the most urban areas, are surely testimony that people do wish for a way of life that embraces nature's natural rhythm rather than pillages its limited bounty.

Most people involved in game shooting are conservation-minded individuals, who seek to maintain and sustain the wildlife they hunt and shoot, and for the most part the relationship between shooter and quarry is one of respect, if not outright love, of nature. However, the hand of politics and social change have played a pivotal role in shaping attitudes to game shooting in Ireland and in the way that it is organised, which is uniquely different from Great Britain. In Ireland today, organised game shooting is a marginal sporting activity compared with, say, the recreational sport of golf. This is not so in Great Britain today, nor was it always the case here. In former times, organised game shoots were one of the most popular forms of big-house entertainment. In fact, what has struck me most while carrying out the research for this book was just how widespread the sport of game shooting was; almost every estate in the country had a shoot. What is more, the bag records relating to them and social features like attendance were written down meticulously in Game Books at the time. With the demise of landed estates in Ireland, from about 1880 much of the cultural tradition and social networking associated with organised shooting was lost, although there are striking examples, too, of continuity, adaptation, change and indeed renewal, especially from the 1960s, as the economic strength of the professional middle class increased. I consider it to have been my privilege to be a first-hand witness to the contents of these records, which have been lovingly preserved, for the most part, by the descendants of those families to whom they relate.

The landed gentry were an important and colourful feature of life in Ireland well into the first half of the twentieth century. Their lifestyles and pursuit of recreational field sports such as hunting, shooting, fishing and other equestrian sports like horse racing and show-jumping, are an important legacy of their time. Furthermore, the social occasions provided by hunts, shoots and the associated house parties, served a number of functions of a more serious nature than sport, conviviality and carousing. For example, they provided the opportunity for members of younger generations to meet suitable marriage partners, ensuring continuity and strengthening of family alliances and economic ties. They also were a means by which natural habitats were preserved. Many point out that the preservation was for their exclusive use and to the exclusion of the majority of ordinary citizens. This is true. However, the habitats were preserved ultimately for the benefit of the wildlife which depended upon it.

Now, conservation of important and threatened habitats is most frequently achieved by agencies of government and other public bodies, most usually through a framework of EU Directives. A difficulty with this approach is that it tends to establish 'museum' sites. To be fair, there is usually provision of some sort for public access or participation, but this certainly falls short of the kind of 'living' connectivity between people and nature and her wildlife that might be achieved through private property rights and public policy incentives that encourage them to be used in a way that protects their intrinsic conservation attributes. There are, I believe, lessons which can be learnt from our past in this regard.

My purpose is to recall the social history of game shooting in Ireland, tracing the stories of shooting on former estates and elsewhere in Ireland from the late nineteenth century and providing, I hope, some insights into issues I have touched on above, such as the relationship between shooting and the balance of nature, and maintaining the fragile habitats on which species depend. It does not pretend to cover the history of every shoot in Ireland. I have learnt this would be a much bigger task, but there is, I believe, a sufficiently representative sample to provide an account of the society involved in shooting in Ireland: their lives, relationships, personalities, and the economic and social milieu which brought them shooting in the first place.

At the time of writing, the Irish economy is engulfed in a crisis born of unsustainable indebtedness which has severely compromised the sovereignty of a State born less than a century ago. In my professional life as an economist, I have had some involvement with the policy responses to this dilemma. In part, the joy of writing this has been the change of scene it has provided from the incessant drip of bad economic news and the depressing commentary that has accompanied it. However, I had not expected to find that the self-same seed of indebtedness and unsupportable lifestyles which lie at the heart of today's drama were also at the centre of the social revolution that engulfed Ireland a century ago and changed its social landscape forever.

Peter Bacon
Ballyrane
March 2012

1

THE ASCENDENCY AND SUBSEQUENT
EVOLUTION OF SHOOTING IN
EDWARDIAN IRELAND

By the 1870s, game shooting had become very fashionable in both Great Britain and Ireland. Until the 1860s, the practice was for shooters to walk through woods and shoot game as it flew away. As a result of developments to the shotgun – breech loading rather than muzzle loading from the 1850s, hammerless action from the 1870s, later still the ejector and the single trigger – a much faster shooting and reloading action became possible. This resulted in it becoming easier to shoot more birds while standing and having game being driven to guns, rather than walking up from behind as previously. Thus, a *new* sport of 'driven' game shooting was born and was applied in particular to pheasants, grouse and hares; quarry species which lent themselves most easily to this approach. This development was to have far-reaching consequences socially, especially amongst the landed gentry, who had the resources and inclination to apply to the development of the sport, which brought an additional dimension to field-sports enthusiasts engaged in fox hunting and angling.

However, it is important to understand that recreational shooting was a popular pastime long before the emergence of the driven approach. Moreover, it was practised across a wide spectrum of society. Classics like William H. Maxwell's *Wild Sports of the West*, first published in 1832, provide testament to the popularity of shooting and the social aspect surrounding the sport:

> Every one shoots Grouse; the operation is so commonplace, that none but a cockney would find novelty in its detail. Our morning's sport was excellent. The dogs were in good working condition and under perfect command … The particulars of the evening compotation I shall be excused in passing over. I must allow that the portion of wine allotted to sportsmen was awfully exceeded … but a man must exercise and carouse with a Grouse shooter to conceive the deep and delicious repose which attends the sportsman's pillow.[2]

Similarly, *The Diary of Colonel Peter Hawker*, commencing in 1802, 'my second season of sporting (age 16½ years)' records a life-long passion for (or obsession with) game and wildfowl shooting stretching over half a century.[3]

These developments to the shotgun (and the quality of cartridges) from the 1860s facilitated the growth of a pastime that was already popular in Victorian times. Another major influence on its popularity and growth was the involvement of Edward VII of England (as Prince of Wales until his coronation in 1901) from about 1864, the year of his wedding. 'From that date the ascendancy of the Prince of Wales over Society was complete until his death nearly fifty years later. His personal

15

1 'Mixing it'
– Members
of the Irish
Aristocracy at a
Royal Shoot at
Sandringham,
c. 1904.

tastes and in particular his love of shooting became the taste of his smarter and richer subjects.'[4] By all accounts he wasn't a particularly accurate shot. However, his sons were; Eddie, before his premature death in 1892, and in particular his second son who became George V and whose deep involvement in shooting – including in Ireland – helped to sustain and maintain the popularity of shooting as a fashionable pastime of the leisured classes throughout the United Kingdom. The Sandringham Estate in Norfolk, purchased by Edward in 1863, the year before his marriage to Princess Alexandra, became a focal point for royal shooting parties. He increased the bag from 7,000 per annum to 30,000 head of game.[5] With 8,000 acres of some of the best game-holding land available, the estate was to become the royal couple's favourite home and a place to which an invitation to shoot was deeply coveted by the aristocracy, including its Irish members.

The point is well made by the illustration above, which was taken at Sandringham, and includes a section of the most powerful and influential members of society, including a good sprinkling of Irish aristocrats. The royals included are King Edward VII (eleventh from left, standing); his son, subsequently George V, then Prince of Wales (sixteenth from left, standing); Princess Victoria of Hesse (1863-1950), maternal grandmother of Prince Philip, the Duke of Edinburgh, and mother of Lord Louis Mountbatten (fifth from left, standing); Prince Charles (seventh from left, standing), and Princess Charles (second from left, seated).

The Irish peers are John Henry Crichton, 4th Earl Erne (1839-1914) (second from left, standing); James Butler, 3rd Marquess Ormonde (1844-1919) (sixth from left, standing); his wife, Lady Ormonde, *née* Lady Elizabeth Harriet Grosvenor, daughter of the 1st Duke of Westminster (fourth from left, seated); their daughter Constance Mary Butler (1879-1949) (first from left, seated); Henry Petty-Fitzmaurice, 5th Marquess of Lansdowne (and 6th Earl of Kerry) (1845-1927) (second from right, seated); his wife, the Marchioness Maud Evelyn Hamilton, daughter of the 1st Duke of Abercorn (fourth from right, seated); Charles Stewart Vane-Tempest-Stewart, 6th Marquess of Londonderry (1852-1915) (third from right, seated), and his wife, the Marchioness Lady Theresa Susey Helen Talbot, daughter of the 19th Earl of Shrewsbury (fifth from right, seated).

Also pictured is Klemens-Wenzel Prinz von Metternich-Winneburg (1869 at Vienna, Austria-1930) (thirteenth from left, standing), who was the son of Paul Prinz von Metternich-Winneburg and Melanie von Zichy-Ferraris, and grandson of Chancellor Metternich. He married

Isabel de Silva y Carvajal on 4 October 1905 in Madrid, Spain. Hans Georg Hermann von Plessen (1841-1929), Kaiser Wilhelm II's orderly *aide-de-camp*, can also be seen (ninth from left, standing).

As this example shows, shooting parties – as well as being enjoyable occasions – provided a very valuable means of networking and social climbing, and were occasions where future marriage partners and family alliances could be developed and fostered.

In Ireland, according to Terence Dooley:

> Organised shoots were one of the most popular forms of big-house entertainment and almost invariably an expensive one … Shooting parties were male-dominated although the ladies did often go out in brakes and joined the men for lunch, sometimes held in a tent that could be moved according to the location of the shoot.[6]

In *The Irish Country House*, Peter Somerville-Large records that:

> Shooting or fowling was part of everyday life in that age of abundance. At Dromoland Sir Edward O'Brien wrote and illustrated a long piece of doggerel in praise of shooting and its culinary results:

> 'A hare shall grace the head, Woodcocks the foot.
> Snipe shall a side dish make and Grouse be put
> With Wigeon, duck and Teal in balance true,
> To Partridges and quails and curlews …'

> In Wicklow, Mrs Smith appointed two young friends to wander over the mountains shooting game to be served at her daughter's wedding. During the Famine landlords like Lord Sligo shot game to be put in the famine pot. Dudley Persse always carried a shotgun with him to shoot at game as he made the rounds of Roxborough, and his little dogcart would be full of birds and rabbits by the time he had finished his rounds.[7]

Referring to Charleville, County Wicklow, home of Henry Monck, 5th Viscount Monck, he states:

> As if there were not enough duck or Wigeon, Charleville reared its own Pheasants for slaughter. Henry Monck was described as 'the best shot in Ireland'. In the game larder beyond the kitchen was a tall wrought-iron stand like a six-fingered signpost, each arm comprising a different day of the week. 'Each in their proper season,' wrote Elizabeth Batt, 'hare and Grouse from the hills, the occasional wild Pheasant and the inexhaustible supply of rabbits, hung on massive iron hooks attached to the relevant arm according to when they were killed. Game had to be retrieved and there were many dogs at Charleville, eight terriers and numerous Irish Setters, both the red variety and the less common black-and-tan. There were also Newfoundlands, the stock of which was increased annually whenever Lord Monck returned on his summer holiday from Canada, where he was Governor General.[8]

Somerville-Large also emphasises the contrasts of shooting in Ireland:

> The best shooting was casual, going out with a gun under your arm. Lord Dunsany … used to visit his relations at Kilcooley Abbey among the bogs of the flat midlands. The talk at Kilcooley

was much of these bogs and of Wigeon and Teal and of Woodcock, which were more taken for granted, and of geese. But a lot of shooting was very formal indeed. At Ashford Castle, at Glenart, Abbeyleix, Moore Abbey, Mount Juliet and a hundred other estates volleys from guns thundered over the trees and bogs … Although the system of slaughter was identical to that in Edwardian England, many English visitors enjoyed shooting in Ireland. On two occasions the Duke of Connaught [i.e. the third son of Queen Victoria] visited Glaslough to shoot, both occasions full of suspense. Embarrassment came from the butler hired from Belfast, drunk as was customary. 'Your Royal 'ighness, there's 'am and cold rabbit pie on the sideboard.' He assured the duke that the blinds were still down in Portadown, 'in mourning for your Royal 'ighness's Ma' … Great agony is endured by those responsible for a royal shoot.

On the duke's next visit there was a shortage of birds and other guests were under orders not to shoot at Woodcock, 'Derry Rossmore claimed that he had refrained from shooting three Woodcock on their way to the royal gun and in consequence expected a step up in the peerage'.[9]

However, game shooting for some sections of society was neither frivolous nor economically rewarding. Payne-Gallwey refers to professional fowlers (see also, Chapter 7: The Wildfowl of Wexford Harbour and Sloblands) in the following terms:

> The professional shooters are men who, making a livelihood as fishermen or boatmen during the summer, find little to employ them in winter. Though they seldom expect to earn any profit by the birds they kill, they have other chances that would not be thrown in their way in Ireland. The wild coasts of that country and the immense lakes and estuaries where fowl collect abundantly are quite unsafe for the small punts generally used in England. If English professional fowlers came to Irish waters, they would have to depend for their support on the result of their shooting. There would be no visitors to employ them and worst of all very poor markets for selling fowl. At the most available shooting stations such as Wexford, Limerick, Cork, Belfast and the northern marine loughs and bays, fowlers abound to their own disadvantage. In out of the way spots such as the bays of Kerry, Clare, Galway, Mayo, Sligo and Donegal swivel guns are less numerous; but professional shore-shooters by the dozen. To keep these men in pleasant temper and prevent their spoiling sport by firing up the fowl, they must be liberally dealt with in the way of a good share from the bag. Once offend the shore men, demand but one wounded Wigeon that may flutter into their dog's mouth, or come to their hands and your sport is spoilt in *that* locality for years to come. These poor shooters trudge to the nearest town of a Saturday to sell what birds they may happen to have killed during the week. A stranger visiting their estuary with his fowling punt is looked upon as a thief come to rob them of their living …[10]

He addresses also the Snipe shooters who abounded, the likes of:

> Patrick O'Halloran, the well-known Snipe-shooter of County Clare, [who] on unpreserved ground obtained the following total in the season just past (1880/81). I have before me his record of birds killed day by day and the receipts for same when sold, both of which correspond. It gives a good idea of what can still be done by an energetic and hardworking shooter. The fame of this man is widespread and sportsmen are in the habit of staying at an inn hard by, to whom he acts as a guide. He is a perfect Snipe-shot and one of the few men living who can account for five Snipe out of seven fired at, from the beginning to the end of the day. His total bag for the season 1880/81 was fourteen hundred and twenty cock and Snipe. The heaviest bag of Snipe in a day, forty-five.[11]

Game shooting represented an important pastime of the rich, a livelihood for talented and knowledgeable locals, and a means of survival for some sections of society who would otherwise have been hungry. The result of this was that it had the potential to provide a focus for common interest in a diverse society, but also to create a source of friction and disharmony in communities. The latter was more often than not the case. Consequently, the issues of regulation, access and protection were never far from the surface, especially as more and more resources were expended by landowners on the development of shooting over their estates.

MATTERS OF SHOOTING

The Gamekeeper

Good game keeping is essential to providing quality shooting. Accordingly, talented gamekeepers were much sought after by shoot owners anxious to provide themselves and their friends with enviable shooting. A gamekeeper was an upper servant who would have been properly and formally dressed in a uniform provided by the master. At the turn of the twentieth century there were no fewer than 533 gamekeepers employed on estates in Ireland. The number had declined to 444 a decade later.[12] During the same time, the number of gamekeepers on estates in Great Britain increased from 17,000 to 23,000.[13] Details of the distribution of gamekeepers by county in Ireland are contained in Appendix 2 and this gives a good impression of the scale and concentration of sporting estates in Ireland at the time.

Gamekeepers were highly mobile and while some stayed in one place for long periods, like Michael Quaid (illustrated) who spent almost half a century at Adare Manor, it was usual for young gamekeepers to move about from estate to estate, learning their trade. One account of such a man is contained in *The Banville Diaries: Journals of a Norfolk Gamekeeper*, which tells the story of Larry Banville (1796-1869) from Cullenstown in County Wexford, who emigrated and became a gamekeeper on the estate of Sir Thomas Fowell Buxton, 1st Baronet (1786-1845) in Norfolk, from 1822 to 1844. His diary contains accounts of his game-keeping life, including being sent to collect Capercaillies from Sweden for the successful reintroduction of those birds to Scotland.[14]

The growing popularity of shooting during the Edwardian period and in particular of driven shooting in the second half of

2 Michael Quaid (1858-1929), gamekeeper at Adare Manor for the last forty-seven years of his life. The portrait shows him standing before the Rathkeale Gate entrance to the Deer Park of Adare Manor, with Woodcock in hand. The artist is Leo Whelan, RHA (1892-1956). The painting was commissioned by Windham Thomas Wyndham-Quin (1841-1926), 4th Earl of Dunraven and Mount-Earl.

3 The Bracken family. The photograph is contained in an album of the Wynne family of Hazelwood, County Sligo, and shows members of the Bracken family dressed in game-keeping attire outside a cot-tage believed to be on the Hazelwood Estate. Evidently the family were regarded highly by the estate owners to merit inclu-sion in the family photo-graph album.

the nineteenth century, meant that landowners required ever increasing numbers of workers to artificially rear and release Pheasants, manage moorland heather in order to promote Grouse numbers, preserve Partridges through nest management, manage coverts and rides to attract Woodcock, preserve land from poachers and intruders, control vermin, and liaise with tenant farmers in relation to crop planting.

A clear hierarchy emerged, with the head keeper at the top of the tree, wielding considerable influence within the estate and wider community. In Ireland, he might have a staff of up to a dozen or more, including under-keepers, beat keepers, bog-watchers,[15] trappers and occasionally a deer-park keeper. For example, one of the Brackens discussed below resided at the Deer Park, Calry, County Sligo. Game Departments of estates had become quite significant in many cases and their incomes and outlays were monitored and accounted for meticulously by the Head Gamekeeper. For example, at the Mahon Estate in Castlegar in the late nineteenth century, there are detailed and precise annual accounts relating to the management of the shooting.[16] There are similarly detailed account ledgers surviving at Ballynahinch Castle, recording the shoot there at the turn of the twentieth century.

Very often the art of game keeping was passed on from father to son. In *Game keeping Past and Present*, David Jones focuses on the prominence of the Grass family, of which he is a descend-ant, on British shoots. In Ireland, the Bracken family was undoubtedly the most prominent and widespread game-keeping family, and one with a very intriguing history.

According to several people with insight on the matter, an Earl of Enniskillen, who lived at Florence Court, County Fermanagh, was not permitted to marry his childhood sweetheart, who was a daughter of the groom. She was married off instead to the son of another groom –

Bracken by name. Many of her sons and descendants became gamekeepers and bear a striking resemblance – in both appearance and demeanour – to the Enniskillens!

The family can trace itself back to Hugh Bracken (b. 1809), who in 1837 married Margaret Berry (d. 1870, at Deerpark, Calry, County Sligo) at Killesher, County Fermanagh. They had eleven children, the last two of whom were girls. Their second son, Robert Bracken (1839-1924) was a gamekeeper at the estate of Henry Bentinck Boyle, 5th Earl of Shannon (1833-1890) at Castlemartyr, County Cork. He returned to Classiebawn in 1901 as head gamekeeper. He was married to a Margaret Addersley and with her he had eight children, six of whom were boys. The third son, Hugh Bracken (1842-1877), became gamekeeper at the estate of the Hon. John Massy at Lissinagroagh, County Leitrim. He married a Sarah Huey in 1868 and with her had five children, all girls. On his death at the age of thirty-five from drowning on Lough Melvin, County Leitrim, his younger brother William (1848-1937), a gamekeeper at the same estate, married his brother's widow, took over her five children and went on to have a further four with her. In later

4 Richard Bracken (1854-1925), head gamekeeper at Hazelwood Estate, County Sligo.

life, William moved from Lissinagroagh to Lurganboy, County Leitrim, the original seat of the Wynnes. Another brother, Henry Bracken (1851-1930), was a gamekeeper living at Trohanny, County Meath in 1901 and subsequently lived at Hazelwood. He was married to Mary Frizell and with her had eight children, three of whom were boys. Richard Bracken (1854-1925) (see Illustration 004), was head gamekeeper at Hazelwood. He was married to a sister of the wife of his older brother Hugh. After Hugh's day, his brother William married Hugh's widow, Sarah Huey. They had five children, two of whom were boys. Christopher Bracken (1856-1895) was head keeper at Castlegar, the Mahon Estate in East Galway. He was married to Mary Berry and they had three daughters.

In the next generation, James Bracken (b. 1875), son of James Bracken (1838-1880) and Mary Bourke, was a gamekeeper at Glenfarne Hall, Enniskillen, the estate of Arthur Loftus Tottenham (1838-1887), landowner and Conservative politician who sat in the House of Commons from 1880 to 1887. Hugh Bracken (b. 1880), eldest son of William (1848-1937) and Hugh's widow Sarah Huey, was a gamekeeper at Castletown House, County Kildare. His younger brother William Henry (b. 1882) succeeded his father William as gamekeeper at estate of the Hon. John Massy at Lissinagroagh, County Leitrim. The youngest of that family, Richard James (b. 1884) was married to his cousin Mary Florence (b. 1889), daughter of Richard Bracken (1854-1925) of Hazelwood. He was a gamekeeper, in County Cork before he moved to Temple House in County Sligo when his cousin (and brother-in-law) Hugh (b. 1879), eldest son of Richard (1854-1925), became too ill to continue in work (see Illustration 005).

Thomas Bracken (b. 1889), second son of Henry (1851-1930) and Mary Frizell, was a gamekeeper at Deerpark, Hazelwood, while his cousin Arthur (1890-1918) was also there.

Robert James Bracken (b. 1875), second son of Robert Bracken (1839-1924) and Margaret Addersley, was the keeper at the Earl of Wicklow's estate, Shelton Abbey, in County Wicklow, before he moved to Markree Castle in County Sligo. The next son, Arthur (b. 1878), was at Florence Court. His younger brother Jules Bracken (1880-1959) was at Classiebawn (see Illustration 006) and was joined there by the youngest of that family, Walter (Watty) Bracken (b. 1886), who previously was a keeper at Castle McGarrett, the seat of Lord Oranmore and Brown.

Finally, Harry Bracken, son of Robert James Bracken, succeeded his father at Markree Castle. In 1959 he was all packed ready to move to Classiebawn following the demise of Jules Bracken. However, Lady Edwina died and he was 'asked' to go to Broadlands, where he spent the rest of his life.

Game keeping was an overwhelmingly male-dominated occupation and remains so today. However, there were rare exceptions. Polly Fishburn was the first recorded female gamekeeper in Great Britain, where she was a beat keeper on the Holkam Estate in the early years of the nineteenth century. In Ireland, the first female gamekeeper is believed to have been Ann Holland, who was employed on the Mountain Lodge Estate in County Monaghan of the 5th Baron Rossmore.[17] In fact, this woman is more likely to have been a bog-watcher than a gamekeeper. (Women were often employed as bog-watchers, due to the lower wages involved.)

The gun which Ann Holland is carrying in the illustration on the following page is actually a rifle – a very early breech loader called a Monke Tail Carbine. Unquestionably, one of the most famous firearms to be invented in the nineteenth century was the Westley Richards Breech Loading Carbine of 1858, more commonly known as the 'Monkey Tail' Carbine. Its numerous variants and respective cartridges kept it in manufacture until 1881, with more than 20,000 being produced for military use. It was to set new standards in rifle design, as it was the first breech-loading rifle with combustible cartridges.

5 *(left)* Hugh Bracken (b. 1879), game-keeper at Temple House, County Sligo.

6 Jules Bracken at Classiebawn Castle.

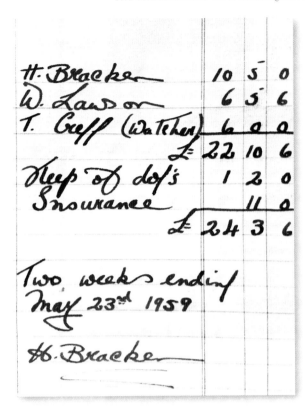

7 **Harry Bracken's last wage slip from Markree Castle, for two weeks ending 23 May 1959.**

8 (right) **Ann Holland.**

It was used by some heavy cavalry regiments and Yeomanry (and probably also by the mounted police, such as some detachments of the RIC) and was usually made in .450 calibre. It did not become obsolete until 1890 or later, so this picture is probably from 1905-1910. Until then, this rifle would have been restricted to military or police use.

Clearly this cabin is from one of the more mountainous areas and from a place where game was preserved but not reared. This rifle is for something big, such as deer – or for scaring people! The idea that such a scruffy-looking female was a principal keeper, responsible for organising shoot days and dealing with guests simply isn't credible. In all likelihood the image is from an English magazine, poking fun and suggesting she is a gamekeeper when she was really just a bog-watcher.

Beating and Picking-up: The Importance of Working Dogs

Working dogs are an integral part of game shooting. Gamekeepers require them in order to flush game and 'dog-in' after shoot days; beaters need biddable and controllable dogs, which can drive game over the Guns. Guns require dogs to hunt game and retrieve killed or wounded birds. Hence, with the rise in popularity of shooting there was a parallel increase in demand for sporting dogs that would do their job efficiently. Gun-dog field trials emerged as a means of testing gun dogs, and field trialling has evolved into a popular and competitive sport in its own right. Estates desired to have their own lines of working gun dogs and estate owners took an active interest in their development. Thus, for example, the Adare line of Labradors was developed by Richard Southwell Windham Robert Wyndham-Quin, 6th Earl of Dunraven and Mount-Earl (1887-1965), of Adare Manor, County Limerick during the first half of the twentieth century. Similarly, Maj. Hales Pakenham-Mahon was instrumental in developing the Strokestown line of Labrador.

However, Labradors are a comparatively modern breed of dog. In the nineteenth century other breeds, now unfashionable, were more favoured. Flat-coated and curly-coated retrievers were used more commonly than Labradors, and their main task was retrieving. The development of the golden retriever from the beginning of the twentieth century owes much to the notorious Lord Lewis Harcourt (1863-1922)[18] under his Nuneham prefix (Nuneham was the name of the estate of Lord Harcourt), which he subsequently changed to Culham for some reason in 1909.

At Glenstal Abbey in County Clare, famous for its Woodcock shooting, the Barringtons laid great store by the Irish Water Spaniel for hunting Woodcock and developed a line named Annagh, which became synonymous with the breed. More widely popular in late-nineteenth and early twentieth-century Ireland was the Cocker Spaniel, which along with the English Springer Spaniel has remained the favourite hunting dog for Woodcock.

For Grouse shooting the Irish Setter was a firm favourite, along with the English Pointer. These breeds were popular also when shooting Woodcock and Snipe. The history of the Irish Red Setter has been comprehensively documented by Raymond O'Dwyer in his *The Irish Red Setter*.

However, for most shooting people, the main requirement from a working dog has been (and remains to this day) an honest shooting companion to enhance the day's sport and enjoyment. For some, this seemingly simple requirement has proved difficult to find. The Game Book of Lord Maurice FitzGerald (1852-1901) of Johnstown Castle, County Wexford, contains the following passage about dogs:

Lulu … Bl. Retriever … Given by Lady Sophia Forbes … Gave Lulu to Mabel.

Hector …Bl. Retriever … Given to Adelaide by Mr D. Morgan … This pup is the most mischievous dog alive and shot May 1884 – bad leg.

Nigger … Bl. Retriever … Given by Ld Conyngham … Shot – useless – no ear, 1886.

Nero … Bl. Retriever pup … Son of Nigger by Bitches of Mr B. McP … Shot as useless.

Nadine … Black retriever bitch … Bought from Cowper 3rd Keeper at Glenart, one year old, £5.5.0 … Died pupping, 1888.

Sailor … Bl. Retriever … 14 months old … Bought from Mr Harty, Glenart … Shot for killing peafowl, Feb. 1891.

Jumbo … Black retriever … Bought from Mr Bewley 30/- as present to Ade … died of distemper …

… and on and on! He didn't have much luck with dogs, or in life, it would seem. He died at forty-nine years.

Shooting Equipment and Accessories: Gun and Game Book

There was a strong tradition of gun-making in Ireland and indeed at least one individual, John Rigby, achieved recognition and acclaim internationally for the quality of his work.[19] Richard Garrett has identified 380 Irish gun-makers meeting the self-protection and sporting requirements of the Irish market over the years.[20] Given the popularity of game shooting, this is unsurprising, although it is likely that at the top end of game shooting most weapons employed would have been from Birmingham or London gun-makers.

An important aspect of shooting game was the recording of what was shot, where and in whose company. The contents of this book have, in large measure, been sourced from Game Books, either of individuals, estates or gamekeepers employed on estates. Game Books take a number of forms. The estate Game Book was generally a substantial, leather-bound book of large format, usually maintained by the estate owner, in which was recorded the shoot dates, the participants, the number of game shot according to species and sometimes comments regarding the weather or how individual guests were performing on the day. The most ornate Game Book found in the course of the work for this book was that of Annaghmore, maintained by Charles Kean O'Hara from 1904 for over a decade. What is unique about this book is the fact that it is both a game record and a visitors' book, containing the autographs of those in the shooting party and many photographs, sketches and line drawings relating to days shooting at Annaghmore, Temple House, Markree Castle and Cooperhill, all in County Sligo. Browsing through it is like reliving the past in real time.

The personal Game Book of an estate owner, as the name implies, usually describes the experience of the individual on his own shoot and at visiting shoots, and comprises the same information listed above. Some are laid out in a manner that enables the total shot by the party to be recorded, as well as that accounted for by the owner of the record. The personal Game Books of Sir Henry William Gore-Booth, 5th Baronet (1843-1900) (Lissadell) are so designed, with printed columns labelled 'self' and 'total'.

The gamekeepers were also sometimes furnished with a Game Book. For Classiebawn, the records used here have been extracted from the book of Jules Bracken (d. 1959), gamekeeper. In addition, there is a gamekeeper's book belonging to Christopher Bracken (1856-1895) of Castlegar, as well as a personal Game Book belonging to Sir William Henry Mahon (1856-1926).

The Lissadell Estate Game Books deserve special mention. The format is extremely large. They are more in the character of a game register, recording not only what was shot by shooting parties and guests, but also records of game and rabbits shot by gamekeepers in every month of the year and descriptions of how game was disposed of – between the house, supplied by way of gifts, or sold off the estate. It is most likely that this register was maintained by the head keeper. Interestingly, the format and layout is very similar to a manuscript game record relating to 1845 (See Illustration 046).

Regardless of the form, Game Books are a rich source of information on the shooting society to which they pertain. The time and trouble taken to record such information is a windfall without which this book would not exist.

Shooting Accommodation: The Shooting Lodge

It is worth pointing out that while much estate shooting was conducted from the comfort of the Big House, there were a large number of purpose-built lodges constructed around Ireland, often in remote places, to accommodate shooting parties to inaccessible locations. The history of this architectural form has been described in some detail in *Irish Sporting Lodges* by Patrick Bowe.[21]

A lodge is a house built for occasional use only. As a result, it is usually smaller in scale and more compact in design than a house constructed for year-round habitation. Shooting, of course, was not the only use for which lodges were built; fishing, hunting, yachting and bathing are just some of the other recreational uses identified by Bowe in this connection. But the focus here is on shooting lodges.

They were built close to the location of wild game. Ballycroy Lodge, at the mouth of the Owenduff river celebrated by W.H. Maxwell in *Wild Sports of the West*, is a very good example of an isolated lodge. Many lodges were associated with Grouse shooting and were located close to the moor or bog. For example, Bowe identifies Grouse Lodge in County Wicklow, Grouse Hall in County Donegal and Grouse Hall in County Kerry, and there were numerous other lodges for

Grouse shooting. Some bore the name 'Grouse' and others did not, like Luggala and Lough Bray Lodges in County Wicklow.

Lodge design evolved to meet its own set of requirements, accommodations and to reflect the environment which hosted it. Being required to accommodate friends, the design was usually compact, often of single-storey construction with a long and rectangular plan. The internal layout reflected the fact that it was designed to accommodate a party of friends rather than a family in permanent residence. Therefore, a disproportionately large number of bedrooms were provided – the majority of them single – and were frequently small and narrow. Many had surprisingly long rear returns to allow for large number of bedrooms required for a sporting party. Larger lodges were sometimes of one storey to the front and two storeys behind, where bedrooms and service rooms were housed. In that way, high-ceilinged reception rooms and two-storeyed low-ceilinged bedrooms and service rooms could be under the same roof. The lodge kitchen was usually of a substantial size, often with an adjoining drying room in which wet clothes could be dried and aired. All rooms, including bathrooms, had large fireplaces. Specialist rooms, such as a gun room with a secure cabinet and places for cartridges, gun bags, game bags and all the paraphernalia of shooting, were also provided.

The internal decoration and furnishings were of the hard-wearing kind, with leather-covered armchairs and sofas, fender seats and large log boxes. Sporting engravings, sporting books and lodge records (often leather bound) and mounted trophies would add adornment and comfort. In the hallway there would have been a barometer and a large coat and hat stand, along with a container for walking sticks and crooks.

Outside the lodge there was usually a yard, which sometimes included a small cottage where a gamekeeper would reside with his family. In addition, there were stables and tack rooms laid on for the ponies and donkeys and carts, which were used to transport the elaborate gear of shooters over considerable distances of frequently rough terrain and to bring home the bag of game at the end of a day. A game larder with a north-facing aspect was another feature that was incorporated in the yard. Finally, kennels were required for the working dogs of the shooting parties. Bowe quotes from Maxwell's description of these at Ballycroy thus, 'nor are the dogs forgotten: a warm and sheltered kennel is fitted with benches and well provided with straw'.

What stands out in all of this is the care and thought (not to mention resources) that went into ensuring that shooting could be carried out in the most remote and wild places of Ireland in conditions that made for the comfort of Guns and ensured that there were sufficient creature comforts to make the occasions sociable and hospitable.

Women and Shooting

Shooting was (and continues to be) a male-dominated sport. However, as the photograph on the following page attests, it was not an exclusive preserve of men. It will be seen from numerous subsequent illustrations that while women participants in shooting was a rarity, shooting parties were often conducted with women present at some point during the day, frequently joining Guns for lunch at a lodge or shooting hut and partaking fully in evening entertainments afterwards. Peter Somerville-Large points out that:

> Shoots were seldom enjoyed by women. Lady Clodagh Anson considered shooting parties 'awful things … The men went off after breakfast and all the wives sat around in the drawing room making unattractive things in wool, generally in very bright colours if they were for the "poor".

9 Women
shooting at
Mount Juilliet,
County
Kilkenny.
(*Getty Images*)

Later the ladies changed into tweeds and thick boots and joined the Guns for luncheon at some keeper's lodge. 'Afterwards you walked with the Guns generally getting home gratefully at dusk, changing into a tea gown for tea, then you "rested", why I don't know, unless the hostess wanted to get rid of you to write letters. You changed again for dinner, of course a very long affair with six or seven courses. How does one live through such things?'[22]

Clearly, Lady Clodagh Anson, to judge from the above, was not a fan of shooting or shoot parties. Lady Clodagh Beresford (1879-1957)[23] married the Hon. Claud Anson, son of Thomas George Anson, 2nd Earl of Lichfield, and Lady Harriett Georgiana Louisa Hamilton, in 1901. She was the daughter of John Henry de la Poer Beresford, 5th Marquess of Waterford, and Lady Blanche Elizabeth Adelaide Somerset. However, it is difficult to know how representative this opinion was, and certainly there were female fans that, such as those pictured, were keen shots. For example, Mary Rose Bacon (d. 1943), wife of Sir Charles Barrington of Glenstal, was known to be a 'crack' shot at Woodcock. Similarly, Nancy Yuille, wife of the 6th Earl of Dunraven and Mount Earl, is reputed to have taken a 'left and right' at Snipe on one occasion.

POLICIES, THE LAW AND REGULATORY FRAMEWORK OF GAME SHOOTING

Game Laws and Regulation of Game Shooting

Until the Game Reform Act of 1831, the right to shoot game was vested exclusively in landowners and poaching of game was a serious criminal offence, punishable with harsh penalties. This Act principally introduced a change whereby, in law at least, the monopoly of landowners' rights to shoot game was broken. Game shooting became open to any purchaser of a game certificate and game trading could be carried on by any purchaser of a game dealer's licence. However, a Lords amendment to the Bill ensured that game was the property of the landowner rather than the occupier of the land. In practice, not much appears to have changed:

> If the reformers expected dramatic confirmation of their theories they were disappointed. Far from declining, poaching seems to have remained at the same level or even increased a little in the year following the passage of the *Game Reform Act*. Parliamentary returns indicate that in the first twelve months of the Act's existence, 2,800 persons were sent to prison in England for game offences. This was well above the figure for each of the previous two years ... Not until 1880 was it that Parliament conceded to farmers the right to kill hares on their land without the permission of landowners.[24]

In the meantime, in 1870 a House of Commons Select Committee had been established to examine the Game Laws and it reported in 1872 and 1873.[25] It contained evidence on the situation in Ireland and evidence on reform was elicited from eight witnesses. The principal focus of attention of the committee in regard to Ireland was the disparity with Great Britain in the open season for Red Grouse (12 August in Britain against 20 August in Ireland) and Grey Partridge (1 September in Britain and 20 September in Ireland). A memorandum subscribed to by 185 signatories, principally representing owners of landed estates in Ireland, was submitted in favour of harmonising the open seasons in Ireland and Great Britain. The main rationale for these proposed changes was to reduce poaching by eliminating the possibility of Irish game being passed off as British game during the few weeks when the season was open in Britain but closed in Ireland. The committee recommended that the season for Red Grouse and Grey Partridge should commence on 12 August and 10 September respectively. The Game Bird (Ireland) Act 1874 gave effect to the proposed change for Grouse but the position of Grey Partridge remained unchanged until 1899, when the Partridge Shooting (Ireland) Act 1899 brought forward the opening date to 1 September and put the closing date back from 10 January to 1 February.

In reality those concerned appear to have had little faith in the power of the law to achieve protection of rights with respect to game. In this respect, landowners in Ireland were not significantly different in attitude from those in Great Britain, although the increasing political instability in Ireland, coupled with the precarious economic position of the landed estates around this time (see Chapter 2), probably resulted in even greater scepticism about orderly regulation of game shooting in Ireland. Therefore they formed their own Representative Association to protect the interests of game.

Irish Game Protection Association

The Irish Game Protection Association was formed in 1891 and continues in existence to this day. It was founded by members of the landed gentry, with many of the names which arise in subsequent chapters being found as members of its executive committee or acting as county representatives. Its objectives were:

To prevent game being killed out of season.
To prevent game being killed on Sundays.
To prevent the illicit sale of game.
To assist the Excise in obtaining convictions against persons killing or dealing in game without a licence and to press the government to direct the Royal Irish Constabulary to assist in enforcing the law in these respects.
To take such other steps for the preservation of game as may be deemed advisable.

The funds of the association could not be used for the enforcement of private shooting rights. A Resident Inspector was retained in any county where subscriptions exceeded £50 per annum.

It is clear that the association was born out of frustration with the laxity of the authorities in respect of enforcing existing laws to protect game. By working closely with the Royal Irish Constabulary, a considerable amount of game licence fees were collected and the association was constantly pressing the Inland Revenue authorities to institute proceedings against offenders whom their inspectors had apprehended.

However, while the same issues remained on the agenda, the Annual Report for the year ending 28 February 1926, the thirty-fifth year of the association, held a note of hope to the 156 members who subscribed £192 15s 0d in total that year:

> … the Government have been obliged owing to the great pressure of other legislation to post-pone until the Autumn session 1926 the promised new Game Act, but we feel confident that they are fully alive to the importance of the subject and we have reason to suppose there will be no undue delay in its introduction. Your attention is drawn to the Advisory Report sent you last year … during the past year several important prosecutions were successfully carried out by the Association and the Committee are glad to be able to record that the Civic Guard continue to enforce the existing Game Statutes and render valuable help in most parts of the Free State.

Nevertheless, the report goes on, 'your Committee consider that the outlook for the protection of game and the furtherance of this object by the Government is more promising than for many years past and have consequently decided to maintain the Association'. In fact, it was 1930 – another four years – before the said piece of legislation was enacted in the shape of the Game Preservation Act 1930.

Game Council Initiative

From around the late 1920s, the Land Commission began to compile and publish lists of sporting rights – both shooting and fishing – in respect of lands which came into its ownership which it offered by way of lettings for up to five years' duration. These were aimed mainly at (and taken up by) non-resident sportsmen and in effect were tourist lettings.[26] There is little information as to what the level of demand for these was or as to the trend in letting revenue over time.

However, by the mid-1950s, concerns were being expressed in periodicals such as *Stream and Field in Ireland* about the poor state of game stocks.

Stanislaus Lynch, who was a founder of the St Hubert Club of Ireland, in about 1954, commenced a lobby to replenish game stocks in Ireland. Lynch was an all-round field-sports enthusiast whose first love was riding to hounds.[27] When the Irish Tourist Board (Bord Fáilte) was awarding grants to riding schools Lynch was appointed a Board Inspector. He also wrote promotional literature that was used to attract visitors to Ireland for hunting and horse-riding holidays.

Through the St Hubert Club, he convened a meeting in Cahir, County Tipperary in May 1958 of rural organisations (the National Farmers' Association, Muintir na Tíre, Macra na Feirme, Irish Countrywomen's Association) and shooting interests to set out the bones of a national game policy which involved: the establishment of Regional Game Councils, constituted from accredited representatives of rural bodies at county executive level; the maintenance of a satisfactory level of farmer interest; and proposals for a statutory Game Board to give direction, technical and financial assistance to the overall movement for the development of game resources.

Various meetings were subsequently convened, with correspondences also being exchanged. Regional Game Councils which corresponded to administrative County Council areas were established. These were then organised into a National Game Council on 30 March 1960, at a meeting of Regional Game Councils held at Jury's Hotel in Dublin. This comprised representatives of the rural organisations and Regional Game Councils, the St Hubert Club, Bord Fáilte and the Department of Land. However, there was dissension along the way. Suspicions were aroused after it was alleged that Bord Fáilte had taken out an advertisement in a British newspaper advertising free shooting in County Monaghan. The Bord Fáilte representative on the Game Council pointed out that they had not placed any such advertisement and referred to its policy on the matter contained in its Annual Report of 1958. The Irish Game Protection Association requested representation on the National Game Council and were told their interests could be looked after at county level! The representations for a statutory game board were never realised.

However, a government response did come in 1961, when a scheme sponsored by Dr Erskine Childers, Minister for Lands, entitled 'The Native Resident Sportsman Game Development Scheme' was introduced, and it continued in existence for twenty years. In essence, the scheme sought to promote game stocks by financially supporting the rearing and releasing of game birds, in association with local gun clubs. However, from the outset there was resentment and distrust of the scheme and its objectives by many local gun clubs, which saw the development of any kind of tourism shooting as being in conflict with their narrow interest of controlling access to game-shooting land (and the cost thereof) through membership of local clubs, frequently at parish level, although they were quite happy to receive financial support for rearing and release programmes.

A further evolution occurred in 1968, when the National Game Council assumed the name 'National Association of Regional Game Councils' as a national lobby organisation looking after the interests of *resident* sportsmen and sportswomen through assisting in the development and implementation of national wildlife policy, legislation, research, education, habitat purchase and development, financing, game release programmes, etc.

In the early 1980s, the Game Development Scheme was ended in the face of intensifying opposition to tourism shooting and increasing pressures on the public finances.

2

The Influence of Economics and Politics: the Irish Land Question

In recording the social history of game shoots in Ireland in the late nineteenth and early part of the twentieth century, it is important to recognise that the economic and social context within which it was taking place was collapsing irretrievably. In certain respects, it is difficult to understand how it was possible to devote such time, energy and resources to a pastime like shooting in the face of such economic pressure and force for social and political change. The answer is probably that it wasn't simply a pastime. Rather it was an integral part of the way of life of those privileged enough to be able to pursue it. It was how people met socially, it was a means by which they would be regarded socially; it was a way of finding suitable husbands and wives to perpetuate that way of life into future generations. It was an essence of what being a country landowner was. Therefore, shooting and the social round of shooting parties through the autumn and winter seasons continued to be pursued even in the face of great economic adversity, political pressure for change and social upheaval involving violence and crime.

During the Edwardian heyday of shooting, the Irish landed class became increasingly constrained by high indebtedness and political turmoil. The Land Acts from 1870 to 1903 were to have a major influence on the estates and land ownership, and political agitation was growing, often with violence against the land-owning class. Many ultimately fled Ireland, abandoning their estates and leaving their residences in burnt ruins. Others who remained were in some cases legally compelled to sell their estates after 1923, under Land Acts introduced by the Free State Government, most notably the Land Act of 1926.

Unsustainable Indebtedness

Somewhat like the Ireland of today, unsustainable indebtedness incurred in boom years was the principal source of economic pressure. Following nearly three decades of post-Famine prosperity, a long-term agricultural depression began in 1877. The parallel with the Celtic-tiger years is revealed starkly by Terence Dooley, who states:

> For landlords, the seeds of economic decline, somewhat ironically, had been sown during the boom years from the mid-1850s to the late 1870s. This was when many landlords had gone in search of mortgages. They had failed to exploit the commercial values of their estates by raising rents in accordance with price increases or continued to live extravagantly, spending as if there was going to be no future downturn in the economy.[28]

Dooley goes on to describe the 'plight' of George Arthur Hastings, 7th Earl of Granard (1833-1889), and his relationship with the trustees of St Patrick's College, Maynooth, in respect of his mortgage of £91,592 (the largest single mortgage on their books) as being fairly typical of many landlords.[29] Some of Lord Granard's shooting exploits are described later. In short, the Granard mortgage became such a huge embarrassment to Maynooth College that:

> … nobody seemed to want to investigate or quantify the final damage caused to the college … It is not quite clear what happened either to the residual estates or the castle. In the case of the former, it seems that the college trustees agreed to their sale at lower rates because of the impoverishment of the tenantry … In the case of the castle the trustees seem to have accepted the report of R.D. Cochrane that it would be futile attempting to sell it … The final overall loss, counting non-repaid capital, arrears of interest and legal costs was therefore in the region of £35,000 [in 1910].[30]

Other institutions, such as the Law Life Assurance Company, had significantly larger mortgages and greater defaults. Dooley remarks:

> All the available evidence points to the fact that most landlords were unable to meet their interest obligations in the 1880s. In 1886 arrears of interest to the Representative Body of the Church of Ireland (RCB) stood at £35,000; by 1890 they had risen to £81,000 and by 1901 to £135,000.[31]

These kinds of losses and their prevalence would be comparable in scale with the Irish banking collapse, which resulted in the establishment of the National Asset Management Agency in 2009. Thus, the landed gentry of the late nineteenth century were about as solvent as the property development class in Ireland a century later. However, they still attempted to maintain the lifestyle and consumption patterns of better times. Sound familiar?

The Irish National Land League

The Land League was founded at the Imperial Hotel in Castlebar, County Mayo, on 21 October 1879. Charles Stewart Parnell was elected president and Andrew Kettle, Michael Davitt and Thomas Brennan honorary secretaries. And so, practically all the different strands of land agitation and tenant rights movements were brought together in a single organisation.

The aims of the Land League, as stated in the resolutions adopted in the meeting, were twofold: firstly, to bring about a reduction of rack-rents, and secondly, to facilitate the obtaining of the ownership of the soil by the occupiers (tenant farmers). It was believed that the league's objectives could best be attained by: promoting organisation among the tenant farmers; defending those who may be threatened with eviction for refusing to pay unjust rents; facilitating the working of the Bright clauses of the Irish Land Act during the winter, and by obtaining such reforms in the laws relating to land as would enable every tenant to become owner of his holding by paying a fair rent for a limited number of years.

Charles Stewart Parnell and others, including Michael Davitt, then went to America to raise funds for the league, with spectacular results. Branches were also set up in Scotland, where the Crofters' Party imitated the work of the Land League and secured a reforming Act in 1886.

The ensuing Land War of 1879-82 saw a collapse in the payment of rents, with them frequently being withheld from landlords altogether, causing irreparable damage to many. Agitation for land reform became inextricably entwined with demands for political Home Rule. For the ruling landed gentry this was a toxic combination which posed an even more worrying threat than economic depression. Furthermore, an aspect of the Land War involved organised direct challenges to field-sports participation over tenanted land. This centred on opposing fox hunting in particular, but extended also to shooting and fishing. The former aspect is discussed in detail in L.P. Curtis's *Stopping the Hunt, 1881-1882: An Aspect of the Irish Land War*.[32]

The Land Acts

There were established mechanisms for dealing with economically encumbered estates dating from 1848 and 1849 in the form of Encumbered Estates Acts and their associated Encumbered Estates Commission, which was to implement the terms of the legislation. This legislation was further adjusted a decade later, bringing about a Landed Estates' Court, the functions of which were absorbed in 1879 by the Land Judges' Court, part of the Court of Chancery.[33]

However, the process of land redistribution, which began under the auspices of the Encumbered Estates Acts, was greatly accelerated by a series of Land Acts. The first of these, the 1870 Land Act, obliged landlords to compensate tenants for improvements made on their holdings. However, it was the 1881 Land Act, enacted in response to widespread social unrest and agitation orchestrated by the Land League, which posed the first serious challenge to the *status quo*, by guaranteeing fixity of tenure, a fair rent (to be adjudicated where necessary by an independent tribunal which the Act established – the Land Commission), and freedom to sell their particular interest in a holding. The Land Commission was charged also with assisting tenants with the purchase of their holdings by advancing up to three-quarters of the purchase money and with the purchasing land for resale to tenants. An inherent deficiency of the legislation was the fact that terms of purchase were the same regardless of the size of holding, the quality of the land and demographic conditions. This problem was addressed by the enactment of the 1891 Land Act, which established the Congested Districts Board.[34]

The torrent of legislation, combined with fundamental economic insolvency of estates and continued social unrest, disruption and hostility, left the landed estate class besieged but doggedly hanging on. With the Wyndham Land Act of 1903 there came a tipping point. It provided that landlords disposing of significant portions of their estates would receive a bonus of 12½ per cent. The bonus was an important incentive to sell, resulting in a rush to acquire benefits from the Act. The proceedings of the sale of an estate went towards clearing landlord debts, but the bonus could not be touched, unless the landlord was incredibly indebted. It was his to use as he pleased.

This 'bail-out' element included by the government of the day secured significant redistribution of land. While many landlords took their money and ran, so to speak, a significant number remained, living off the investment portfolios generated by land sales and continuing to pursue the life which they had had for so long.[35]

It was the 1930s before the landed gentry were finally vanquished, as global economic recession took its toll on the investment portfolios which had been accumulated earlier and the Free State Land Acts compulsorily acquired the residual estates on which they survived. Frequently bad advice and naivety played a part in their bankruptcy, as well as the recession. The Russian Revolution of 1917 also played a role, as many had invested in mineral deposits in Russia prior to the Bolshevik Revolution.

The Great Shoots of the
North-West: Woodcock,
Snipe and Grouse

If a sportsman is fond of cock shooting, it will repay him well for his trouble to take a trip to Ireland; it is not material what part to recommend, as it is impossible almost to go to a bad place for sport. As to asking leave, it is needless; as the only cause of jealousy that can subsist between the visitor and the owner of the ground will be for not acquainting him of his coming, in order that he might have it in his power to receive him with the usual hospitable manner, by providing beaters to show him sport, giving him the best of fare, a bottle of good claret, a sincere and hearty welcome, assuring his guest the longer he stays and honours him with his company, the more welcome he is, and the happier he will make him.[36]

Thornhill Sporting Directory (1804)

There are many places in Ireland which are famous for Woodcocks, amongst which perhaps the best are Baron's Court. Belonging to the Duke of Abercorn, Castle Bernard, in County Cork, where Lord Bandon often has excellent sport, Markree Castle, County Sligo, belonging to Captain Cooper, R.A., Glenstall, County Limerick, where Sir Charles Barrington has before now secured over 50 couple in the day – it was here that, on the first occasion of this being effected, on the hundredth cock being shot that all the beaters stopped and gave three rousing cheers, a proceeding which shows the keener of the Irish beater but would considerably astonish some of us in England – Muckross and Ashford, both belonging to Lord Ardilaun, the latter being the place being famous as the best of all and it is in one beat here –'Ballykyne' – that in 1892, 1894 and 1903, 209, 205 and 211 cock were killed on the day.

Arthur Acland-Hood, *Notes on Shooting in the British Isles* (1909), p. 56

The Woodcock

Elusive, mysterious, crepuscular, shy, magical, eerie: just some of words that have been used to describe the Woodcock, a bird that has fascinated and excited the interest of man for centuries, mainly because of its curious character and also because of its quality as a game species, which has been revered by shooters.

10 (left) Woodcock, Philip Rickman.

There is a resident population which breeds in suitable wooded habitat. Late winter and spring are the best times to see Woodcock, for then, in the twilight hours, the males perform display flights – known as roding – above or amongst the treetops. Following a wide circuit of the woods on broad, rounded, owl-like wings, Woodcock often use woodland rides as route markers whilst alternately croaking like demented frogs and uttering repeated, high-pitched 'tsiwick' calls.

Roding Woodcock are often first seen twenty minutes or so after sunset and again immediately before sunrise.[37] Commencement of the roding season seems to be heavily influenced by weather. Woodcock roding often starts at the beginning of March, or exceptionally in February. They rode over a relatively wide area in an effort to tempt female Woodcock up to join them, or, alternatively, to encourage females on the ground to reveal themselves. Another curious supposed feature of their behaviour is the question of carrying their young, a controversial issue which has not been put beyond dispute by incontrovertible photographic proof but yet remains alive in Woodcock lore.

It is the influx of migratory Woodcock, which swells the resident population for the winter months, which stirs the spirit, curiosity and instincts of field-sports men most. Their habit of arriving on the full moon – 'Woodcock moon' – most usually of November (but sometimes October) and the subsequent months of December and January signals a season that has been captured in words and on canvas for generations and for many defines the essence of winter field sports.

There are two main criteria for Woodcock habitat: firstly, earthworms, and secondly, suitable roosting cover, where their mottled rich plumage provides them with a perfect camouflage in the leaf litter and can provide the solitude which they crave:

> The cover a mixture of brambles, gorse bracken, fir plantations of varying ages, underwood of chestnut, hazel, rhododendrons and laurels, great beeches and ash trees, hollies and planes, an ever-changing layout, an olla-podrida of West of Ireland woodland growth; the ground now rising up to stony places, now sinking into marshy hollows. These woodlands, these wild places here and there, have blotted out erstwhile parks, demesnes – aye, mansion house and castle.
>
> Lord Dorchester, *Sport: Foxhunting and Shooting* (1935)

Permanent pasture is especially favoured, as constant grazing and manuring by cattle ensures an abundance of worms. The feeding areas tend to be near the roosting areas and definite paths are followed between the two at dusk and dawn, making them unsporting quarry at these times of day.

The climate and geography of the West of Ireland has always been attractive for wintering Woodcock; the tempering influence of the Gulf Stream, the pattern of agriculture, and availability of suitable cover have all contributed to the attractiveness of the area. In former times, significant efforts were applied on many of the former landed estates (most notably, Ashford, Baronscourt, Lissadell, Temple House, Classiebawn, Hazelwood) to understand the comings and goings of wintering Woodcock using private ringing experiments. These have been faithfully recorded in the Game Books of these estates and in other literature (see the sections relating to these estates for further discussion and references to this early research). In addition, Woodcock coverts were strictly preserved from disturbance of any kind, sometimes ruthlessly, in order to ensure the peace and solitude that would attract and hold the maximum number of Woodcock in order to facilitate a small number of 'big-bag' days. Nowhere were greater resources applied to this end than at Ashford Castle during the tenure of Lord Ardilaun, at the turn of the twentieth century.

However, the curiosity and interest in Woodcock behaviour and their population dynamics is probably as great today as ever. The status of Woodcock continues to be something of a mystery and certainly an issue around which there is still much debate, although the question of where they come from can now be answered with greater certainty. There is reasonably good evidence to suggest that, in the case of Ireland, Scandinavia and north-west Russia are the principal sources of many of the birds found in winter along the western seaboard, which arrive via the North Sea and western isles of Scotland, with a second line arriving from Eastern Europe and central Russia via Wales and the Irish Sea.[38]

Whether Woodcock are more or less plentiful than formerly is a much more open question and not just in relation to Ireland. For example, Trotman notes:

> ... based on the flimsiest of evidence the European Union Draft Management Plan for Woodcock 2006 and 2007 claimed unfavourable conservation status. However, Birdlife International/EBCC (2000) showed that in the majority of European and Baltic countries with sizeable numbers of breeding Woodcock, numbers were in fact stable. In fact an increase in numbers was reported from Denmark, Ireland, Holland and Spain. In France the monitoring of roding males since 1988 shows the French breeding population to be stable and probably increasing.[39]

The National Woodcock Association of Ireland[40] carries out an annual 'wing survey' in conjunction with other organisations to monitor and analyse population trends and its age profile. Statistical comparison with earlier times is not, of course, possible, because comparable data for the present does not exist, but the picture portrayed in annual reports of recent years suggests a relatively benign position. For example, of the season 2007/8 it is stated that it was:

> ... regarded as the best season for Woodcock in the last 40 years ... Woodcock appeared in larger than normal numbers during last season, the first large fall of Woodcock on the full moon in October was replicated through the following months including January. Calm clear weather on the days and nights on either side of the full moon contributed to a minimum of Woodcock fatalities on their migration to Ireland. The east coast of the country did not hold the normal number of birds as in previous years and likewise the midlands had a hit and miss population over the season.[41]

Of 2008/9, the chairman reported:

> Woodcock appeared in constant numbers during last season [20]08/09; the first fall of Woodcock came in October and was replicated through the following months including January. Again this year calm clear weather on the days and nights on either side of the full moon contributed to a maximum number of Woodcock arriving to Ireland. Throughout the country, Woodcock were reported in numbers and there appeared to be a blanket of Woodcock covering the whole of the country.[42]

Again, in 2009/10, the picture was strong, at least in the early part:

> This season [20]09/10 has seen a great number of Woodcock migrating to Ireland, the migration began early due to very cold weather in Europe and this weather followed the Woodcock to Ireland where we had one of the coldest winters in history. This cold weather created great difficulties for wildfowl and waders who require soft ground to feed and a suspension of hunting was imposed in the early part of January.[43]

Similarly, in 2010/11:

> As Woodcock numbers were building up in November the sudden change of temperature in
> December caused probing birds and in particular Woodcock severe hardship and it could be
> suggested that many juvenile Woodcock on their first migration to Ireland did not survive the
> severe cold. The wing survey would tend to support this contention as there were many more
> adults in the wing analysis results that normal.[44]

Of course this picture does not 'prove' whether Woodcock are more or less abundant than they
were formerly, but it does suggest that the wintering population remains strong and the habitat
is there to support it. Undoubtedly, the afforestation programme supported by successive Irish
governments over the past seventy or so years, especially on upland moorland areas of the West,
has meant a reduced concentration of the wintering population, a factor which has probably at
least compensated for increased general levels of disturbance in woodlands. The effect of lower
densities on overall bag numbers is rather more difficult to ascertain, but it has had the effect of
making the kind of very large bags that were a feature of a small number of estates' shoots a thing
of the past. Whether this is a good or bad thing for the sustainability of Woodcock numbers,
however, is rather difficult to judge.

The Snipe

> Ireland has for centuries been remarkable for the abundance of its Snipe in the shooting season
> – 'to which', as Watters says, 'the sister kingdom can offer no comparison' ... It is said, however,
> that the numbers have fallen greatly since the introduction of breech-loading guns. At any rate,
> the larger bags of former times are no longer obtained ...[45]

These words were written in 1953 and as the game records of many shoots presented in the following pages demonstrate, Snipe represented a significant element of estate shooting in Ireland.
It was well represented in the bag of a mixed day's shooting or as the outcome of days spent on a
bog in their pursuit. Many pages of many books record escapades of Snipe shooting in the latter
part of the nineteenth and early part of the twentieth centuries. A stalwart like Payne-Gallwey's
The Fowler in Ireland (1882) has much to say of Snipe shooting, including, importantly, the following remark:

> It is a mistake to think that the best [Snipe] shooting is in bogs and marshes. The birds, no
> doubt, collect in such places, but will rise in wisps and not afford pleasant sport in consequence.
> Where Snipe rise and lie best is in the large wet green fields, in which the water, though splash-
> ing nearly every step, rarely reaches the ankle.[46]

Wild Sports in Ireland by John Bickerdyke (the *nom de plume* of Theodore Cook), written at
Paradise, County Clare, the family home of the Henn family in the closing years of the nineteenth
century and *Seventy Years of Irish Life* by W.R. Le Fanu, first published in 1893, are but two others
which contain detailed and colourful accounts of the glory days of Snipe shooting in Ireland.

There are several factors which account for the popularity of Snipe shooting. One author in
the late nineteenth century pointed out:

11 Snipe in the Reeds, Archibald Thorburn.

Snipe shooting has one great advantage: it can be enjoyed by the poor man as well as the rich. No high rents, no keepers, no army of beaters, no highly preserved ground are necessary for its enjoyment – nor could the veriest curmudgeon of a farmer make any claim for damages inflicted by Snipe.[47]

Another feature of Snipe shooting which makes it so attractive is the fact that:

> … the unreliability of the Snipe is only equalled by the unreliability of one's shooting … but [in the view of Hugh Pollard] they are the 'Austin Sevens' of the game world and three thousand acres of Irish bog and mountain will hardly yield the sportsman of restricted means the sport he will get on three hundred acres of decent English rough shooting, though he will get more exercise.[48]

Many would disagree!

In the past half century, however, although hard statistical evidence is not available to *prove* the point, few would argue that there have not been further substantial declines in Snipe numbers. The main cause has been the loss of the kind of habitats precisely described by Payne-Gallwey above through drainage in support of improved agricultural output.

The Irish Red Grouse

Red Grouse are essentially a territorial bird and towards the end of October the cock birds begin to re-establish their territory. The most sought-after areas contain a diversity of habitat, including patches of differently aged heather, other edible vegetation and water. The size of the territory is between two and thirty acres, depending on the quality of the habitat. During harsh weather, the birds abandon their territories and congregate in large packs. As the weather becomes milder again, they disperse and territories are resumed. Grouse often pair up at this time, sometimes resuming the relationship of the previous year, and the male will defend the territory vigorously.

Apart from vagaries of weather and habitat, Grouse are prone to two diseases. The first is the strongyle worm – a tiny parasitic nematode which burrows into the wall of the gut – and the second is louping ill, which is spread by ticks. Their susceptibility to these diseases depends in some measure on the overall density of Grouse left after a shooting season and on the ratio of old to young in the population. In addition to very precise and active habitat management, healthy Grouse stocks also require precise management of stocks during the shooting season. Too many birds left to over-winter tends to leave the population exposed to disease and resultant mortality, which can be catastrophic; too few birds left and there is an insufficient number to breed and sustain the population at an optimal level. Great game-keeping skill is required to manage Grouse to their full potential.

No doubt surrounds the status of the Red Grouse in Ireland; it has suffered catastrophic failure and barely hangs on in a remnant of its former habitat. As a game quarry species it no longer exists in any meaningful way. This contrasts with the position a hundred years ago, when Grouse bags on many shoots in the west, north-west, parts of the midlands, and in County Wicklow were a feature and integral part of the shooting season in Ireland. At no time did the shooting compare with moors on the east coast of Scotland, but as the following pages attest, there was good Grouse shooting on many Irish moors.[49]

However, their loss is a tragedy: the Irish Red Grouse is a separate sub-species. It is, therefore, the only indigenous game-bird species. Its demise is due entirely to the loss and mismanagement of the moorland heather habitat on which it depends. There was a partial resumption of moor management following the First World War, but this was short-lived, as political turbulence and changes to the system of land tenure took their toll on Grouse moor management. Grouse management was simply not on the agenda of the landowners of the newly born State. Declining Grouse populations were also a feature of Scottish (and English) moors in the 1930s and '40s.[50] As in Ireland, the causes were the same: reduced effectiveness of moor management and overgrazing by sheep and cattle.[51] In Ireland, additional causes of decline were habitat degradation and fragmentation resulting from afforestation and peat land exploitation.

Frequent attempts have been made to halt and reverse the trend of decline, but none have succeeded. The first and probably the most serious initiative came in the 1960s on foot of representations from the National Farmers' Association. As a result, in 1966, the Minister for Lands commissioned An Foras Talúntais (The Agricultural Institute) to create a research programme which would provide recommendations on increasing Grouse populations. The project was undertaken at the Glenamoy Research Station in County Mayo, under the guiding hand of Mr P.J. O'Hare, who led the project in collaboration with Mr Adam Watson of the (then) Game Conservancy (now the Game and Wildlife Conservation Trust). While much was learnt through this collaboration, by the time the second phase of the project was underway in the early 1970s, it was found that 'there was a big decline in Grouse numbers on all areas, including experimentally treated ones, though the treated ones continued to have more Grouse relative to their respective control areas. The decline was associated with increased sheep stocks after entry to the EC and higher headage subsidies.'[52] These influences continued to exert a negative effect over the following two decades on the already fragile status of the Red Grouse, while issues of commonage and

12 *Spring Grouse*, Archibald Thorburn.

the adverse risk/reward profile of investment in moorland renewal prevented *effective action* on the ground to save the Red Grouse in Ireland.

There has been recent renewed effort to halt the decline of the Red Grouse, with the establishment in November 2010 of the Irish Red Grouse Association, under the auspices of Countryside Alliance Ireland. At its recent conference in October 2011, it set out a programme of possible actions aimed again at addressing the issue of declining Red Grouse in Ireland.

THE ASHFORD ESTATE, CONG, COUNTY GALWAY: THE BEST WOODCOCK SHOOT IN THE WORLD

Ashford was acquired by Sir Benjamin Lee Guinness (1798-1867) for his eldest son Arthur (1840-1915) from Lord Oranmore and Browne in 1852. He purchased other estates from the Encumbered Estates Court, including the Doon Estate from Sir Richard O'Donnell, the Cong Estate from Alexander Lambert and part of the Rosehill Estate from Lords Charlemont and Leitrim. He bought the Elwood Estate of Strandhill, just across the river from Ashford, in 1871 and Lord Kilmaine sold him Inishdoorus islands on Lough Corrib. In all there were about 29,000 acres accumulated in and around Ashford.

In 1868, Sir Arthur inherited Ashford from his father (along with St Anne's in Clontarf, County Dublin, where he was to die in 1915). He married Olive White (d. 1925), of Bantry House, in February 1871, in what has been described as an arranged marriage:

> Guinness was wealthy, but socially ill at ease and keen to disguise his unconventional private life. Lady Olivia was aristocratic in bearing and anxious to become a leading society hostess and patron of the arts. She was happy to accept what was always understood to be a wholly platonic marriage in exchange for an unusual degree of personal and material independence.[53]

Sir Arthur was educated at Eton and Trinity College Dublin. More interested in politics than business, on Sir Benjamin's death he was returned to his father's seat at a by-election and represented the City of Dublin at Westminster. He was returned again in the general election of 1868. However, it was discovered that his agent had bribed an elector without his knowledge and he

13 Ashford Castle, Cong, County Mayo.

14 **Lord Ardilaun at work.**

was unseated on a petition the following year. Nevertheless, he was re-elected in 1874, holding the seat until 1880 when he was raised to the peerage as 1st Baron Ardilaun of Ashford. Politically he was a staunch Unionist and strongly opposed to Home Rule.

Following his father's death, Arthur was jointly responsible, with his younger brother Edward Cecil, for the entire running of the Guinness Brewery, a subject in which he seems to have had not much interest. His brother, by contrast, had been his father's secretary for many years and had accumulated a good deal of knowledge of the business. The collaboration was not an easy one and Arthur sold his shares to Edward Cecil for £680,000 in instalments between 1877 and 1880.

Along with his inheritance from his father and private investments, Lord Ardilaun was a millionaire. In effect he had limitless resources to devote to his passion for Woodcock shooting and indeed a lifestyle that couldn't even be imagined by most people, then or now. From the time the estate had been acquired, a careful programme of planting and covert management had been commenced and put in place with a view to making it an attractive habitat for Woodcock.[4] 'Every covert was planted with the timber or shrubs most favoured by 'cock; as soon as any deteriorated they were uprooted and replaced, and even broad leaved timber was banned because of its tendency to drip.'[55]

By the late 1800s, there is evidence to show that his investment was starting to pay dividends, as the following data contained in the shoot records for Ashford shows:[56]

Date	Guns	Duration (Days)	Bag over duration of shoot	Best one day
1878	6	5	320	116
1879	5	4	350	117
1880	6	5	336	165
1881	6	3	216	88
1882	no shoot			
1883	no shoot			
1884	6	2	196	172
1885	7	5	280	112
1886	7	5	301	154
1887	7	4	278	145
1888	6	5	210	102
1889	no shoot			
1890	6	4	297	183
1891	7	5	273	209
1892	no shoot			
1893	7	6	336	145
1894	7	6	336	145
1895	8	6	512	209
1896	8	4	247	126
1897	5	6	307	128
1898	7	6	300	118
1899	7	6	400	168
1900	7	5	273	140
1901	8	4	234	117
1902	7	5	284	130
1903	no shoot			
1904	8	6	554	211
1905	8	6	444	181

In addition, Acland-Hood (1915) records that:

There are several beats on the estate which are only shot once a year, as a rule at the end of January; the most famous being Ballykine, Toberbearoge, which come into the same day. Ross Hill – Cong Rocks and Pigeon Hole – and Doon, which is some twelve miles away, at the end of Lough Corrib. Each has its distinctive features. At Ross Hill nearly the whole morning is taken up in beating two islands in Lough Mask, two Guns generally guarding the outside flank in boats. When the water is rough it is an exciting experience, and most difficult to shoot at all to say nothing of shooting successfully. Doon, which is generally best in very hard weather, is an old large wood on the side of a very steep hill, with very old and deep heather for under covert. Birds flushed from the top dart straight down the hill towards the Guns below and then turn sharply and apparently fly for the next man's head, twisting and turning in every direction and affording perhaps the most difficult chances one gets at Ashford. The best beat of all is Ballykine, as the records will show. Ballykine itself is an old wood, consisting principally of hazel, with a few hollies and a little bracken, all springing from the limestone rocks. Being an old demesne, it is surrounded by a high wall, and no doubt it is this wall which has made it such a favourite with the 'cock as it is so perfectly undisturbed. The first beat in Ballykine proper is the best, and we have known fifty-eight 'cock killed in this one long strip, one Gun being fortunate enough to annex sixteen birds. There is another covert called Toberbearoge, which is shot the same day, a very long larch covert, perhaps eighteen years old and of late years this has proved almost as productive as Ballykine itself.[57]

The Royal Shoot of January 1905

In 1905 there was a great shoot (despite unsuitable weather conditions: it was generally sunny) and an even greater social occasion. The principal guest of Lord and Lady Ardilaun was the Prince of Wales (soon to be King George V). The event was exhaustively reported in the papers of the time including the *Court Circular*, *The Irish Field*, *Vanity Fair*, *The Times*, *The Irish Times*, *Westminster Gazette* and *Madame*, amongst others.[58] A selection of extracts from these is contained in O. FitzGerald's *Ashford Castle: Through the Centuries*.[59]

The other house party guests included Sir Charles Cust, Equerry to HRH the Prince of Wales, Lord Bandon, Lord Rathmore, Col. the Hon. Robert Villiers Dillon, Maj. Arthur Acland-Hood and Mr Percy La Touche.

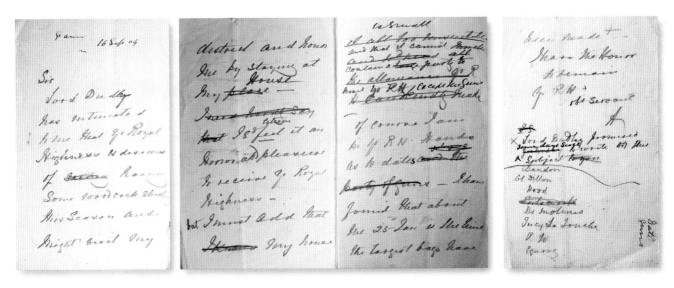

15 A draft by Lord Ardilaun, written in pencil, of his invitation to HRH the Prince of Wales, dated 16 September 1904. It is evident from this that the instigation of the invitation was from HRH the Prince of Wales himself through Lord Dudley, who was Lord Lieutenant of Ireland between 1902 and 1905. The opening lines read, 'Sir, Lord Dudley has intimated to me that Yr Royal Highness is desirous of ~~seeking~~ having some Woodcock shooting this season and might visit my district and honour me by staying at my ~~place~~ House. ~~I need hardly say that~~ I sd feel it an honour and pleasure to receive yr Royal Highness but I must add that my house is small …'

So who were these invited guests?

HRH the Prince of Wales (from 6 May 1910, His Majesty King George V), George Frederick Ernest Albert (1865-1936)

Included in the 'Top Shot' list of the 100 greatest shots of all time, compiled by *The Field* (2009), where he is described as, 'A King among men on the stand and a gifted shot. He was in the party at Hall Barn, Buckinghamshire in December 1913 when 3,937 Pheasants were shot, the largest Pheasant bag made in the UK at the time.'

George was a grandson of Queen Victoria and Prince Albert of Saxe-Coburg and Gotha. From 1877 until 1891 he served in the Royal Navy. On the death of Victoria in 1901, George's father became King Edward VII and George was made Prince of Wales. On his father's death in 1910, he succeeded as King-Emperor of the British Empire. He was the only Emperor of India to be present at his own Delhi Durbar.

In 1917, he became the first monarch of the House of Windsor, which he renamed from the House of Saxe-Coburg and Gotha as a result of anti-German public feeling. His reign saw the rise of socialism, communism, fascism, Irish republicanism and the first Labour ministry, all of which radically changed the political landscape. He was plagued by illness throughout much of his later reign and was succeeded by his eldest son, Edward VIII.

Born on 3 June 1865 at Marlborough House, London, George was the second son of the Prince and Princess of Wales, Albert Edward and Alexandra. His father was the eldest son of Queen Victoria and Prince Albert of Saxe-Coburg and Gotha. His mother was the eldest daughter of King Christian IX of Denmark.

16 **The Royal Party at the lunch pavilion.**

As a younger son of the Prince of Wales, there was little expectation that George would become King. He was third in line to the throne, after his father and elder brother, Prince Albert Victor. The death of his elder brother effectively ended George's naval career, as he was now directly in the line of succession. George was created Duke of York, Earl of Inverness and Baron Killarney by Queen Victoria on 24 May 1892. The Duke and Duchess of York lived mainly at York Cottage, a relatively small house in Sandringham, Norfolk, where their way of life mirrored that of a comfortable middle-class family rather than royalty. George preferred a simple, almost quiet, life, in marked contrast to the lively social life pursued by his father.

On 9 November 1901, George was created Prince of Wales and Earl of Chester. King Edward VII wished to prepare his son for his future role as King. In contrast to Edward himself, whom Queen Victoria had deliberately excluded from State affairs, George was given wide access to State documents by his father. George in turn allowed his wife access to his papers, as he valued her counsel, and Mary often helped write her husband's speeches.

On 6 May 1910, King Edward VII died and George became King. He inherited the throne at a politically turbulent time. The Liberal Prime Minister H.H. Asquith led a minority government dependent upon the support of Irish Nationalists. As part of his Irish policy, Asquith sought to introduce legislation that would give Ireland Home Rule, but the Conservatives and Unionists were opposed to it. Desperate to avoid the prospect of civil war in Ireland between Unionists and Nationalists, George called a meeting of all parties at Buckingham Palace in July 1914 in an attempt to negotiate a settlement. Before an agreement was reached, political developments in Britain and Ireland were overtaken by events in Europe, and the issue of Irish Home Rule was shelved.

George preferred to stay at home pursuing his hobbies of stamp collecting and game shooting, and lived what later biographers would consider a dull life because of its conventionality. He inherited his father's passion for shooting and for Woodcock shooting in particular, a point recalled by John Betjeman in his verses on the death of the King:

17 **HRH the Prince of Wales's letter of thanks to Lord Ardilaun, dated 31 January 1905.**

> Spirits of well-shot Woodcock, Partridge, Snipe
> Flutter and bear him up the Norfolk sky[60]

His passion was to be fulfilled in strong measure during his week at Ashford.

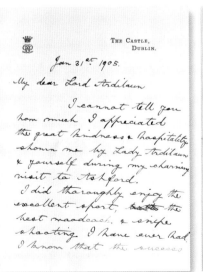

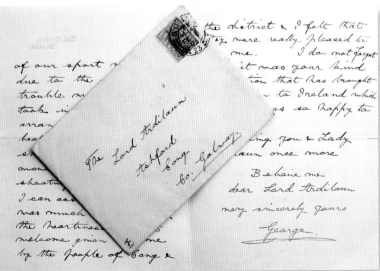

Sir Charles Leopold Cust (1864-1939)
Equerry to the Prince of Wales. He succeeded in that role after the Prince's coronation. He was responsible for creating The Queen Mary photograph collection on India, while accompanying the Royal Tour of 1905/1906.[61]

James Francis Bernard, 4th Earl of Bandon, KP (1850-1924)[62]
A British Deputy Lieutenant in Ireland and representative peer. Lord Bandon was a cousin of the Earl of Middleton (head of the southern Irish Unionists at the time of the Anglo-Irish War, 1919-1921). He was married in 1876 to 'Doty', a daughter of Lord Carbery. They were, by all accounts, an immensely hospitable and showy couple, known locally as 'the King and Queen'. He was a great practical joker and fond of rollicking parties.[63] He was a keen shot and was at practically every worthwhile shoot in the country. His name appears more consistently across every Game Book than any other member of the landed gentry.

Castle Bernard, his estate near the town of Bandon, County Cork – a famous Woodcock shoot in its own right – was one of the last great houses burned during the troubles of the 1920s, by an Irish Republican Army party under Sean Hales on 21 June 1921 as a reprisal measure against British policy to burn Irish homes in districts where martial law had been declared. Tom Barry, the leader of the local IRA, claimed they burned two 'Big Houses' for every one Irish peasant's cottage destroyed.

Lord Bandon was also kidnapped by the local IRA and held hostage for six weeks before being released on 12 July. The IRA threatened to execute him if the British went ahead with executing IRA prisoners. During his captivity, Bandon coolly played cards with his captors, who treated him well. Tom Barry later stated he believed the kidnapping helped move the British towards the Anglo-Irish Treaty of 1921 and the cessation of hostilities.

Part of the family moved to Scotland in the late thirties. James Owen Bernard, the son of Robert Bernard, were last heard of in a small town called Cardenden (Bowhill), close to Lockgelly in Fifeshire, Scotland. The only surviving son of James O. Bernard is Robert Mitchell Bernard.

David Robert Plunket, 1st Baron Rathmore PC, QC (1838-1919)[64]
Irish lawyer and Conservative politician. He was the third son of John Plunket, 3rd Baron Plunket, second son of William Plunket, 1st Baron Plunket, and Lord Chancellor of Ireland. His mother was Charlotte, daughter of Charles Bushe, Lord Chief Justice of Ireland, while the Most Revd William Plunket, 4th Baron Plunket, Archbishop of Dublin, was his elder brother, who was married to Anne Lee Guinness, sister of Lord Ardilaun. He was educated at Trinity College Dublin and was called to the Irish bar in 1862.

After practising on the Munster Circuit for a number of years, Plunket was made a Queen's Counsel in 1868 and became legal adviser to the Irish Government that same year. In 1870, he was elected Conservative Member of Parliament for Dublin University, and was Solicitor General for Ireland under Benjamin Disraeli from 1875 to 1877. He was then briefly Paymaster General under Disraeli (then the Earl of Beaconsfield) in 1880 and was sworn of the Privy Council the same year. In 1885, he became First Commissioner of Works in Lord Salisbury's first ministry, a post he held until January 1886. He resumed the same post in August of the same year when the Conservatives returned to power, and held it until 1892. On his retirement from the House of Commons in 1895 he was elevated to the peerage as Baron Rathmore of Shanganagh in the County of Dublin.

Apart from his political and legal career, he was a director of the Suez Canal Company, chairman of the North London Railway for many years, and was also a director of the Central London Railway at its opening in 1900.

In Dublin, Rathmore was a member of the Kildare Street Club. He died in August 1919, unmarried, at the age of eighty, in a hotel in Greenore, County Louth, and his peerage became extinct on his death.

Colonel the Hon. Robert Dillon (1838-1923)[65]

Robert Villiers Dillon was son of Robert Dillon (1807-1893), 3rd Baron Clonbrock, and his wife, the Hon. Caroline Spencer (1805-1864). After attending Carshalton and Woolich schools, he commenced a career with the army in August 1853, as a Gentleman Cadet of the Royal Artillery Regiment. In 1857, he was sent to Hong Kong, where he was stationed until his return, initially to Athlone in 1863 and then to the Curragh. Both stations worked well in terms of facilitating hunting and getting home to shoot, which he did frequently. His sisters loved having him, George's diary recording, 'it is so jolly having him home again and how much he was missed … he is so merry'. In 1864, he was appointed extra ADC to Lord Carlisle and during the summer of that year he spent a good deal of time playing cricket at the Viceregal Lodge.

In 1873, he became engaged to Harriet (always known as Harrie) Gladstone, daughter of Mr Adam Gladstone, a first cousin of W.E. Gladstone, the Prime Minister. On his engagement, he received a letter from his father offering him his good wishes:

> I will add most sincerely and truly that no son had ever more faithfully earned a father's blessing than you have all your life through. You have, I am deeply thankful to say, been ever and always the very best of sons and have never been the means of giving me one moment's uneasiness.[66]

They were married on 3 June 1873 at Beckanham church, near Harrie's home, and honeymooned in Ireland.

He continued to serve with the Royal Artillery until his retirement in 1887, with the honorary rank of major general – a title he never used, favoring instead colonel. They then went to live at Wootton House, near Bedford, and stayed there almost for the rest of his life. He was attracted to Wootton House by the hunting and enjoyed many years of it. However, he came back to Clonbrock every winter in time for the first shoot and stayed for some Snipe shooting. He was an extremely good shot and on this account he received an invitation annually from Lord Ardilaun.

Their only son, Charles Henry ('Charley'), attended Eton and Sandhurst before his Commission with the Rifle Brigade. In 1901, at the age of twenty-three, he was killed in the Boer War. They placed a brass tablet to his memory in Ahascragh church, Ballinasloe. It was found in the ruins of the church after the fire of 1922 – the only thing in the building that had survived. There were two daughters: Hilda and Stella Margaret.

Major Arthur Acland-Hood (1859-1929)

Son of Sir Alexander Bateman Periam Acland-Hood, 3rd Baronet, and Isabel Harriet Fuller-Palmer-Acland. Married Miriam Anne Reynardson, daughter of Col. Charles Birch Reynardson in 1896. Held the office of Deputy Lieutenant and the office of Justice of the Peace (JP). Invested as an Officer, Order of the British Empire (OBE).

A writer and shooting legend, Acland-Hood was included in the 'Top Shot' list of the 100 greatest shots of all time compiled by *The Field* (2009), where he is described as, 'in the front rank of Edwardian shots. With Payne-Gallwey and Rimington-Wilson, he was on Broomhead Moor in August 1913 when 2,843 Grouse were bagged. A low Partridge or Pheasant on the left was his Achilles heel.'

He authored *Notes on Shooting in the British Isles* (London, 1909) and a chapter on Woodcock contained in *The Gun at Home and Abroad* in four volumes, which he co-authored with Millais, *et al.* These were published between 1912 and 1915. The former is a collection of essays, most of which had been published previously as articles in *The Times*. In the preface he states:

I was encouraged by several friends [that] … if you publish these articles in a small book, which would slip easily into the great coat pocket (and *mind* and have a good clear print), many people will buy it to while away a tedious journey or wet Sunday afternoon and they are sure to go to sleep and dream of many good days they have previously enjoyed and recommend it to other victims of insomnia.

The Gun at Home and Abroad, by contrast, is truly encyclopaedic in scope. It encompasses all aspects of shooting, from stag hunting technique and statistics, to tips on burning Grouse moors in autumn, to accounts of African big-game hunts that blend solid observation with colourful anecdotes. It is a lavishly produced and richly informative work, documenting the sporting life of a bygone era. Each volume contains a photogravure frontispiece of King George V. It is unclear what his connection to Ardilaun may have been. It is presumed that he was present as part of HRH's party.

Mr Percy La Touche (1846-1921)

There are three branches of the La Touche family in Ireland, namely: the Bellvue, Delgany, County Wicklow, family; the Harristown, County Kildare, family, and the Marlay, Rathfarnham, County Dublin, family. Percy La Touche comes from the Harristown branch.

He was son of John 'The Master' (John being Master of the Kildare Hounds, 1841-45) La Touche (1814-1904) and Maria (b. 1824), only child of the Dowager Countess of Desart, County Kilkenny, who was a very cultured lady, with a particular interest in botany, drawing, languages and poetry. John Ruskin called her 'Lacerta'. She was an avid letter-writer and wrote a number of tracts on religious and social themes. She also wrote two novels, *The Clintons* (1853) and *Lady Willoughby* (1855). She had a horror of blood sports, and complained often about the neighbouring gentry, whose chief delight was in such country pursuits.[67] They had three children: Emily, born 1844; Percy, born 1846, and Rose, born 1849.[68]

When 'The Master' died in 1904 in his ninetieth year, his son Percy succeeded to the estate at the age of fifty-eight and spent his time in those pursuits abhorred by his mother. He rode several winners in steeplechases in his early years and along with Lord Drogheda. He played a major part in managing Punchestown racecourse and the Irish Turf Club. He presented a cup (known to this day as the La Touche Cup) for competition at the Punchestown Spring Festival, over four miles of banks, fences, stone walls and hurdles. He moved in the highest levels of society and was a favourite of Edward VII. He was closely involved in Punchestown Races, which Edward VII and Queen Alexandra attended on 26 and 27 April 1904.

La Touche married Lady Annette Scott, a sister of the 4th Earl of Clonmel, but they had no children. Percy and Lord Enniskillen (a fellow steward of the Turf Club) were sometimes included on English shooting parties in the company of King Edward and other social luminaries.[69] After his death in 1921, Annette having died six months earlier, his sister Emily's son Ernest Ottway Ward succeeded, and the estate passed through two other owners before being sold in 1946 to Maj. Michael Wentworth Beaumont, who had connections with shooting on the South Slob in County Wexford.

18 *Percy La Touche* by Sarah Purser.

Commencement of Shooting: Wednesday 25 January
The *Westminster Gazette* of 31 January 1905 reported that shooting commenced on Wednesday 25 January:

> … early in the morning, and was very satisfactory, though the bag did not come within thirty of the record established at Ashford a couple of years earlier when 211 Woodcock were killed. By half past eight the Guns were on their way to Clonbur covert, a mile from the house, where shooting began at once with about 50 beaters driving the birds out into open glades. The Prince was in great form and shot magnificently, only one of the party exceeding by a single bird His Royal Highness's first day's record. Lunch was served in the Lunch House at Ballycoyne and the sportsmen shot on until dark, the day's count including 180 Woodcock and a few Pheasants. The shooting on Thursday was over the Ross Hill Estate which skirts Lough Mask and on two of the islands on the Lough – the smallest of which covers 150 acres. Glorious sunshine prevailed each day which was most disappointing for the host as hard frost is what is so essential for Woodcock shooting. The bag on the concluding days of the week seldom held more than from 90 to 100 Woodcock but a number of Pheasants Partridges and other birds were also shot.[70]

Country Life of 4 February 1905 reports similarly:

> The first beat shot was Ballykyne, the most famous collection of Woodcock coverts in the British Isles. The Guns, seven in number, were placed some in line some ahead of the flanks … the next beat called Black Wood was not so good as usual. After this a very typical beat is taken over the rocks of Drineen … His Royal Highness, walking in front of the line of Beaters had some capital shooting here … a further beat in the afternoon at Pigeon Hole rocks provided a good many birds being flushed. At the end of the day the total was found to be 181 Woodcocks and a few Pheasants. His Royal Highness headed the score by killing 40 Woodcock. On the next day a further 11 birds were shot at Rosshill on Lough Mask; 85 'cock on the following day around Ashford itself and 30 at Doon on Saturday.

1905

DATE.	GUNS.	No. of Guns.	Woodcock	Pheasants	Snipe.	Duck.	Rabbits.	Hares.	Various.	BEAT.
Jan: 25.	Lord Ardilaun. Lord Bandon. Sir C Cust. Col. Hon. R Dillon. Maj. A. Hood. H.R.H. Prince of Wales. Lord Rathmore. Percy la Touche. 8 Guns	181.								Ballykine. Ross Hill.
26.	The Same.	92.								
27.	The Same.	85.								
28.	The Same.	29.								
30.	The Same.	32.								
31.	The Same.	25.								
		Total. 444								

19 The game card for the Royal Shoot, 1905, showing the Guns and bag for each day of the shoot.

At the shoot honouring the Prince of Wales, held between 25 and 31 January 1905, 444 birds were killed. The seven Guns shot 211 Woodcock on a single day. On another day, the Prince and Maj. Acland-Hood went Snipe shooting and shot eighty birds between them. The Prince was delighted and told Lady Ardilaun that evening he had 'never had such a day in his life'.[71]

The Organisation of the Beats

Shooting was organised with meticulous attention to detail. Each 'beat' varied in width from 100m to 250m, and were from 500m to 1,000m in length. They were flanked on all sides by shooting paths and worked to obtain the longest drive.

There were a large number of people involved in the organisation and presentation of birds to the Guns, which usually numbered seven. These comprised the gamekeeper, head beater, beaters (around fifty), pickers (at least two), loaders (one to each Gun), and dog-men (no fewer than three).[72]

> Your stick is a terrible giveaway, since nothing can hide the fact of it is empty or poorly furnished with birds; on the other hand if you have been lucky, you regard your bulging stick with pride, for there is the symbol of your prowess plain for all folk to see.[73]

The role of the gamekeeper is that of Director of Field Operations. He was also responsible for cleaning and oiling the guns at the end of each day's shooting.

Guns were positioned on the shooting paths, usually four on the right and three on the left. Each Gun was numbered according to his position, which was allocated by a draw of numbers.

20 **Lord Ardilaun with beaters.**

To eliminate any advantage, the position of each Gun was changed, usually down (i.e. seven to six; six to five; etc.) following each beat.

At the beginning of each beat, all the beaters are lined across the starting line and the game-keeper gives the starting signal (usually a whistle or horn blow). The head beater then leads his beaters along the beater paths, making as much noise as possible. The distance between beaters was usually maintained at twenty metres, or closer in some instances. On flushing a bird, the beaters would scan its line of flight and shout to the Gun nearest it. If the Gun is successful, the gamekeeper may signal a halt to allow the bird to be retrieved. When the Woodcock is bagged, a signal to recommence is given. This process is repeated as often as necessary until the beat is completed.

The picker's role is to anticipate where the bird is likely to have fallen and to retrieve it. Injured birds were 'marked' and picked with dogs as speedily as possible. The picker was responsible also for keeping an account of the number of birds shot by each Gun. The dead birds were carried along the beat on a game stick. Acland-Hood (1909), remarks:

> … it is dangerous and almost useless to employ a retriever so each gun is accompanied by a 'picker' or particularly smart and keen-eyed beater, who, directly a bird falls, instantaneously marks the spot and dashes into the covert – and it is rarely that one has to wait long before the welcome cry of 'I have him your honour' comes from the depth of the covert. I have known a picker collect successfully six birds all knocked down into seemingly impossible rocks and under-growth at one stand and in different directions and it is by no means uncommon for a picker to gather over 40 'cocks for his patron on a big day at Ballykyne without losing one, or having to ask for the services of the one brace of retrievers that is brought out on these occasions.[74]

Surrounding Social Activities

The visit attracted a lot of public attention, to which the following press report extracts, taken from FitzGerald's *Ashford Castle: Through the Centuries*, attest:

> On Friday morning the Prince drove through the village of Cong on his way to the Cong Rock coverts and had an extraordinarily enthusiastic reception from the people who had put up the most wonderful decorations in his honour. Lord and Lady Ardilaun drove with His Royal Highness through the little town, but Lady Ardilaun returned to the house before the shooting began. She is in no sense of the word a sportswoman and seldom joined the Guns even at lunch. She is a sweet retiring woman with a charming face. A few outside guests came to dinner on several nights; otherwise the party spent a quiet evening at Bridge and retired early after the fatigues of the day. Lady Ardilaun wore some lovely dinner gowns during the week, that on the evening of the Prince's arrival being especially beautiful, being of white crepe de Chine, trimmed with bands of ostrich feathers, the bodice draped with a fichu of exquisite old Irish point. Lord Ardilaun did everything in Princely fashion during the week and forgot nothing which could add to his Royal guest's comfort and pleasure. The Prince must have found it hard that he was in far-off Connemara, that odd wild corner of the earth which is supposed to have escaped the wand of civilisation.

An important concern relating to the visit was security. There is a letter from the Prince's private secretary, the future Prime Minister Neville Chamberlain, to Lord Ardilaun, contained in the Memorabilia Room at Ashford, which describes the arrangements that were planned.

However, it may be noted that there was great emphasis, too, that security should not be at the expense of disturbing any of the coverts, 'You may rely on the Royal Irish Constabulary keeping a vigilant eye "outside" the coverts.'

22
Chamberlain's letter to Lord Ardilaun regarding security arrangements for the Royal Shoot.

Shoot Returns at Cong, Selected Years, 1906-1983

The subsequent bag record history from Ashford is summarised in the table below. It demonstrates a generally strong trend up to the early 1950s, after which the returns shrank until shooting ceased in 1983.

Shoot Returns Cong Selected Years, 1906-1983

Year	Duration of Shoot (Days)	No. of Guns	Bag	No. of Birds Flushed
1906	6	7	280	–
1907	6	7	393	–
1908	6	7	434	–
1909	6	7	454	–
1910	6	7	587	–
1917	4	7	390	–
1918	4	7	182	–
1919	4	7	203	–
1928	8	7	636	–
1929	11	7	752	–
1930	11	7	569	–
1931	14	7	656	–
1932	13	7	522	–
1933	9	7	522	–
1934	10	7	509	–
1937	9	7	722	–
1938	7	7	526	–
1940	7	7	400	–
1941	6	7	326	–
1951	10	7	485	–
1961	5	6	88	–
1971	6	8	104	–
1974	6 (Dec. only)	7	48	243
1975	12	7	129	392
1976	6	7	81	345
1977	12	7	118	424
1978	12	7	79	406
1979	9	7	106	427
1980	11	7	168	699
1981	13	7	251	902
1982	12	7	187	708
1983	6 (Jan. only)	7	80	332

The Record Shoot of January 1910

Shoots were held annually up until 1910, after which there was a lapse until 1917. Presumably this reflected the declining health of Lord Ardilaun, who died at St Anne's in Clontarf, Dublin, in 1915. Thus, the shoot of 1910 was his last. It is also famous because of the record for a *single day* that was established on 31 January, when the bag was 228 Woodcock. To date, this has not been repeated anywhere. The 1910 shoot took place over five days from January 1928 to 2 February.

23 Shoot
card for the
record shoot
of January 1910
showing the
Guns.

DATE.	GUNS.	No. of Guns.	Woodcock	Pheasants	Snipe.	Duck.	Rabbits.	Hares.	Various.	BEAT.
	1910. Record Shoot.									
Jan: 28.	Lord Ardilaun. Lord Bandon.	77.								Ross Hill.
	M͏ʳ E. Becker. M͏ʳ C.P. Coote.									Ballykine.
	The O'Connor Don. Percy la Touche.									
	Hon: E. O'Brien. 7 Guns.									
29.	The Same.	86.								
31.	The Same.	228.								
Feb: 1.	The Same.	110.								
2.	The Same.	86.								
		Tot. 587								

The total bag was 587 Woodcock. However, the record bag for a *shoot* at the estate was established 1929, when 752 birds were shot over eleven days shooting by seven Guns.

Weather conditions were perfect during the period of the shoot.[75] There was snow, hail and fog, with minimum temperatures of -13 to -14 degrees Celsius. The previous couple of weeks also had sleet, snow and hail, and freezing temperatures.

The shooting party comprised seven Guns, namely: Lord Ardilaun, Lord Bandon and Mr Percy la Touche, who had participated in the Royal Shoot of 1905; and Mr C.P. Coote, the O'Conor Don, Mr E. Becker and the Hon. E. O'Brien.

Major Charles Robert Purdon Coote (1875-1954)

Son of Charles Purdon Coote and Hariette Louisa Maxwell. He married Noel Margaret Jephson Stracey, daughter of Lt-Col. Ernest Henry Denne Stracey and Faith Dorothy Neatrice Mounteney Popham, on 30 September 1933 and had five daughters. He gained the rank of temporary major in the service of the Royal Army Service Corps. He fought in the First World War and was decorated with the *Croix de guerre* (Belgium).

He lived at Bearforest, Mallow, County Cork, and Ballyclough Castle, County Cork. He died on 28 March 1954 aged seventy-nine years and was considered by Lord Oranmore and Browne, who took over the shooting at Ashford in 1940, to be the 'best shot of all'.[76]

The O'Conor Don

It is believed this was Charles William O'Connor (1878-1963). He was the son of Denis Maurice O'Conor Don (1840-1883), who was an Irish politician, serving as a Liberal (pro-Home Rule) MP for County Sligo from December 1868 until his death, and Ellen Kevill Davies of Croft Castle, Herefordshire, England. He married Evelyn Lowry Corry (1879-1963), daughter of Admiral the Hon. Armar Lowry Corry and Geraldine King, and had retained associations with both Clonalis House, Roscommon, the ancestral home of the O'Conor Don family, and Croft Castle, where he lived.

Sir Eustace Becher (1859-1934)

Son of Sir John Wrixon-Becher, 3rd Baronet, and Lady Emily Catherine Hare. He married Constance Gough-Calthorpe, daughter of Augustus Cholmondeley Gough-Calthorpe, 6th Baron

Calthope, and Maud Augusta Louisa Duncombe, on 8 October 1907. He died on 14 October 1934 at age seventy-four. Sir Eustace William Windham Wrixon-Becher, 4th Baronet, gained the title of 4th Baronet Wrixon-Becher. The original seat of the family was Aughadown, a neighbouring estate to Bantry, from which Lady Ardilaun came.

The Hon. Edward Donough O'Brien (1867-1943)
Third son of Sir Edward O'Brien (1839-1900), 6th Baronet (14th Baron Inchiquin), by his first marriage to Emily Holmes à Court (1842-1868):[77]

> He attended Wellington College, after which he joined the Clare Artillery for a few years. When Robin Vere O'Brien finally succeeded in resigning as agent, Edward stepped into his shoes and managed Dromoland. He married Lady Beatrice Hare, younger daughter of the Earl of Listowel at Ballyhooley, Co. Cork, in 1899. They lived at Roslevin, a house on the Tulla side of Ennis. They spent several thousand pounds on improvements to the house, which was burned subsequently in 1922, during the Civil War. It is now in ruins.[78]

He was a keen sportsman and a frequent guest at Ashford. He also appears frequently at Dromoland and Eden Vale, often in the company of Eustace Becher.

Shooting after Lord Ardilaun's Death in 1915

The shoot of 1910 was the last before Lord Ardilaun's death in 1915. The next shoot did not take place until 1917. By this time, the Honourable Arthur Ernest Guinness (1876-1949), second son (of three) of Edward Cecil Guinness (1847-1927), had taken over the running of the estate, which had been bequeathed to his father Edward Cecil, then Viscount Iveagh, on the death of Lord Ardilaun.[79]

Ernest was married to Marie Clotilde Russell (d. 1953), a granddaughter of Lord Arthur Lennox, in 1903. His finest moment came during the First World War when he arrested a British officer cycling behind the lines on suspicion of being a German spy. No soldier so young could have rightfully earned all the medals which adorned his chest. It turned out the 'spy' was the Prince of Wales.

Ernest had three daughters, Aileen Sibell Mary (1904-1999), Maureen Constance (1907-1998) and Oonagh (1910-1995), collectively known as the 'Golden Guinness Girls'. They were the true-life prototypes for the 'It' crowd of the 1920s – social show-offs of note.

All three married well; Aileen to Brinsley Plunket (1903-1941), a grandson of Lord Ardilaun's sister who had married Bishop Plunket. Maureen married, firstly, Basil Sheridan Hamilton-Temple-Blackwood, 4th Marquess of Dufferin and Ava, son of Frederick Temple Hamilton-Temple-Blackwood, 3rd Marquess of Dufferin, and Ava and Brenda Woodhouse, in 1930. Secondly she married Maj. Harry Alexander Desmond Buchanan, son of Lt-Col. James Claud Buchanan, in 1948, from whom she divorced in 1954. Thirdly, she married John Cyril Maude, son of Cyril Francis Maude and Winifred Emery, in 1955. Oonagh, married the 4th Lord Oranmore and Browne, the great-grandson of the man who had originally sold Ashford to Sir Benjamin Lee Guinness in 1868 and the man who, with the Marquess of Sligo, was to lease and manage the shooting at Ashford from 1940.[80]

When Ernest Guinness took over in 1917 he employed up to 100 beaters on each shoot, many more than were needed. By then, shoots were held twice annually: in December and again at the end of January.[81] The four-day shoot in late February 1917 returned a bag of 390 Woodcock for seven Guns. Shoots were held also in 1918 and 1919, with bags of 182 and 203 respectively. The record books are blank for the period 1920-1927, and it is unlikely that shooting took place. This may have been due to unrest in the country. The shoot restarted in all its splendour in 1928, with an eight-day shoot for seven Guns and a bag of 636 birds.[82] With the exception of the years 1935 and 1936, shoots were then held annually until 1938, under the direction of the Hon. A.E. Guinness. The shoot of 1930 was noteworthy for the fact that it was the first time Lord Oranmore and Browne participated. He was to become involved, one way or another, with the evolution of the shoot for the following fifty years.

However, the beaters continually went on strike for more money. Finally, one day during the 1939 shoot, the beaters went on strike in the middle of the day's shooting, just as the Guns were to be brought by boat to Inchagoill Island on Lough Corrib. Had they struck at the beginning of the day he might have negotiated, but this was too much for Ernest Guinness. He abandoned the shoot and carried off the Guns in his aeroplanes to Scotland. The following week, the Iveagh Trustees placed 22,000 acres of the estate for sale. It was bought by the State in 1939 for £20,000. Ten thousand acres were placed under the Forestry Service, with the remainder divided up by the Land Commission and sold to tenant farmers.

Dominick Geoffrey Edward Browne, 4th Baron Oranmore and Browne, 2nd Baron Mereworth (1901-2002)[83]

The longest-serving British peer and legislator. Born the Hon. Dominick Geoffrey Edward Browne in 1901, he was eldest son of the 3rd Lord Oranmore and Browne and Lady Olwen Verena Ponsonby, daughter of Edward Ponsonby, 8th Earl of Bessborough. He was educated at Eton and Christ Church, Oxford, before joining the Grenadier Guards.

In 1927, he succeeded his father, who died in a car accident in Southborough, Kent, and took his seat in the House of Lords as Baron Mereworth, a UK peerage, although he primarily used his Irish title.[84] He had the distinction of sitting in the House of Lords for seventy-two years, the longest by any peer, and during that time was one of the few peers to have never spoken in the House.

In 1930, the English residence of the Browne family, Mereworth Castle, was sold and he went to live in his Irish residence, Castle MacGarrett, in County Mayo. Castle MacGarrett, its 3,000 acres (1,200 ha) and 150 employees, gave him the chance to breed race horses and farm on a large scale. Lord Oranmore was also an aviator.

In 1939, Oranmore and Browne tried to join the British Army, but he was told that, at thirty-eight, he would be more useful if he concentrated on farming; as a result his war service was with the Local Defence Force in County Mayo.

In the early 1950s, the castle was acquired by the Irish Government's Irish Land Commission and turned into a nursing home. Lord Oranmore and Browne went to live in London.

He married three times. Firstly in 1925 to Mildred Helen Egerton, daughter of the Hon. Thomas Henry Frederick Egerton of the Earls of Ellesmere and Lady Bertha Anson of the Earls of Lichfield (marriage dissolved in 1936). Secondly in 1936 to Oonagh Guinness, daughter of Ernest Guinness and an heir to the brewery fortune (marriage dissolved in 1950). Thirdly, in 1951, he married Constance Stevens, an actress with the stage name Sally Gray, famous for her roles on the stage and in various movies in the 1930s and '40s. He died in London on 7 August 2002 at the age of 100.

Lord Oranmore and Browne and the Marquess of Sligo, following a tendering of the shooting rights, gained a ten-year lease of same for £1 per annum.[85] A syndicate was established which included as its guests some of the best and most aristocratic shots in the world. As well as Irish neighbours, Guns included the Duke of Devonshire, Signor Chiano (who shot for Italy in Mexico in 1968), the Duke of Grafton, Prince d'Arenberg, Prince de Caraman-Chimay, Monsieur L'Abbé de la Motte, Count de Ganay, Count de Gramont, Monsieur Alain de Rothchild, Mr Raymond Guest, the O'Conor Don, the Marquess of Dufferin and many others.

However, even at the first shoot of 1940 under the new management (lasting seven days and resulting in a bag of 400 birds) there was trouble. The beaters withdrew their labour three times! Thereafter, the number of beaters was gradually reduced to twelve. However, bags began to decline as covert maintenance was reduced and alternative habitat became more abundant. The halcyon days of Woodcock shooting instigated by Lord Ardilaun were over, although the social round continued undiminished until the early 1980s.

Assessment: Keys to Success and Decline

What was it that made Ashford such a great habitat for Woodcock? The provision of quiet and undisturbed cover of a suitable kind is considered to be essential. Acland-Hood (1909), who was a guest on the Royal Shoot of 1905, makes useful remarks in this regard:

> There is no doubt that Woodcocks frequent the same woods year after year – any instances of their doing so are on record; I know certain sheltered spots under holly bushes or in bracken under a sunny bank, close to good springs, which are a sure find, season after season, for a ''cock'. It is a curious fact that the record days obtained at Lord Ardilaun's famous beat of Ballykyne in county Galway on at least three occasions were preceded by 'jubilee' years for some reason or another – i.e. the beat was never shot. This almost proves that the birds who found out this happy winter resort in the previous season bore it in mind, and returned with their families in the succeeding year. With regard to the foregoing remark, Lord Ardilaun was unable to shoot his coverts at Ashford last season, 1908/9, and it will be interesting to see whether the next Woodcock week will be more prolific than usual. There are many woods in England, Scotland and Ireland more or less noted for their Woodcock-holding propensities; in many cases their glory has departed, probably because the woods are not left quiet, or else they have not been properly thinned.
>
> The Woodcock loves quiet above all things and he cannot bear living in a covert full of Pheasants or ground game … On the other hand, the covert of Ballykyne, belonging to Lord Ardilaun, has always been kept religiously quiet; Pheasants are not tolerated in it and no one can disturb the principal beats as they are surrounded by a high wall. The result is that for the last thirty years the average bag has been rather over 140 birds each season; it is only shot through once a year. With regard to 'thinning' it is well known that the Woodcock, in addition to quiet loves warmth and a dry bed, where he can comfortably digest and doze throughout the day. If coverts are allowed to get overgrown and out of hand they will not be used half as freely by Woodcock as they would be if certain patches were cut from time to time, on which bracken and low hazel would speedily spring up. The model covert is that which is kept quiet, lies dry, and has a mixture of hazel, hollies, young larch, bracken and gorse, with a good feeding ground within convenient distance.[86]

Clearly, ideal conditions of the kind described above may exist naturally. What the records at Ashford demonstrate is that benign intervention and careful management, painstakingly undertaken, and with great commitment of financial resources and time, can enhance the underlying natural habitat to provide a haven for wildlife and a social outlet for man – both in harmony.

When this commitment of resources was reduced, numbers fell back from the peaks recorded in the Ardilaun days.

ANNAGHMORE MANOR HOUSE AND COOPERSHILL, COLLOONEY, COUNTY SLIGO

Annaghmore and Coopershill have been home to the O'Hara family for centuries. The shooting record – logged meticulously in the Game Book, which also is a kind of scrap book, containing autographs, photographs and occasional watercolours – extends from 1904 to the present day, making it a true record of shooting society in the area in its many facets. The O'Haras are related to the Coopers of Coopershill, the Percevals of Temple House, the Wynnes of Hazelwood and probably also to the Coopers of Markree Castle.

These families maintained strong social ties. Indeed, shooting at these estates was reciprocal and it appears the shooting was carried out on a systematic and co-ordinated basis between these estates, presumably to rest the beats and ensure good overall management of stocks of birds. Other local landed families (related and unrelated), as will be seen below, appear regularly each season in the Game Book records, as well some names from further afield. A comprehensive account of the genealogy of these families is contained in McTernan's *The Light of Bygone Days: Houses of Sligo and Associated Families & Chronicles of Sixty Families Past and Present* (Sligo 2009). The summary that follows draws on this work and the accounts of surviving relatives.

The estate of Charles William O'Hara (1817-1898) extended to over 21,000 acres in 1878.[87] He was born Charles William Cooper, second son of Arthur Brooke Cooper (1757-1854) of Coopershill and Jane Frances O'Hara (1783-1874) of Annaghmore.[88] He inherited Annaghmore from his (unmarried) uncle, Maj. Charles King O'Hara (1785-1860), his mother's brother, on condition that he change his name to O'Hara, which he did by royal licence in 1860, thereby becoming Charles William Cooper O'Hara.

24
Annaghmore
House,
County Sligo,
c. 1900. From
Annaghmore
Game Book.

Charles William Cooper O'Hara had eight sons and six daughters by his marriage in 1858 to Anne Streatfield of Sussex. Their eldest son, Charles Kean O'Hara (1860-1947), who achieved the rank of major with the Sligo Militia, succeeded to Annaghmore, where he presided over his sporting estate, developing the shoot and his own pack, known as the 'O'Hara Harriers'. He, it was, who founded the Annaghmore Game Book.[89] He remained a bachelor all his life. A sister, Charlotte Jane, married Alexander Perceval (1859-1887) of Temple House in 1881, thus establishing a link to that estate, while another brother, Frederick William Cooper O'Hara (1875-1949), was to succeed to Coopershill, following the demise of his (unmarried) brother Arthur Cooper O'Hara (1862-1934). These two brothers figure prominently in the Annaghmore Game Book, as does the autograph of Frederick William's wife Muriel (*née* Henn).[90]

On Charles Kean's demise in 1947, Annaghmore passed to his nephew Donal Frederick Cooper O'Hara (1904-1977), a son of Frederick William of Coopershill and his wife Muriel. Meanwhile, Francis Cooper O'Hara (1906-1982), another son of Frederick William, succeeded to Coopershill.

The line of O'Haras at Annaghmore has continued to the present day, passing from Donal Frederick and his wife Elizabeth Linnell of Cheshire, to Dermot Charles (who was born in Kenya and married firstly Frances Rosemary Fulcher) and to Kean and Durcan, the present occupant, in 2005.

Meanwhile, Francis Cooper O'Hara and his wife Joan Bridgman of Essex passed Coopershill on to their sons Brian and Timothy. The present owner, Simon O'Hara, is second son of Brian and Lindy.

25 Coopershill, County Sligo, 1906. From Annaghmore Game Book.

Neither Annaghmore nor Coopershill were damaged during the Troubles of the 1920s. As landlords, the Cooper O'Haras were regarded as exemplary, and had extremely good relations with their tenants.

However, the estate today, at about 1,100 acres, is a fraction only in extent compared to what it was at the turn of the twentieth century. The estate was reduced by the sale of tenanted lands under the Land Acts, with the process continuing into the 1920s.

The Shoot, 1904-1918

A summary, by season, extracted from the Annaghmore Game Book is contained in the following table. In addition to records relating to the Annaghmore Estate, there are accounts of bags obtained from Cooperhill, Temple House, Hazelwood and Markree, emphasising the interrelated nature of the shooting on these estates, as well as entries from farther afield, such as Glenfarne Hall, County Leitrim, home of Col. John George Adamson and his family.[91]

There was a wide range of shooting habitats within the 21,000 acres which comprised Annaghmore prior to its break-up, and a wide range of beats are identified, including: Home-side (Woodcock, Pheasant); Far-side (Bog avenue: Woodcock, Pheasants); Collooney Plantation (Woodcock); Collooney Mountain (Grouse); Carrowmore; Mulligans and Killinden's Woods (Woodcock); Rathmore, Ranaghan, Ratbarran, Quigleystown Bogs (Snipe); Barnhill, Blackwood (Woodcock, Pheasants); Dromore (Grouse); Longhill; Springwell, and many more besides.

Summary Extract of Return from Annagmore Game Book, 1904-1918

Year	Guns	Woodcock	Snipe	Grouse	Pheasant
1904/05 September	7/8	–	–	Scotland 437 + 8 Black	–
October	–	10	–	–	–
November	–	53	31	–	180
December	–	15	64	–	50 CH
January	–	28	16	–	61+40 CH
February	2	3	130	–	–
1905/06 September	8	–	3	Scotland 519+ 70 Black	–
October	2/3	–	40	–	–
November	–	34	11	–	154+78 CH
December	–	96	34	–	109
January		32	9	–	39+37 CH
February	2	10	258	–	–
1906/07 September	6/7	–	–	Scotland 237+14 Black	–
October	2/4	–	66	–	–
November	–	30	92	–	156
December	–	41+52HW	43	–	165+55CH
January	–	115	53	–	38+163HW+30CH
February	–	2	97	–	–

Year	Guns	Woodcock	Snipe	Grouse	Pheasant
1907/08 September	8	–	–	Scotland 920+16 Black	–
October	2/3	–	38	–	–
November	–	33+22HW	47	–	104+277HW
December	–	79+20M	40	–	69M
January	–	53	65	–	55
February	–	36	46	–	–
1908/09					
October	–	–	–	–	–
November	–	37+42 HW	9	–	174+269 HW
December	–	15+6 CH	24	–	89+49CH
January	–	24+4CH+27 TH	19	–	32+13CH
February	1	1	36	–	–
1909/10 September	8/9	–	–	Scotland 665+25 Black	–
October	2/1	–	29	–	–
November	–	44+71*	34	–	62CH
December	–	43+94 TH (incl. 82 record 2/12)	11	–	111+223 TH
January	–	65+44 HW	90	–	41+148HW+30CH
February	2/3	11	103	–	–
1910/11 September	8	–	–	812+36 Black	–
October	2	–	23	–	–
November	–	26+5CH+14TH +13M+26*	25	–	164+168TH+22CH 104M
December	–	38+36TH	86	–	106
January	–	10+25M+29HW	10	–	59CH+53M+139HW
February	1/2	2	138	–	–
1911/12 September	1	–	–	Scotland 9 Black	–
October	2	–	31	–	–
November	–	20+97TH	6	–	625TH
December	–	36	36	–	188
January	–	45+16M	21	–	120+86M
February	2/3	1	181	–	–
1912/13 September	2/3	–	–	32	–
October	2/3	–	53	–	–
November	–	65+59HW	35	–	220+428HW+ 47CH
December	–	55+73 TH	24	–	84+273TH
January	–	21+14TH	23	–	148TH+18CH

Year	Guns	Woodcock	Snipe	Grouse	Pheasant
February	2	10	131	–	–
1913/14 September	8	–	–	Scotland 462+14 Black	–
October	1/2	–	27	–	–
November	–	46+11TH	2	–	149
December	–	41+8CH	43	–	45CH
January	–	26+35TH	20	–	22+88TH+19CH
February	2/3	9	114	–	–
1914/15 August	2/4	–	–	70	–
September	2	–	–	20	–
October	–	–	–	–	–
November	–	25+38HW	11	–	140+276HW
December	–	21+4CH+13*	12	–	80+34CH
January	–	37+6CH+38TH	29	–	24CH
February	1	12	50	–	–
1915/16 August	2/3	–	–	85	–
September	2	–	–	22	–
October	2	–	5	6	–
November	–	25	1	–	–
December	–	2+7CH+60HW	23	–	68HW+41CH
January	–	51	10	–	15+33CH
February	2	16	61	–	–
1916/17 August	2	–	–	80	–
September	1/3	–	–	20	–
October	1	–	8	2	–
November	2/3	8	10	–	–
December	–	61+11CH	33	2	50CH
January	1/4	2	17	–	15
February	–	–	–	–	–
1917/18 August	2	–	–	49	–
September	–	–	–	–	–
October	2	–	12	–	–
November	–	10+5CH	4	–	33+42CH
December	2/4	9	24	–	–
January	–	36+5CH+36HW	5	–	37CH+63HW
February	4	14	–	–	–

Note:

CH: Coopershill   HW: Hazelwood   M: Markree   TH: Temple House   *Glenfarne/Florenscourt

The Adamsons were regular guests at Annaghmore. In addition to Col. Adamson's, the autographs of Lina, Muriel and Eve Adamson appear regularly in the Game Book.

There is a well-defined pattern to the seasons during this period. In most years (September 1912 and the years September 1914-1918 were the exceptions) Charles Kean O'Hara went to Scotland (usually Kinveachy Forest) and spent about a week shooting Grouse in September in a party of about eight Guns.

On his return in October, the usual quarry was Snipe, but this was generally not more than a couple of Guns out together for a day and typically there were four or five days, consecutively in the month, spent like this. The company on these outings comprised mainly Charles Kean along with younger brothers Arthur Cooper and/or Frederick William Cooper. The only non-family guests whose names appear with regularity for Snipe shooting in October are Count Enrique O'Brien (with Mona O'Brien) and Wilfred F. Tempest (b. 1846) (with Florence Tempest), both of whom arrived for a few days' Snipe shooting in October most years.[92] Count Enrique O'Brien is believed to be a member of the Inchiquin O'Briens, a branch of which family settled near Cadiz, Spain, in the early 1700s.[93]

Most years, in early November, there was a visit to Glenfarne Hall, County Leitrim, for Pheasants. There, Col. Adamson's party (of about eight Guns) usually comprised (in addition to Charles Kean): Capt. W. Knox, G.R. Willis-Sandford, Capt. C. Vesey, W.S. Hunt, L. Thompson and H. Warren. The shooting was carried out over about four days and the bag was generally in the range of 60 to 100 birds per day.[94]

From about mid-November to the end of January there was significant concentration on Woodcock, with shooting revolving between Annagmore, Coopershill, Temple House, Hazelwood and Markree Castle. Typically there was shooting on six to eight days a month during this time, with the number of Guns ranging from three to eight (but usually five to seven).

The core of the party comprised Charles Kean O'Hara and his brothers Frederick William Cooper (Coopershill) and Arthur, Arthur Ascelin Perceval (1885-1967) (see Temple House), his uncle, Philip Dudley Perceval (1865-1939) (see Hazelwood House), and Bryan Cooper (1884-1930) (see Markree Castle).

GAME KILLED AT KINVEACHY FOREST. *1905*

Date	Beat	Grouse	Black Cock	Grey Hen	Part-ridges	Wood-cock	Snipe	Wild Fowl	Hares	Rabbits	Roe	Various	Remarks
September.													Party.
" 18th	Foregin West.	119.	1.					3.	1.				Sir J. Maryon-Wilson Bt.
" 19th	Pile.	134.	4.	1.				33.					Sir A. Peyton Bt.
" 20th	Bt of Garten Flats.	47.	8.	9.				1.		2.		1.	Hon. E. L. Parker.
" 21st	Slock.	158.	1.					10.	1.				Major C. Stanton.
" 22nd	Dochern & Wood.		34.	12.	2.		.	4.	1.	3.		1.	C. K. O'Hara Esq.
" 23rd	Foregin Pastl.	137.					1.	16.					G. Maryon-Wilson Esq.
													H. Pickersgill-Cunliffe Esq.
													J. A. Parle Esq.
25	Boat of [untitled]		8.		11		1	1	1	107. 1 Stag ft.D.		4	Jimmy. McKenn. CK&Co
26	Blackleun									1 Stag	1 Salmon		
27.	Boat [untitled]	5					2	57.	1		1		Stmw. & John. McKenn CK&Co
28	Boat of Julie			1				1					McKenn CK&Co
	TOTAL	595.	48.	22.	2.	.	.	1.	467.	3.	5.	2.	

26 Kinveachy Forest game card, September 1905.

27 (right) *Annaghmore: In the Bog Avenue, 21 Dec. 1909, J. Percy Gethin (1859-1934). Watercolour, 11.5cm x 17.5cm.*

J.P.G
21st Dec '09

28 *Temple House Lake and the Footbridge – Coopershill* Percy Francis Gethin (1874-1916). Watercolours, each 9cm x 6cm, pasted opposite 11 December 1905.

Evidently, the Guns were joined by their wives and other female members of the families, presumably in the evening, at Annaghmore, where they would have stayed. The autographs of Muriel O'Hara (*née* Henn), wife of Frederick William, Muriel Perceval (*née* Wynne of Hazelwood), wife of Philip Dudley, Dorothy and Madeline Wynne, Elenora Perceval (*née* Mac Dowel), wife of Alexander Ascelin, and Nora MacDowel appear frequently in the Game Book during these years.

Percy Francis Gethin (1874-1916)

Another circle of regular guests at the shooting parties were neighbouring landed families of County Sligo. These were principally comprised of members of the Gethin family, notably Percy Francis Gethin, second son of Capt. George and Maria Connellan of Hollywell House, who was an artist of note, studying painting in London and Paris before taking up teaching posts at

Plymouth and Liverpool.[95] He was unmarried and was mortally wounded at the Battle of the Somme. The Game Book contains two small watercolours by him of the *Temple House Lake and the Footbridge – Coopershill* (see Illustrations 028), pasted opposite 11 December 1905.

On that day, shooting was at Temple House (Kilbratten, Derreen and Shrunagh beats). The Guns, in addition to Gethin, comprised brothers Charles Kean and Arthur O'Hara (Annaghmore), Alexander Ascelin Percival (Temple House), Sir Malby Crofton (Longford House), H.G L'Estrange (1869-1929) of Lisnalurg, and Roger Palmer (probably of Keenagh Lodge, Castlebar). The bag for the day was eighty-nine head, comprising eleven Pheasants, forty-six Woodcock and the rest in rabbits and hares.

Captain John Percy Gethin, JP, DL (1859-1934)
A more frequent visitor was Capt. John Percy Gethin, of Ballindoon, which he inherited along with 2,500 acres on his grandfather's death in 1885.[96] He was a cousin of Percy Francis and appears every season during this period, with his mother Emmeline (*née* Horsfall). In 1919, he transferred Ballindoon to a cousin, Randolph George, and settled in York, birthplace of his mother, where he died without issue in March 1934.[97]

Henry George L'Estrange of Lisnalurg (1869-1929)
Master of the Sligo Harriers and also a frequent shooting guest, along with his wife Evelyn (*née* Wynne, of Hazelwood). He succeeded his father, Christopher Carlton L'Estrange (1813-1889) as agent for the Ffolliot, Perceval, Phibbs and Wynne Estates, with all of whom he had close personal relations. The L'Estrange family was related through marriage to the Coopers of Markree Castle (Sophia married Edward Joshua Cooper), the Percevals of Temple House (Jane Anne married Alexander Percival), Wynnes of Hazelwood (H.G. married Evelyn Mary Wynne), and Coopers of Coopershill (in 1852 Christopher Carlton L'Estrange married Charlotte Anne, youngest daughter of Arthur Brooke Cooper (1757-1854)).[98]

Sir Malby Crofton (1857-1926)
Eldest son of Henry Bliss Crofton and Sophia Horsfall of Yorkshire. In 1880, he married Louisa Margaret, daughter of Richard J. Verschoyle of Tanrego. According to McTernan:

> Sir Malby was widely known as a 'popular country gentleman', a progressive farmer and an active member of the County Sligo Agricultural Society. He was an ardent supporter of Sir Horace Plunkett's Co-Operative Movement and for a time acted as President of the Skreen Co-Operative Society … In a letter to *The Irish Times* shortly before his death he stated that from his experience Protestants were well treated and need not fear their future in an Irish Free State. His passing in 1926 severed one of the few surviving links with the old landed gentry of another era and he was the last of his race to reside at Longford House on a permanent basis.[99]

The Longford House Estate amounted to about 3,500 acres at the time.[100]

Count Casimir de Markievicz (1874-1932)
Another notable shooting guest was Count Casimir de Markievicz. He was with the shooting party of 5-6 January 1910, when the shooting was at Hazelwood Demesne and the Big Wood and Bog the next day on the same estate. The bag was 162 and 116 on each day respectively. This included

DATE	NAME	PLACE	NO OF GUNS	GROUSE	PHEASANTS COCKS	HENS	PARTRIDGES	BLACK GAME	WOODCOCK	SNIPE	WILD FOWL	WOOD PIGEON	HARES	RABBITS	DEER	VARIOUS	TOTAL
1910																	
Jan 5	R.S. Percival. A.A. Percival, Maj. H.W. Studd. G. Hinson	Hazlewood. Demesne	6		93				11	2	Teal 4		52				162
" 6	C. de Markievicz. C.K.O.H.	Do Bigwood. Bog	6		55				33				27	1			116
" 22	R.B. Hanston C.K.O.H.	Bella. Rathmore. Rathbraven	2		4				2	25				5			36
" 24	R.B. Hanston. C.K.O.H.	Island Bog. Ranaghan Rathmore Langley Lew. Curnomacatrick	2		2				14		1	1	6				24
" 25	R.B. Hanston. Col. R. Money. R.C. Money C.K.O.H.	Small Plantations Except Rathbraven plantation	4		6				5	1		2					14
" 26	R.B. Hanston. A.C. O'Hara. Fitzgerald Col. R. Money - R.C. Money - C.K.O.H.	Annaghmore Home side & Bogland	6		28				4	2	Teal 4		2	19		Teal 3	62
" 27	Same	Do Far side. Ardeen & Bog wood	6		13				5	2	1	2	8	10	Hawk 1	Teal Tomtit 2	44
" 28	R.B. Hanston. Fitzgerald Col. Money. R.C. Money C.K.O.H.	Calleen Mulligan's Kilbride Wood	5		1				14	3		2			Mole 1	Plover Tomtit 2	23
" 29	Same (C.K.O.H.M) Jun Fitzgerald	Annaghlig. Bella. Hinnogrelly Magh	2½		2				12	1	Duck		1	1	Cuckoo 1	Plover Grey Hen 5	24
" 31	R.B. Hanston. Bob. R. Money	Bella Bog. Rathmore. Burnt House Sta. Half quarter. Magunisbough	3		3				3	19					Cuckoo 1	Plover 1	27
Feb. 1	Same	Rathbraven Callison & mowing Bush by Laurence to Coolaney	3							13					Mole 1	Plover 1	15
" 19	Fitzgerald. E.K.O.H. C.K.O.H.	Kinnard Wood. Lower. Barnfield. Black wood - Clean - waterfall. Doyle's at Ardeen - (For Rabbits)	3						2	3		1	30		Cat 1	Rat 1	38
		TOTALS															

29 Page from Annaghmore Game Book, 5-6 January 1910.

ninety-three Pheasants and eleven Woodcock on the first day to six Guns, and fifty-five Pheasants and thirty-three Woodcock on the second day to the same Guns.

Markiewicz's fame, of course, has been secured through his marriage to Constance Gore-Booth (1868-1927) of Lissadell. He was from a wealthy Polish family who were landowners in what is now the Ukraine. He became a portrait and landscape artist. He met Constance in Paris and in 1900 they married in London. Their daughter Maeve was born the following year. Their home was in Dublin from 1902, but owing to declining health in his later years, Markievicz moved to Warsaw, where he died in 1932.

There were other regular guests from beyond the borders of Sligo. The Adamsons of Glenfarne Hall, County Leitrim, and Quinn Longworths of Glynwood, Athlone, have been mentioned already. Other names to appear to shoot are Edward (1882-1914) and quite regularly Charles Mulholland (1886-1936) (3rd Baron Dunleath) of Ballywalter, Newtownards, County Down, and Richard Blakiston-Houston of the Orangefield Estate and Beltrim Castle, Gortin, County Tyrone, especially in February (see below).

Ballywalter Park, Newtownards, County Down, has been home to the Mulholland family since it was acquired by Andrew Mulholland in 1846 from the Mathews family. In 1892, John Mulholland was raised to the peerage as 1st Baron Dunleath, for his services as a Member of Parliament. Edward and Charles were first and second sons respectively of Henry Mulholland (1854-1931), 2nd Baron Dunleath, and his wife Norah (née Ward, d. 1935), known universally as 'Gogo'.[101]

Ballywalter thrived as a centre of entertainment whilst Gogo was châtelaine, with grand house parties, shooting weekends and dances. The social round was resumed after the First World War, in spite of Edward being killed at Ypres in the opening months of the war whilst serving with the Irish Guards. Charles succeeded to the title and Ballywalter. In 1920 he married Sylvia Brooke, following his younger brother Harry, who had married Sylvia's sister Sheelah. They were both daughters of Sir Arthur Brooke of Colebrooke and sisters of Basil, later 1st Viscount Brookeborough. Sylvia died soon after the marriage. Charles remarried in 1932, when he wed

30 (right)
Annaghmore,
9 January 1908,
keepers and
beaters.

31
Annaghmore:
coming to a
day's end, with
a mixed bag
of Pheasants
and Woodcock
being carried
by the gentle-
man on the
right of the
picture.

Grace, daughter of Charles D'Arcy, Archbishop of Armagh and Church of Ireland Primate of All Ireland.

The style of Woodcock shooting around these estates was quite different from the grand formality of Ashford in its heyday around the same time. It was certainly organised, with keepers and beaters employed, but the shooting was on a lesser scale and there was more informality. The social round of these shooting parties was more frequent. Over the period from late November to the end of January, they appear to have managed twelve to sixteen days per season across the four estates – Annaghmore, Temple House, Hazelwood and Markree Castle – primarily focused on Woodcock. By the end of January there was probably an amount of social fatigue from so much socialising at shooting parties.

February allowed a return to two or three Guns spending a day on a bog after Snipe, similar to the pattern of October. In almost every year during this period, Richard Blackiston Houston appears with Charles Kean O'Hara and his brother Frederick.[102] He was a regular guest during the Woodcock months but appears not to have missed a February for Snipe shooting. The pair of Guns would typically spend six to nine days in the month shooting Snipe, with a few Woodcock thrown in and some hares and rabbits. February 1906 was a particularly good month, with eleven days' shooting yielding a bag of 258 Snipe to two Guns (about a dozen a day per Gun) and 10 Woodcock, picked up as singles or in brace. Bags in the range of 130 to 180 were more usual; 8 to 12 birds per day per Gun, still very pleasant shooting! However, it is noticeable that after 1913, the number shot fell to fifty or sixty per month. Were birds becoming less abundant, or were the Guns simply slowing?

1950 to Date

There was no shooting between 1918 and 1950. Charles Kean was in his late fifties as the First World War ended and then there was the process of selling large chunks of the estate and the adverse consequences which this had on the ability to shoot. By the time the estate was settled again Charles Kean was an elderly man, with Arthur only two years younger than him. However, shooting recommenced in November 1950, at which time the estate was much reduced from its former scale. Shooting was confined to the Demesne, Bella, Rathmore and the Bog area. The parties comprised the same core families, namely: Donal Frederick O'Hara (1904-1977), eldest son of Frederick William Cooper O'Hara (1875-1949) of Coopershill and his wife Muriel (*née* Henn), who succeeded to Annaghmore after Charles Kean (followed by his son Dermot Charles from 1962); his brother Francis Cooper O'Hara (1906-1982), who succeeded at Coopershill in 1949 (and in due course his son Brian); Edward Francis Cooper (1912-1982) of Markree Castle, eldest son of Bryan Ricco Cooper (1885-1930) (followed by sons Edward and Charles), and, for a time, Ascelin Perceval (1885-1967), then his son 'Alec' (1913-1986) and his son 'Sandy' (from 1961), and so on to the present day!

From outside the families, a frequent member of the parties of this period is Richard ('Dick') Wood-Martin (b. 1929), nephew of Henry Roger ('Hal') Wood-Martin (1875-1933) of Cleveragh, the seat of the Martin family, who made frequent appearances at Temple House. For the decade of the 1950s, the shooting averaged about four days per season, with six to eight Guns per party. On average, the bag of Woodcock amounted to thirty-two birds per season. In the 1960s, fewer numbers of days were shot; typically two or three for a dozen or two birds. The shooting then lapsed again from 1967 until 1990, when it was revived by Durcan, the present occupant of Annaghmore.

The pattern now is two or three days per season for a couple of dozen Woodcock. Much has changed over the century-and-more history of shooting at Annaghmore, but one thing has remained unchanged: for over a hundred years the Coopers, O'Haras and Percevals have enjoyed

32 Guns having been joined by the ladies towards the end of a day. The game cart can be seen in the background

33 (right) One Woodcock receiving a lot of attention.

a few days' Woodcock shooting together during the months of winter and the Woodcock have usually obliged!

TEMPLE HOUSE, BALLYMOTE, COUNTY SLIGO

Percevals trace their ancestry at Temple House back to the seventeenth century, when George Perceval married Mary Crofton of Temple House in 1665; Temple House being part of Crofton land at that time. The shooting records go back to 1898 and there is a fine Woodcock shoot there at present, managed by Roderick Perceval. The estate extended to over 7,000 acres in the late nineteenth century but now consists of around 1,200 acres, of which about half is native wood-land. The estate today retains some of the prime beats, such as Kilbratten and Derreen, as well as the Demesne. In addition, now the shoot is managed over a further 4,000 hectares of forestry leased from Coillte.

Temple House has had an eventful history, surviving bankruptcy, the Famine and the Troubles of the 1920s, when there was systematic burning of Big Houses. For over a century, Woodcock shooting has been pivotal in its social calendar. Its survival is owed to the strength of character, compassion and adaptability of many members of this remarkable family. They are related to the O'Haras of Annaghmore: Charlotte Jane, younger sister of Charles Kean (1860-1947), the bachelor brother who was the doyen of shooting up to 1918, married the short-lived Alexander Perceval (1859-1887), while his younger brother Philip Dudley (1865-1939) established a link to Hazelwood through his marriage to Muriel Wynne.

Prior to this generation, Alexander (1787-1858) and his wife Jane Anne (d. 1847) had a strong influence on Temple House well beyond their own day. She was a L'Estrange of Moystown, in what was then King's County (County Offaly today). She and Alexander married in 1808. Her nephew Christopher Carleton L'Estrange (1813-1889) married Charlotte Anne, youngest daughter of Arthur Brooke Cooper of Cooperhill (and sister of Charles William (1817-1898) who succeeded to Annaghmore in 1860). He became agent to the Perceval, Ffolliot, Phibbs and Wynne Estates, and he would also play a pivotal role in Temple House's evolution.

34 Temple House, County Sligo. The early nineteenth-century family seat was enlarged and embellished in the 1860s.

35 Jane Anne Perceval (née L'Estrange) (1790-1847) by Carl Vogel.

McTernan found that:

> In 1822, when famine and fever was widespread, Alexander paid regular visits to the homes of the afflicted and provided them with food and other assistance. During the cholera outbreak a decade later both he (i.e. Alexander) and his wife (i.e. Jane Anne) were 'indefatigable in their exertions' to feed the poor and needy. With the onslaught of the Famine in 1846 the *Mayo Telegraph* reported that Col. Perceval (he attained that rank in the Sligo Militia) was supplying hundreds of his tenants daily with Indian meal and oatmeal at reduced rates from a depot at Bunninadden. His wife, Jane, was tireless in her efforts to attend to the poor and needy and as a result she contracted fever and died in January 1847.[103]

'Sandy' (Alexander Robert Hugh) Perceval tells of his understanding gained from a story told in the letters of Sommerville to Ross that, in fact, Jane, on her deathbed, asked of her daughters with respect to their tenants, 'please do not neglect these people during my funeral' and so the daughters delivered food to the needy on the day of their mother's funeral.

In the late 1960s, Sandy Perceval attended a function in Sligo at which a figure believed to be a member of the IRA was also in attendance. Sandy asked to be introduced and when he was, he asked why it was that Temple House was not burned during the Troubles. The man to whom the question was posed related how the kindness and compassion of Jane Perceval was remembered by his family and his predecessors when saying the family rosary and that that was the reason why Temple House had been spared.[104] However, there is a large bundle of correspondence contained in the Temple House papers between Maj. A.A. Perceval and his wife, Eleanora Margaret ('Nora', eldest daughter of Effingham Carroll MacDowell MD of The Mall House, Sligo – these individuals are discussed in greater detail later) related to the period 1914-1920, which concentrates mainly on the first months of the First World War and on 1920, following an attack by the IRA on Temple House in the latter year, when Mrs Perceval was severely injured and lost the baby she was then carrying.[105]

Alexander and Jane had ten children together. Their third son, also Alexander (1821-1866), was known as the 'China-man', for he worked in the tea trade in China with the firm of Jardine, Matheson & Co. He went there seeking his fortune and foreseeing that his father's election expenses were putting the family estate in peril. Indeed, the estate was lost when, on Alexander's death, it was offered for sale in the Encumbered Estates Court for £80,000. It was bought by Robert Westley Hall-Dare of Newtownbarry, County Wexford (members of this family figure prominently in the early days of shooting on the North Sloblands in County Wexford). The Hall-Dare connection in County Wexford commenced only in 1861.[106] The family are descended from Robert Westley Hall Esq. of Wyefield and Craanbrook, High Sheriff of Essex (1821) and MP for South Essex.

However, in May 1860, Hall-Dare was convicted of common assault on Elizabeth Montague, the gamekeeper's wife, and as a result had little option but to leave the area and offer the property for sale.[107] News of these events was relayed to Perceval in Hong Kong by the former agent Christopher L'Estrange, Jane Anne's nephew, who was authorised to purchase the estate for a reputed £120,000. Thus, the estate came back to Perceval ownership in March 1861 to great rejoicing locally.[108] He brought families previously evicted back to the estate and improved housing, which had been allowed to fall to ruin. One such family was the Carneys, who, when they returned, retrieved goats which they had previously husbanded from a feral state. A member of this family, Mel Carney, was to become gamekeeper on the estate until his death in 1869.[109]

However, Alexander's life came to a premature end in May 1866, at the age of forty-four. The estate passed to the eldest son, also Alexander (1859-1887), when he was only seven years. As noted earlier, he married Charlotte Jane O'Hara of Annaghmore in 1881. His life was also short-lived, although in his brief life he established a reputation as a fine shot and a resident and improving landlord. He left a son, Alexander Ascelin Charles Philip Spencer (1885-1967), and a daughter, both of tender years. Alexander Ascelin was to become a keen sportsman and shot, gracing the pages of both the Annaghmore and Temple House Game Books for many years. Charlotte Jane, his mother, with the assistance of Henry L'Estrange, kept her hands firmly on the reins of Temple House during Ascelin's minority. Following Ascelin's marriage, Charlotte Jane went to live in Staffordshire, where she maintained her lifelong interest in hunting.

Following an education at Cheam School and Eton, Ascelin returned to the estate. His coming of age, as with those of his predecessors, was a time of celebration and rejoicing. He married Eleanora Margaret MacDowel, eldest daughter of Surgeon Effingham MacDowel of Sligo Infirmary. Her autograph, and that of Muriel MacDowel, appears in the Annaghmore Game Book.

Ascelin served as a major with the Irish Guards Regiment in the First World War, where he received serious injuries which were to impair his mobility but not, evidently, his spirit for shooting, which he practised frequently, transporting himself

36 Mel Carney (d. 1869), gamekeeper, Temple House.

37 (right) The Guns' autographs following a day's shooting at Markree Castle and Temple House, 17-18 January 1912.

38 Mulligan's Wood showing horse and trap (note top-hat livery of driver).

from covert to covert in a trap. According to present family members, he was dragged from the rubble of a building, having been buried for three days, with not much hope of survival. He had major abdominal surgery, following which he was advised by his surgeon to have a glass of port after every meal and several whiskeys every evening.[110]

Nor did his injuries impair his participation in local affairs. He was High Sheriff in 1919 and a member of Sligo Harbour Board, the Race Committee and the Board of Fishery Conservators. He was elected president of the County Sligo Agricultural Society in 1947. Following the death of his wife Nora in 1957 he moved to Dublin, where he died a decade later.

Ascelin's eldest son Alexander ('Alec') Robert Charles Perceval (1913-1986) returned to Temple House following a distinguished military career with the Indian Army during the Second World War, in which he was seriously injured and was a recipient of military honours. For some time there he was also manager of a tea plantation. On his return, he established a renowned Frisian dairy herd and married Yvonne de Hamel. He was a keen country sportsman, enjoying both fishing and shooting until his death in 1986, and his inscription describes him as, 'Tea planter, Farmer and Sportsman'.[111]

The present generation comprises Alexander Robert Hugh Perceval ('Sandy') (b. 1934), his wife Debonnaire (*née* Hardcastle), and their children Roderick, Serena and Charlotte. In 2004, Roderick and his wife Helena Raggett took over the management of the estate and the shoot from his father, 'Sandy'.

The Temple House Alphabet

A somewhat witty but insightful commentary on the social life surrounding shooting parties at Temple House in the early twentieth century is provided in the *Temple House Alphabet*, written in 1910 by E.A. Shaw:

A is for Ascelin who guides us around,
He thinks we are under control, I'll be bound.

B are the Brackens, for all things they're able,
They're Keepers and equally good for the table.

C are the cakes, oh so temptingly shaped –
Not all of the party the pitfall escaped.

D are the dangers we always are in,
To frighten us thus is distinctly a sin.

E are the evenings might merrily be spent
Playing tricks of all kinds – on amusement we're bent.

F is Sir Frederick – no doubt he is pleased,
At owning a daughter who always is teased.

G is for Grace, poor misunderstood child,
And people declare she is noisy and wild.

H are the hundreds of Pheasants they slay,
Which means that the Guns have enjoyed a good day.

I are the idiots, of course they're not here,
If y'd said that they were 'twould indeed have been queer.

J are the jokes that they practise on us,
It is best on the whole not to make too much fuss.

K are the kicks which at dinner exchanged,
Incline us to think that the party's deranged.

L are the ladies who numbering five,
To make the house pleasant increasingly strive.

M is Mulholland who sleeps in his chair,
Till discreetly awakened by kind ladies fair.

N is for Nora, misunderstood child,
And people declare she is noisy and wild.

O, The O'Haras, who join with the lot,
Who deem it essential to make our lives hot.

P are the Percevals, all good and kind,
Who most of our antics too kind are to mind (but)

Q are the questionable things we are taught
By people who really to know better ought.

R is the result when we're shocked and we're fussed
And together retire in deepest disgust.

S is the Smoking room – all rights reserved
From Poachers, however, not always preserved.

T are the tunes both melodious and sweet,
To which all the party we thoughtfully treat.

U's the upheaval immense and complete,
'Tis caused by annoying maids usually sweet.

V is the victory – soon 'twill be ours,
When driven at last to displaying our powers.

W is Webster so mixed by the 'courses',
He hands us in turn such a mixture of sauces.

X are the Xcellent manners of all
And none from this height of great Xcellence fall.

Y is for You, whom we still will pay out
And we leave you to guess who were talking about.

Z is the zero to which spirits fall,
When from this gay visit there comes the recall.

Ascelin obviously refers to Alexander Ascelin Charles Philip Spencer (1885-1967), who was host at Temple House. The Nora referred to later is probably either a daughter or indeed his wife, Eleanora MacDowel.

The reference to Brackens is quite interesting. As we read early in Chapter 1, according to several people with knowledge of the matter, the Earl of Enniskillen, who lived at Florence Court, County Fermanagh, was not permitted to marry his childhood sweetheart, who was a daughter of the groom. Instead she was married off to the son of another groom – whose name was Bracken. However, many of her sons and descendants became gamekeepers and bore more than a passing resemblance to the Earls of Enniskillen!

There are numerous references in the Temple House Game Book to Brackens being in attendance at shoot days. For example, in the seasons of 1910 to 1915, there are references to 'six Brackens', 'four Brackens' or 'three Brackens', and there are various entries for 'R. Bracken', 'Richard Bracken', 'H. Bracken', 'Henry Bracken', 'Dickie Bracken', 'Jules B[racken]', 'Hugh (J.) B[racken]' and 'Arthur Bracken'. Their names appear alongside the Guns and they are not distinguished as keepers. Indeed, the reference in the Alphabet suggests they may have been included with guests 'at the table'. A Christopher Bracken was also employed as a keeper at Mahon's Castlegar Estate in County Galway.

The Sir Frederick referred to is Sir Frederick Shaw, a frequent guest, to judge from the Game Book; it is presumed that the author of the Alphabet is a relation, probably his wife. Mullholland is probably Charles Mullholland of Ballywalter, who was the most frequent member of this family in the list of Guns, although on one date during the 1910/11 season there was five members of that family shooting: Lord Dunleath, Henry Lyle Mulholland (1991-1931) and his sons Charles (1886-1952), Henry (1888-1971) and Godfrey (1892-1942).

There is a clear sense of the fun, entertainment and the house-party atmosphere that prevailed at Temple House in these lines, as well as the Guns withdrawing to the Smoking Room to leave the ladies after dinner.

Summary Extract of Return from Temple House Game Book, 1898-1918

Year	Beat	Guns	Grouse	Woodcock	Snipe	Pheasant
6 Jan. 1898	Derreen and Kilbratten	7		31	1	13
7 Jan.	Demesne	6		6	1	23
20 Dec.	Derreen and Kilbratten	7		28	1	24
21 Dec.	Demesne	7		19		28
27 Dec. 1899	Derreen and Kilbratten	7		41		21
28 Dec.	Demesne	6		30	1	31
22 Jan. 1900	Demesne			5		5
27 Dec.	Derreen and Kilbratten	6		30		10
28 Dec.	Demesne	4		22		20
21 Jan. 1901	Inside and Outside	6		17		21
20 Dec.	Derreen and Kilbratten	7		29		11
21 Dec.	Demesne	6		21		30
9 Jan. 1902	Inside and Outside	6		17		32
30 Dec.	Derreen and Kilbratten	6		32		7
31 Dec.	Demesne	5		25		13
14 Jan. 1903	Inside and Outside	6		18		8
17 Nov.	Markree Cloonmacduff	7		9	46	25
5 Dec.	Coopershill	7		8	2	63
9 Dec.	Derreen and Kilbratten	6		26		6

Year	Beat	Guns	Grouse	Woodcock	Snipe	Pheasant
10 Dec.	Demesne	6		33		33
21 Dec.	Annaghmore Demesne Walk	6		4		16
23 Dec.	Annaghmore Inside and Bog	6		23	2	23
1 Dec. 1904	Annaghmore Inside and Bog	8 5		15	3	115
22 Dec.	Coopershill			1	4	50
1 Dec. 1909	Demesne East	7		12		199
2 Dec.	Derreen and Kilbratten	7		82	1	24
3 Dec.	Demesne West	5		17		25
10 Jan. 1910	Lake				2	
11 Jan.	Demesne East			7		82
12 Jan.	Derreen and Kilbratten			23		13
13 Jan.	Demesne West			3		17
4 Nov.	Hazelwood Keelogybog	11	24	4	3	
7 Nov.	Hazelwood Deer Park	4		14		
8 Nov.	Markree Union Wood	6		16		12
29 Nov.	Temple House Lake and River	9			23	
30 Nov.	Temple House Demesne East	7		14	1	168
1 Dec.	Derreen and Kilbratten	7		37		22
2 Dec.	Demesne West	6		25		45
6 Dec.	Hazelwood Cairns	5		33	1	13
7 Dec.	Hazelwood Dark trees/Percy Mount	6		23	1	109
8 Dec.	Hazelwood Pumpstore and Bog	6		35		156
9 Dec.	Hazelwood Rockwood	5		26	1	
10 Dec.	Hazelwood Doonee	4		15		2
17 Jan. 1911	Temple House Lake	6			7/18 duck	
18 Jan.	Temple House Demesne East	7		4		59
19 Jan.	Derreen and Kilbratten	6		27	1	3
20 Jan.	Demesne West	6		13	2	18

Year	Beat	Guns	Grouse	Woodcock	Snipe	Pheasant
18 Oct.	Hazelwood Gilmartins	10	22		3	
19 Oct.	Hazelwood Doonee	5	9	1		3
16 Nov.	Hazelwood Rockwood	4		26	1	4
18 Nov.	Hazelwood Kilsillan	2	1	2	20	
21 Nov.	Hazelwood Cairns	4		1	4	8
22 Nov.	Hazelwood Percy Mount	7		18	4	141
23 Nov.	Hazelwood Pumpstore and Bog	7		38		218
24 Nov.	Hazelwood Deer Park and Stone Park	4		24		
28 Nov.	Temple House Lake and River	9			10/17 duck	
29 Nov.	Temple House Demesne East			9		229
30 Nov.	Dereen and Kilbratten	7		32		45
1 Dec.	Temple House Demesne West	6		23	1	48
6 Dec.	Annaghmore Home side	7		5	2	88
7 Dec.	Annaghmore Far side	7		8	1	76
12 Dec.	Hazelwood Far Holywell	3		6	3	1
13 Dec.	Hazelwood Glencar	4		5	2	1
28 Dec.	Annaghmore Carrowmore	3		2	18	10
2 Jan. 1912	Annaghmore Carrowmore	2		1	15	
	Annaghmore Home side	6		11	1	61
4 Jan.	Annaghmore Far side	6		5		59
9 Jan.	Hazelwood Rockwood	5		22		2
10 Jan.	Hazelwood Dark trees Percy Mount	6		5	2	94
11 Jan.	Hazelwood River and Bog	6		28		79

Year	Beat	Guns	Grouse	Woodcock	Snipe	Pheasant
12 Jan.	Hazelwood Cairns and Doonee	4		16	2	6
16 Jan.	Temple House Lake and River	8			13 duck	
17 Jan.	Temple House Demesne East	7		2		116
18 Jan.	Derreen and Kilbratten	7		18	1	12
19 Jan.	Temple House Demesne West	6		13	1	21
25 Jan.	Annaghmore			6	2	31
23 Oct.	Hazelwood Millbrook	2			41	3
24 Oct.	Hazelwood Whites and Fox Hills		25	1		
20 Nov.	Annaghmore Home side	8		8	2	147
21 Nov.	Annaghmore Far side Bog Avenue	8		23	4	69
26 Nov.	Hazelwood Cairns	5		21		31
27 Nov.	Hazelwood Percy Mount	8		22	2	276
28 Nov.	Hazelwood Bog Beat	7		45		155
29 Nov.	Hazelwood Deer park	4		31	2	5
10 Dec.	Annaghmore Coolloney Plantation	5		22	1	7
2 Jan. 1913	Annaghmore Carrowmore	4		1	6	5
7 Jan.	Hazelwood Doonee	4		17	2	
8 Jan.	Hazelwood Percy Mount and Dark Trees	7		12		103
9 Jan.	Hazelwood Bog and Bog Avenue	7		18		41
10 Jan.	Hazelwood Rockwood	5		56		
23 Jan.	Markree Farm side			6		44
24 Jan.	Markree Ballygawley			26	11	2
27 Jan.	Annaghmore	5		10		26

The Shoot 1898-1915

The Temple House beats were shot twice a season, with one shoot usually before Christmas and a second later in January, which allowed for six to eight days of shooting. The beats are both consistent and productive and the yield has been remarkably consistent over the past hundred years. At the time under review, it is clear from the way the Game Book is organised – and similar to that of Annaghmore – that shooting at the estate was part of a rotation with neighbouring estates comprising Annaghmore, Hazelwood, and Markree Castle.

The Kilbratten and Derreen Wood beats have consistently yielded thirty to forty Woodcock. Exceptionally, on 2 December 1909, there were eighty-two Woodcock shot by seven Guns on this beat. There was clearly a lot of Woodcock around Temple House that season, with a further twelve and seventeen Woodcock being taken on 1 December and 3 December at Demesne East and Demesne West respectively, giving a bag of 111 Woodcock for that December shoot. In addition, there were 199 Pheasants shot in Demesne East, a further couple of dozen at each of Kilbratten and Demesne West, and a smattering of ground game and occasional Snipe and Wood Pigeon. All in all it was a delightful few days' shooting. The Guns comprised: Ascelin Perceval of Temple House; brothers Charles Kean and Frederick William O'Hara, Annaghmore; Philip Dudley Perceval, Hazelwood; Charles Mulholland, Ballywalter; Sir Frederick Shaw, and J. Harvey.

The shooting parties at Temple House at the turn of the twentieth century, as one might expect, were very much a gathering of Percevals (both of Temple House and Hazelwood), O'Haras (especially brothers Charles Kean and Frederick William), Coopers of Annaghmore and Coopershill, and Coopers of Markree Castle, notably Maj. Bryan Ricco Cooper and his uncle Brig.-Gen. Richard Joshua Cooper, CB (1917), CVO (1909) (1860-1938), of Blackwell Hall, Buckinghamshire, and 28 Lowndes Square, London.

Other neighbouring families found at Annaghmore and discussed earlier, such as L'Estranges and Gethins, were frequent guests also at Temple House, as indeed were others from further afield like Count Markiewicz, who was present from 17-20 January 1911, along with Ascelin Perceval, Henry L'Estrange, Godfrey Mulholland, Philip Dudley Perceval, Frederick William O'Hara and his brother Charles Kean (only on 18 January). They shot forty-four Woodcock and eighty Pheasants over the four days, as well as a few Snipe and some ground game.

Another guest who appears at this time more frequently in the Temple House records is Henry Manly Palmer. The Palmer family was resident at Sriff (or Shriff) from at least the end of the eighteenth century. They held lands in the parishes of Drumlease and Drumreilly, in the Barony of Dromahair in the mid-nineteenth century. Henry Manly Palmer of Sriff was a member of the Grand Jury for Leitrim in 1851. Isabella Palmer of Drumkeel is recorded as owning over 1,300 acres in Leitrim in 1876. Thomas Robert Palmer, living at Friarstown in the 1870s, owned over 1,600 acres in County Leitrim at that time. This family intermarried with the Cullen family of County Leitrim on a number of occasions.

William Arthur Saunders-Knox-Gore (1854-1925)

Another Gun at Temple House, William Arthur Saunders-Knox-Gore was from Belleek Manor, County Mayo. He was son of Maj.-Gen. William Boyd Saunders (who assumed the additional surname of Knox-Gore by royal licence in 1891) of Ardmore, Torquay, Devon, who married Matilda Knox-Gore of Belleek Manor in 1854.[112]

Ernest Henry Knox of Greenwood Park (b. 1859)

Son of Albert Henry Knox (1827-1915) and Jane Harriet (daughter of James Annesley Knox of Crosspatrick). Greenwood Park was built by John Henry Knox (1786-1861), the sixth son of Francis Knox (1726-1818) of Rappa Castle, and Mary, fourth daughter of Paul Annesley Gore of Belleek Castle.

The Knox and Gore families were large landowners in north-west County Mayo and County Sligo who intermarried frequently to give rise to a bewilderingly complicated family, which extended to become Saunders-Knox-Gore and Pery-Knox-Gore. The Knox-Gore Estate was centred round the town of Ballina and it included lands in the parishes of Doonfeeny, Kilmoremoy and Ballysakerry (Barony of Tirawley), the parishes of Bohola, Killasser and Kilgarvan (Barony of Gallen), the parish and Barony of Burrishoole, County Mayo, and in the Barony of Tireragh, County Sligo. In 1876, the estate amounted to 22,023 acres in County Mayo and 8,569 acres in County Sligo. John Henry Knox built Greenwood Park in 1814. He married Adelaide Handy, daughter of Samuel Handy, in 1830 and together they had five children, of which there were two sons. However, these died in 1869 and 1875, and the house was occupied by daughter Florence, who sold Greenpark to a Knox cousin of Mount Falcon – probably Utred Knox. Other members of this family, including Col. Knox-Gore and P. Knox-Gore, make occasional appearances at Temple House.

Harry Knox's Game Book, relating to his shooting between 1895 and 1919 – and he did rather a lot – shows that most of his outings were around his own extended family's estates, each of which, to judge from the returns, had a thriving shoot, showing good returns of Pheasants, Woodcock, Snipe, and, in certain places, Grouse. Notably, these shoots included: Belleek Manor, which was in the hands of Maj.-Gen. William Arthur Saunders Knox-Gore at the time; Rappa Castle, the ancestral home dating back to Francis Knox; Mount Falcon, then in the hands of Utred Knox and his wife Nina Knox-Gore; Netley Park, which was in the hands of Henry William Knox, fourth son of Francis and Mary of Rappa Castle; Palmerstown, the home of Henry Arthur, the fifth son of Francis and Mary, and Owenmore, which was owned by the Orme family and probably leased by Knoxes at the time. In the latter part of the twentieth century, this property was associated with the McCausland family. Another estate not in his family which was visited rather frequently by Knox was Enniscoe, owned by Mervyn Pratt (1807-1890) and subsequently by his son Joseph Pratt (1843-1924). The Pratts were related to the Tynte family of Tynte Park, County Kildare, for some time part owners of the South Slob, County Wexford.[113] Enniscoe House today is in the hands of Susan Kellett, a descendant of the Pratts. Susan has hosted a Woodcock shooting syndicate at Enniscoe for the past thirty years.

Captain Graham Owen Robert Wynne (1862-1932)

Of Clogherevagh, a frequent member of the Temple House shooting parties, he was married to the Hon. Maud Anna Morris, daughter of Michael, 1st Lord Killanin. He served with the Royal Irish Regiment and was son of Maj. Charles Bradstreet Wynne of Clogherevagh and Emily Frances Gore-Booth of Lissadell. Graham of Clogherevagh and Muriel Wynne of Hazelwood were cousins, their mothers, Emily Frances Gore-Booth and Stella Gore-Booth respectively, were sisters.[114]

Finally, amongst the early regulars at Temple House, it is worth mentioning Henry Roger ('Hal') Wood-Martin (1875-1933) of Cleveragh, the seat of the Martin family. He was second son of William Gregory and Dorothy Robinson (Woodville). He spent much of his time managing his estate and the Robinson Estate office. He died unmarried at the age of fifty-eight. His nephew Richard ('Dick') Wood-Martin (b. 1929) played an active role in the Annaghmore shoot in the 1950s. He was involved also in the Classiebawn Shoot, where he was shoot manager from 1980.

1950 to Date

The recent history of Temple House is remarkably similar to those off Annaghmore Manor and Markree Castle, with a very considerable overlap in the *dramatis personae*. However, in more recent years, Roderick Perceval has taken significant steps to expand the scope of the shoot. He can now manage to shoot about sixteen days over the season, these divided about equally before and after Christmas. Moreover, he would not usually cover the same ground more than once a season. He has achieved this through lease arrangements with Coillte Teo, including incorporating parts of the shooting rights of the residual estate of Lissadell. The shooting at Temple House, in contrast to Markree, is not syndicated, although there is a high level of repeat party shooting between one year and the next.

HAZELWOOD HOUSE, COUNTY SLIGO

The Wynnes of Hazelwood had a strong shooting tradition and some shooting diaries of John Arthur Wynne (1801-1865), have survived from 1829. He was Under Secretary of State for Ireland and a Privy Councillor, and grandfather of Muriel Wynne (1892-1932). He was married to Lady Anne Butler, second daughter of the 1st Marquess of Ormonde.

His shooting diary relating to the period 1829-1833 is the earliest consistent record of Woodcock shooting uncovered in the course of researching this book. It is a meticulously kept little diary, giving details of the dates, places, number of guns, bag and remarkably, the number of shots fired. It also contains a brief account of weather conditions on each day.

Thus, from 1829-30, shooting took place on thirteen days, with the first shoot on 16 December and the final one on 25 January. Weather conditions were generally frosty with snow. Over this period there were 155½ brace of Woodcock shot, 12½ brace of hares and 34 brace of 'sundries'. The number of Guns ranged from two (four occasions) to six (two occasions). The number of shots fired was 1,024, a remarkable ratio of 2.5:1. The best day was at Lurganboy on 23 December 1829, when six Guns took 21½ brace of Woodcock for 176 shots (4:1). It is noted there was, 'Hard frost. Snow on the ground. Birds plenty. Some very bad shots out'!

On 31 December in Rockwood, 6 Guns had 15 brace of Woodcock for 108 shots (3.6:1). 'Sleaty, frost not very hard. Birds not plenty. One Gun killed nothing.' Shooting took place on thirteen days in 1830/31 and twelve the following season. The bag was ninety-two and a half brace and

39 Hazelwood House, County Sligo.

40 Diary entries, 1829-1830, of John Arthur Wynne (1801-1865).

eighty-two and a half brace of Woodcock respectively. In 1832/3, shooting over eight days, fifty-three brace of Woodcock was shot by between two and four Guns. In contrast with 1829/30, the weather on most days is described as mild, on occasions with thick fog, or 'Fine, mild and calm. Birds very scarce.'

Muriel Wynne was the eldest of four daughters of Owen Wynne VI (1843-1910) and Stella Gore-Booth, youngest daughter of Sir Robert Gore-Booth (1805-1876). Owen Wynne, too, had a keen interest in shooting. The 2nd Marquess of Ripon, formerly Earl de Grey, is considered to be one of the finest game shots ever to have lived. In forty-seven seasons from 1867 to 1913 he shot a total of 2,771 Woodcock, the vast majority of these on winter covert shoots when Pheasants were the main quarry. His Game Books show that he used come to Ireland, usually after Christmas, especially to shoot Woodcock. He was a regular at Lissadell in the 1870s and shot also at Hazelwood. For example, on 9 February 1874, when he paid his second visit of the season to Lissadell, five Guns shot the Wynnes' coverts at Hazelwood bagging fifteen Woodcock, but de Grey only accounted for one, 'not a d...d cock would come near me'.[115]

Muriel married Philip Dudley Perceval (1865-1939), who was the younger brother of Alexander (1859-1887) and uncle of Alexander Ascelin (1885-1967) of Temple House, which was also steeped in shooting tradition. Philip and Muriel would have had frequent contact through the shooting parties shared by their families. They married in 1892 and spent some years in Queensland, Australia, before returning to settle in Hazelwood. Hazelwood was designed for Owen Wynne by the architect Richard Castle and built between 1720 and 1740. The estate comprised 13,000 acres.[116]

Philip was a strong advocate of the Union and spoke at a number of local anti-Home-Rule rallies and at Women's Unionist Alliance meetings in 1912 and 1913. He and Muriel subsequently

41 Hazelwood shooting party: Back row (left to right): Lady Stella Gore-Booth (1846-1887) (wife of Owen Wynne); Richard Joshua ('Ricco') Cooper (1860-1938); Sarah Wynne (d. 1903) (daughter of Owen and Stella); Venetia Cooper (1872-1951) (sister of Ricco); Lord Grey; Unknown. Front row (left to right): Unknown; Grace Wynne (d. 1914) (daughter of Owen and Stella); Owen Wynne (1843-1910); Madeleine Wynne (d. 1933) (daughter of Owen and Stella); Geraldine [?] and Lee Norman[?].

42 Shooting party, Hazelwood House, including Owen (O.), Stella (S.) and Grace (G.) Wynne, Capt. Lamb, Matthew Cole and two indecipherable names.

settled in England, where she died in 1932 and he seven years later. The estate was sold to the Land Commission in the 1920s and the house has had various uses including army accommodation, psychiatric hospital and more latterly, part of an industrial building. Though neglected it survives intact.They were survived by their only child, Dorothy.[117]

Philip was a regular in the round of shooting parties which involved Hazelwood, Temple House, Annaghmore and Markree. He was keenly interested in particular in the breeding and migratory habits of Woodcock. In common with a number of other owners of estates in Ireland and Great Britain at about this time, he engaged in a scheme of ringing, or 'marking' as it was called, of Woodcock to learn more about their habits.[118] The results were reported in an article by him in *The Irish Naturalist* of November 1913:

I started marking Woodcock here for my own information only, as both my keeper (who has had a lifelong experience amongst Woodcock) and myself had come to the conclusion that we are now mainly dependent for our stock during the shooting season on the birds that are bred here; it is seldom of late years that a migration of foreign birds can be noticed as they used to be in former times. While referring to this particular neighbourhood only and to what has come under my own observation, I am of the opinion that the flights of foreign birds are of late years inclined to remain in England and the eastern counties of Ireland than used to be the case and that here in the west our home bred birds are principally to be relied on for our stock of birds during the shooting season.

I first entertained the idea of putting rings on young Woodcock in 1908, in order to try to get some idea as to whether we got any, and if so, how many, relatively, of the birds that were bred in the place. In [the following year] 1909 … we were able to mark 16 young Woodcock. The following winter seven of the marked birds were shot, all except one being got here and that one was got a couple of miles from where it was ringed. The following year 1910 … we were unlucky in dropping on but few young birds, though there were plenty about and only a dozen had rings put on. Of these, four were shot the following winter, as well as two birds ringed the year before [1909]. In 1911, we were again unable to catch many young birds and I can only account for 10 rings having been put on and that winter we shot 3 of these birds, also one of 1909 and one of 1910 and the same season two of our 1911 birds were shot in the vicinity. At the moment of writing (17 March), there appeared to be more Woodcock in this place than there have been all the winter … These birds we look upon as responsible for the stock we may expect next season.

The accepted theory amongst many sportsmen is that the birds that are bred here go away and that possibly some may return. I admit that some may and do leave us, but from my own observations and from those of others better qualified to give their opinion than I am, I believe that most of the birds bred here remain with us all through the year. There is not a month during which plenty of Woodcock cannot be seen here; sometimes they are in the old woods, sometimes in spinneys and sometimes on heather. Where they are depends on the time of the year and the conditions of weather.

Hazelwood, Sligo.[119]

A number of points of interest emerge from this article. Firstly, it is clear from this experiment, and those referred to on other estates, that the status of Woodcock was not something taken for granted. These were privately sponsored schemes aimed at learning and achieving greater

43 Philip Dudley Perceval (1865-1939).

understanding of the population dynamics of Woodcock and in particular to the sustainability of that population. The latter point is amply demonstrated in the belief, expressed in the piece above, concerning the local breeding population forming the stock for the season ahead, rather than reliance on migratory birds.

The second point of interest is the apparent abundance of Woodcock outside the winter months, 'There is not a month during which plenty of Woodcock can be seen here'. Is there anywhere in Ireland today where that could be said to be the case? It certainly suggests that suitable breeding (and probably feeding) habitat was more abundant and probably managed to support a large resident breeding population.

Finally, there is the intriguing remark that: 'it is seldom of late years that a migration of foreign birds can be noticed as they used to be in former times'. At the time of the article (1913) and the seasons prior to that, Woodcock bags at Hazelwood were consistently high. For example, in December 1910, five Guns over the same number of days had 132 Woodcock, followed by 101 to the same number of Guns over four days from 21 to 24 November 2011, and seventy-one the following January and 119 for the four days 26-29 November 1912. These bags would appear to be very strong to be reliant on a resident population, or if they were, then resident populations were much stronger than they are today. As with many aspects of Woodcock, we shall never know!

Sadly, Hazelwood, unlike Temple House, Annaghmore and Markree Castle, is no more. Philip Dudley Perceval and Muriel left Hazelwood for England. They were the last in their line to reside there and the estate was broken up after their departure.

MARKREE CASTLE, COLLOONEY, COUNTY SLIGO

Markree is the oldest inhabited residence in County Sligo, having been founded by Cornet Cooper in the mid-seventeenth century and has been the seat of the Cooper family since then. The estate extended to over 34,000 acres, including a walled demesne of 1,000 acres and a deer park of 200 acres. The main part of the estate was sold under the Land Acts, and after the First World War the house became vacant. It came through the Troubles unscathed, although it was occupied by a contingent of the National Army, which successfully resisted attempts by Irregulars to gain possession.

It remained vacant until 1927, when Bryan Cooper (1884-1930) resumed occupation for a short period and carried out essential repairs and maintenance. In the 1950s the estate experienced difficult times; the castle fell into disrepair and was abandoned, following the death of Lt Commander Edward Francis Cooper. In 1988, his second son, Charles, came into possession from his older brother Edward Joshua. He undertook extensive renovations, converting the castle to use as a hotel.[120]

The Game Book of Brig.-Gen. Richard Joshua Cooper (1860-1938) and his successors provides a comprehensive record of the Markree shoot and Richard's many visits to neighbouring and other shoots around the country. His name appears in the Game Books of both Temple House and Annaghmore, and his autograph appears in the Game Book.

He is worth mentioning, also, for the fact that in his capacity of Private Secretary to the Lord Lieutenant of Ireland, Earl of Dudley, between 1904 and 1905, he was involved with the arrangements of the Prince of Wales's visit to Ashford in 1905. A letter he wrote to Lord Ardilaun can be seen above. Lord Dudley appears in this book – in more colourful terms – in the section dealing with Screebe House.

44 Markree Castle, County Sligo.

Richard Joshua rose to the rank of brigadier-general, having commenced his army career with the Coldstream Guards in 1880. He served in Egypt in 1882, saw action at Mahuta and at the Battle of Tel-el-Kebir. He then transferred to the Irish Guards in 1900, when that regiment was established, as lieutenant-colonel commanding a battalion. He served in the Boer War before his stint as Private Secretary to Lord Dudley. During the First World War he served as Commander of the 29th Infantry Brigade at Gallipoli in 1915, where he was wounded and mentioned in despatches. He married Constance Mary, youngest daughter of Alexander William Thorold Grant-Thorold of Weelsby House, Lincs., England, in 1904 and he died without issue in 1938.[121]

Bryan Ricco Cooper (1884-1930)
Eldest son of Maj. Francis E. Cooper, who died on active service in South Africa in May 1900. He succeeded his grandfather, Edward Henry Cooper, at Markree on his attaining twenty-one years of age in June 1905. He was educated at Eton and the Royal Military Academy at Woolwich and subsequently attained the rank of captain in the Sligo Artillery. He was a frequent member of the shooting parties of Markree, Temple House, Annaghmore and Coopershill in the seven years or so from his accession to Markree. However, on the outbreak of the First World War he joined the Connaught Rangers, with whom he served with distinction at Suvla Bay, Gallipoli and Salonika. He was mentioned in despatches several times and was raised to the rank of major.

He returned to a changed world at home and appears to have moved away from traditional country life, becoming involved in politics; he fought the general election of September 1923 and again in 1927, successfully on both occasions. He was interested in the stage and also in writing. He died in Dublin, following a brief illness, at the young age of forty-six years.

Bryan's eldest son with his first wife, Marian Handcock of Buckinghamshire, Edward Francis, Cooper (1912-1982) succeeded at Markree. With his wife, Elizabeth Clarke of Sussex, whom he married in 1936, he had three sons and two daughters. Edward, the eldest, inherited. However, he sold his interest to his younger brother and hotelier Charles in 1988. Following the Lloyd's collapse of 1994, a further 600 acres were sold to meet commitments.

The shooting tradition at Markree has been sustained through these generations and is faithfully recorded in the Game Book, which was initiated by Richard Joshua. The book itself was a Christmas present given to him in 1895 by his brother Arthur Charles (1864-1921), a frequent shooting companion, who died unmarried. However, the records contained in it date from 1886. (Presumably the earlier records were transcribed from an earlier book.) In 1902, the Game Book was 'closed and given to Bryan "Ricco" Cooper to continue, February 26th 1902'. No reason is given for this. Bryan was eighteen years of age, which may have had some significance. Also, a year earlier, on 20 January 1901, it is noted that it was 'Bryan's first experience as host.' Pressures may have been growing on Richard Joshua's time, as he was to become Private Secretary to Earl Dudley, Lord Lieutenant, between 1904 and 1905.

Records are contained thereafter for each season until the end of January 1914, when Bryan went off with the Connaught Rangers to the First World War. During the period of the war, there are records contained for 1914 and from 1916 to 1920. However, in many cases then the shooting parties were confined to the keeper 'Bracken' and Edward Stanley Handcock (and a J.H. Handcock), Bryan Cooper's father-in-law, who, it appears, was there most of the time from 1916 through to 1920. These three Guns had good shooting, especially of Woodcock, where the daily bag ranged from sixteen to twenty-six.

There was a further break from then until 1948, when records recommence and cover the period to the mid-1990s. This latter period was compiled by Edward Francis, Bryan's eldest son, and, in turn, his eldest son, Edward Joshua (b. 1940).

As a young man in his middle to late twenties, Richard Joshua was very much a man about the shooting scene. In the season of 1886/87, he spent thirty-two days shooting and succeeded in maintaining that kind of commitment for most seasons of the ensuing decade! In addition to Temple House, Annaghmore, Coopershill, Hazelwood and Markree, he managed to get around to Lissadell (Gore-Booth, County Sligo), Knockranny (Tennison, County Roscommon), Kilronan (King/King-Tennison, County Roscommon), Longford Lodge (Crofton, County Sligo), Rockingham (Lord Kingston, County Roscommon), Ballindoon (Gethin, County Sligo) – spending a few days at each! For example, in the five days from 28 December 1886 inclusive at Lissadell, there were ninety-three Woodcock and fifty-nine Pheasants shot by a party comprising: R.J. Cooper, Sir Henry Gore-Booth and son Jocylyn, Lord de Grey (subsequently 2nd Marquess of Ripon), Gerrard Macklin Eccles (1857-1940) and another Eccles.

The Eccles' were of Moneygold House. Gerrard was born in Bombay and a local government auditor by profession. He attained the rank of major with the Sligo Artillery Militia. He was a keen country-sports man, a leading member of the Sligo Harriers, point-to-point follower and owner of a number of outstanding horses.

Twelve months later, almost to the day, the same party, with the addition of Owen Wynne of Hazelwood, were back in Lissadell on 20 and 21 December 1887, where they shot twenty-three and twenty-six Woodcock on the Cat Corner and Oxfield beats respectively. They then moved to Hazelwood, shooting Glencar (22 December), Hazelwood Bog (23 December, with the addition of brothers George and Frank Gethin, Ballindoon, on that day only) and Rockwood (26 December), accounting for sixteen, thirty-one and forty-four Woodcock on each day respectively. Then it was back to Lissadell, for 27 and 28 December, with the addition of Lord Kingston (Rockingham), where six and twenty-one Woodcock were shot respectively, the latter on the Mountain Plantation. All in all a busy Christmas shooting party!

The summary shooting record for Markree for the ten seasons 1886/7-1895/6 is summarised in the following table. It is representative of the period to the commencement of the First World War and provides a good view of the extent and pattern of shooting over the seasons of this period.

Summary Shooting Records Markree Castle, 1886-1896

Date	Beat	Woodcock	Pheasants
1886/7, 7 Dec.	Union Wood	17	8
8 Dec.	Grove Side	8	78
9 Dec.	Farm Side	20	76
10 Dec.	Union Wood	26	14
4 Jan.	Cloonmacduff	1	66
5 Jan.	Union Wood	17	14
6 Jan.	Grove Side	9	53
7 Jan.	Farm Side	14	56
1887/8, 9 Nov.	Union Wood	12	22
10 Nov.	Farm Side	26	136
11 Nov.	Grove Side	10	146
28 Nov.	Cloonmacduff	4	78
8 Dec.	Union Wood	16	7
9 Dec.	Farm Side	10	146
5 Jan.	Union Wood	15	15
6 Jan.	Grove Side	5	60
1888/9, 28 Nov.	Farm Side	26	65
29 Nov.	Cloonmacduff	5	46
30 Nov.	Grove Side	8	69
14 Dec.	Union Wood	9	1
9 Jan.	Union Wood	19	13
10 Jan.	Farm Side	11	38
11 Jan.	Cloonmacduff	3	29
1889/90, 27 Nov.	Grove Side	19	69
28 Nov.	Union Wood	23	14
29 Nov.	Farm Side	31	73
30 Nov.	Ballygawley	16	–
19 Dec.	Cloonmacduff	12	60
7 Jan.	Union Wood	21	22
8 Jan.	Cloonmacduff	1	42
10 Jan.	Grove Side	11	47
29 Jan.	Farm Side	14	45
1891/2, 11 Nov.	Grove Side	15	86
13 Nov.	Union Wood	20	24
15 Nov.	Farm Side	20	45
6 Jan.	Farm Side	20	19
7 Jan.	Union Wood	35	4
8 Jan.	Grove Side	15	92

Date	Beat	Woodcock	Pheasants
13 Jan.	Ballygawley	27	14
14 Jan.	Cloonmacduff	8	44
1891/2, 11 Nov.	Grove Side	13	70
12 Nov.	Union Wood	16	9
1 Dec.	Cloonmacduff	3	66
2 Dec.	Ballygawley	18	3
3 Dec.	Farm Side	16	54
12 Jan.	Ballygawley	23	2
13 Jan.	Farm Side	17	32
16 Jan.	Union Wood	32	16
1892/3, 22 Nov.	Farm Side	19	66
23 Nov.	Ballygawley	13	–
24 Nov.	Union Wood	25	12
3 Dec.	Cloonmacduff	13	63
6 Dec.	Ballygawley	14	–
10 Dec.	Grove Side	5	94
14 Dec.	Creagh	19	–
29 Dec.	Farm Side	10	35
6 Jan.	Union Wood	23	12
11 Jan.	Cloonmacduff	7	38
12 Jan.	Grove Side	7	48
16 Jan.	Ballygawley	12	1
17 Jan.	Creagh	14	1
18 Jan.	Union Wood	26	7
1893/4, 21 Nov.	Cloonmacduff	8	54
22 Nov.	Farm Side	18	69
23 Nov.	Union Wood	18	19
30 Nov.	Grove Side	11	91
17 Jan.	Creagh	22	2
18 Jan.	Ballygawley	28	4
23 Jan.	Farm Side	10	64
24 Jan.	Cloonmacduff	10	39
25 Jan.	Grove Side	9	40
26 Jan.	Union Wood	25	9
1894/5, 13 Nov.	Farm Side	27	77
14 Nov.	Union Wood	30	18
15 Nov.	Grove Side	20	98
16 Dec.	Creagh	19	2
17 Dec.	Cloonmacduff	3	43
18 Dec.	Ballygawley	23	4
19 Dec.	Union Wood	13	10
8 Jan.	Union Wood	29	16
9 Jan.	Ballygawley	14	2
10 Jan.	Grove Side	12	58
11 Jan.	Farm Side	27	45
26 Jan.	Cloonmacduff	6	52
1895/6, 26 Nov.	Grove Side	12	143
27 Nov.	Union Wood	27	22
28 Nov.	Farm Side	19	133

Date	Beat	Woodcock	Pheasants
29 Nov.	Union Wood	17	24
17 Dec.	Ballygawley	19	7
18 Dec.	Cloonmacduff	9	100
21 Dec.	Creagh	15	3
2 Jan.	Union Wood	4	27
7 Jan.	Farm Side	15	92
8 Jan.	Union Wood	4	27
9 Jan.	Grove Side	10	115
23 Jan.	Cloonmacduff	6	65

Shooting took place on an average of ten days from November to January. Fourteen days was the maximum (in 1892/3) and seven days was the fewest (1888/9). On average, the bag each day comprised fifteen Woodcock and forty-five Pheasants to five Guns. The best season was 1890/1, when the average bag of Woodcock was twenty per day, and the biggest single day was on 7 January 1891, when thirty-five Woodcock were shot. In both 1887/8 and 1888/9, the daily average of Woodcock was a dozen. The poorest day was 4 January 1887, when only one Woodcock was shot at Cloonmacduff. However, there were sixty-six Pheasants in the bag, so some compensation. Union Wood was the most prolific and consistent beat, and appears not to have been stocked with Pheasants, presumably to keep the wood quiet for Woodcock, although there were good Woodcock numbers in both Farm Side and Grove Side, which clearly held the bulk of the Pheasants.

The pattern over this decade was repeated with consistency over the next twenty years, with similar bags being recorded. The participating Guns also remained constant with local families, L'Estranges, Gethins, Sir Manley Crofton, Manley Palmer, the Wynnes, Percevals and O'Haras making up a core, along with Richard Joshua Cooper, his brother Arthur Charles, and, from about 1900, Bryan Cooper.

There were some notable guests that joined occasionally. Amongst these was Maj. Acland-Hood, considered to be one of the finest of Edwardian shots, who appears on 18 January 1904 for shooting over five days, with Richard Joshua, Bryan Ricco, Edward Gethin, Arthur O'Hara and Lord Kingston. In addition to half a dozen or so Pheasants a day, the party shot ninety-seven Woodcock on Markree's main beats.

On 3 January 1905, in a party which included the Earl of Dudley and Lord Holmpatrick and Guy Edward Cooper (1891-1941), Bryan's younger brother, there were twelve Woodcock and fifty-nine Pheasants shot on what was described as 'Guy's first covert shoot'. In the next season, on 4-6 December 1905 a shooting party comprising Arthur Charles Cooper, younger brother of Richard Joshua, and his nephew Bryan Ricco, hosted Sir Neville Chamberlain, the Hon. R. Butler, Col. Ward, and R. Grant Thorold over three days, in which they shot Union Wood (thirty-one Woodcock and fifteen Pheasants), Farm Side (twenty Woodcock and sixty-four Pheasants) and Ballygawley (twenty-two Woodcock and thirty-seven Pheasants).

So the seasons ran until 1920. After this date there was a gap until 1946. For the last ten years of his life, Bryan spent most of his time in Dublin, professionally as a politician and recreationally pursuing his interest in the theatre. His son Edward Francis was serving in the Royal Navy during the Second World War, while Peter, his brother, was at Markree. He was a 'horsey' man and did not have an interest in shooting.

1946-1968

When shooting resumed in 1946 after the Second World War, much had changed and yet much remained as before. Markree Castle was in the hands of Edward Francis Patrick Cooper (1912-1982), eldest son of Bryan Ricco and his first wife, Marian Handcock. He was then thirty-four years old, and had retired from the Royal Navy in 1945 with the rank of Lieutenant-Commander. In 1937, he married Elizabeth Mary, eldest daughter of the late Venerable Charles Philip Stuart Clarke, Archdeacon of Chichester. By this stage they had Deirdre Ann (b. 1938), Edward Joshua (b. 1940), and Pricila Elizabeth (b. 1946). Charles Philip (b. 1948) hadn't yet arrived.

Harry Bracken (of the keepering dynasty) was keeper, like his father (Robert James) before him, a position he held until he went to Broadlands, Hampshire, in 1960, to take up a post of gamekeeper there.

The round of shoots which was attended retained continuity in respect of Temple House, Annaghmore and Coopershill. Hazelwood was no more and Lissadell no longer appears, the shooting having ceased there in 1944. However, the shoots of other estates, not previously mentioned, are included regularly. For example, Tanrego House, Beltra, a plain two-storey, five-bay, L-shaped Georgian residence, which looks onto 100 acres of parkland, close to Ballisodare estuary, and has excellent views to both sea and mountain. It was home, successively, to Richard John Verschoyle, from 1864, and William D. Verschoyle. In 1932, it became the property of Capt. Gordon H.C. McCormick, solicitor, who in turn was succeeded by Col. Francis R. Palmer, of the Huntley Palmer biscuit family from Scotland, and then by Sir John Farr, a Conservative MP.[122] All four of these appear shooting at Markree and were involved also at Annaghmore and Temple House from the 1940s through to the 1960s and later. On 28 January 1948, six Guns, including Edward Francis, shot twelve Pheasants, eight Woodcock and a few rabbits there, in continuous drizzle.

Strokestown Park, home of the Pakenham-Mahon family, was another shooting estate which was visited by Edward Francis, and Pakenham-Mahon was a visiting Gun at Markree. On 12 October 1948 a rather poor bag at Strokestown comprised ten Snipe, one Pheasant and two plover to three Guns, including Edward Francis. Strokestown has an extremely vibrant history, which is well worth recalling here. It was the family home of the Pakenham-Mahons from the 1600s until 1979. By the early eighteenth century, the estate comprised over 11,000 acres, scattered throughout north-east Roscommon, put together from the later seventeenth century as a result of land acquisitions by Capt. Nicholas Mahon around 1660. Later, his great-grandson Maurice Mahon purchased additional lands, following his elevation to the peerage of Ireland, as the 1st Baron Hartland, in 1800. After the assassination of Maj. Denis Mahon in November 1847, at the height of the Famine, his only daughter, Grace Catherine, vowed never to return to her ancestral seat. She was on honeymoon at the time, having been married only weeks earlier to Henry Sandford Pakenham, son of Dean Henry Pakenham of Tullynally, and heir to the vast Pakenham and Sandford Estates in Counties Longford, Westmeath and Roscommon. The marriage alliance (by which Henry Sandford Pakenham assumed the additional surname of Mahon) united the estates of both families to comprise over 26,000 acres, and the Strokestown Estate remained one of the largest in Roscommon until his death in 1893.

Grace Catherine never returned to Strokestown, but her son Henry Pakenham-Mahon loved the house. He married the only daughter of Col. Sidney Burrard:

> …such a great beauty that people would stand on walls and on each other's shoulders to catch a glimpse of her. Their daughter, Olive, inherited her mother's looks, large expressive eyes and soft mouth. She grew up at Strokestown but spent half the year in their house at Bond Street.[123]

She fell in love with and married Edward Stafford-King-Harmon, heir to the Rockingham Estate, County Roscommon. However, she was to be married, widowed and become an expectant mother all within five months, for her husband was killed at Ypres in November 1914. She went on to marry Maj. Wilfred Stuart-Atherstone-Hales in 1921. But after only one month, her grandfather Henry Sandford-Pakenham died and stipulated 'that if she were to enjoy Strokestown, her heritage, she must revert to her maiden name of Pakenham-Mahon'.[124] Her new husband adopted his wife's name and their children, Nicholas, twin Denys, and sister Elizabeth, all became Pakenham-Mahons.

Castledargan was a local estate in Ballygawley. Originally the home of the Ormsby family:

> … it was bought in 1876 through the Landed Estates Court by William Middleton, a Sligo merchant, for £12,000, from his son-in-law, John R. Ormsby and comprised 959 acres. Middleton mortgaged the estate to Andrew Hosie, a Miller from Dromahaire, for £10,000. Following Middleton's death in 1882, the property was offered for sale in 1883 and purchased by John Hosie, nephew of Andrew for £7,750. The house became home to three generations of Hosie: John who died in 1919, his son James and his grandson, John Christopher, who died in 1997.[125]

Both James and John Christopher were regulars at Markree in the 1950s, as indeed they were at Annaghmore. In addition, a G. Middleton and W. Middleton also appear in the Game Books of both Markree and Annaghmore in the 1950s. They may be related to William Middleton, the Sligo merchant who died in 1882, however, it has not been possible to establish a precise relationship. Castledargan itself appears to have been a poor enough shoot. The record indicates a bag of three Pheasants and five Woodcock on 22 January 1955, when Edward Francis Cooper and five other Guns shot it; about the same as two years earlier on 2 December 1953, when three Pheasants and a couple of Woodcock were shot.

Hollybrook, originally the home of a branch of the Ffolliott family in the mid-seventeenth century, became a hotel and in 1946 the property of Desmond R. Sherriff, who catered especially to visiting anglers and retained it until 1960. At a shoot on its 300 or so acres on 26 November 1949, it yielded thirteen Woodcock and three Pheasants to six Guns. Sherriff was a regular at Annaghmore and Markree from 1946 into the 1960s.

The individuals of these estates, along with the Percevals of Temple House, Coopers of Coopershill, O'Haras of Annaghmore, Richard ('Dick') Wood-Martin, and Alexander P. MacArthur of Ardaghowen (proprietor of Sligo's premier bakery in O'Connell Street), as well as the keeper, Harry Bracken, whose name appears frequently with those of the Guns, dominate the Game Records for Markree over the twenty years or so to about 1968. Much the same as Annaghmore, and for that matter Temple House. By and large the quality of the shooting remained comparable with that of the late 1800s. There were fewer Pheasants, because fewer were put down, but in terms of Woodcock the bag records are comparable to those early days, ranging from eight to eighteen or so per day, although there are certainly fewer days when the total is above twenty-four, compared with the earlier period.

1990 to Date

The next major change came when Charles Cooper took over from his elder brother Edward in 1988. Faced with the challenge of restoring the property and establishing Markree as a fine country house hotel, he came up with the rather novel idea of providing an investment opportunity through a business expansion scheme and a shooting opportunity in the form of a syndicate which would have exclusive shooting rights over Markree. The idea worked, both as an investment and in terms of delivering continuity of the shooting. The investors, of whom there were about fourteen in number, have been also a remarkably stable shooting syndicate for the past twenty years or so. As a group, they include names such as Dick Wood-Martin, who has been associated for generations with Woodcock shooting in the area, and Donal O' Hara of Annaghmore, who has similar associations. The shooting, which usually takes place over perhaps ten days in a season, is organised very much from a social point of view. The shooting is driven, with the Cooper family supplying most of the beating firepower, both human and dog along with some input from syndicate members. It is a very good example of adaption and change that has enabled continuity of a shoot with a long and distinguished tradition.

LISSADELL, COUNTY SLIGO

Lissadell was the childhood home of Irish revolutionary Constance Gore-Booth, her sister, the poet and suffragist Eva Gore-Booth, and their siblings, Mabel Gore-Booth, Mordaunt Gore-Booth and Jocelyn Gore-Booth. It was also the sometime holiday retreat of the world-renowned poet William Butler Yeats. He made the house famous with the opening lines of his poem 'In memory of Eva Gore-Booth and Constance Markiewicz':

> The light of evening, Lissadell,
> Great windows open to the south,
> Two girls in silk kimonos, both
> Beautiful, one a gazelle.

William Butler Yeats, *The Winding Stair and other Poems* (1933).

The Gore-Booths of Lissadell were described as 'an enlightened family of the Protestant ascendancy, [and] were part and parcel of the history of Sligo for close on four centuries'.[126]

Sir Robert Gore-Booth (1805-1876)

The first of the family to achieve prominence in relatively modern times, he was the eldest son of Sir Robert Newcomen Booth Gore, 3rd Baronet, who had assumed the additional surname of Booth by sign manual.[127] His mother was Hannah Irwin of Streamstown, Achonry. His father died when he was nine years old and so he became a ward of court for twelve years. He was educated at Westminster and Queen's College, Cambridge. He succeeded to the title and family estates in 1826. He quickly adapted to life as a resident landlord and country gentleman, and was prominent in the public life of the county as High Sheriff, Magistrate and JP.

The present Lissadell House was built by Sir Robert in the 1830s, replacing an earlier, eighteenth-century house nearer the coast. In addition, he purchased the Fitzmaurice Estate at Ballymote for £130,000, bringing his estate holding to about 32,000 acres.

45 Lissadell House, County Sligo, June 2007, showing the south-facing front with the curved bay, and also the west side which comprises two wings and a sunken courtyard, from which a tunnel leads to the main avenue at the intersection with the coach house/forge avenue. The Woodcock or other game was probably brought from the shoots down the tunnel, through the courtyard and into the kitchen or pantries.

46 Sir Robert Gore-Booth's (1805-1876) Game Book, 1840. The manuscript provides a template for the very large-format printed Game Books of the Lissadell Estate, which record its shooting history until 1944.[129]

'Sir Robert had the reputation of being a model country gentleman, kind hearted and liberal and ever ready to aid and improve the condition of his tenants. As a landlord he must be classed with the best,' wrote a correspondent with *The London Times* in 1881. 'He let his lands at their value and never pressed for rent, allowing his tenants plenty of time to wait and sell in the best market.'[128] During the Famine he mortgaged the estate to the extent of £50,000 in order to provide his tenants with food and clothing. He was a keen sportsman and had his own private pack of hounds known as the 'Lissadell Harriers'. Sir Robert was also a shooting man but the historical record of shooting at Lissadell really commences with the next generation of Gore-Booths and the families with which they married. Sir Robert had five children: two boys, Robert Newcomen (1831-1861) and Sir Henry William (1843-1900), 5th Baronet; and three daughters, Augusta Elizabeth (d. 1906), Emily Frances Graham and Stella Anne.

Sir Henry and his son and successor Sir Jocelyn (1869-1944) were the driving forces behind the strong shooting tradition at Lissadell in the half century up until 1944. In addition, as will be shown below, this shooting tradition was reinforced through the marriages of Stella Anne to Owen Wynne (1843-1910) of Hazelwood House, and Emily Frances to Maj. Charles Broadstreet Wynne (d. 1890) of the Cloherevagh branch of the Wynne family, whose husbands and offspring were keen shooters at Lissadell parties.

Sir Henry William Gore-Booth, 5th Baronet (1843-1900)[130]

Notable Arctic explorer and adventurer, as well as the owner of the 32,000 acres which comprised the Lissadell Estate, he married Georgina May Hill of Tickhill Castle, Yorkshire. They lived at Lissadell House and were visited frequently by a childhood friend, the poet W.B. Yeats, and his daughters. Together they had five children, two boys, Sir Jocelyn (1869-1944) and Mordaunt (1878-1958), and three girls, Constance (1968-1927, later Countess Markiewicz), Eva (1870-1926), who became involved in the labour movement and women's suffrage in England, and Mabel Olive (1876-1955).

Unlike his father, Henry was not involved in public affairs or hounds, preferring instead the rod and gun. He was interested primarily in the development of his estate and the welfare of his tenants, and he served both as the president of the Sligo Agricultural Society and the chairman of the Sligo, Leitrim & Northern Counties Railway.

He was also a prolific writer on a variety of topics, including Arctic exploration, yachting, whaling, polar-bear hunting and shark fishing. He sailed his own yacht to the Arctic. He also hunted big game in Africa and some of his fellow explorers, like Benjamin Leigh Smith, in whose rescue Henry partook in 1882, and Admiral Markham were shooting guests at Lissadell (see below). Henry was a correspondent of Sir Ralph Payne-Gallwey, who notes that:

Sir H. Gore-Booth tells me that during frost and snow they find Cock in large numbers. Some years since one hundred and fifty couple were killed in three days by a party of eight guns, close around the house at Lissadell. During the last few days of January and the beginning of February 1867, three hundred and thirty-eight 'cock were killed in six days, at the same place, by a party averaging seven Guns. The winter of 1878/79, Sir Henry tells me, was a fairly good one in Sligo. Two Guns at Lissadell in that year obtained twenty couple in a day; four Guns thirty-two couple and the next day, thirty couple. The best bag in 1880/81 was thirty-three couple to four Guns.[131]

There is no doubt that Lissadell's reputation as a premier Woodcock shoot was well established by this time and it was a place where shooting was taken seriously. This is reflected in a number

47 **Sir Henry Gore Booth (1843-1900) with Woodcock bag.**

of ways. For one thing, there were three keepers – Wood, Magee and Cadden – working there during the early decades of the twentieth century.[132] In addition, the estate Game Books are of unusually large format and contain very detailed information of game shot (including trapped game, in the case of rabbits), noting the numbers obtained from each beat. Moreover, and unusually, there are records for the months of March through July, relating mainly to rabbits shot and trapped by location by the keepers, including the name of the keeper responsible. There is also a parallel record of what game was sent to the house and the game sold off the estate. Thus, they are more a game register maintained by the keepering staff than a Game Book maintained by the estate owner.

Lissadell, like Ashford, Barons Count, Classiebawn and Hazelwood also undertook a study of Woodcock movements using ringing techniques. The reports of ringing and recoveries are noted in the Game Books.

It has been noted elsewhere that Lissadell was included in the annual Irish shooting tours of Lord de Grey during the 1870s, when his own diaries show him visiting also Hazelwood and Muckross.[133]

Sir Jocelyn Gore-Booth, 6th Baronet

A personal Game Book of Sir Jocelyn Gore-Booth, 6th Baronet, picks up the story from 1895-1900. Jocelyn loved fishing as well as shooting, but, as noted by McTernan:

> On his accession to the family estate he was not content to live what now appears to have been the idyllic life of a country squire. Instead he took up farming on an extensive scale and became a noted livestock breeder. He also developed an extensive bulb farm. He also recognised the economic possibilities of timber and planted a large are of his 32,000 acre estate … A century ago Lissadell was one of the principal agricultural and horticultural farms in the country giving employment to more than two hundred workers.[134]

Date 1913..	NAMES OF BEAT	GUNS	Rabbits Trapped	Rabbits Shot	Hares	Pheasants Cocks	Pheasants Hens	Geese	Partridges	Snipe	Woodcock	Sundries
			3113	931	211	175	167	58	.	132	107	41
Decr 12th+13th	Hill fields &c		15									
„ 15th	Ballinfull + Upper Glen	Wood					6					
„ 16th	Glen + Road fences		12	6								
			13									
„ 17th	Glen + Road fences		9	10								
„ 18th	Glen + Road fences		8									
19th+20th	Glen + Road fences		10	10								
„ 23rd	Nursery White Wood &c		12	7	1							
„ 24th	Nursery White wood &c		8									
„ 26th												
„ 27th	Seafield	Mr Coffey										
„ 26th	Nursery whitewood &c	Mr Coffey	26									
„ 29th	Johnsport Breaffy + Ballinfull	Capt L'Estrange Malone				2				11	1	
30th	Carney + Coole drumman	Capt Malone + Major Hildyard		1						9		
„ 30th	Crushmou		8									
„ 31st	Rahelly + Sea Field	Major Hildyard + Mr D. Coffey										
			20									
			62	26								
						2	2	1				1
			3316	991	216	177	174	58	..	152	109	41

No of Woodcock ringed in 1913.
1 Woodcock No 34, ringed at Mountain Wood
2 Woodcock Nos 14, 15. ringed at Cat Corner (right leg)
2 Woodcock Nos 4. 5. ringed at Tunnel
1 Woodcock No 16, ringed at Clancy's Young Wood
1 Woodcock No 17. ringed at Cregoran
1 Snipe No 2 ringed at Ballintrillick, (Thrush Mountain)

Novr 18th 1913. 1 Woodcock shot at Oxfield with ring No 17.

48 Lissadell Game Book, note of Woodcock ringed in 1913.

He became a leading proponent of Horace Plunkett's Agricultural Co-Operative Movement and devoted much time and energy to the establishment of creameries at Drumcliffe, Ballinfull, Ballintrellick and other locations around the county.

Jocelyn married a second cousin, Mary L'Estrange Malone, in 1907,[135] and had eight children: Michael, Brian, Hugh, Angus, Rosaleen, Bridget, Rosaleen, Aideen and Gabrielle.[136]

When the Wyndham Land Bill was enacted in 1903, Sir Jocelyn was one of the first proprietors to become involved in the scheme that encouraged landlords to allow their tenants to buy out their holdings. 'More than 1,000 tenants purchased between them some 28,000 acres of the original 32,000 acres that Jocelyn had recently inherited, leaving the demesne surrounding the house as the principal block of remaining land.'[137]

Jocelyn's Game Books show the shooting parties comprising a combination of family, local neighbours and guests from further a field and abroad. His father, Sir Henry, who appears as 'HWGB', appears on most days shooting during the five seasons covered by this diary. Jocelyn's uncle, Owen Wynne (1843-1910) of Hazelwood, married to Stella Gore-Booth, and his cousin Capt. Graham Wynne (1862-1932) of Clogherevagh, son of his aunt, Emily Frances, and Maj. Charles Broadstreet Wynne, are also very frequent shooters. Jocelyn's younger brother, Mordaunt (1878-1958), appears only occasionally, notably at the end of December 1891.

There are also a number of occasional shooters during this period who are probably relations by marriage, such as Lt-Col. Hon. George Henry Morris (1872-1914), who became the first commanding officer to lead an Irish Guards battalion into battle. He was born in Spiddal, County

Galway, and was the second son of Michael Morris, 1st Baron Killanin, and therefore a brother to Anne Morris, the wife of Capt. Graham Wynne. He is probably the Capt. Morris who appears shooting with Jocelyn on 9 December 1891, before his departure to join the Rifle Brigade in India as second lieutenant in 1892. Similarly, from 12 to 21 October 1891, an E. Ussher is found shooting on most days. Mary Rowland Egerton Warburton, widow of Robert Newcomen Gore-Booth (1831-1861), Sir Henry's elder brother, married a John Ussher in 1865. It is suspected that the Ussher referred to is an issue of this marriage.

There are a number of Guns who appear in these early records who are frequent shooters during the period and for many years into the twentieth century. Most notable of these are William Seymour Bird and Revd Fletcher Sheridan Le Fanu.

William Seymour Bird (1846-1919)

William Seymour Bird, Churchtown House, Dundrum, County Dublin, was the eldest son of John James Bird MD, FRCSI, of Banagher, County Offaly, and Hannah Moore, BA (TCD). He was a gold medallist in History and English Literature at Trinity. Admitted as a student in Trinity term 1867, he was later admitted to Middle Temple, Easter term 1868, and was then called to the Bar at Michaelmas term 1870, becoming QC in June 1889. He was appointed County Court Judge for the West Riding of Cork on 27 February 1892 and he resigned from this position in 1915. He appears to have been shooting very frequently from 1895 to about 1912, at which time he was sixty-six years of age. In addition, he appears to have had a lease, or some kind of exclusive arrangement in respect of the shooting, on the Ballymote Estate, in regard to which there is a separate note (in red ink) recording the summary of 'Judge Bird's shooting at Ballymote' for each season over the decade or so to 1910.

Revd Fletcher Sheridan Le Fanu (1860-1939)

The son of William Richard Le Fanu (1816-1894) and Henrietta Victorine Barrington, aunt of Sir Charles Burton Barrington of Glenstal. His father, William Richard, was a civil engineer and Commissioner of Public Works in Ireland, and he authored *Seventy Years of Irish Life* (1893). He lived at Summer Hill, Enniskerry, County Wicklow. He married Jane Hore, daughter of Walter Hore, on 18 November 1885 and died without issue in 1939. Revd Fletcher Sheridan Le Fanu was educated at Haileybury College, Haileybury, Hertfordshire, England. He graduated from Trinity College Dublin with a Bachelor of Arts (BA) and he was the rector at St John's, Sandymount, County Dublin. Again, he was a very frequent shooter up to about 1906.

Frederick Oliver Robinson, 2nd Marquess of Ripon, GCVO (1852-1923)[138]

The most renowned guest Gun, from a shooting point of view, he was styled Viscount Goderich between 1859 and 1870 and Earl de Grey between 1870 and 1909. He was a British courtier and Liberal politician. Ripon was the only son and only surviving child of George Robinson, 1st Marquess of Ripon, and grandson of Prime Minister Frederick John Robinson, 1st Earl of Ripon. His mother was Henrietta Anne Theodosia, daughter of Henry Vyner. Lord Ripon entered Parliament for the Ripon constituency in 1874, a seat he held until 1880. In 1909, he succeeded his father in the marquessate and took his seat in the House of Lords. He also served as Treasurer to Alexandra of Denmark, Queen Consort of the United Kingdom. In 1885, Lord Ripon married Lady Constance Gladys, daughter of Sidney Herbert, 1st Baron Herbert of Lea, and widow of St George Lowther, 4th Earl of Lonsdale. They had no children. She died in October 1917, aged fifty-eight years. Lord Ripon survived her by six years and died in September 1923, aged seventy-one years. McKelvie notes of him:

The second Marquess of Ripon, formerly Earl de Grey, was probably the finest game shot who ever lived. He certainly devoted his energies to shooting on a Homeric scale, even by the standards of the spacious days in which he lived. Between 1867 and 1923 his Game Books record a total of 556,813 head of game, wildfowl, rabbits and 'various'. In forty-seven seasons from 1867 to 1913 he shot a total of 2,771 Woodcock. The vast majority of these were shot on winter covert shoots when Pheasants were the main quarry. Ripon's lifetime total was 241,224 Pheasants, giving a rough ratio of almost 100 Pheasants shot for every Woodcock he bagged.[139]

He is recorded shooting from 30 December 1890 to 14 January 1891, a period of 'fine, hard frost'. The party comprised: Sir Henry; Jocelyn; Maj. Fletcher Le Fanu; Gerrard Macklin Eccles (1857-1940), who appears regularly and frequently at Lissadell from this time through to 1930; Owen Wynne (1843-1910); Capt. Graham Wynne (1862-1932), and Wilfrid Ashley, 1st Baron Mount Temple (1867-1939) of Classiebawn Castle. There was a close relationship between Lissadell and neighbouring Classiebawn, which went back to the time of Sir Robert Gore-Booth and Lord Palmerstown.[140] Ashley, it is suggested, was probably a suitor of Constance Gore-Booth (elder sister of Jocelyn), whom she described as 'a young nobleman living on a nearby estate'.[141] In summary, the bag for the ten days of shooting comprised 332 Woodcock, 201 Snipe, 36 wildfowl (including 4 geese) and 104 Pheasants, as well as numerous hares and rabbits. Jocelyn's Game Book was unusual in that it contained a column entitled 'self' alongside the 'total'. He was in the habit of completing this column for Woodcock and Snipe at least, and in this regard he accounted for forty-six Woodcock and forty-four Snipe. He also notes that, 'W.A. [Wilfrid Ashley] and I shot 11 Golden Plover off the car.'

Admiral Sir Albert Hastings Markham, KCB (1841-1918)

Another notable guest in these years is Admiral Sir Albert Hastings Markham, a British explorer, author, and officer in the Royal Navy who was there again in December 1894. He married Theodora Grevers in 1894, with whom he had one daughter. He was the fifth son of Capt. John Markham, who had retired from the navy because of ill health with the rank of lieutenant. His grandfather, William Markham, had been Archbishop of York. Markham joined the Royal Navy in 1856 at the age of fifteen and spent the first eight years of his career on the China Station. He became acquainted with a British consulate official who encouraged an interest in ornithology and shooting Snipe. Throughout his life he enjoyed hunting all manner of beasts. The only killing at which he showed disgust was the drawn-out deaths of whales, which he saw on Arctic voyages.

In 1879, he accompanied Sir Henry Gore-Booth aboard the *Isbjörn* to Novaya Zemlya, a remote island in northern Russia. He served for many years on the Council of the Royal Geographical Society, along with his cousin Sir Clements Markham, whose biography he would later write. In addition, he wrote numerous books and articles about his explorations. While stationed in the Pacific from 1879 to 1882, he compiled a list of Pacific Gulls which was published in 1882 by the ornithologist Howard Saunders and republished in 1883 by Osbert Salvin. Salvin named a bird, Markham's Storm-Petrel, after him, in honour of his contributions to science.

Julian Russel Sturgis (1848-1904)

Also present during several of these seasons was Francis Spring Rice (1852-1937), 4th Baron Monteagle of Brandon, son of the Hon. Stephen Edmond Spring Rice, and, for the Grouse shooting in August and September 1893, Julian Russell Sturgis (1848-1904), who was an American-born novelist, poet, librettist and lyricist who lived and worked in Britain nearly all of his life. He

49 Lissadell party including, back row from left, Julian Sturgis (1848-1904), Sir Henry Gore-Booth (1843-1904), Capt.Constable and William Richard Le Fanu (1816-1894).

played soccer as an amateur for Wanderers FC, winning the English FA Cup in 1873, and becoming the first American to play in an FA Cup-winning team.

Sturgis was born in Boston, Massachusetts, but moved to England when only seven months old, when his father, Russell Sturgis, a successful Boston and Far East merchant (1805-1887), joined Baring Brothers in London. Sturgis's mother was Julia Boit, his father's third wife. He was a pupil at Eton College, where he played an active role in the mixed Wall and Field XIs in 1867, being keeper of the field in 1867, and editing the *Eton College Journal*. On leaving Eton, he went up to Balliol College, Oxford, where he rowed for three years for the college. After graduating, he became a barrister and acquired British nationality. He subsequently became a novelist, librettist and lyricist. In 1885, Sturgis wrote the libretto for Arthur Goring Thomas's opera *Nadeshda*, which was first performed at the Drury Lane Theatre on 16 April 1885 and was considered to be Thomas's best.

In 1863, he married Mary Maude Beresford (d. 1952), only daughter of Col. Marcus Wylly de la Poer Bereford (1825-1902). Sturgis's connection is unclear but may have come through Constance Gore-Booth.[142] As Sturgis died in April 1904, it was probably his son Sir Mark Beresford Russell Sturgis (1884-1949) who is referred to on subsequent shoots in the period from August 1905 to August 1914. (In 1893 he was too young to have been shooting.) He married Ellen Rachel Montagu-Stuart-Wortley-Mackenzie, daughter of Francis John Montagu-Stuart-Wortley, 2nd Earl of Wharncliff, and Ellen Gallwey, in 1914. He was Joint Under-Secretary for Ireland during 1920-1922. He died on 29 April 1949.

Sir Edward James Harland, 1st Baronet (1831-1895)

Finally there was Sir Edward James Harland, shipbuilder and politician, who was shooting during the Christmas and New Year shoot of December/January 1894. Born in Scarborough, North Yorkshire, he was educated at Edinburgh Academy. In 1846, aged fifteen, he took an apprenticeship at the engineering works of Robert Stephenson & Co. in Newcastle upon Tyne. Afterwards he was employed in jobs in Glasgow and again in Newcastle, before moving to Belfast in 1854 to manage Robert Hickson's shipyard at Queen's Island. Four years later he bought the yard and renamed the business Edward James Harland & Company, and in 1861 he formed a business partnership with Gustav Wilhelm Wolff, his former personal assistant, creating Harland & Wolff. Later, Harland recruited William James Pirrie as another partner. Edward Harland, Gustav Wolff and William James Pirrie maintained a successful business, receiving regular orders from the White Star Line before Harland's retirement in 1889, leaving Wolff and Pirrie to manage the shipyard. In 1860, Harland married Rosa Matilda Wann, of Vermont, Belfast, who was the daughter of Thomas Wann, a stockbroker and insurance agent. In 1885, he was granted a knighthood and a baronetcy. Harland was a member of the Conservative and Unionist Party, and served as Mayor of Belfast; later he moved to London and served as Member of Parliament for Belfast North until his death.

A summary of the seasons' bags for 1890/91-1894/5 achieved by this group of Guns is contained in the table below (excluding hares and rabbits):

	Grouse	Partridge	Pheasant	Woodcock	Snipe	Wildfowl
1890/1	–	–	104	332	201	36
1891/2	77	79	265	572	766	42 (9 geese)
1892/3	Jocelyn shooting Prairie chickens in Manitoba					
1893/4	211	132	268	164	197	–
1894/5	65	86	240	232	106	–

The shooting records for the first decade of the twentieth century are drawn from the Estate Game Books. These provide a comprehensive picture up until 1944, when Sir Jocelyn died. In the first decade, Sir Jocelyn is accompanied by Judge Bird, Fletcher Le Fanu, Capt. Graham Wynne, Col. Wilfrid Ashley, Henry L'Estarange and some *new* family members, as well as certain neighbours who previously had not appeared.

   The first of the new family members to appear shooting is Charles Percival Foster (1872-1946), along with brothers John Kenneth Foster MP (b. 1866), Robert Lionel Foster (b. 1870) and father, John Foster (1832-1910). Charles was married to Mabel Olive Gore-Booth (1876-1955), Jocelyn's youngest sister. They began shooting at Lissadell from 1902.

Count Casimir de Markievicz (1874-1932)

The year 1902 also saw the first appearance of 'Mr' de Markievicz, i.e. Count Casimir de Markievicz (1874-1932), who was introduced to his future wife, Constance Gore-Booth, Jocelyn's older sister, in January 1899 at a student ball by the Polish writer Stefan Kozywoszewski. The two married in September 1900 and came to live in Dublin in 1902. He was from a wealthy Polish family who were landowners in what is now the Ukraine. He became a portrait and landscape artist. He was a regular shooter at Lissadell and indeed at Temple House and Hazelwood, and he appears to have fitted in comfortably with Irish shooting society at the time, although Jocelyn had grave reservations about the match and the validity of his title.[143] This may account for the fact that it is not until 1913 that he is referred to in the Game Book as 'Count'. Finally, 1902 saw the commencement of shooting by Philip Dudley Perceval (1865-1939) of Temple House, who had married Muriel, daughter of Owen Wynne and Stella Anne Gore-Booth in 1892.

Major Harold Charles Thoroton Hildyard (1872-1958)

Later in the decade, another of Jocelyn's in-laws joins the shooting parties and commences a long association with the shooting at Lissadell. Major Harold Charles Thoroton Hildyard was from a distinguished military family and on 15 August 1909 he married Selina L'Estrange Malone, older sister of Mary Sibill, wife of Sir Jocelyn. His father, Gen. Sir Henry John Thoroton Hildyard, GCB (1846-1916) was a British Army general who saw active service in the Anglo-Egyptian War of 1882 and the Second Boer War. He was General Officer Commanding-in-Chief, South Africa, from 1905 to 1908. He had two brothers: Gerald Moresby Thoroton Hildyard (1874-1956) and Gen. Sir Reginald John Thoroton Hildyard (1876-1965), who was a British Army general who saw active service in the Second Boer War and the First World War, and he was Governor and Commander-in-Chief of Bermuda from 1936 to 1939. The latter made a number of appearances shooting in 1925.

Cecil John L'Estrange 'Colonel' Malone (1890-1965)

Another brother-in-law of Jocelyn who would have a long shooting association which commenced in 1909 was Cecil John L'Estrange 'Colonel' Malone, who became Britain's first Communist member of the House of Commons. He was brother of Mary Sibill, Jocelyn's wife.

Born in Dalton Holme, Yorkshire, on 7 September 1890, he was a rector's son and joined the Royal Navy in 1905, attending the Royal Naval College at Devonport. He played a pioneering role in naval aviation and rose to become a commander, and later a lieutenant-colonel, in the British Army. He saw action in the First World War, commanding HMS *Ben-my-Chree*, for which he was awarded the Order of the Nile. In the 1918 UK general election, Malone joined the anti-communist Reconstruction Society and was elected as the Coalition Liberal MP for Leyton East, although he later claimed never to have actually joined the Liberal Party. He was also awarded the Order of the British Empire.

In September 1919, Malone, along with another traveller, arrived in Petrograd. There he met and spoke with key leaders of the trade union movement before proceeding by train to Moscow, where he met with Maxim Litvinov, then a top official in the People's Commissariat of Foreign Affairs. He later met with Foreign Minister Georgii Chicherin and Red Army leader Leon Trotsky on an inspection of troops at Tula aboard Trotsky's special train. During his visit, detailed in his memoir, Malone toured factories and theatres, power stations and government offices. He found the mission of the Bolshevik government in attempting economic reconstruction to be compelling and emerged from his trip a committed communist. 'The history of Allied negotiations and transactions with Russia appears to have been a chain of catastrophes and mistakes,' he wrote.[144]

Malone married in 1921 and worked to promote the affiliation of the CPGB to the Labour Party, which was under consideration as a tactical matter, urged by Lenin. Malone later left the CPGB and to join the Independent Labour Party, which was affiliated to the Labour Party. He unsuccessfully stood as the Labour candidate for Ashton-under-Lyne at the 1924 UK general election, but was elected in the Northampton by-election of 1928 and held the seat until the 1931 UK general election.

Finally, this decade saw a number of neighbours commence shooting at Lissadell. Sir Malby Crofton, like Jocelyn, was an ardent supporter of Sir Horace Plunkett's Co-Operative Movement and for a time acted as president of the Skreen Co-Operative Society, and on this account alone would have been a likely companion of Jocelyn.

Gregory Gonville Wood-Martin (1878-1934)
The third son of Col. William Gregory Wood-Martin (1847-1917), the antiquary and historian. His elder brother 'Hal' was a frequent shooter at Temple House. Gregory Gonville returned to farming at Woodville following a distinguished career in the navy, which included commanding a gunship in the Battle of Jutland. He married Dorothea Hosie of Castledargan in 1925 and they had a son, Richard ('Dickie'), who in turn succeeded at Woodville. The latter was an increasingly frequent shooter from the early 1950s (when he shot with his father at Lissadell and Classiebawn) at Temple House, Markree, Annaghmore and especially Classiebawn, where he was shoot manager up to its cessation in 1991.

A final recruit to the Liassadell shooting field in 1909 was Capt. William Henry Parke, JP, a land agent who resided at Dunally for a time before enlisting in the Connaught Rangers. His shooting career, however, was brief. He was killed in action in Germany in 1916.

Shooting during the decade was intense, commencing in August with Grouse and working through to Pheasants from October, and Woodcock and Snipe from late November through December and January, when shooting took place on most days.

The season of 1910 is typical of most years of the opening decade of this century. Shooting commences on 22 August, with Henry Wynne out with the keeper Wood on Ballintrellick bog for nineteen Grouse. The following day he takes five on Benbulben and ten the day after at Upper Glen. In early September, Sir Mark Sturgis arrives to shoot, and over a few days with the keeper Wood, the Grouse bag for August and September is brought to seventy-five for about six days shooting by one Gun and a keeper.

Sir Mark remained into October, during which the shooting was slow, comprising mainly of rabbit, hares and the odd Snipe and plover, taken in and around Crushmore and the White Wood. By early November, Maj. Hildyard was shooting also and by 19 November, covering Seafield, Johnsport and Ardtarmon, the bag included seven Snipe, sixteen Woodcock, a goose and several Golden and Green plover.

The main shooting commenced on 29 November with a party comprising Sir Jocelyn, Capt. Wynne, Judge Bird, Maj. Eccles, Gregory Wood-Martin and Capt. Parke. The shooting took place over Oxfield and Cat Corner, the two most consistent Woodcock beats on the estate, and moved on over the following two days to Holywell, Upper Glen and Foresters. Over the three days, the bag included 184 Pheasants and 76 Woodcock. The following week, basically the same Guns continued, though frequently in twos and threes, taking odd Pheasants, hares and rabbits, about eighteen Snipe and twenty-one Woodcock.

On 2 January 1911, Sir Jocelyn was back out shooting, following a brief stop over Christmas. He was accompanied by Maj. Hildyard, who spent Christmas at Lissadell, and by Count de Markiewicz, who was also at home for the holiday. Other guests were '2 Creightons and Leveson-Gower'. Shooting took place over the following four days at Holywell, Upper Glen, Churchill, Ballintrellick, Mountain Wood and Argaron. The bag comprised ninety-six Pheasants and ninety-nine Woodcock (nineteen to twenty-six each day, save for one when the total was six).

Vice-Admiral William Spencer Leveson-Gower
It is likely that the 'Leveson-Gower' referred to in the Game Book was Vice-Admiral William Spencer Leveson-Gower, 4th Earl Granville, KG, GCVO, CB, DSO (1880-1953),[145] a British sailor and governor, styled the Hon. William Spencer Leveson-Gower until 1939, when he acceded the title following his elder brother Granville's death in that year. Born the younger son of Granville

George Leveson-Gower, 2nd Earl Granville, William Leveson-Gower joined the Royal Navy in 1894. He was promoted to sub-lieutenant in 1900, lieutenant in 1902 and Commander in 1913. He served in the First World War and was awarded the Distinguished Service Order in 1919.

Appointed, in turn, Chief of Staff to the Commander-in-Chief, The Nore, in 1924, *aide-de-camp* to the King in 1929, and Commander-in-Chief, Coast of Scotland, in 1931, William was made a Companion of the Bath in 1930 and retired in 1935. In 1945, he became Governor of Northern Ireland, serving until 1952. He was made a Knight of the Garter that same year. In 1916, Lord Granville married Lady Rose Constance Bowes-Lyon, the second surviving daughter of the 14th Earl of Strathmore and Kinghorne and elder sister to Queen Elizabeth, the Queen Mother. She died in 1967, while he predeceased her at the age of seventy-two.

The '2 Creightons' could be of the Earl of Erne's family, given the spelling of the name, rather than the Sligo family from Carrowgarry.[146] However, it more likely refers to Alexander Joseph Crichton (1861-1934), who succeeded to the family estates at Carrowgarry on the death of his father in 1888. He became an active member of the Irish Agricultural Organisation Society and was for many years president of the Skreen and Dromod Co-Operative Agricultural Society. 'Co-operation was the guiding principle of his life and in many respects he led the way for others of his class and social standing to follow.'[147] He would thus have been an easy soulmate to Jocelyn, whose ideals were very similar. His brother Eric Cuthbert Crichton (1886-1961) graduated in medicine from Trinity College Dublin. During the First World War, he held the rank of captain in the RAMC, serving in Egypt and Palestine. Following his return he was appointed Assistant Master of the Rotunda Hospital in Dublin but moved to South Africa as Professor of Obstetrics and Gynaecology at the University of Durban. The third brother, Dr Brian Dodwell Crichton (1887-1950), succeeded to Carrowgarry and was a more regular shooter than his older brother at Lissadell and also at Classiebawn.

The intervention of the First World War does not appear to have disrupted shooting at Lissadell as it did at many other estates. A noticeable feature during those years is the frequent appearance of J[ules] and W[atty] Bracken, the Classiebawn gamekeepers, at Lissadell shoots, as guest shooting at Classiebawn was suspended during these years.

About 1915 sees the first involvement of Frederick William Cooper O'Hara (1875-1929) of Coopershill, along with his brother Arthur Cooper O'Hara of Annaghmore. Their association lasted for more than a decade. Another new shooting visitor from this time was Christopher G. Orme (d. 1929) of Owenmore House (County Mayo) and Orme's Lodge, Enniscrone. He married Mary Kathleen, daughter of Michael Morris of Spiddal (subsequently Lord Killanin) and niece of Capt. Morris. He was a frequent guest in the Lissadell shooting line-up until his death.

The summary shooting record for the first two and a half decades of the twentieth century is shown below (in calendar years):

	Pheasant	Grouse	Partridge	Snipe	Woodcock
1900	645	51	11	234	135
1901	727	79	34	514	130
1902	518	59	21	473	262
1903	413	63	–	395	128
1904	525	86	5	440	154
1905	643	120	–	400	123

1906	189	136	2	232	65
1907	416	83	7	316	269
1908	514	91	–	225	113
1909	358	76	–	244	98
1910	370	75	–	252	185
1911	171	96	–	201	83
1912	760	99	–	246	170
1913	341	58	–	152	109
1914	434	19	–	66	188
1915	193	85	–	210	117
1916	390	57	6	126	120
1917	325	57	8	54	29
1918	316	62	–	154	109
1919	321	21	5	130	152
1920	298	15	–	142	138

In 1926 we see the first of many appearances with Jocelyn of his sons 'master Michael', 'master Hugh' and 'master Bryan', who appear regularly each season during the next ten years or so. Also making his first appearance about this time is Maj. Michael Nicholls, a trustee of the estate. Years later, he was to play a significant role when the estate was being managed by Jocelyn's sister Gabrielle, in the so-called 'Lissadell Affair'.[148]

From about this time, too, Maj. Ascelin Perceval (1885-1967) of Temple House makes increasingly frequent appearances, as does Capt. Jimmy Hamilton (1913-1987) of Brown Hall, County Donegal. Indeed it appears that most of those who are found shooting at Classiebawn from the 1930s became involved at Lissadell from about the same time, including T.H. Blackburn, Dr McCready, Dr Crichton, Coulthard Nelson, Thomas Troubridge Stubbs, and Stanley Pettigrew.

50 Shooting party, Lissadell. From left: Brian Gore-Booth (1912-1940), Gabrielle Gore-Booth (1918-1973), Unknown, Angus Gore-Booth (1920-1996), HughGore-Booth (1910-1943) – in a bomber jacket, Unknown, Rosaleen Gore-Booth (1914-1991), Unknown, the keeper.

51 A bag of Barnacle geese: Angus Gore-Booth (1920-1996) with the keeper on his right.

However, Lissadell was in decline by the mid-1920s. 'Gabrielle, Jocelyn's youngest daughter, later wrote that after 1920 "something of the spirit of the place and wellbeing had vanished". She was alluding to the effect which the political upheavals were having on the estate'.[149] In addition, the loss in 1922 of Cooper, Jocelyn's estate manager, who went on to become a director of the Bank of England, was a devastating blow. Furthermore, the emergence of mental ill-health in Sir Michael, his eldest son, and the loss of two other sons, Hugh (1910-1944) and Brian (1912-1940), in the Second World War, took a fatal toll on Jocelyn. Even before these final sad years, the shooting record for most of the last two decades before Jocelyn's death was one of decline, as the table opposite shows:

	Pheasant	Grouse	Partridge	Snipe	Woodcock
1925	35	1	–	91	24
1926	26	3	–	21	15
1927	76	–	–	53	34
1928	72	–	–	91	16
1929	104	2	–	41	50
1930	148	13	–	358	71
1931	88	16	–	307	75
1938	52	–	–	8	59
1939	88	6	–	1	29
1940	107	–	–	2	16
1942	36	1	–	1	9

The shooting rights over part of the residual Lissadell Estate are now exercised under lease, mainly by Roderick Perceval of Temple House.

CLASSIEBAWN CASTLE, COUNTY SLIGO

He [Mountbatten] was happier there 'than anywhere else on earth' and I [Timothy Knatchbull] felt the same. Before each holiday there I was filled with intense excitement, and when the time came to leave Classiebawn, I felt like crying. My cousin Ashley invariably had tears running down his face. We sensed that we were leaving a place where normal life was suspended and dreams were played out, impossible to be regained in another time, another place.

Timothy Knatchbull, *From a Clear Blue Sky* (2009), p.37.

Classiebawn Castle is undoubtedly a place of haunting beauty, with a history marred by enormous tragedy dating from the Famine years and culminating in the murder of Lord Louis Mountbatten in 1979. The story of Classiebawn, as it relates to the Mountbatten murder, is compellingly told by his grandson in *From a Clear Blue Sky*, to which the reader is referred for this numbing episode of its history. However, in its time it was a Woodcock shoot of considerable renown and there was serious resource devoted to understanding the habits and migration of Woodcock. It was also a good habitat for wintering Snipe.

The castle was commissioned by Henry John Temple, 3rd Viscount Palmerston, KG, GCB, PC (1784-1865), known popularly as Lord Palmerston, who was a British statesman who served twice as Prime Minister of the United Kingdom in the mid-nineteenth century.[150]

Palmerston's greatest contribution to the area was the development of the stone harbour in Mullaghmore, which still stands. Work on it began in 1822 under the direction of the engineer Alexander Nimmo and it was completed in 1841. Palmerston had big plans for it as an exporting harbour, but they never came to fruition; it is now used mostly for pleasure craft and it served the fishing community very well in past times.

Palmerston presided over Mullaghmore and North Sligo during the years of the Great Famine. His record during that period is bad. During the summer and autumn of 1847, nine vessels, carrying over 2,000 persons, left Sligo port with tenants evicted and 'shovelled out' from his Sligo estates. They arrived in Canada half naked and totally destitute. The city of St John in Quebec

52 Classiebawn Castle, County Sligo.

province had to take many of Palmerston's evicted tenants into care and, outraged, sent a scathing letter to Palmerston expressing regret and fury that he or his agents 'should have exposed such a numerous and distressed portion of his tenantry to the severity and privation of a New Brunswick winter … unprovided with the common means of support, with broken down constitutions and almost in a state of nudity … without regard to humanity or even common decency'. The graves of many of these victims can be seen today on the old quarantine station, now a museum, at Grosse-Île, near Quebec.

On the death of Lord Palmerston, Classiebawn (with its castle incomplete) passed to his stepson William Francis Cowper-Temple, 1st Baron Mount Temple, PC (1811-1888), of Broadlands, Hampshire, also a British Liberal Party politician and statesman. The castle was completed in 1874. After William's demise, it passed to his nephew the Hon. (Anthony) Evelyn Melbourne Ashley PC (1836-1907),[151] another British Liberal politician and fourth son of Anthony Ashley-Cooper, 7th Earl of Shaftesbury (see below), and Lady Emily Cowper, eldest daughter of Peter Cowper, 5th Earl Cowper, and sister of William Cowper-Temple, 1st Baron Mount Temple. He was educated at Harrow and Trinity College, Cambridge. He was Private Secretary to Lord Palmerston from 1858 to 1865 and was a Barrister on the Oxford Circuit from 1865 to 1874. He was married firstly to Sybella Charlotte Farquhar in 1866, with whom he had two children: Wilfred William Ashley, later Baron Mount Temple (1867-1939), and Lillian Blanche Georgiana Ashley (1875-1939). Following Sybella's death in 1886, he married Lady Alice Cole, daughter of William Cole, 3rd Earl of Enniskillen, on 30 June 1891. She died on 25 August 1931.

In 1907, Classiebawn was inherited by the son of the Hon. Evelyn Melbourne Ashley, Wilfrid William Ashley, 1st Baron Mount Temple (1867-1939), a Conservative politician who was Minister of Transport in the Government of the United Kingdom between 1924 and 1929. In 1901, he married Amalia Mary Maud Cassel, a daughter of financier Sir Ernest Cassel. The couple had two daughters: Edwina Mountbatten, Countess Mountbatten of Burma, and Ruth Mary Clarisse (later Cunningham-Reid, later Gardner, later Lady Delamere). Later, in 1914, he married Muriel Emily ('Molly') Forbes-Sempill, the former wife of Rear-Admiral Hon. A.L.O. Forbes-Sempill.

Shooting records for Classiebawn are contained in a privately owned Game Book (1912-1959) of Jules Bracken, gamekeeper at Classiebawn.[152] However, shooting was taking place at Classiebawn long before this. For example, de Grey was shooting there in the 1870s, when he was also a visitor at Muckross, Lissadell and Hazelwood.[153] There are also references and accounts of shooting at Classiebawn contained in the Game Books of Sir Jocelyn Gore-Booth relating to the late 1890s.[154]

Another important source of information on Woodcock at Classiebawn are two articles by Dr S.R. Douglas, MRCS, LRCP (Lond.), Captain IMS (retired), dating from 1917 and 1929.[155] Dr Douglas (1871-1936) was a regular shooter, appearing frequently in the Game Book during the period 1912-1929. He was born in 1871 and educated at Haileybury College and St Bartholomew's Hospital. After taking the double diploma MRCS, LRCP in 1896, he joined the Indian Medical Service in 1898 as surgeon lieutenant. He served with the Plague Commission in 1899 and with the China Expedition in 1900-1, being promoted to captain. He was invalided home at the end of 1901, but in spite of poor health he soon took up work at St Mary's Hospital with Sir Almroth Wright and his work was to play a significant role in new studies on vaccines and vaccine therapy.[156]

The articles in question report the findings of ringing experiments of Woodcock carried out at the instigation of Col. Wilfrid Ashley, 'under the direction of Mr Jules Bracken, Col. Ashley's keeper and Bailiff'.[157] The experiment commenced in 1910 and continued until 1928. The total duration of the experiment was therefore nineteen years, and during that time 658 Woodcock were ringed and the results analysed in Douglas's two articles.

Douglas sets the scene as follows:

Col. Ashley's property consists of a strip of country lying between the Ben Bulben range and the southern shore of the Bay of Donegal, in the County of Sligo … It is composed largely of small holdings, which have been vested in tenants under the various Land Acts, but it also contains a considerable extent of bog land and some fine coverts made up of both hard and soft wood trees. These woods during the winter months harbour a considerable number of Woodcock affording excellent sport: in exceptional years large bags have been made, for instance in January 1892, 92 and 98 cock were shot on consecutive days: the more usual bags, however, are about 120 cock for two Guns in a week's shooting. Woodcock have only comparatively recently nested regularly in these parts, for, from information received from a former keeper of Col. Ashley's, Mr R. Bracken, who had been brought up in this part of the country and who has

53 Wilfrid William Ashley, 1st Baron Mount Temple (1867-1939) (centre), at Lissadell House.

54 **Recovery records (1914-1915) of Woodcock ringed at Classiebawn Castle.**

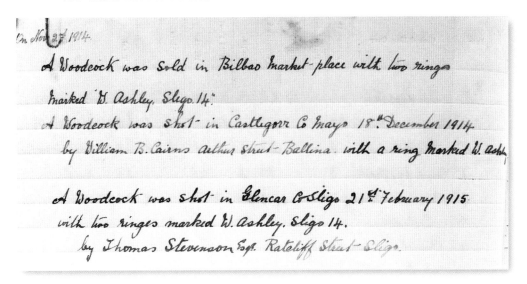

On Nov 27 1914

A Woodcock was Sold in Bilbao market-place with two rings marked "D. Ashley, Sligo. 14."

A Woodcock was shot in Castlegore Co Mayo 18th December 1914 by William B. Cairns arthur Street Ballina. with a ring marked W. Ashley

A Woodcock was shot in Glencar Co Sligo 21st February 1915. with two rings marked W. Ashley. Sligo 14. by Thomas Stevenson Esq. Ratcliff Street Sligo.

several relatives keepers on neighbouring estates, it appears quite certain that a Woodcock's nest was considered the greatest rarity before the year 1875. Since that date they have become more and more numerous. On Col. Ashley's property and especially in respect of the principal breeding ground described below, Woodcocks' nests were practically unknown before the year 1900. The principal breeding ground is a wood about 150 acres in extent, situated about the centre of the property. This wood, which was planted about 1830, consists almost entirely of Scotch and Maritime fir and lies within half a mile of the sea. The soil is very sandy and the ground between the wood and the seashore is occupied by sand dunes covered with bent grass. That part of the wood where most of the Woodcock nest is occupied by well-grown pine-trees and is practically destitute of any undergrowth, the ground between the tree-trunks being thickly carpeted with moss and fallen pine needles, with here and there, heaps of fallen sticks.[158]

As regards the Bracken family of gamekeepers who served at Classiebawn, they are described eloquently by local historian Joe MacGowan as follows:

Bachelor Watty Bracken, his brother Jules, his wife Felicity and daughter Yvonne lived in a spacious two-storey stone-built house on the estate. Prior to Mountbatten's time, Lord Ashley, successor to Palmerston, employed the Brackens as gamekeepers and managers of Classiebawn, its grounds, cattle, rabbits, Pheasant and peasants. They protected the teeming rabbit warrens, hatched and raised flocks of Pheasants that shrieked and primped on tree branches and hid in the long grass. The two brothers managed the woods and grazing, poisoned predators, controlled and trapped the rabbit warrens. Raising and releasing the Pheasants in season they also conducted the hunting parties that shot them. Wearing tweed knickerbockers, jackets and hats, the Brackens' manner of dress alone, apart from religion, pointed them out as different to everyone else in the village. Their relationship with the villagers was a Jekyll and Hyde one. On pitch-black winter nights they patrolled the Classiebawn demesne with shotguns and flashlights, protecting Lord Ashley's rabbit warrens. The poachers with their carbide lamps and hounds played cat and mouse with them. There was nothing personal in their encounters. The Brackens had law on their side; the hunters felt they had a moral right. Laws were made for the rich, the rabbiter claimed; they had a God-given right to the lands of their ancestors. Sometimes the poachers won and carried off a haul of rabbits; sometimes the Brackens succeeded and the miscreants were forced to plead their case before a hard-faced DJ in Grange District Court. When morning came it was business as usual. Poacher and gamekeeper exchanged civilities and engaged in the commerce of a small village as if nothing at all had happened. Men who skirmished with the gamekeepers and stole the landlord's rabbits the night before now went to the Brackens for permission to cut a load of firewood in the Classiebawn woods. A cartload of timber cost five shillings. It was all very civilised, a game almost, and no one thought it odd. It was as if nothing at all had happened the night before. If the firewood could be removed as easily as the rabbits there would be no question of paying. The Brackens kept a dairy too. When our cows ran dry we bought milk, and delicious salty homemade butter, from those people who were so different from us, but still in a detached sort of way, were yet a part of our community. Old ghosts live there now, but I remember the Bracken family for the efficient and homely dairy they kept, for well-scrubbed flagstone floors, for the smell of fresh buttermilk, for the men's strange tweed hats and baggy plus-four trousers, for Mrs Brackens kindness to a small boy, for the fresh milk we bought when our cows went dry, for the rich, salty taste of their delicious homemade butter. Sights and sounds so commonplace long ago, exotic now, but etched forever in a child's mind. Acknowledging local sensitivities and politics, these agents of a foreign landlord knew when to look the other way. There were invisible lines that were respected. Republicans were billeted in Classiebawn during the War of Independence. Hostages were taken once and held there to secure the release of condemned IRA prisoners, Johnson, O'Shea and MacBride. The castle was mined with dynamite: any attempt at rescue and it would be I blown sky high! If the Brackens noticed anything unusual in their patrols, and they must have, they said nothing. 'Less said is easiest mended.' was an old country saying. They were on Lord Ashley's payroll and then Mountbatten's, but the people who lived in the small community of Mullaghmore were their friends and neighbours.[159]

The description of their relationship with the wider community could probably be validly repeated at many other landed estates in Ireland at the time.

The shooting record commences with Count G.F.W. Metternich, Count P.W. Metternich and Count A.W. Metternich, shooting 199 rabbits in eight days during June and July 1912.[160] In August, September and October, forty-five Grouse were shot at Glengarrah, Clonkeen and Clonduff, along with twelve Snipe and eight wildfowl. The shooting was done by gamekeeper Jules Bracken and the birds were sent to 'The Grove, Stanmore' and 'Mrs Kincaid'. 'The Grove' was the home of Wilfrid Ashley's wife's family. Sir Ernest Cassel bought the property in 1906 for £17,000 following the death of its owner, naturalist Mrs Eliza Brightwen, who lived there from 1872 to 1906. The Kincaids were the Sligo agents of Lord Palmerstown, through the firm of solicitors Stewart & Kincaid, which was the largest estate agency in the country for many years.[161] A Col. W. Kincaid appears shooting at Classiebawn in October 1912.

December saw the bulk of the shooting. In the period 18-21 December, Col. Wilfrid Ashley, Dr Douglas and R.D. Bloominfield, Esq., accounted for sixty-five Woodcock, one hundred and thirty-two Pheasants, nineteen Snipe and twenty-six wildfowl, shooting Classiebawn, Cloontybawn, Cloonkeen and Glengorrah. After Christmas, from 26 to 31 December, Ashley was the only one out and he got seventeen Woodcock, thirteen Snipe and twenty-six Pheasants. In January and February, the shooting was carried out only by keeper Jules Bracken, the others presumably having vacated Classiebawn. Over seven days he shot four Woodcock and sixty-five Snipe, most of which was forwarded to Mrs Kincaid.

55 Jules
Bracken taking
a shot.

August 1913 saw Wilfrid Ashley back for Grouse, with fifty-four shot on 16-17 August at
Glengorrah and Ardnaglass bogs, and a further eighty-nine in four days in September, to his own
Gun it seems. Later in the year, again with Dr Douglas and a Douglas Everrett, Esq., in two days'
shooting at the end of December and beginning of January 1914, the three Guns took forty-nine
Woodcock at Cloontybawn and Classiebawn, as well as nineteen wildfowl on the lake. Seven days in
early January saw the same three Guns with seventy-two Woodcock, fifty-eight Snipe and seventy-
two Pheasants from Glengorrah, Cloonkeen and Cornduff. It is also noted in the Game Book that
there were 5,830 rabbits shot and trapped in 1913-14. Indeed, there were large numbers of rabbits
trapped and shot every year, and the numbers for 1913-14 are representative and not exceptional.

During the years of the First World War, shooting continued at Classiebawn but in a low-
key way, and it was carried out mostly by the gamekeepers. Thus, in 1914-15, Jules Bracken shot

twenty Grouse and twenty Snipe in October 'for Wilfrid Ashley'. There was no further shooting that season, and in 1915/16 there were sixty Grouse shot between August and October by J[ules] and W[atty] Bracken, thirty of which were 'for Broadlands'. Ashley was back for August and September 1916, shooting sixty-four Grouse, twenty-four Snipe and thirty-one wildfowl at the Lake in August and a further fifty Grouse in September, but there was no further shooting that season.

Hostility and violence in 1917 were sufficient to drive the Ashley family away from Classiebawn and leave it in the care of their trusted gamekeepers, Jules and Walter Bracken. Under their care the castle survived the Troubles. Apparently, according to a local historian:

> … the IRA had planned to destroy it but it was saved by the intervention of local members. Instead the IRA secretly billeted men in it and at one point held hostages there to secure the release of condemned IRA prisoners. If the Brackens noticed anything unusual, and they must have, they said nothing.[162]

August 1917 saw Jules on the moor at Glengorrah taking sixty-two Grouse in two days. In early January 1918, Ashley and Douglas had ninety-eight Woodcock in four days, and later in the month a further twenty-eight, along with eighty Pheasants and thirteen Snipe. The fact that the coverts were undisturbed in the previous two seasons may have had a bearing on the strong showing of Woodcock at this time.

With the end of the First World War on the 'eleventh hour of the eleventh day of the eleventh month' of 1918, the scene of social shooting quickly resumed, with a five-Gun party shooting six days between 30 December and 7 January 1919, and good shooting it was. In all, the bag comprised one hundred and twenty-eight Woodcock, eighty-three Pheasants, fifty-two Snipe and twenty-four wildfowl. The shooting party comprised the Earl of Shaftsbury and his son Lord Ashley, the Marquess of Linlithgow, Maj. Charles Mulholland (later 3rd Baron Dunleath of Ballywalter), who was Military Secretary to the Lord Lieutenant of Ireland between 1919 and 1921, and Col. Noel Corry.

Anthony Ashley-Cooper, 9th Earl of Shaftesbury, KP, PC, GCVO, CBE (1869-1961)[163] was the son of Anthony Ashley-Cooper, 8th Earl of Shaftesbury, and Lady Harriet Augusta Anna Seymourina Chichester (d. 1898), the daughter of George Chichester, 3rd Marquess of Donegall, and Lady Harriet Anne Butler. He would have been a first cousin of Col. Wilfrid W. Ashley, their respective fathers, Anthony Ashley Cooper, the 8th Earl (1831-1886), and Evelyn Ashley (1836-1907), being brothers and the sons of Anthony Ashley Cooper, 7th Earl of Shaftesbury.

In 1899, the 9th Earl married Lady Constance Sibell Grosvenor (1875-1957), the daughter of Victor Alexander Grosvenor, styled Earl Grosvenor (son and heir of Hugh Lupus Grosvenor, 1st Duke of Westminster), and his wife, Lady Sibell Mary Lumley, daughter of Richard George Lumley, 9th Earl of Scarborough.

The 9th Earl of Shaftesbury and his wife, Lady Constance, had five children, of whom Maj. Anthony Ashley-Cooper, Lord Ashley (1900-1947) was the eldest. Ashley (Col. Wilfrid's nephew) was married twice. His first wife was the former Edith Louisa Sylvia Hawkes, known as Sylvia. They were married in 1927 and divorced in 1934. Upon her marriage, she became Lady Ashley, while her legal married name was Ashley-Cooper. Lord Ashley shocked London society by marrying Hawkes, an English model and actress from the chorus line. They were divorced after she began an affair with American actor Douglas Fairbanks Sr, who was named as co-respondent in the petition for divorce.

After Lord Ashley's divorce, Lady Ashley went on to marry Fairbanks; Edward John Stanley, 6th Baron Sheffield; American actor Clark Gable, and Prince Dimitri Djordjadze. Although she was married to four other men after her first divorce, she continued to use the name Lady Ashley throughout her life.

Lord Ashley's second wife was the French-born Françoise Soulier, daughter of Georges Soulier of Caudebec-en-Caux. Lord Ashley and Soulier were married in 1937 and remained married until his death in 1947. Their two children were Anthony Ashley-Cooper, 10th Earl of Shaftesbury (1938-2004), and Lady Frances Mary Elizabeth Ashley-Cooper (b. 9 April 1940).

Lord Ashley was heir apparent to the earldom, scheduled to inherit upon the death of his father. During the Second World War, Maj. Lord Ashley served as a British Intelligence Officer with the Auxiliary Units, which were highly covert Resistance groups trained to engage and counteract the expected invasion of the United Kingdom by Nazi Germany. However, at age forty-six, Ashley died unexpectedly of heart disease, before his father. At that time, his son, Anthony Ashley-Cooper became heir apparent, inheriting the earldom in 1961 upon the death of the 9th Earl of Shaftesbury.

Victor Alexander John Hope, 2nd Marquess of Linlithgow, KG, KT, GCSI, GCIE, OBE, PC (1887-1952)

British statesman who served as Governor General and Viceroy of India from 1936 to 1943. He was born at Hopetoun House, South Queensferry, Linlithgowshire, Scotland, the elder son of John Adrian Louis Hope, 7th Earl of Hopetoun (afterwards 1st Marquess of Linlithgow), and Hersey Everleigh-de-Moleyns, Countess of Hopetoun and later Marchioness of Linlithgow, daughter of the 4th Baron Ventry. His godmother was Queen Victoria. He was educated at Eton College and succeeded his father as 2nd Marquess of Linlithgow on 29 February 1908. Linlithgow served as an officer on the Western Front during the First World War, ending the war with the rank of colonel. He commanded a battalion of the Royal Scots and was appointed an Officer of the Order of the British Empire.

He then served in various minor roles in the Conservative Governments of the 1920s and 1930s. From 1922 to 1924 he served as the Civil Lord of the Admiralty, then as chairman of the Unionist Party for two years. He also served as president of the Navy League from 1924 until 1931.

He became the Viceroy of India in 1936, where he pushed nutrition to the top of the research agenda and he implemented the plans for local self-government embodied in the Government of India Act of 1935, although the recalcitrance of the princes prevented the full establishment of Indian self-government. With the outbreak of the Second World War, Linlithgow's appeal for unity led to the resignation of the Congress ministries. Disputes between the British administration and Congress ultimately led to massive Indian civil disobedience in the Quit India Movement in 1942. Linlithgow suppressed the disturbances and arrested the Congress leaders. He retired in 1943, his seven-year tenure as Viceroy having been the longest in the history of the Raj. He was considered by his British obituarists to have been one of the most skilful colonial officers to have held the highest office. Indians were less kind and he is partly blamed for the Bengal famine of 1943. A devout Presbyterian, he served as Lord High Commissioner to the Church of Scotland in 1944 and 1945. He died in 1952.

Brigadier-General Noel Armar Lowry-Corry (1867-1935)

Another cousin of Wilfrid Ashley. He was the son of Armar Henry Lowry-Corry and Alice Margaret Greg, and grandson of Henry Thomas Lowry Corry and Lady Harriet Anne Ashley, sister of the 7th Earl of Shaftsbury. He married, firstly, Rosalind Gertrude Lloyd-Anstruther, daughter of Lt-Col. Robert Hamilton Lloyd-Anstruther and Gertrude Louisa Georgiana FitzRoy, in 1895. He married, secondly, the Hon. Clare O'Brien, daughter of Edward Donough O'Brien, 14th Baron of Inchiquin, on 26 July 1904.

Brigadier-General Noel Armar Lowry-Corry fought in the Boer War between 1899 and 1901. He was Colonel of the 2nd Battalion, Grenadier Guards, in 1900 and he was decorated with the award of Companion, Distinguished Service Order (DSO) in 1900. He held the office of JP for Breconshire and gained the rank of honorary brigadier-general, fighting in the First World War between 1914 and 1915.

However, the situation at Classiebawn became very disturbed and between 1920 and 1925 there was no shooting. In 1925, Wilfrid Ashley mothballed Classiebawn and arranged the distribution of its contents. A party of four Guns, comprising Gen. R. McCalmont, Maj. Lord Templemore, Sir Clive Morrison Bell MP, and Maj. J. Ewing were present at the beginning of 1926 and shooting between 2 and 6 January. They bagged forty-one Woodcock, thirteen Pheasants, twenty-one Snipe and twenty-five wildfowl. The same Guns again, between 7 and 9 January, had twelve Woodcock, eighty Snipe and nineteen wildfowl. And in the first half of February, over ten days' shooting, the bag was thirty Woodcock, one hundred and seventy-six Snipe and twenty-four wildfowl.

Robert McCalmont (1881-1953)

From a prominent County Antrim family, Robert McCalmont became an army colonel and honorary brigadier-general. He succeeded his father, James Martin McCalmont (1847-1913), who also was a British Army officer and Conservative politician, who reached the rank of colonel and was ADC to the Duke of Marlborough, Viceroy of Ireland.

Robert, who was knighted in 1952, was a Member of Parliament from 1913 to 1919, representing East Antrim, and was the recipient of numerous awards and achievements. He first married Mary Caroline Skeen (d. 1941) in 1907. After her death he married Iris Heather Flinn in 1950.

Brigadier-General Robert McCalmont was involved with the establishment of the British Field Sports Society (BFSS) in 1930 in an effort to counter a growing number of attacks on all forms of field sports (in the press and elsewhere).

Arhur Claud Spencer Chichester, 4th Baron Templemore, KCVO, OBE, DSO (1880-1953)

A British soldier and politician, he was educated at Harrow and Sandhurst before being commissioned into the Royal Fusiliers in 1900. He fought in the Boer War and also served in Tibet. Chichester distinguished himself in the First World War with his service in France and Italy, becoming a major with the Irish Guards and winning, along with many other awards, the DSO (1918) and an OBE (1919). In 1924, he succeeded his father as 4th Baron Templemore, and three years later was appointed Parliamentary Private Secretary to the Earl of Onslow as Under-Secretary of State for War and Paymaster General. Lord Templemore was a Lord-in-Waiting to George V from February to June 1929 and again between 1931 and 1934. He was also Captain of the Yeomen of the Guard for eleven years (1934-1945), and served as Conservative Chief Whip in the House of Lords (1940-1945). He was appointed KCVO in 1938.

In 1911, Templemore married Clare Meriel Wingfield, daughter of Mervyn Wingfield, 7th Viscount Powerscourt by his marriage to Lady Julia Coke, daughter of the 2nd Earl of Leicester, of Holkhom, Norfolk.

Sir Arthur Clive Morrison-Bell, 1st Baronet (1871-1956)

British soldier, Conservative Party parliamentarian and a brother-in-law of Lord Templemore. Educated at Eton and Sandhurst, he was commissioned in the Scots Guards in 1890. He served in the Boer War, was appointed major in 1908, and retired from the army that year. At the January 1910 general election he was elected MP for Honiton and remained in the position until 1931, when he retired due to ill-health. He rejoined the army at the beginning of the First World War, was captured in 1915, and returned to England in 1918. He married Lilah Wingfield, a great beauty and younger sister of Clare Meriel Wingfield, in 1912 and they had two daughters, Sheila and Patricia. He was made a baronet in 1923 but his title became extinct upon his death.

During the 1930s and up until about 1947, the shooting was taken on lease by a group which at various times throughout that period included: Dr G. McCready, a medical practitioner from the Mall, Sligo; Mr T.H. Blackburn, Dean of Sligo Grammar School; Dr and Mrs McCarthy; Dr Brian Crichton (1887-1950) of Carrowgarry, County Sligo, a paediatrician who was attached to both Temple Street and Harcourt Street Children's Hospital, before he returned to Carrowgarry in 1933; Coulthard Nelson (subsequently, in the 1950s, his son Drummond was involved), and William Ardill, son of Dean Ardill, a founder of Sligo High School and rector at Calry, County Sligo, who was Dublin based but came occasionally to shoot. Major Ascelin Perceval was also there shooting in 1930, along with two sons – 'Master A. and Master J.'. Ascelin's father-in-law, Surgeon Effingham McDowel of the Sligo Infirmary, was also involved in Classiebawn at this time. In addition, a Thomas Troubridge Stubbs appears for much of the time until the middle 1940s. He was probably a descendant of the Ballyshannon family.[164] Colonel Prioleau, a retired British Army Officer who leased Fortland, Easkey, from Benjamin McKinley of Kilglas and Dublin, was there regularly, until he rejoined the colours on the outbreak of the Second World War. Garvell Warrington, Rector of Kinlough, County Leitrim, Stanley Pettigrew, retired miner, living at Keeble near Woodville, County Sligo, and Alexander McArthur, proprietor of Sligo's premier bakery in O'Connell Street, who purchased Ardaghowen House in 1941, were also actively involved.

A summary of the shooting record for the period 1933/34-1946/7 is contained below:

	Grouse	Woodcock	Snipe	Wildfowl	Pheasant
1933/4	25	101	507	101	56
1934/5	54	36	252	42	121
1935/6	30	83	221	71	66
1936/7	51	50	254	83	120
1937/8	47	60	209	83	124
1938/9	32	81	179	69 (inc. 9 Geese)	120
1939/40	37	134	90	26	140
1940/1	22	55	97	60	120
1941/2	12	37	56	76	152
1942/3	6	13	36	32	43
1943/4	9	51	104	27	109
1944/5	11	245	57	33	104
1945/6	7	44	33	85	41
1946/7	–	–	7	36	15

Date 1945.	Ground Shot Over	Pheasants.	Partridges Pigeons	Grouse	Woodcock	Snipe	Wild Fowl	Hares	Rabbits	*(illegible)*	Total	Guns
January 24th	Classiebawn	3	3		83				3	1	93	J. Coulter Nelson Esq U.S. S. Pettigrew W.H. McCready T.H. Blackburn T.T. Troubridge Wardell Esq S. Pettigrew Gun
„ 27th	Classiebawn		2		101	1					104	T.T. Stubbs Esq & friend W. Wardell Gun T.T. Stubbs Esq
„ 31st	Cloonaghbawn + Classiebawn		4		34		1			2	41	A. McArthur Esq JP
2 good woodcock days with hard frost & Snow												
		3	7		218	1	1		3	3	238	

Rabbits Trapped & Shot 1150 Couple

56 'Two good Woodcock days with hard frost and snow,' Classiebawn Castle Game Book, 1945.

As would be expected, the Grouse shooting took place mostly in August and September and the bag was taken over four to six days by two to four Guns. There is evidently a serious falling off in numbers from the early 1940s, with the shooting effort still in the range of three to six days. Woodcock and Snipe shooting were the main strengths of the shoot, and with four Guns usually shooting (occasionally five or six), the record is quite consistently strong, especially up to 1941/42. The bags recorded were shot over about ten to twelve days, with the end of November and December accounting for most of the yield.

Exceptionally good Woodcock shooting in 1939/40, and again in 1944/45, is down to a few very strong days. On 24 January 1940, Dr McCready, Coulthard Nelson and Thomas Troubridge Stubbs had seventy-two in Classiebawn wood. In 1944/45, there were two exceptional days on 24 and 27 January 1945, when Coulthard Nelson, T.T. Stubbs (again), T.H. Blackburn, Stanley Pettigrew and Miss McCready shot 83 and 101 Woodcock respectively in Classiebawn.

It is noticeable, also, that the Snipe bag was falling in the 1940s. Whether this was the result of ageing Guns, loss of Snipe habitat, or something else, is not known. It is interesting that in 1944/45, it was Miss McCready rather than Dr McCready who was out. For whatever the reason, change was in the air. Edwina, who inherited Classiebawn in 1939 on the death of her father, visited in 1943 and again in 1947, when renovations were being completed. General Robert McCalmont returned in 1947 to shoot at Classiebawn, following an absence from the end January 1927, and was out each season until his death in 1953. During his later years he had a residence at Glen Lodge, Strandhill, County Sligo. He appears shooting alone, for the most part, until 1951, when, like McCalmont, Lord Templemore made a return to Classiebawn. He was there in both 1951 and 1952 along with his son Maj. the Hon. Dermot Richard Claud Chichester (1916-2007). Dermot succeeded as 5th Baron Templemore in 1953 and became a regular Gun during the 1950s, along with his cousin Mervyn Patrick Wingfield (1905-1973), 9th Viscount Powerscourt, who was an occasional visitor during the mid-1950s.

Captain Richard Outram Hermon (1898-1976)
Another change was the leasing of the shooting to Richard Hermon of Necarne Castle from 1950 until about 1965. Captain Richard Outram Hermon was only son of Sidney A. Hermon, JP,

the White House, Belcombe, Sussex. He married Coralie Adelaide Mervyn Porter, daughter of John Porter-Porter and Josephine Henrietta Lloyd of Belle Isle, County Fermanagh, in 1927. He bought Necarne Castle, near Irvinestown in County Fermanagh – once known as Castle Irvine Castle – in 1925, turning it into a haven for shooting parties. A former officer in the Coldstream Guards (1916-21), he was 'Championship Marksman' of Great Britain in 1936 and was considered to be the best shot in Northern Ireland. Richard ('Dick') Wood-Martin (b. 1929), who also commenced shooting at Classiebawn in 1951, described Hermon as the 'shooting companion you

57 Captain Richard ('Dick') Outram Hermon (1898-1976) of Necarne Castle.

wished not to be near: he missed nothing'.[165] It was Richard Wood-Martin, along with his wife Elizabeth, who would retrieve a critically injured Timothy Knatchbull from the sea amid the wreckage off Mullaghmore following the bombing of *Shadow V* on Monday 27 August 1979.[166]

Captain Hermon had a summer house at Mullaghmore, chosen, it appears, because of his friendship with Lord Mountbatten (Admiral of the Fleet, the 1st Earl Mountbatten of Burma). They were both keen sportsmen, and shot and fished together. Captain Hermon and Lord Mountbatten both kept seagoing boats at Mullaghmore.

However, the shooting was not strong, even considering that the shooting effort was reduced to about ten days in total over the season. A couple of dozen Woodcock was the average per season in the 1950s, and about fifty Snipe and a similar number of wildfowl. In 1965, the shooting was taken by Capt. Jimmy Hamilton, who ran it until 1980. Thereafter, Richard Wood-Martin took it over until 1991, when it ceased, as Classiebawn came to be the full-time residence of Mr Hugh Tunney, following his twenty-one-year lease of the property from January 1976.[167]

Since then, there has been much change which would have reduced the attractiveness of Classiebawn to Woodcock. Knatchbull, returning there in 2003, found that:

> The tumbledown stone wall that had run for a mile or more around the estate had been beautifully repaired. Beyond it the woods I remembered had vanished and now beef cattle were grazing on neat paddocks. Much of the tall, wild Marram grass, which had spread over the land from the sand dunes, had been removed, and in its place was lush new pasture. The face of the landscape had changed …[168]

However, with that, the Woodcock wintering habitat has largely disappeared.

BALLYNAHINCH CASTLE, BALLYNAHINCH, COUNTY GALWAY

The story of Ballynahinch is well told by Tim Robinson in *Connemara, Listening to the Wind*. Indeed, it would be difficult to find a better account of the history of Ballynahinch, which, in some respects, remains shrouded in mystery, including the early shooting records, unfortunately. The passages below draw heavily on Robinson.

The Martin family was one of the seven tribes of Galway and owned Ballynahinch Castle. They ran up large debts with the Law Life Assurance Company and when they failed to meet the loan obligations, the mortgagees sued Martin in the Encumbered Estates Court. However, owing to the failure to sell the estate, the Law Life Assurance Company ended up buying the property. More than twenty later, in 1872, Richard Berridge (*c.* 1810-1887) negotiated with the Law Life Assurance Company for the purchase of 160,000 acres, including the castle, the fisheries, oyster beds, rights to hold fairs, etc., in addition to Clare Island and another five small estates in Mayo for the sum of £230,000, of which half was paid at the time and uncertainty regarding the balance!

Robinson notes of the first Richard Berridge that he 'is especially obscure, to the point of being mysterious, in both his doings and his motivation'.[169] It seems that his name was not originally Berridge but MacCarthy. His father was thought to be Florence MacCarthy from Kerry, an officer in the 60th Regiment of Foot who served in the Leeward Islands, where he married a Miss Berridge. Their son Richard was born in Lambeth, Surrey, but even the date of birth is not unambiguous, being either 1809 or 1813. Neither is it known why he forsook his father's name in favour of his mother's maiden name, but a result was that his father disowned him.

58
Ballynahinch
Castle, County
Mayo.

He is reputed to have made three fortunes and lost two of them. His money was made from his partnership in the Meux Brewery. According to family lore, Lady Meux offered him the family fortune if he changed his name to Meux. However, he declined.

He married twice. The name of his first wife is not known, but there was a daughter from this marriage. His second marriage was to a Mrs Wilson (*née* Laura Isabella Dove) and took place after they had four children together. One of these children, also named Richard, was born in 1870, but according to Robinson, 'there is a scintilla of doubt as to whether this Richard was indeed Berridge senior's son'.[170]

On his death in 1887, Richard's estate (and £200,000) passed to his son Richard Berridge (1870-1941). The elder's tenure had not been a distinguished one: having paid a fortune to acquire it, little effort was expended to maintain it and he didn't live there, though his land agent George Robinson did. Moreover, his reputation as an absentee landlord was a poor one.[171] In contrast, son Richard, who did not appear to regard his father well, was resident from the beginning and took the estate in hand. He was a keen sportsman and shot, and divided his time between Connemara and big-game hunting in Africa. Sadly, the whereabouts of his shooting records are a mystery.

However, some insights into the shooting of the time can be obtained through the game records of his wife's uncle, Arthur V. Wilcox (1865-1924). Wilcox was a descendant of Thomas Wilcox of Exeter, England, who settled at Concord, west of Philadelphia by 1725, where he built paper mills. He married a Marion Cozzens (1868-1952) of New York. In 1897, Arthur came to Ballynahinch on the new railway to stay at the Anglers Return, Toombeola, to shoot and to fish. He was accompanied by his wife, son and daughter and his niece Mary Eulalia Lesley (1881-1957), daughter of Robert Lesley. Arthur took a ten-year lease on Glendollagh House, Recess (long since gone), from Richard Berridge.

Richard Berridge met with Mary Eulalia Lesley while she was at Glendollagh and the two were married in 1905, at her home in Haverford, Pennsylvania, before returning to Ballynahinch. Arthur Wilcox acquired a site from Richard Berridge and developed Lisnabrucka Lodge, a mansard-roofed mansion overlooking the eastern end of Ballynahinch Lake, which was completed in 1910.

A Game Book of Arthur Wilcox relating to the period 1898-1904 has survived and from it, a glimpse is provided of the shoots and those participating on at least part (Glendollagh) of the Berridge Estate over these five years. Even though the number of seasons concerned is short, a clear pattern can be discerned; commencing with Grouse shooting in August, September and into October, with some Partridge also. This was followed by Pheasant and Woodcock in November and December. Between sixteen and twenty days were spent at Grouse from 12 August each year, for a bag of 80-100 brace of Grouse, walked-up by between two and four Guns (quite a small team).

By and large, the team of Guns comprised the same individuals from one year to the next. These usually included: Arthur Wilcox; his father-in-law, F.K. Cozzens, who appears to have been present only for Grouse shooting; his secretary, Arnold Matthews of Derrada (Anglers Return) Lodge; William Sharp Waithman of Merlin Park, Galway (d. 1922), who was known as the 'Squire'[172] and was married to Lady Leicester Philippa Stanhope, daughter of Charles Wyndham Stanhope, 7th Earl of Harrington, and Elizabeth Still-de-Pearsall, on 6 September 1883, and his son Wyndham (b. 1887). The Waithmans acquired Merlin Park in 1876 and it continued in the family's ownership for three generations until it was donated to the Irish State as a tuberculosis sanatorium.

Wilcox's son James commenced shooting on 18 August 1900 at the tender age of twelve and is recorded frequently out and about in both August and September. He also appears in subsequent seasons with his father during Grouse shooting in August and September.

Less frequently at Grouse shoots is 'Fenton', who appears alone on 19 and 20 September 1899 on the College Lands, where he shot eight Grouse, and the following season on 11 September 1900, along with Arthur and his father-in-law. The three Guns had fifteen Grouse. It is unclear who this Fenton is. Various branches of the Fenton family held estates in the Barony of Tireragh, County Sligo. One branch was centered on a house at Dromore, in the village now known as Dromore West. Information in the OS name books suggests that the house was built around 1786 and purchased by Capt. Fenton from Mr Jones of Fortland, Easkey. In June 1864, Thomas Fenton, together with John Nesbitt Malleson, offered the mansion house and lands at Dromore for sale in the Landed Estates Court. In June 1865, James Fenton offered for sale lands at Clooneen, Barony of Tireragh, with the estate being acquired by William Lougheed in the latter part of the nineteenth century.[173]

The Grouse shooting took place around the townlands of Cappahoosh, Lettershanna (where a few Partridges were usually shot, but only around half a dozen. The biggest bag of Partridges was at Roundstone, with Richard Berridge on 20 September 1898, when eleven brace of Partridge were shot), Lisoughter and Garoman, all within the Ballynahinch Estate at the time and generally in the area of Recess.

The Pheasant shooting was conducted principally within the demesne of Ballynahinch and the parties tended to be of eight Guns. The bag ranged from 97-306 Pheasants, with up to 13 Woodcock also being accounted for per day. About six days in November and December were devoted to Pheasants. The Guns, in addition to Wilcox, Waithman and Matthews, included most frequently Richard Berridge, Thomas Hazell of Doon Cottage (later Doon House), who was the principal buyer of kelp in Connemara, and Henry Robinson of Letterdife House, land agent for Berridge.

In addition, there were other guests of whom only their names are known. These included Montgomery Campbell, Trevor Lewis, Howard and Eustace Henry, J.C. Gardner and Gen. Sir John Davis. On 27 November 1901, the party of five included Baron von Dalwyg, who was married to a sister of Richard Berridge.[174] He appears on only one occasion, unsurprisingly, perhaps: the bag for the six guns comprised twenty-two Pheasants and thirteen Woodcock!

On two occasions, the presence of Fr Gleeson, parish priest of Roundstone, is recorded. On 1 December 1898, the party comprised, in addition to Gleeson: Richard Berridge, Thomas Hazell, Henry Robinson and Arnold Matthews. They were shooting the demesne and the bag was fifty-one Pheasants and seven Woodcock. He was there again the following season on 12 November, along with Berridge, Gen. Sir John Davis, Trevor Lewis, Howard Henry, J.C. Gardner and Wilcox, when they had a bag of seventy-seven Pheasants and two Woodcock. Gleeson's presence is interesting for the fact that he was one who was pushing for the estate to be acquired and broken up by the Congested Districts Board in conjunction with the Land Commission, and was critical of their tardiness in coming to grips with the estate.[175] The fact that he doesn't appear again may suggest he became disenchanted with Berridge and his circle. He was certainly frustrated with the Congested Districts Board, claiming in 1910 that the estate had been offered to it five years earlier. In 1914, the CDB finally took over the estate of 143,325 acres for £95,441.[176] Berridge retained the castle and the immediately surrounding demesne (though some land was sold to the Forestry Commission) for another decade, before finally selling the remainder of the estate and castle to the Maharajah Ranjitsinhji ('Ranji') in 1925, although not Screebe Lodge, which they retained until 1960. In fact, the Berridges spent little time after 1914 at Ballynahinch, which was subject to a number of 'intrusions' from Black and Tans, and the IRA. These episodes are described in some detail by Robinson. The Maharajah provided another colourful chapter in the life of Ballynahinch, told with eloquence by Anne Chambers in her book *Ranji*.[177] However, it is a short-lived tale. Ranji died in April 1933 and Ballynahinch was sold in further fragments.

To judge from ledger records which have survived relating to the rearing of game and game keeping during the Berridge era, there was more shooting taking place than is indicated by the relatively short records that have been cited above from Wilcox's Game Book of 1898-1904.[178] However, little more can be added in the absence of the shooting records. Another limiting feature of Wilcox's records is that they are very much those of a visitor, who, as might be expected, has more limited social contact than would be the case of a resident shooter. When combined with their relatively short duration, the result is a less indepth view than one would like.

There is no doubt either, that for long periods of the twentieth century, there was no formal shooting taking place. Under the auspices of the hotel's management, managed shooting of Woodcock has been provided over the past thirty years or so, and shooting packages arranged primarily around Woodcock are part of the hotel's winter programme.

SCREEBE LODGE, SCREEBE, COUNTY GALWAY

Screebe House or Lodge today is a sporting estate of 44,000 acres of rights, providing quality fishing (salmon and sea trout), shooting (Woodcock and duck), stalking (of red deer) and country pursuits (like walking, boating, etc.) from luxury accommodation at the lodge. As such, it continues its historical roots as an angling and shooting lodge, primarily associated with the Berridge Estate, the centre of which was Ballynahinch Castle.

The lodge dates from at least the 1880s[179] and has had a colourful, and indeed sad, history through the lives of some of its occupants. The Earl and Countess of Dudley, Lord Lieutenant of Ireland and instigator of HRH the Prince of Wales's invitation to Ashford by Lord Ardilaun, leased Screebe for a time from Richard Berridge, with whom he became lifelong friends. However, he appears to have taken no interest in shooting at Screebe, being preoccupied with other matters, as discussed below.

William Humble Ward (1867-1932), 2nd Earl of Dudley[180]

Born in London, William Humble Ward was the son of William Ward, 1st Earl of Dudley, and Georgina, daughter of Sir Thomas Moncreiff, 7th Baronet, and was educated at Eton. From 1895 to 1896, he was Mayor of Dudley. His father died in 1885 and the 2nd Earl inherited his empire of Black Country mines and businesses. Dudley became part of the social circle of the Prince of Wales (later King Edward VII), who attended his wedding to Rachel Gurney in 1891. He enjoyed racy Edwardian society, whereas his wife Rachel set store on solid Victorian virtues. At the age of only twenty-eight he became Mayor of Dudley and he quickly succeeded though a flurry of political appointments, including Member of the Privy Council, Lord Lieutenant of Ireland (1902) and 4th Governor General of Australia. He and Rachel had four sons and three daughters.

59 Screebe Lodge, County Galway.

Lady Rachel Dudley (1876-1920), before she was married, was awarded a CBE for her work establishing field hospitals in South Africa. She was also responsible for setting up the district nurse system in Ireland. In 1918, she was awarded the OBE and was also decorated with the Royal Red Cross. It is speculated that her popularity was the main reason that Screebe Lodge was not burned or vandalised during the War of Independence.

While they separated in 1912, both continued to visit Connemara regularly. Lord Dudley would stay at nearby Inver with his long-time lover, the music-hall actress Gertrude 'Gertie' Millar, wife of the British composer and writer Lionel Monckton. However, tragedy struck in June 1920, when it was announced that:

> The Countess of Dudley, wife of a former Viceroy of Ireland, was drowned on the Connemara coast on Saturday. Lady Dudley arrived at Recess, County Galway, on Saturday morning and drove to Screebe Lodge. After lunch Lady Dudley and her maid went to bathe in the sea at Camus bay. She was very fond of bathing, and on entering the water swam out from the shore. Soon, however, she collapsed and sank within sight of her maid who was powerless to help her. Assistance was summoned and the body was recovered half an hour later.[181]

Lord Dudley went on to marry his lover Gertie four years later. Gertie's previous husband, Lionel Monckton, had refused to allow his wife a divorce but when he died in 1924 she at last became Lady Dudley. Lord Dudley died in 1932 and Gertie in 1952.

An old faded photograph still hangs in the entrance hall of Screebe. Did she drown? Was it a heart attack? Suicide? It has long been said that Screebe House has a ghost. Doors are mysteriously locked, shadowy figures flit across landings. Room number six is said to have its secrets; indeed, one regular visitor to number six ties his foot to the bed because he says Screebe is the only place that he sleep walks, and has found himself down at the harbour on several occasions. Perhaps it's just the creaking and groaning of an old house, but if Screebe does have a ghost it must be Lady (Rachel) Dudley!

Howard St George (b. 1857)

Along with his wife, Howard St George came to Screebe in 1896 at the invitation of the Berridge family to manage the estate. Richard St George, originally a member of a Cambridgeshire family, came to Ireland in the seventeenth century and was appointed Governor of the town of Athlone. His grandson Richard St George, of Carrick-on-Shannon was founder of the Hatley Manor, County Leitrim, branch of the family, and Mary St George married James Mansergh and they were the parents of Col. Richard Mansergh St George of Headford, County Galway.

Members of the family served as High Sheriffs of Leitrim in the eighteenth century. The family also held lands in Counties Offaly, Roscommon, Tipperary (629 acres in the parish of Donaghmore, Barony of Iffa and Offa East) and Waterford, where Christina St George is recorded as the owner of over 1,000 acres. Another branch of the St George Estate was centred on the house at Tyrone, parish of Drumacoo, Barony of Dunkellin, County Galway, built about 1779. This had originally been a French estate but the family assumed the title of St George in 1774 due to inheritance from the St George family of Hatley Manor, County Leitrim.

In the 1870s, the family owned 15,777 acres in County Galway. By the early 1900s, however, some of the estate had been sold and the house at Tyrone had been left empty for long periods. In 1914, over 3,000 acres of an estate described as St George and Concannon was vested in the Congested Districts Board.

Howard St George came from the Kilcogan branch of the family. He became the estate manager at Screebe and was a strong conservationist during his time. The Game Book, containing
entries for both fishing and shooting (and referred to below), is kept in his own hand. Indeed, he
planted the pine trees on the islands nearby and the peninsular opposite the lodge, making it a
most picturesque comer of the south Connemara coast. Unfortunately this was not to be his total
legacy to Screebe. His beautiful and strong-willed American wife, Evelyn Florence, eldest child of
George Fisher Baker, founder and president of the First National Bank of America, proved to be
rather a handful. They had married against her father's wishes in 1891 and came first to Screebe
to start their married life. Evelyn was unhappy with life in the west of Ireland so they moved to
Clonsilla Lodge at the edge of Phoenix Park, Dublin, in 1905. It would seem that Howard continued to manage Screebe up until 1913. Whilst in Dublin, they were introduced to William Orpen
through the artist's mother, Annie. Orpen was commissioned to paint several pictures of Evelyn
and their three children. During this time, William Orpen and Evelyn St George became lovers.
She is well documented as his sitter, muse, lover, companion and patron. In 1912, she was even to
bear him child, Vivian.

Sotheby's, who were selling one of Orpen's most famous paintings of Evelyn St George, the
property of the Jefferson Smurfit Group, which was sold for £924,000 in 2003, state that:

> While Mrs St George's demeanour perfectly reflects her self-awareness as a women of immense
> social standing (not to mention the last word in sartorial elegance), there is evidence, in this
> portrait, of something beyond the haughtiness and superiority that is to be expected as the
> undisputed preserve of a member of the Edwardian *beau monde* …

Orpen and Evelyn exchanged many letters throughout their long friendship. The known tally of
surviving letters is over 800, with around 365 in the collection of the National Gallery of Ireland.
This extensive correspondence permits a privileged insight into the relationship; over the years
the two were to console, amuse, berate and regale each other in equal amounts, sharing their
affections and observations easily on the page, whether communicating by word or image.

After the St Georges moved back to London in 1912, the affair became more or less public
knowledge. Bruce Arnold has commented that 'to all intents and purposes it was a second marriage for each'.[182]

The early game records of Screebe Lodge (both fishing and shooting) are dominated by the
Crozier family. Croziers were associated with Fermoyle Lodge and fishery, built by the Berridges
in 1880 as part of their estate. Interestingly, there is a connection between this family and Hewett
Barrington Jellett, long-time shooter at the North Slob, County Wexford, and elsewhere, as his
mother, Iris Kathleen Crozier, was a daughter of Tom Crozier.

Thomas F. Crozier (1872-1930)
Through his firm, Thos F. Crozier & Son, Solicitors, of Banbridge, County Down, and 17 Granby
Row, Rutland Square West (and sometime also of 12 Ely Place), Dublin, Crozier acted for Richard
Berridge and, according to descendants, was agent of Berridge's estate, although this position seems
also to have been held by his father-in-law George Robinson and brother-in-law Henry Robinson.
His first wife, Georgina, was a Robinson from Letterdyfe House, Roundstone, County Galway,
and is presumed to be a daughter of George Robinson, who was, for a time, Berridge's land agent.
He had three children with her. She died comparatively young and he then married Isabel Morna

60 Lord and Lady Dudley with Tom Crozier setting off for Screebe.

Pollock, with whom he had two children. The family party which attended Screebe in the 1890s was rather large, numbering almost a dozen, including several couples, and that is besides 'Miss Crozier and party'. Inferring from initials, it is possible to assemble a picture of who comprised the party.

F.R.M. Crozier was probably Francis Rawdon Moira Hastings Crozier, who died in 1902. He was a solicitor and he lived at some time in Dominick Street in Dublin. His wife was Catherine Sophia Magee. He was the father of Thomas F. Crozier. F. Crozier Jr was probably Francis Rawdon Moira Crozier (b. 1876), who married Constance Geraldine Millar. They had three children. W.M. Crozier was probably William Magee Crozier, who was born in 1873 and died at the Somme in 1916. H. Crozier is considered to have been Louis Herbert Crozier (b. 1877). He was a commander in the Royal Navy. His wife was Blanche Dalglishe and they died without issue. G.F. Crozier was most likely George Francis Crozier, who was born in 1875. His wife was Blanche Atkinson and they had two children. Miss M.E. Crozier may have been Marion Crozier (b. 1843), the sister of Francis Rawdon Moira Hastings Crozier. She was living with the family around the turn of the century at 19 Monkstown Road, Dublin. A likely candidate for G. Crozier is George Darley Crozier (b. *c.* 1826), who was the eldest brother of Francis Rawdon Moira Hastings Crozier.

It is worth noting that Thomas F. Crozier was a grandnephew of Capt. Francis Rawdon Moira Crozier (b. 1796), who came from a wealthy Banbridge family. His father, George Crozier, was a leading solicitor who acted for two of Ireland's most powerful landowning families: the Downshires and the Moiras. Francis, one of thirteen children, was named after Francis Rawdon, the Earl of Moira. His story is told in a biography by Michael Smith entitled *Captain Francis Crozier – Last Man Standing?* (2006). It demonstrates that he was among an exceptional band of men who opened the doors to the unexplored regions of the Arctic and Antarctic. It was the feats of Crozier and his fellow explorers in the mid-nineteenth century who paved the way for the more well-known exploits of men like Amundsen, Scott and Shackleton in the early years of the twentieth century. There would have been no heroic age of polar exploration without men like Francis Crozier.

The party engaged in both fishing and shooting, with the shooting commencing in August and continuing through November. An early summary record of the shooting for 1889 gives the following returns:

	Grouse	Partridge	Snipe	Duck	Hares	Cock
Mr Davies-Longworth Party	240	–	3	2	17	–
Mr Crozier's	86	17	18	3	6	4
	326	17	21	5	23	4

Edward Davies-Longworth lived at Glynwood, Westmeath, and appears shooting at Annaghmore around this time, and indeed O'Haras were visitors to Glynwood. To judge from the composition of the bags above – higher numbers of Grouse and no 'cock – the Longworth party was shooting earlier than Croziers. What is most striking, however, is the overall strength of the Red Grouse bag. The parties were also involved in fishing at this time, and a summary record of the salmon and sea trout catch is contained within the record, showing some of the 'Miss Croziers' being quite effective with a rod.

There are a number of others who were part of the Crozier party, including Bernard Arthur Forbes (1874-1948), 8th Earl of Granard, and D.C. Palmer. Along with Thomas F. Crozier, these Guns appear to have walked-up Grouse on most days in September, usually for four to six couple of Grouse on a morning. For example, a typical entry, for 15 September 1890, reads, 'Earl of Granard and T.F. Crozier, three brace of Grouse, one Snipe, one Teal and one rabbit. Rose four salmon caught one brown trout two lbs.'

The Game Book contains notes like these practically every day, as some or other of the party went shooting while others angled. Typically, two or three Guns made up the shooting party and spent a few hours of the morning walking-up Grouse and taking Snipe, Teal, or the odd rabbit and hare. The party varied from day to day, but Thomas F. Crozier featured on practically every morning's outing. And every year the pattern was the same. Thus, on 'Thursday 30 August 1894 T.F. and W.M. [Crozier][183] shot twenty brace of Grouse, two hares and one Snipe and on Friday the same Guns shot eleven brace and three hares. Both days birds plentiful and strong notwithstanding wet breeding season.'

The Robinson family, comprising George, son Henry and certain Miss Robinsons, shared with the Croziers in 1890, and Henry, with some of his sisters, was there again in 1891, his father having died in 1890.

George Robinson, of Thomastown in Mayo, was the land agent of Law Life Assurance, sometime owners of the Ballynahinch Estate, and was to succeed in that capacity when Richard Berridge acquired Ballynahinch from Law Life Assurance in 1872. Indeed it appears that from 1857 until 1885, when they built their own mansion, Letterdife House, near Roundstone, they lived at Ballynahinch.[184] George's wife, Rebecca, was a descendant of the Martins and Wood-Martins of County Sligo. George's son Henry succeeded his father as land agent to Berridge. After the estate was bought out by the Land Commission in 1914, Henry remained on as agent.

The bags for 1890 and 1891 are comparable and summarised as follows, where the total figure includes birds shot over Christmas:

	1890		1891	
	August–November	Total	August–November	Total
Grouse	69	69	109	116
Woodcock	1	39	–	63
Snipe	15	78	55	181
Hares	14	15	5	21
Plover	2	12	4	4
Duck	7	10	2	6
Widgeon	3	43	6	37
Teal	4	10	1	11
Heron	1	1	–	–
Partridge	1	1	14	27
Total head		267		466

In 1892 and 1893 there was 'no account or report of shooting done over Xmas', but the autumn shooting comprised seventy-eight Grouse, fifteen Partridges and thirty Snipe in 1892, and two hundred and nine Grouse and 16 Snipe the following autumn.

Shooting was actively managed by Henry St George, who in 1896 records that, 'In 1896 I turned out at Screebe Lodge, 10 brace of Hungarian Partridges, and I turned out 65 brace of Scotch Grouse on different parts for shooting.' Introduction of birds seems to have been made every few years. In 1902, for example, there is mention of '20 brace of Yorkshire Grouse turned down Oct. 1902'.

Vermin control was pursued ruthlessly and excessively as the following table, extracted from the records, shows:

Vermin killed on Screebe shooting by H.B. St G.'s Keepers, winter, 97/98, verified by him.

Foxes	19	77 more cubs
Badgers	11	–
Otters	7	–
Hawks	20	10 young ones
Stoats	7	–
Cats	1	–
Herons	112	12 old ones
Cormorants	4	–
Herring Gulls	5	–
Margansers	3	–
Magpies	18	77 young ones
Total	207	

Sadly, there are similar records for other years.

The seasons had their ups and downs, too. For example, in respect of the 1901 season, St George records that:

> There was a wretched show of Grouse as generally in Ireland the day hatching and rearing being cause of poor turn-out. We only shot to 24 Oct. twenty-four brace Grouse, four brace of Partridge, and twenty two hares. Total shooting eighty-nine duck and Wigeon – forty-one Woodcock – eight-four Snipe – twenty-one Grouse – four Partridge – thirty-two hares – two Pheasants.

In contrast, in 1911 he was able to write:

> A fine breeding season for Grouse and good show of birds on Leam and Shanamore but very few on Screebe Flats. Birds have become very wild after 25 August. Total Grouse shot 235, Snipe 83, Hares 36, Wigeon and duck 18, Woodcock 19, Teal 5, Partridge 1. Total 400 head.

The summary record for 1912, St George's last year at Screebe, is described by Peter Divorty,[185] the gamekeeper, as 'A very poor game season, very few Snipe and duck. A good stock of Grouse left.'

List of Game Killed on Screebe, Season 1912/13

Grouse	159
Snipe	48
Widgeon	17
Mallard	2
Teal	1
Woodcock	12
Hares	22
Pochard	1
Total	262

St George adds, 'The Grouse were about ½ the No. of last year, many broods were drowned – it was a miserable year not only here but all over the Kingdom, crops ruined and everywhere bad weather.' Not the best note on which to end his term at Screebe!

It is unclear if shooting took place after Howard St George's departure. Richard Berridge, who had sold Ballynahinch, took Screebe Lodge back in hand from 1925 until 1959, when his son Lt-Col. Robert Lesley Berridge sold it to Lord Islwyn Davies and his wife Camilla. They ran it as a hotel during the 1960s. They had an interest in the fishing, and renovated and operated the disused hatchery.

In 1982, the property came into the hands of the present owner, Albert Burkart, and he has invested heavily in and developed the sporting resource of the estate, in particular the fishery and the wild salmon stocks, which were close to extinction. At the time the Burkart family acquired Screebe, it consisted of about 20,000 acres of shooting and fishing rights. However, these have been added to with the acquisition of the rights of Fermoyle and the Currarevagh Estates, bringing it to around 44,000 acres of sporting rights.

The demesne at Currarevagh comprises 200 acres and there are an additional 8,000 acres of mountain shooting which have been acquired by the owners of Screebe Lodge. There were detailed Game Books at Currarevagh but their whereabouts are now unknown. However, Maurice Semple had access to them, and a summary is contained in his *Where the River Corrib Flows*, which is referred to below.

As may be seen from Semple's text, these Game Books confirm an active shoot at Currarevagh and good bags of Grouse, Woodcock, Snipe and Grey Partridge (the last at least until the mid-1870s, after which they seem to have become scarce). This pattern of declining Grey Partridge numbers from the 1870s is similar to other estates where they once were plentiful.

Clues of the shooters are scant and insufficient to provide reliable positive identification. However, a number of suggestions can be deduced. For example, the Oswalds, who were recorded frequently around the 1870s, may have been the family of Capt. James Townsend Oswald (1820-1893) of Dunniker, Scotland, who was a descendant of the Rt Hon. James Oswald (1715-1769), Treasurer of Ireland, and Revd Dr John Oswald (c. 1716-1780), Bishop of Clonfert. Wedderburne, another name appearing in the Game Book in the 1870s, is also a Scottish name; the Wedderburn (later Ogilvy-Wedderburn) Baronetcy of Balindean in the County of Perth being a title in the Baronetage of the United Kingdom created in 1803. William Shoolbred (d. c. 1880) may have been the co-founder of Shoolbred & Loveridge of Wolverhampton. The firm was involved in the manufacture of tin-plate goods and so Hodgson's mining interests may have been a link between them. Finally, it is plausible that 'R.J. Martin' was a relative of Col. Richard Martin (1754-1834), politician and animal rights activist, who became known as 'Humanity Dick'. He was born at Ballynahinch Castle, County Galway, and was raised at Dangan House, situated on the Corrib, four miles upriver from the town of Galway.

	Grouse	Partridges	Woodcock	Snipe	Wildfowl
1866	46	40	121	72	2
1867	81	68	90	93	6
1868	70	63	119	287	6
1869	146	171	140	206	18
1870	284	115	212	258	32
1871	362	60	147	558	64
1872	210	35	173	171	–
1873	368	116	220	605	9
1874	273	18	218	173	16
1875	261	30	302	438	62
1884/85	421	16	158	93	2
1885/86	352	34	47	38	2
1886/87	283	1	127	98	7
1887/88	437	31	185	135	24
1888/89	492	14	147	168	25
1889/90	606	19	169	194	32
1890/91	260	9	343	210	32
1891/92	325	52	257	203	11
1892/93	240	29	223	290	52
1893/94	324	12	222	192	40
1894/95	273	11	486	279	64

In addition, the Currarevagh records show that 'in 1912/13 they shot 169 Grouse, forty-four hares, fifty rabbits, thirty-three Pheasants, one hundred and ninety-seven Woodcock, three hundred and seventy Snipe, eight Mallard, twelve Teal, six wild geese, three Golden Plover and one fox. They also saw [only] two Partridge.'[186]

The sporting tradition of Screebe is maintained today by the Burkhart family. The emphasis is on managing and stalking red deer but there is also syndicated duck shooting and Woodcock shooting on the estate.

4

SOME SHOOTING ESTATES
IN NORTHERN COUNTIES

BARONSCOURT, COUNTY TYRONE

A shoot with a distinguished history under the management of the Hamilton family, Dukes of Abercorn, which continues to thrive in the present day.

The Dukedom of Abercorn

61 Baronscourt, County Tyrone.

James Hamilton, 2nd Marquess of Abercorn, who had been given the Garter in 1844, served as Lord Lieutenant of Ireland from 1866 to 1868 (and again from 1874 to 1876); and on 10 August 1868, during his first term, he was created Marquess of Hamilton, of Strabane, and Duke of

139

Abercorn (in the peerage of Ireland).[187] He had fourteen children, thirteen of whom survived into adulthood, including seven sons, several of whom were keen shots.

The account of shooting presented here is based substantially on the personal Game Book of James Edward Hamilton, 4th Duke of Abercorn (1904-1979), who was the son of James Hamilton, 3rd Duke of Abercorn (1869-1953), and Lady Rosalind Cecilia Caroline Bingham. He was variously styled Viscount Strabane (1904-1913), Marquess of Hamilton (1913-1953), and finally inherited his father's peerages on 12 September 1953.

Lord Hamilton (as he then was) attended Eton. After being commissioned into the Grenadier Guards, he rose to the rank of captain. He was appointed Honorary Colonel of the 5th Battalion, Royal Inniskilling Fusiliers (Territorial Army unit). In 1928, he married Lady Kathleen Crichton (1905-1990), a daughter of Henry Crichton, Viscount Crichton (1872-1914, son of the 4th and father of the 5th Earl of Erne) and Lady Mary Cavendish Grosvenor (1883-1959, daughter of the 1st Duke of Westminster). They had two sons and a daughter. In 1946, he was elected to the County Council of County Tyrone, served as High Sheriff of Tyrone, and then served in the Senate of Northern Ireland, becoming Lord Lieutenant of County Tyrone from the death of his father until his own death in 1979, at the age of seventy-five.

The eldest son, James Hamilton, 5th Duke of Abercorn, KG (b. 1934), is the current Duke of Abercorn, having succeeded his father in June 1979. He was educated at Eton College and the Royal Agricultural College. In 1952 he was commissioned into the Grenadier Guards. In 1964 he became Ulster Unionist MP for Fermanagh and South Tyrone (when he held the courtesy

62 The Baronscourt Game Department posing at the anchor of the French vessel *Lausun*, on which King James II embarked after the Battle of the Boyne in Waterford Harbour accompanied by his *aide-de-camp* and kinsman Claud Hamilton, 4th Earl of Abercorn. It was presented to James Hamilton, 1st Duke of Abercorn (1811-1885), when he was Lord Lieutenant of Ireland, by the Waterford Harbour Commissioners.

title Marquess of Hamilton), succeeding his first cousin Lord Robert Grosvenor (later Duke of Westminster). He held his seat in the 1966 election but lost it to Unity candidate Frank McManus in 1970 by 1,423 votes. In 1986, he was appointed Lord Lieutenant of County Tyrone and he stood down in 2009. In 1999, he was appointed a Knight of the Order of the Garter, and was Colonel of the Irish Guards from 2000 to 2008. Additionally, he was appointed Lord Steward of the Household in 2001, serving until 2009.

In 1966, he married Alexandra Anastasia 'Sacha' Phillips (b. 27 February 1946), eldest daughter of Lt-Col. Harold Pedro Joseph Phillips (1909-1980) and Georgina Wernher (1919-2011), elder daughter and co-heiress of Sir Harold Wernher, 3rd Baronet of Luton Hoo, Bedfordshire. The duchess is the elder sister of Natalia, wife of the Duke of Westminster.

The Duke and Duchess of Abercorn have two sons and a daughter: James Harold Charles Hamilton, Marquess of Hamilton (b. 1969), currently manages the shooting at Baron's Court. He was married on 7 May 2004 at the Guards Chapel, Wellington Barracks, to Tanya Marie Nation (b. 1971), eldest daughter of Douglas Percy Codrington Nation, senior managing director of Bear Stearns (1942-2001) and his wife Barbara 'Bobbie' Brookes. They have two children, James Alfred Nicholas Hamilton, styled Viscount Strabane (b. 30 October 2005), and Lord Claud Douglas Harold Hamilton (b. 12 December 2007). Lord Nicholas Edward Hamilton (b. 5 July 1979) is the Duke and Duchess's younger son and his sister, Lady Sophia Alexandra Hamilton (b. 8 June 1973), was a model before 1996. She married British war journalist Anthony Loyd in 2002, but they divorced, without children, in 2005.

Lord Claud Anthony Hamilton (b. 1939), the 4th Duke's second son, held the office of Deputy Lieutenant of County Fermanagh in 1978 and in 1991 he was JP. In 1982, he married Catherine Janet Faulkner (niece of Lord Faulkner of Downpatrick). They have a son and a daughter. He is related to the late Diana, Princess of Wales, through Diana's paternal grandmother, Cynthia Spencer, Countess Spencer, who was the daughter of James, Marquess of Hamilton, later the 3rd Duke of Abercorn.

Shooting at Baronscourt

Shooting at Baronscourt has a long, distinguished and well-documented history, going back at least to the tenure of James Albert Edward, the 3rd Duke of Abercorn, which commenced in 1913, when the estate extended to about 60,000 acres. Thus, an entry in a diary of Lord Cloncurry for 4 January 1887, states that he was 'impressed by the [3rd] Duke of Abercorn's claim that 12,644 Woodcock had been shot at Baronscourt over a period of forty years'.[188] That's 316 per season *on average* – certainly an extraordinary bag. However, there is considerable evidence in support these kinds of numbers. For example, *The Field* of 19 December 1883 reports on seven days of shooting at Baronscourt over the period 6-17 December, when five Guns accounted for 353 Woodcock (i.e. twenty-five brace per day or five brace per Gun per day). On 13 December, the best day, the bag was eighty-one Woodcock, with twenty-eight – the lowest daily bag – on the previous day. In addition, there was a bag of Pheasants of 458 (over thirty-two brace per day).

Lord Claud J. Hamilton (1843-1925) and Lord Ernest William Hamilton (1843-1925)
The lucky Guns in that party comprised: Viscount Newport, MP; S.W. Hart Dyke, Bart, MP' Mr John Bowen; Lord Claud J. Hamilton (1843-1925), MP, and his younger brother Lord Ernest Hamilton (1858-1939). The last of these were the second and seventh (youngest) sons of the 1st Duke.

Lord Claud John Hamilton (1843-1925) was educated at Harrow School. In 1865 he became Conservative MP for Londonderry City, a position he held until 1868, when he was appointed a Lord of the Treasury in Benjamin Disraeli's first ministry. In 1869, he became MP for King's Lynn (until 1880), for Liverpool from 1880 to 1885, for Liverpool West Derby from 1885 until he resigned his seat in 1888, and for Kensington South from January 1910 to 1918.

Hamilton married Carolina Chandos-Pole (a granddaughter of the 5th Earl of Harrington) on 20 July 1878 and they had two children. Lord Claud had been an *aide-de-camp* to Queen Victoria from 1887 to 1897 and was appointed to the Privy Council in 1917.

Lord Ernest William Hamilton (1858-1939) was a British soldier and Conservative politician. He was educated at Harrow School and the Royal Military Academy, Sandhurst and he became a captain in the 11th Hussars. In the 1885 general election, Hamilton was elected Member of Parliament for Tyrone North and he held the seat until 1892. Hamilton was the author of several novels, two of which – *The Outlaws of the March* and *The Mawkin of the Flow* – are set on the Scottish Borders in the late sixteenth and early seventeenth centuries. Another novel, *Mary Hamilton*, is based on the ballad of the same name.

Hamilton married Pamela Campbell (d. 1931) in 1891. She was a granddaughter of Sir Guy Campbell, 1st Baronet, by his son Capt. Frederick Augustus Campbell (1839-1916). They had two sons and two daughters.

George Cecil Orlando Bridgeman, 4th Earl of Bradford (Viscount Newport), DL, JP (1845-1915)

British soldier and peer. He was the elder son of the 3rd Earl of Bradford and Selina Louisa Forester. Bridgeman was educated at Harrow School and served in the 1st Life Guards and the Shropshire Yeomanry Cavalry, reaching the rank of captain. In 1869, Lord Bradford married Ida Frances Annabella Lumley, daughter of the 9th Earl of Scarborough, in Maltby, Yorkshire. They had seven children.

He succeeded his father in his titles on 9 March 1898. Bridgeman was Member of Parliament for North Shropshire from 1867 to 1885. He was Deputy Lieutenant of Warwickshire and Shropshire, as well as Justice of Peace for Staffordshire, Warwickshire and Shropshire. He died in London and was buried in Weston Park, Staffordshire, on 6 January 1915. His sister, Lady Mabel Selina Bridgeman (d. 1933), married Col. William Kenyon-Slaney on 22 February 1887, and a son of theirs, Capt. Robert Orlando Kenyon-Slaney, married Mary Cecillia Rhodesia Hamilton (1896-1984), daughter of the 2nd Duke of Abercorn.

Sir William Hart Dyke, 7th Baronet PC, DL, JP (1837-1931)

English Conservative politician. The second son of Sir Percival Hart Dyke, 6th Baronet, and Elizabeth Wells, Hart Dyke, he was educated at Harrow School and was Conservative MP for West Kent (1865-1868), Mid Kent (1868-1885) and Dartford (1885-1906). He was a Conservative whip from 1868 to 1874, and he held ministerial office under Benjamin Disraeli, as Parliamentary Secretary to the Treasury (1874-1880), and under Lord Salisbury, as Chief Secretary for Ireland (1885-1886) and as Vice-President of the Committee of the Council on Education (1887-1892).

He succeeded his father to the baronetcy in 1875 and was appointed a Privy Counsellor in 1880. Hart Dyke married Lady Emily Caroline Montague, daughter of the 7th Earl of Sandwich, in 1870. He died in July 1931, aged ninety-three years, and was succeeded in the baronetcy by his fourth and only surviving son, Oliver.

Further evidence of the importance of the shoot is contained in Acland-Hood (1915), who quotes Mr R. Taylor,[189] head keeper to the Duke of Abercorn, who wrote to him as follows:

The following is a list of Woodcocks shot on this estate since 1905:[190]

Year	Number shot	Year	Number shot
1905	432	1909	403
1906	385	1910	402
1907	360	1911	345
1908	418		

Clearly, these are impressive numbers and they point to a first-class wintering habitat and a serious commitment to its management in the interests of maintaining a strong population. As regards active management, Mr Taylor, again writing to Acland-Hood, reminds him that:

The marking of young Woodcocks was begun at Baronscourt in the year 1905. The earliest date we have put rings on is April 6 and the latest July 18. When gathering Pheasants' eggs in the latter end of April and beginning of May we see young Woodcocks on the wing and a lot of old birds sitting. The distinguishing mark on the ring affixed to the young bird's leg is B.C., and the date. The following is a record of Woodcocks ringed at Baron Court and of birds shot with rings on them:

Year	No. ringed	When and Where Shot
1905	15	1 shot at Baronscourt
1906	68	1 shot at Baronscourt, 1 at Harrow, 1 in Cornwall; all with 1905 ring
1907	65	2 at Baronscourt with 1905 ring
1908	65	2 at Baronscourt and 1 at Ardouries, Inverness, 1908 ring
1909	58	2 with 1907 ring, 3 with 1908, and 4 with 1909, all at Baronscourt
1910	47	2 with 1907 ring, 3 with 1908 and 2 with 1910, all at Baronscourt
1911	16	2 with 1905 ring, 1 with 1908, 1 with 1911; all Baronscourt

A great many Woodcock are seen flying about here in June and July, but towards the end of the latter month, they begin to leave the place and during the month of August and September very few are to be seen. The first flight generally reaches us about the second week in November.[191]

Clearly, this is a more ambitious scheme than that at Hazelwood around the same time.

The Game Book of James Edward Hamilton (1904-1979), 4th Duke of Abercorn, covering the period 1916 to 1938 inclusive, provides a detailed insight to the consistency of the Baronscourt shoot up until the Second World War and the many shooting guests to which it played host. The record is particularly interesting for the fact that it commences in 1916, when he was a mere boy of twelve years, and grows with him to adulthood, recording consistent and diverse shooting and a widening social circle of relations, friends and associates of the family who came to shoot at the estate. In addition, it provides accounts of shooting visits to Colebrooke (home of the Brookes, Viscounts Brookeborough) and Crom Castle (home of his in-laws, the Crichtons, Earls of Erne).

There was considerable Grouse moorland available in the shape of Moorlough (a mountain near Strabane with a considerable wilderness of 30-40,000 acres), Bessy Bell (a mountain behind Baronscourt) and Manis (a hill beside Bessy Bell), and not surprisingly, shooting commenced on

Shoveler

Sheld-duck

Gadwall

Mallard

these in August and continued in September. Later in the season, the shooting – Pheasant and Woodcock – was at Cloonty, the wood around Baronscourt; around the lakes at Baronscourt; at Envagh, two to three miles from Baronscourt, where there was a rough wood of about 300 acres around the lake; the townlands of Mullaghcroy, a hill on the other side of Baronscourt, which at the time was good Woodcock country (now planted with Sitka spruce), and Aughassey, on the other side of the valley.

In the earliest years of 1917 to 1920, outings recorded mainly comprised of himself, his father, the duke (on occasions), his brother Lord Claud David (1907-1968) (almost always) and Taylor the gamekeeper (always). In August 1919, the two young Hamilton brothers, were accompanied on Bessy Bell by their uncle Lord Bingham (George Charles Bingham, 5th Earl of Lucan (1860-1949), a brother of their mother, Lady Rosalind Bingham (1869-1958)) and his son the Hon. John (1904-1992), the Hamiltons' cousin. Notwithstanding their young ages – they were only seventeen and fourteen respectively in 1920 – and the small parties involved, the shooting was quite impressive and provides a foretaste of what lay ahead:

63 Vignettes of duck painted by James Edward Hamilton, 4th Duke of Abercorn (1904-1979), in his Game Book.

	Grouse	Pheasants	Snipe	Woodcock	Duck
1917/18	55	35	14	42	4
1918/19	142	7	13	24	6
1919/20	39	12	8	11	2
1920/21	-	7	1	21	-

In the course of the following years, as James Edward progressed into adulthood, the shooting circle widened progressively. Family members continued to be at the heart of that circle. Lord Claud Nigel Hamilton, James's uncle, and his brother-in-law Capt. Robert Orlando Kenyon-Slaney were frequent and regular shooters throughout the 1920s.

Captain Lord Sir Claud Nigel Hamilton (1889-1975)[192]
Educated at Wellington College, Berkshire, England, he was decorated with the award of Companion, Distinguished Service Order (DSO), in 1914. He fought in the First World War in 1918, where he was mentioned in despatches. He held the office of Equerry-in-Ordinary to HRH the Prince of Wales in 1919. Invested as a Companion, Order of St Michael and St George (CMG) in 1920, he held the offices of Deputy Master of His Majesty's Household in 1921, of Extra Equerry between 1922 and 1924, and of Equerry-in-Ordinary to HM King George V between 1924 and 1936. Lord Claud was Comptroller, Treasurer and Extra Equerry to Queen Mary between 1936 and 1953, and he fought in the Second World War between 1939 and 1942. Invested as a Knight Grand Cross, Royal Victorian Order (GCVO) in 1949, he held the office of Extra Equerry to HM Queen Elizabeth II between 1953 and 1975. Lord Claud married Violet Ruby Ashton, daughter of James Ashton, on 11 July 1933.

Major Robert Orlando Rodolph Kenyon-Slaney (1892-1965)
The son of Col. Rt Hon. William Slaney Kenyon-Slaney and Lady Mabel Selina Bridgeman, he married Lady Mary Cecilia Rhodesia Hamilton, James's sister, on 24 May 1917. They were divorced in 1930. On 25 April 1931, he married Nesta Forestier-Walker, daughter of Sir George Ferdinand Forestier-Walker, 3rd Baronet, and Georgina Emily Chamberlain.

Major-General Frederick George Beaumont-Nesbitt (1893-1971)
Another relation who found himself with a long shooting association was Maj.-Gen. Frederick George Beaumont-Nesbitt (1893-1971). The son of Edward John Downing Beaumont-Nesbitt and Helen Thomas, he married Cecilia Mary Lavinia Bingham, daughter of Maj.-Gen. Hon. Sir Cecil Edward Bingham (brother of Lady Rosalind Hamilton, wife of the 3rd Duke of Abercorn) and Rose Ellinor Guthrie, on 24 April 1915. He later married the Hon. Ruby Hardinge, daughter of Henry Charles Hardinge, 3rd Viscount Hardinge of Lahore and Kings Newton, and Mary Frances Nevill, on 1 March 1928.

Major-General Frederick George Beaumont-Nesbitt was decorated with the award of Military Cross (MC). He was invested as a Commander, Royal Victorian Order (CVO), and gained the rank of major-general in the service of the Grenadier Guards.

Another shooting guest was brother-in-law John Henry George Crichton, 5th Earl Erne (1907-1940), brother of James's wife Lady Kathleen Crichton. In October 1914, his father was killed in action in the First World War and only a month later, aged seven, he succeeded his grandfather as 5th Earl Erne. Erne was commissioned into the Royal Horse Guards from Sandhurst in 1927. He was promoted lieutenant in 1930 and resigned his commission in 1934.

He was active in the House of Lords and served as a Lord-in-Waiting from 1936 to 1939 in the National Government which was led firstly by Stanley Baldwin and later by Neville Chamberlain. He later joined the North Irish Horse and fought in the Second World War as a major.

Lord Erne married Lady Davidema Katharine Cynthia Mary Millicent Bulwer-Lytton, daughter of Victor Bulwer-Lytton, 2nd Earl of Lytton, and Pamela Plowden, in 1931. On 23 May 1940, he died in France from wounds received in action during the German invasion, aged thirty-two. He was succeeded in his titles by his two-year-old only son Henry. Lady Erne later married the Conservative politician 'Monty' Woodhouse.

A cousin of Crichton's, Michael Crichton, who designed the Westminster family's beautiful, classic, wooden motor yacht called *Trasna*, which they kept at Ely Lodge, was also shooting at Baronscourt in the mid-1920s.

James Craig, 1st Viscount Craigavon (1871-1940)

In addition to relations, there were a number of prominent local families who shot regularly at the estate through the 1920s and 1930s. The prominent unionist politician, leader of the Ulster Unionist Party and the first Prime Minister of Northern Ireland, James Craig, 1st Viscount Craigavon (1871-1940), appears at Baronscourt as a guest of the duke in January 1924. Craig was created a baronet in 1918 and raised to the peerage in 1927 as Lord Craigavon. Craigavon was born at Sydenham, Belfast, and was the son of James Craig (1828-1900) a wealthy whiskey distiller. His father owned a large house, Craigavon, overlooking Belfast Lough and his mother, the former Eleanor Gilmore Browne, was the daughter of Robert Browne, a prosperous man who owned property in Belfast and a farm outside Lisburn.

He was educated at Merchiston Castle School in Edinburgh, Scotland. On leaving school he began work as a stockbroker, eventually opening his own firm in Belfast. His wife, Cecil Mary Nowell Dering Tupper (Viscountess Craigavon, d. 1960), whom he married on 22 March 1905 after a very brief courtship, was English, the daughter of Sir Daniel Tupper, assistant comptroller of the Lord Chamberlain's department of the King's household. They had twin sons and a daughter.

He enlisted in the 3rd (militia) regiment of the Royal Irish Rifles on 11 January 1900 and went onto serve in the Second Boer War. In June 1901, he was sent home, suffering from dysentery, and by the time he was fit for service again the war was over. On his return to Ireland, having received a £100,000 legacy from his father's will, he turned to politics, serving as MP for East Down from 1906 to 1918. From 1918 to 1921, he represented Mid-Down, and served in government as Parliamentary Secretary to the Minister for Pensions (1919-1920) and Parliamentary Secretary to the Admiralty (1920-1921).

Craig rallied the Ulster unionist opposition to Irish Home Rule in Ulster before the First World War, organising the paramilitary Ulster Volunteers and buying arms from Imperial Germany. The Volunteers became the nucleus of the 36th (Ulster) Division during this time. Craig succeeded Edward Carson as leader of the Ulster Unionist Party in February 1921. In the first Northern Ireland general election he was elected to the newly created Northern Ireland House of Commons as member for County Down, and on 7 June 1921 (over two weeks before the opening of the Parliament of Northern Ireland), he was appointed the first Prime Minister of Northern Ireland by the Lord Lieutenant of Ireland.

Maurice Marcus McCausland (1872-1938)

Maurice Marcus McCausland of Drenagh, Limavady, County Londonderry, is one of another long-established family associated with the shooting at Baronscourt. He was a son of Conolly Thomas McCausland (1828-1902) and the Hon. Laura St John, a daughter of the 14th Baron of John of Bletsoe.

Maurice Marcus married Eileen Ogilby, daughter of Robert Alexander Ogilby of the Ardnargle Estate, also in Limavady. Conolly Robert (1906-1968), Maurice's son, fought in the Second World War and was so profoundly affected by what he experienced that he changed his faith to Catholicism. This he did despite knowing he had signed a codicil to his father's will barring him from inheriting should he become a Catholic. The will was contested and it was found that although the codicil applied to Conolly Robert, it did not do so to any of his direct descendants. So, on his death in 1968, his son Marcus inherited Drenagh.

Lieutenant-Colonel Henry Sacheverell Carlton Richardson (b. 1883)
Another similarly long-established family associated with the shooting over several decades is that of Lt-Col. Henry Sacheverell Carlton Richardson of Rossfad, Enniskillen. His sister Jane Mary Richardson was the first wife of Field Marshal Alan Francis Brooke, 1st Viscount Allenbrooke.

Mervyn William Charles Nesbitt Knox-Browne, DL (1880-1954)
The Knox-Browne family of Aughentaine Castle, Fivemiletown, County Tyrone, was another family which had an association with the shoot through Mervyn William Charles Nesbitt Knox-Browne. He was the son of Lt-Col. John Hervey Knox-Browne, JP, DL (1841-1927), who was baptised with the name of John Hervey Browne, though his name was legally changed to John Hervey Knox-Browne by Royal Sign-Manual on 16 March 1874. He was *aide-de-camp* to the Lord Lieutenant of Ireland, the 2nd Duke of Abercorn, in 1886; gained the rank of lieutenant-colonel in the service of the 9th Brigade, Northern Irish Division (Royal Artillery), and held the office of High Sheriff of County Tyrone. He, too, lived at Aughentaine. Mervyn's son, also Mervyn (b. 1927), sold Aughentaine to Capt. J.H. Hamilton-Stubber and it was subsequently demolished in 1955.

Captain Sir Charles Norman Lockhart Stronge, 8th Baronet, MC, PC (NI), JP (1894-1981)
It is worth mentioning, also, Capt. Sir Charles Norman Lockhart Stronge, a senior Unionist politician who was shooting at Baronscourt from the 1930s. Prior to his involvement in politics, he was a British Army officer, awarded with the Military Cross for having fought at the Battle of the Somme.

Sir Norman was born in Bryansford, County Down, the son of Sir Charles Stronge, 7th Baronet and Marian Bostock, whose family was from Epsom. He was educated at Eton. In the First World War he served in France and Flanders with the 10th Battalion Royal Inniskilling Fusiliers, as lieutenant and later as captain. He was decorated with the Military Cross and the Belgian *Croix de guerre*. He survived the first day of the Battle of the Somme and was the first soldier after the start of the battle to be mentioned in despatches by Lord Haig. In April 1918, he was appointed adjutant of the 15th Battalion, Royal Irish Rifles.

On the outbreak of the Second World War, he was again commissioned, this time into the North Irish Horse, Royal Armoured Corps, reverting to second lieutenant. In 1950, he was appointed honorary colonel of a Territorial Army unit of the Royal Irish Fusiliers. After his retirement from Stormont politics in 1969, where he served in several government positions from 1941, he farmed the family's several-thousand-acre estate at Tynan Abbey. His positions after the war included Speaker of the Northern Ireland House of Commons (for twenty-three years) and member of the Privy Council of Northern Ireland, to which he was appointed in 1946. In 1981, he was shot and killed, aged eighty-six, along with his son James, by the Provisional IRA at Tynan Abbey, their home, which was burnt to the ground during the attack.

He was married to Gladys Olive Hall, the daughter of Maj. H.T. Hall, originally from Athenry, County Galway. They had four children, including James.

Colonel John Knox McClintock (1864-1936)

This account of notable Guns of the Baronscourt shoot would be incomplete without mentioning Col. John Knox McClintock (1864-1936) of Seskinore, County Tyrone, who was a regular there through many seasons. His family had close ties over the years with the Abercorns. John was the eldest son of Col. George Perry McClintock of Seskinore, who commanded the 4th Battalion Royal Inniskilling Fusiliers from 1881 to 1887, and was ADC to the 1st Duke of Abercorn and Earl Spencer when they filled the position of Viceroy of Ireland.

Colonel John McClintock was educated at Cheltenham College and Oxford Military College. On completing his education, he joined the 3rd Battalion of the Royal Inniskilling Fusiliers. He retired from army life on disbandment sometime after the conclusion of the First World War. A keen sportsman, Col. McClintock succeeded his father as Master of the Seskinore Harriers in 1886, and held the position until his death. The Seskinore Harriers were founded by the McClintock family, and the colonel was an enthusiastic member of the hunting field.

In addition to those mentioned above, there was a long list of peers who made regular forays to shoot at Baronscourt, including Lord Eldin, Lord Harcourt, Lord Hartington, Lord Morven C. Bentinck, Lord Dalhousie, and the Hon. William Coke, Lord Wicklow.

Edward William Spencer Cavendish, 10th Duke of Devonshire, KG, MBE, TD (1895-1950)

Known as Marquess of Hartington from 1908 to 1938 and head of the Devonshire branch of the Cavendish family, Edward was the owner of Chatsworth House, and one of the largest private landowners in the United Kingdom and the Republic of Ireland, where they own the Lismore Estate in County Waterford. He was also MP for West Derbyshire (1923-1938) and a minister in Winston Churchill's wartime government.

64 Page from the Game Book of James Edward Hamilton, 4th Duke of Abercorn (1904-1979).

In 1917, he married Lady Mary Gascoyne-Cecil. They had five children. On 26 November 1950, he suffered a heart attack and died in Eastbourne in the presence of his doctor, Dr John Bodkin Adams, suspected serial killer. Despite the fact that the Duke had not seen a doctor in the fourteen days before his death, the coroner was not notified as he should have been. Adams signed the death certificate, stating that the Duke died of natural causes. Thirteen days earlier, Edith Alice Morrell – another patient of Adams – had also died. The Duke's sudden death meant that his estate had to pay 80 per cent death duties, which would have been avoided had he lived a few months longer. This led to the transfer of Hardwick Hall to the National Trust, and the sale of many of the Devonshires' accumulated assets, including tens of thousands of acres of land.

A summary record of shooting at Abercorn, based on the personal Game Book of James Edward, the 4th Duke, is shown below. It must be stressed that this summary is from a personal record and not the estate record. Therefore, it recalls only those shoots personally attended by the Duke. As a result, there is considerable volatility in returns from year to year arising from variations in the Duke's shooting days and times at Baronscourt. He was a frequent shooting guest at other estates throughout the UK. What stands out quite clearly from his records is the strong performance of Baronscourt for Grouse and Woodcock.

	Grouse	Pheasants	Woodcock	Snipe	Wild Duck
1922/23	15	11	87	213	434
1923/24	220	187	228	121	378
1924/25	3	48	53	113	457
1925/26	5	48	35	42	155
1926/27	58	269	238	44	270
1928/29	0	37	218	43	254
1929/30	193	66	97	111	277
1930/31	196	84	67	91	215
1931/32	56	27	92	101	226
1932/33	89	166	64	170	297
1933/34	124	72	50	49	113
1934/35	119	31	10	44	195
1935/36	41	0	32	17	93
1936/37	84	0	14	98	294
1937/38	66	0	86	57	228

Woodcock Shooting Today

Baronscourt offers specialised driven Woodcock shooting during the winter months of November, December and January. The shoot management adopts a strict limit on the number of days that are allocated to Woodcock shooting for self-imposed conservation reasons. As a result, they offer only two days back-to-back Woodcock shooting per month.

Much of the woodland cover has been carefully managed to create the perfect habitat for Woodcock and yet allows the Guns to take both a sporting and safe shot. Eight Guns is the ideal number and there is a minimum charge per day based on that figure. All the arrangements for shooting are made by the estate, including transport and lunch in a nearby pub. The shoot is led by the head gamekeeper, together with a team of highly experienced beaters and their well-trained dogs.

BROWN HALL, BALLINTRA, COUNTY DONEGAL

Brown Hall Estate has been home of the Hamilton family for two and a half centuries, and the family have resided in Donegal probably since the late sixteenth century. The original estate extended to 20,000 acres when it was inherited by John Hamilton (1800-1884) in 1821, celebrated by Dermot James in his *John Hamilton of Donegal (1800-1884): This Recklessly Generous Landlord*.[193] He was eldest son of James Hamilton (1771-1805) and Helen Pakenham (*c.* 1775-1807), daughter of the 2nd Baron Longford. Thus, his influential family included Arthur Wellesley (later the Duke of Wellington), who was an uncle though his marriage to the sister of John Hamilton's mother.

> The main part of the estate ran inland from Donegal Bay, between Donegal town and Ballintra, almost as far as Pettigo and Lough Erne; and northwards to near Lough Eske and the Barnsmore Gap. Separated from this, about twenty miles further north there was a further very large tract in the Finn Valley.[194]

It appears the estate had lain idle for fourteen years prior to his inheritance, when he 'set himself up in what he called his "bachelor house" with a servant, gamekeeper and a cook/housemaid (the gamekeeper's wife)'.[195] It appears that shooting was being managed at Brown Hall from this early time, although no records seem to have survived.

The game records commence in 1886, during the time of John Hamilton's son Maj. James Hamilton (1824-1915) and they continue through the tenure of John Stewart Hamilton (1864-1952), his eldest son by wife Dorothea Stewart, and through that of James Montgomery Hamilton (Capt. Jimmy) (1913-1987), John's son by his wife Winifrid Weston (d. 1950), to the present John Hamilton (b. 1952), the son of Capt. Jimmy and his wife Alice Lewis, who manages the shooting today with his wife Radine Fernandez.

Historically the shooting was primarily Grouse, Woodcock and Snipe, as the following summary records from the period 1886-1908/9 demonstrate:

65 Brown Hall House, County Donegal.

	Place	Pheasants	Partridge	Grouse	Woodcock	Snipe
5 days, 1886	Fintown	–	–	81	–	7
6 days, 1888	Fintown	–	–	55	–	11
4 days, 1893	Fintown	–	1	56	2	11
1893/4	Brownhall	2	–	13	10	20
1894/5	Fintown	–	1	48	–	6
	Brownhall	10	–	19	70	28
1895/6	Fintown	–	–	65	–	7
	Brownhall	33	–	14	15	6
1896/7	Brownhall	65	–	144	6	37
1897/8	Fintown	–	–	118	–	123
	Brownhall	23	–	120	16	81
1898/9	Fintown	–	–	150	2	128
	Brownhall	30	–	84	25	121
1899/1900	Brownhall	20	–	94	57	183
1900/1	Brownhall	25	–	52	34	104
1901/2	Brownhall	45	–	124	38	122
1902/3	Brownhall	17	–	117	44	103
1903/4	Brownhall	27	–	150	36	93
1904/5	Brownhall	49	11	146	28	151
1905/6	Fintown	–	–	173	–	–
	Brownhall	56	16	170	55	204
1906/7	Brownhall	40	1	105	42	121
1907/8	Brownhall	38	1	98	33	129
	Fintown	–	–	139	–	47
1908/9	Brownhall	51	1	62	48	126
1910	Brownhall	44	–	57	4	7
	Fintown	–	–	171	–	4

It is difficult to be certain about whose record is contained above. It is most likely that of Maj. James Hamilton (1824-1915) father of John Stewart Hamilton (1864-1952), since it describes 'self' and 'JSH' on 19 November 1898 as being shooting at Brownhall. However, in the same handwriting there is a summary record of shooting at 'Parksville B.C.' during the years 1911-19, suggesting the record is that of John Stewart Hamilton, since he was in Canada during those years.

John Stewart Hamilton was over fifty when his father died and in 1919 he returned from Canada, to which he had emigrated in 1910, in order to take on the management of the estate, which was in a precarious financial situation. In his memoir, *My Times and Other Times*, he writes with evident bitterness about its condition and about the profligate manner with which the family fortune had been spent. Dermot James points out that:

> Obviously it would have been difficult, if not politically tactless, for him to have openly faulted John Hamilton for his generosity to his tenants, but what the grandson – and other members of his family at the time – found difficult to accept was that much of the money was wasted because of impulsive decisions and impatience, even though John Hamilton had readily acknowledged his own foolishness in this respect.[196]

Evidently, the shooting at Fintown was principally for Grouse, with smaller numbers of Snipe. Brownhall, by contrast, had Pheasant, Grouse, Woodcock and Snipe, and occasional Partridge.

It is also difficult to be precise about the composition of shooting parties, with little more commentary than 'self and various' or 'self and four Guns' being typically noted in the Game Book. A name which appears with regularity is 'W.A. Hamilton'. While, this is most likely a relation, the Christian initials do not relate to anyone known to be associated with Brownhall Hamiltons. Another regular at this time was Sir Arthur Robert Wallace (d. 1912). This is almost certainly Sir Arthur Robert Wallace, CB, of Ardnamona, a JP and DL for County Donegal, who was Principal Clerk at the Chief Secretary's Office, Dublin Castle (1854-1901), and who died in 1912. Ardnamona appears in the Brown Hall records. For example, on 29 November 1900, 'four Guns shot Ardnamona for a bag of thirty Woodcock and twelve Pheasants'. However, it seems likely that this was by invitation of Wallace, who appears on Brown Hall days regularly.

Another name to appear shooting at Fintown is 'Dunville'. This may be one of the Dunvilles who controlled Dunville Whiskey and whose seat was Redburn House, Holywood, County Down. Of these, the most likely candidates would appear to be Robert Grimshaw Dunville, JP (1838-1910), a Deputy Lieutenant of County Down, a High Sheriff of County Meath, a founder member of the Reform Club and a member of the Liberal Party until William Gladstone advocated Home Rule for Ireland. He then became a Liberal Unionist.

In 1890, Robert's son John Dunville Dunville (1866-1929) was appointed Private Secretary to the Duke of Devonshire. As a young man he had been an enthusiastic cross-country rider and a skilled polo player. While he was at Cambridge, he was Master of the Cambridge Staghounds for two seasons, 1886 and 1887. John Dunville gained an MA at Trinity College, Cambridge, and served as a lieutenant-colonel in the 5th Battalion of the Leinster Regiment (the old Meath Militia).

Henry Herbert Ronald White (1879-1939)[197]

Another shooting companion of the Hamiltons was Henry Herbert Ronald White, son of Maj.-Gen. H.G. White, who had acquired Lough Eske Castle in 1894 from the estate of Thomas Brooke (of the same family as Colebrooke Park). He was a man of great bravery and a highly efficient soldier, who could probably have risen to be a general, like his father, had he concentrated his considerable energies solely on a military career. He was highly respected and admired by the men of the 25th Fusiliers (Frontiersmen).

White was commissioned into the 60th Rifles in 1898 and served in South Africa between 1901 and 1902. On 10 January 1904, he was seriously wounded by a bullet through the right chest at Jidball, Somaliland. In April of that year, he was promoted captain – an unusually fast rise. He became adjutant of 5th Battalion, 60th Rifles from 1906 to 1908. He was due to be posted to Bermuda that year, but he decided to resign his commission after the sudden death of his father in order to run the family estate at Lough Eske Castle.

He modernised the castle, employing a dozen workers, and made sure that half were Republicans and half Unionists. When he returned after the First World War, he found both political factions coming to him asking for the advice of an experienced soldier. His advice was always the same, 'War is the worst of events, and killing a waste which does no person any good whatsoever.' Eventually, the Troubles in Ireland forced him to sell the estate. He was then awarded the OBE. After the war, he returned to the life of a gentleman, travelling the world, fishing, shooting and sailing motorboats.

There were a number of other, less conspicuous, characters, whose identity is difficult to ascertain. One was a Sir H. Stewart, who was shooting from this time. The Hamiltons were related to a number of branches of Stewarts in Donegal. John Hamilton of Brown Hall (1735-1811) was mar-

66 Captain
and Mrs Jimmy
Hamilton.

ried to Isabella Stewart of Killymoon, County Tyrone, while more recently, Maj. James Hamilton (1824-1915) was married to Dorothea Stewart, daughter of William Stewart, MD, of Horn Head, County Donegal. It is most likely that the Stewart in question is a relation, by marriage, of this Maj. James Hamilton. However, it has not been possible to confirm the identity precisely.

Other participants were: R. Cochran, probably of Edenmore, Stranolar, described by Lewis as 'a neat mansion, in a small but handsome demesne, on the south bank of the river Fin'; and the Johnstons, both in the linen-bleaching trade, 'of Woodlands, a handsome modern residence, of J. Johnston, Esq., JP; Summer Hill, of C. Johnston, Esq.' Also in the records of this time is T.T. Stubbs, presumed to be Thomas Troubridge Stubbs of London, who came to Ireland in the 1830s and settled at Ballyshannon, County Donegal. In 1839, he married Elizabeth Chinnery, daughter of Joseph Folingsby of Belfast and Ballyshannon by his wife Eleanor, daughter of Sir Broderick Chinnery. (See Lissadell, where a Thomas Troubridge Stubbs was shooting in the 1940s.)

Records for Brownhall were recommenced in 1919, when John Stewart Hamilton returned to take on the management of the estate following his father's demise in 1915. Soon afterwards, in 1925, he was joined by his son James Montgomery Hamilton (1913-1987), who was, in time, to become a true character of Irish shooting and he devoted much of his life both to the sport and to game conservation. From the beginning, he meticulously kept a game record.

> To see my tenants stout and hale
> And roistering in my hall,
> To see them quaff the nut brown ale
> And know not want at all.
>
> To plant my covers like a king
> And know that they will thrive,
> (These splendid oaks will green with spring
> When I am not alive).

I love the gold October days,
The echo of my gun,
The old cock Pheasant's wily ways,
And how red foxes run.

I like to hear the cheep of mouse,
When all is still and dark,
The creaking of this panelled house,
And owls about my park.

These things I hold and will I hold,
Whatever fortunes come,
And when at last I'm dead and cold,
My heir shall be my son.

Pray God he keep in sacred trust,
This ancient house and lands,
And, when at last, he comes to dust,
Leave it in loving hands!

The Game Book records father and son shooting together, often just the two of them, for much of the period to the end of the Second World War. When Jimmy Hamilton started farming at Brownhall he remarked he had 'a few acres with a bit of a mountain' to contend with. Being a member of the landed gentry did not pose any barriers either. Anyone who shared his interest, regardless of colour or creed, was welcomed equally and it was this direct honesty which allowed him to transcend politics and religion in discussing shooting, and which made him so popular across the spectrum of society.

Moreover, the shooting was cultivated with as much care and attention as any other aspect of the farm, with the result that his shooting days were most popular with those privileged to be invited. There were days when father and son were joined by others: Stubbs, Stewart and the illusive W.A. Hamilton continued through these years, and they were joined by newcomers like William Ramage, the Ballyshannon solicitor, who shot regularly with them. There is also a record of August 1936 in which the guest is 'Conyngham' – probably Frederick William Burton Conyngham, 6th Marquess Conyngham (1890-1974). The Conyngham family had four distinct estates in the county: Boylagh, Mountcharles, the Rosses and Stranorlar (including the Tyrcallen Estate). Alas, there was little success, with only five Grouse being shot over two days.

However, the overall record in the interwar period, through to the end of the Second World War, remained broadly consistent, as the summary below shows:

	Place	Pheasants	Partridge	Grouse	Woodcock	Snipe
1919/20	Brownhall	43	–	130	47	29
1920/1	"	–	–	10	–	1
1921/2	"	'Broke foot in 1921 … [illegible]'				
1922/3	"	6	–	7	3	–
1923/4	"	12	–	22	7	5
1924/5	"	25	–	21	25	127

1925/6	"	25	–	69	16	106
1926/7	"	25	–	49	24	70
'JSH laid up for most of the winter'						
1927/8	"	31	–	61	60	47
1928/9	"	32	10 swans	79	37	125
1929/30	"	25	–	95	49	155
1930/1	"	35	–	84	34	93
1931/2	"	27	16 swans	67	22	81
1932/3	"	49	11 swans	135	32	121
1933/4	"	55	8 swans	146	32	102
1934/5	Fintown	–	–	50	–	6
1935/6	Brownhall	17	2	43	5	46
1936/7	"	16	14	48	5	74
1937/8	"	40	34	43	19	105
1938/9	"	25	13	24	10	43
1939/40	"	13	29	10	5	2
1940/1	"	28	17	13	5	38
'War abroad'						
1945/6	"	20	11	29	1	11
1946/7	"	28	17	13	5	38

The record picks up again from 1953, the year after his father's death. By this time he was to be found shooting at numerous venues, including Classiebawn, Lissadell, Temple House and Annaghmore in County Sligo, and across many shoots in Northern Ireland. He was especially friendly with Richard Hermon, who appears shooting with him during the 1950s, as does Sir Norman Stronge. However, the record below relates to shooting at home and – pointedly perhaps – relates only to 'self'. What a remarkable eight seasons' shooting for one man at home!

	Pheasants	Grouse	Woodcock	Snipe
1953/54	12	93	12	166
1954/55	19	117	40	74
1955/56	18	135	16	95
1956/57	12	92	12	40
1957/58	1	85	11	31
1958/59	1	100	4	22
1959/60	22	79	51	130
1960/61	51	93	42	146

There were, of course, visiting Guns; Richard Hermon of Necarne Castle, Sir Norman Stronge, some of the Sligo Coopers, and Howard Temple (1914-2010), who was chairman of Magee Tweeds until 1983, being amongst the more frequent. The Magee title dates from a previous owner, who founded a drapery shop in Donegal Town in 1866. He owned a hotel and was so impressed with the sales skills of a teenage Robert Temple – who sold him a pair of Woodcock – he recommended him as an apprentice. The apprentice became the owner of the shop in 1900 and decided to keep the name Magee. Robert Temple was joined by his eldest son Howard in 1931, just three years after the family moved from living quarters above the shop to a new home at the edge of Donegal Town. Howard felt a natural drive to become actively involved in the family business and studied at home in the evenings for a university degree.

The format of Hamilton's record keeping changed during the 1970s, his summaries distinguishing his own contribution separately from the total bag (a practice also of Sir Jocelyn Gore-Booth of Lissadell). To judge also from the Pheasant and Woodcock numbers accounted for, these records include 'away shooting'. One wonders if he was becoming more competitive with age …

		Pheasants	Grouse	Woodcock	Snipe
1971/72	Self	126	52	57	111
	Total	935	101	335	493
1972/73	Self	118	15	39	113
	Total	875	34	209	532
1973/74	Self	111	20	53	86
	Total	664	45	281	441
1974/75	Self	86	25	34	89
	Total	513	56	226	454
1975/76	Self	69	34	22	60

Jimmy Hamilton's favourite quarry species were Grouse, Snipe and Woodcock. He was particularly concerned for the future of the Grouse – the dwindling numbers of the 1970s and earlier sounding an alarm – and was instrumental in the establishment of the All Ireland Grouse Council, a group dedicated to understanding the decline of this quarry species. In asking for funding for this, he wrote:

> I should like every man in Ireland who has ever shot a Grouse and would like for his son to be able to do the same, to contribute a fiver to this worthy cause. Are we men or mice? After all what's a fiver these nowadays? It should not be hard to cut out the last round of drinks for once to help such a noble cause as mine.[198]

He was a true hunting conservationist, spending much time on his beloved Grouse mountain, managing heather and trying to control the predators. He was never interested in the size of the bag, but rather the quality of the shooting. 'His infectious enthusiasm for the cause of game survival provided much of the motivation for my writing,' wrote Colin Me Kelvie in his *A Future for Game?*

The Hamiltons' shooting tradition lives on today through Jimmy's son John Hamilton, who provides Guns with a mixture of walked-up shooting and driven Pheasant and ducks.

COLEBROOKE PARK, COUNTY FERMANAGH

Colebrooke Park, County Fermanagh, is the family home and seat of Viscount and Viscountess Brookeborough, and one of Northern Ireland's most important and historic stately homes.

Now set in a 1,000 acre estate, Colebrooke Park a short distance from the tranquillity of beautiful Lough Erne. There is a long shooting tradition on the estate, practised to the present day by the Brooke family, who have owned the County Fermanagh estate for ten generations. This includes stalking of a long-established and carefully managed herd of Fallow Deer.

The family's history lies principally in the military and in politics, and the Brooke family were at the heart of Ulster Unionist politics for several generations. The shooting party guests of Colebrooke Park reflect these twin occupations of the family. In addition, it was at the heart of the cluster of shooting estates that included Baronscourt (Abercorns), Aughetaine (Knox-Browne), Ballywalter (Mulholland), Belle Isle (Porter-Porter), Castle Irvine (Archdale),[199] Crom (Crichton), Florenscourt (Cole), Lough Fea (Shirley), Necarne (Hermon), Rossfad (Richardson), and Tynan Castle (Stronge), all of which were linked by social and political ties (including marriage) and all of whom are to be found shooting with the Brookes of Colebrooke Park.

Sir Arthur Douglas Brooke, 4th Baronet (1865-1907) provides a starting point to the shooting history through his Game Book of 1896 to 1903. In April 1887, Sir Victor Brooke began handing over responsibility for running Colebrooke to his eldest son, (Arthur) Douglas, who took up residence at Colebrooke with his wife, Gertrude Isabella ('Lilah') Batson, daughter of Stanlake Batson of Horseheath, Cambridge, whom he had married in the summer of that year. Thereafter, they lived together on the estate virtually all year around. Within twelve months, Basil, the first of their five children, was born into the somewhat austere, disciplined family atmosphere favoured by their father. Sir Douglas enjoyed shooting, fishing and natural history, but indulged these interests mainly within the confines of his property. He had a genuine interest in farming and worked to build up the stock on the home farm which had been so neglected by Sir Victor. His youngest brother, Alan, was to become Field Marshall, 1st Viscount Alanbrooke (1883-1963).

Sir Arthur continued the family's tradition of public service, particularly at a local level. He served on the Fermanagh Farming Society and the Agricultural Committee, and was a member of the Royal Dublin Society. He was a JP, a Deputy Lieutenant and a sheriff for the county, and represented Maguiresbridge district on the County Council, for a time acting as its vice-chairman. He was also a strong supporter of the Church of Ireland, active in the Temperance Movement, and a vice-chairman of the Clogher Valley Railway Company. He became one of the

67 Colebrooke Park, County Fermanagh.

leading figures in the Orange Order and was also active politically. In 1893, he made known his intention of standing as a parliamentary candidate for South Fermanagh. He did so, according to *The Fermanagh Times*, 'out of a sense of duty', but Sir Douglas's defeat was inevitable, given the size of the nationalist majority. Throughout the years, he continued to serve as chairman of the South Fermanagh Registration Association and was one of the leading subscribers to party funds in the division. Sir Douglas died in 1907 and his widow in 1918.

A summary of the shooting record contained in his Game Book is shown below:

	Grouse	Partridge	Pheasants	Woodcock	Snipe	Duck
1889/90	4	4	730	285	154	107
1890/91	42	2	769	346	97	54
1891/92	30	8	176	32	67	21
1892/93	1,234	–	226	104	66	19
1893/94	56	5	1,179	90	150	70
1894/95	71	3	578	133	87	32
1895/96	132	5	762	15	41	50
1896/97	68	2	1,504	104	137	105
1897/98	385	2	1,671	223	116	134
1898/99	204	2	994	117	67	112
1999/00	45	–	1,294	243	83	176
1900/01	84	–	1,270	182	97	240
1901/02	47	–	672	236	200	246
1902/03	93	–	338	132	108	160

The Grouse were taken, for the most part, from Mullaghfad, which was included in the Colebrooke Park Estate, with some also being taken at Bessy Bell in neighbouring Baronscourt. No details are contained in respect of the very large bag of 1,234 Grouse recorded in 1892/93. Of the bag of 385 Grouse obtained in 1897/98, 195 came from the Powerscourt Estate in County Wicklow, while over half the bag of 204 recorded for 1898/99 came from Kinlough, County Leitrim, the home of the Johnston family. The strong and generally consistent bags of Woodcock and Snipe reflect the strength of the Colebrooke Estate and others in the vicinity, most notably Baronscourt.

A frequent shooting companion of Douglas was Sir Edward Mervyn Archdale, 1st Baronet, PC (Ireland), DL (1853-1943), a Northern Irish politician. Archdale was born in Rossfad, County Fermanagh. Members of his family in subsequent generations were also regular shooters with the Brookes. He was educated at the Naval School in Portsmouth and entered the Royal Navy in 1866. He was promoted to the rank of Lieutenant in 1875 and retired in 1880. He was appointed High Sheriff of Fermanagh for 1884 and was elected Conservative MP for North Fermanagh in 1898. He resigned in 1903 but regained the seat in 1916. In 1921, he resigned to stand for the new Parliament of Northern Ireland and was elected for Fermanagh and Tyrone. He held that seat until 1929, and was then elected for Enniskillen, retiring in 1937. From 1921 to 1925, he served as Minister of Agriculture and Commerce in the Government of Northern Ireland and continued as Minister of Agriculture from 1925 to 1933. As a landowner and practical farmer, he was well-qualified for the job.

Archdale was appointed to the Privy Council of Ireland in the 1921 New Year Honours, entitling him to the style 'The Right Honourable', and he was created a baronet in 1928. He was succeeded by his eldest son, Vice-Admiral Sir Nicholas Edward Archdale, 2nd Baronet (1881-1955), who married Gerda Henriette Sievers, daughter of Frederik Christian Sievers, on 22 July 1920. He fought in

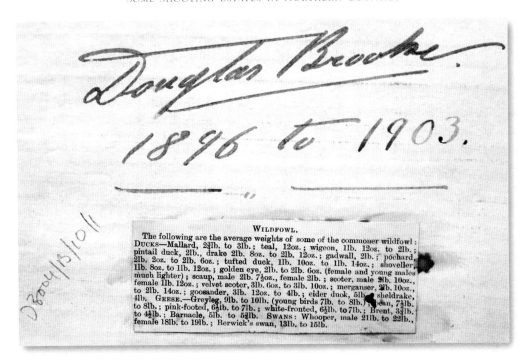

68 Douglas Brooke's Game Book, 1896-1903.

the First World War with the submarine flotillas. He gained the rank of vice-admiral in the service of the Royal Navy and he held the office of *aide-de-camp* to HM King George V in 1929. He was General Inspector, Ministry of Home Affairs, Northern Ireland, between 1931 and 1946 and he succeeded to the title of 2nd Baronet Archdale of Riversdale, County Fermanagh on 1 November 1943.

His son Capt. Sir Edward Folmer Archdale (1921-2009), the 3rd Baronet, was a Royal Navy captain and submarine officer, during the Second World War and a local politician. Nicknamed 'Teddy', he joined the Royal Navy after attending Copthorne Primary School in Sussex. After graduation from Dartmouth Naval College, he was promoted to midshipman and served into the start of the war, aboard HMS *Vindictive* and HMS *Edinburgh*. He completed his training in HMS *Hood* and HMS *Bulldog*, later famous for her capture of the Enigma machine, before volunteering to serve in submarines. He was awarded the Distinguished Service Cross in October 1943, and after submarine service he taught at the stone frigate HMS *Excellent* as a gunnery instructor. He was the gunnery officer of HMS *Daring*, served at the Royal Naval Tactical School from 1959-62, and he attended the Joint Service Defence College at Latimer, and the Canadian National Defence College at Kingston, Ontario. He retired from the Royal Navy and worked in defence sales after retirement, and also became involved in local politics in Northern Ireland. He was a Conservative Party member until joining the United Kingdom Independence Party later in life.

Sewallis Evelyn Shirley, DL, JP (1844-1904)

Members of the Shirley family of Ettington Park Manor at Stratford-upon-Avon and Lough Fea, County Monaghan, appear with regularity shooting with Douglas Brooke. Most notably, perhaps, was Sewallis Evelyn Shirley, a British politician. He is best known for having founded the Kennel Club in Britain in 1873. A member of the Shirley family headed by the Earl Ferrers, Sewallis was the son of Evelyn Shirley and Mary Clara Elizabeth, daughter of Sir Edmund Lechmere, 2nd Baronet. Born at the family's English estate of Ettington Park at Stratford-upon-Avon, he was educated at Eton before matriculating to Christ Church, Oxford, in 1864, though he did not take a degree. Shirley married Emily Jean, daughter of Col. William Macdonald, in 1884, and they had several children.

Throughout his life, Shirley had a keen interest in dogs – both working dogs and pure breeds. He was associated in particular with the development of the Flat-Coated Retriever. In 1873, he brought together a group of similar-minded people with the aim of establishing a governing body which would allow the definition of dog breeds to protect pedigrees and to improve the standards of hygiene at dog shows. Later that year, the Kennel Club was formed, with Shirley sitting as secretary from 1873 to 1899.

Shirley's family had a long connection with County Monaghan and they owned a large estate at Lough Fea.[200] He entered Parliament representing Monaghan (a seat previously held by both his father and grandfather) in 1868, and won the election through a promise to defend the Protestant constitution. He continued to represent the constituency until 1880, but rarely spoke in Parliament, and he lost his seat when opposition Liberal supporters ran a successful campaign based on tenants' rights. He attempted to return to politics in 1885, standing against an Irish nationalist candidate for the newly created seat of South Monaghan, but was heavily defeated. Relations with the tenant farmers on his estates, which he inherited in 1882, were poor. This, combined with forced evictions following the agricultural depression of the 1880s, led to his estate being targeted by the Nationalists.

Basil Stanlake Brooke, 1ˢᵗ Viscount Brookeborough, Bt, KG, CBE, MC, PC, HML (1888-1973)
When Douglas Brooke died in 1907, at the age of forty-two, he was succeeded by his eldest son Basil Stanlake Brooke. He was an Ulster Unionist politician who became the third Prime Minister of Northern Ireland in 1943, holding office until 1963. He was a nephew of Field Marshal Viscount Alanbrooke (1883-1963), Chief of the Imperial General Staff during the Second World War, who was only five years his senior. Brookeborough's sister Sheelah married Sir Henry Mulholland; their son would succeed as Baron Dunleath. Members of the Mulholland family became frequent shooting visitors to Colebrooke.

Brookeborough was also a keen shot and maintained the shooting tradition at Colebrooke. He held several ministerial positions in the Government of Northern Ireland, and has been described as 'perhaps the last unionist leader to command respect, loyalty and affection across the social and political spectrum of the movement'.

He was awarded the Military Cross and *Croix de guerre* for his service during the First World War. In 1920, he left the British Army to farm his estate at Colebrooke. He entered politics, where he had a very long career. When he resigned the Premiership of Northern Ireland in March 1963, he was Northern Ireland's longest-serving Prime Minister, having held office for two months short of twenty years. He had also established a United Kingdom record by holding government office continuously for thirty-three years. However, Brookeborough faced increasing disenchantment amongst Unionist Party backbenchers for what was regarded as his indifferent and ineffectual approach to mounting economic problems. As this dissatisfaction grew, British civil servants and some members of the Unionist Party combined to exert discreet and ultimately effective pressure on Brookeborough to resign to make way for Terence O'Neill who was Finance Minister. In 1963, his health having worsened, he resigned (at the age of seventy-five) as Prime Minister, but he remained a member of the Northern Ireland House of Commons until the 1969 general election, becoming the Father of the House in 1965. During his last years in the legislature, he publicly opposed the liberal policies of his successor as PM, Terence O'Neill, who actively sought to improve relationships with the Republic of Ireland and who attempted to grant the demands of the Northern Ireland Civil Rights Association.

By his first wife, Lord Brookeborough had the following children:

Lieutenant Basil Julian David Brooke, 1920-1943, killed in action;

John Warden Brooke, 2nd Viscount Brookeborough, 1922-1987;

Lieutenant Henry Alan Brooke, 1923-1945, killed in action.

John Warden Brooke, 2nd Viscount Brookeborough, Bt, PC (NI) (1922-1987)

A Northern Irish politician who was educated at Eton. During the Second World War he served in the British Army in North Africa, Italy and Germany. He was on the personal staff of Field Marshal Viscount Alexander of Tunis and an *aide-de-camp* to Field Marshal Earl Wavell, Viceroy of India (1947).

He was elected to Fermanagh County Council in 1947 (until 1973) and was chairman of the council from 1961 to 1973. He was appointed High Sheriff of Fermanagh for 1955 and succeeded his father as the Ulster Unionist Stormont MP for Lisnaskea in a by-election on 22 March 1968, retaining that seat until the abolition of the Parliament of Northern Ireland in 1973. Brookeborough was a member of a dissident group of Ulster Unionist backbench MPs who campaigned for the removal of Terence O'Neill as Prime Minister. When O'Neill finally resigned in April 1969, his successor, James Chichester-Clark (1923-2002) brought some of this dissident group into his government. Chichester-Clarke is recorded shooting at Colebrooke in 1952/53.

Brookeborough was made Parliamentary Secretary at the Ministry of Commerce (1969-70) and then Parliamentary Secretary at the Department of the Prime Minister (1970-12). Under Brian Faulkner's premiership, he was government chief whip (1971-1972) and he also served in the Cabinet from 1971 as Minister of State in the Ministry of Finance. He represented North Down in the Northern Ireland Assembly (1973-74). When the Unionist Party of Northern Ireland was founded by pro-Sunningdale Agreement members of the Ulster Unionists, Brooke joined and he was again elected for North Down to the Northern Ireland Constitutional Convention (1975-76). He also represented the views of the Unionist Party of Northern Ireland (UPNI) in the House of Lords.

Brookeborough married Rosemary Chichester (d. 30 January 2007), daughter of Lt-Col. Arthur O'Neill Cubitt Chichester, MC, of Galgorm Castle, in 1949 and they had five children: Alan, Christopher, Juliana, Melinda and Susanna.

Summary records from the Game Book of Sir Basil Brooke for the period 1920-1926 are shown below:

	Grouse	Partridge	Pheasant	Woodcock	Snipe	Duck
1920/21	952	1	251	171	27	340
1921/22	1,322	342	544	369	173	456
1922/23	1,242	–	372	199	156	597
1923/24	593	1	148	311	144	85
1924/25	442	–	218	238	175	946
1925/26	518	1	125	257	141	457

There are no details provided with respect to the annual Grouse bags and it is considered that these were probably obtained away from the Irish estates and most probably at Scottish ones. The same is true of the Partridge bag of 342 for 1921/22. However, the balance of Pheasants, Woodcock, Snipe and wild duck were obtained in the local area. Aside from Colebrooke Park grounds, the returns reflect visits to Baronscourt, Aughentaine, Florenscourt and Crom, and the

Season, 192........to 192........

Pheasant	Grouse	Partridge	Wood-cock	Wild Duck	Widgeon	Teal	Snipe	Wood Pigeon	Hares	Rabbits	Deer	Etc	Salmon	Trout	Pike	TOTAL
								6						1		7.
															3	3
								16.								16.
								19								19
								37.								37.
								3				J.Dues 2			11.	16.
								16				cat				17.
								23								23.
								14							1.	15
								2.	21			Roots 45y.				582
								2	154			462		1	15	735
									14	1		1			2D	36
								2	171	1		463		1	35	771

Season, 192........to 192........

Pheasant	Grouse	Partridge	Wood-cock	Wild Duck	Widgeon	Teal	Snipe	Wood Pigeon	Hares	Rabbits	Deer	Etc	Salmon	Trout	Pike	TOTAL
													6.			6
	63						2									65
	2						1			14		Flood.				17
										8.				3		11
	31.						1		1			g.Trows. 2				35
	46									1.						46.47
										4.		cat.				4.
										12		1 Rat				13.
										18.		1		1.		20.
										2					2.	4
	142						4		1	1	58		4	6	4	2	227
									2	243	1	463	6	14	35	862.
	142						4		3	1	301	1	487	12	18	37	1084

wild duck were secured for the most part at the Downpatrick Marshes and comprised Wigeon, Teal and Mallard.

John Porter-Porter (1853-1939)

Around this time there are entries recording the presence of John Porter-Porter of Belle Isle, County Fermanagh. Bell Isle Estate today is in the ownership of the Duke of Abercorn (since 1991) and there is an active shoot there, as there was during the tenure of the Porters previously.

John Porter-Porter was baptised with the name of John Porter Archdale. He was the second son of Nicholas Montgomery Archdale and Adelaide Mary Porter of Crocknacrieve, near Ballinamallard, County Fermanagh. On 11 May 1876, his name was legally changed to John Porter-Porter when he assumed the surname and arms of Porter only, in lieu of his patronymic, by Royal Licence. He succeeded at Belle Isle, the home of his uncle, the controversial John Grey Vesey Porter (1818-1903), brother of his mother, who died without issue. Amongst the latter's tribulations was a scandalous affair by his wife, Elizabeth Jane Hall (daughter and co-heiress of Richard Hall of Inishmore Hall, Derrybrusk, near Belle Isle), whom he had married in 1863, when he was forty-seven and she was about eighteen:

> The marriage was desirable from the financial point of view and because the Belle Isle and Inishmore Estates 'matched'. But it was childless and, it would seem, unhappy, partly on account of the disparity in their ages, and partly (it may be conjectured), on account of Porter's cantankerousness. In September 1870, Mrs Porter formed an illicit liaison with one Capt. Leonard Poynter of the 16th Regiment, then stationed in Enniskillen. Porter found out about this affair in December and, with the aid of his butler and other men-servants, lured Capt. Poynter to Belle Isle, where he was considerably knocked about, had his hair and one side of his luxuriant moustache cut off, and was then severely horse-whipped by Porter personally. Capt. Poynter brought an action for assault and battery against Porter and claimed damages of £10,000. Porter would probably have been well advised to have settled out of court. Instead, a packed Dublin courtroom was regaled for almost a week with salacious details of the doings of Mrs Porter and Capt. Poynter at Belle Isle. In the end, the jury – obviously composed of stern Victorian *paterfamiliae* – found for Capt. Poynter, but awarded him a farthing in damages. Shortly afterwards, Porter successfully sued for divorce. His wife and her parents retired to London, where Mrs Porter died, still only in her early forties, in 1887.[201]

John Porter-Porter married Josephine Henrietta Lloyd, daughter of Col. Jesse Lloyd, on 31 January 1884. He lived at Clonbalt, County Longford, before inheriting Belle Isle, seemingly in 1887 when Mrs Porter died.[202] They had five children together.

He held the office of High Sheriff of County Longford in 1879 and the office of High Sheriff of County Fermanagh in 1883.

69 (left) Grouse and Rabbit Vignette, Game Book of Sir Basil Brooke, 1924/25.

A later Game Book covers the period 1938/39-1957/58, a noteworthy feature of which is a consistent record of Pigeon shooting during this period, but no records of Partridge being shot and only few Pheasants.

	Grouse	Pheasant	Woodcock	Snipe	Pigeon	Duck
1938/39	79	45	186	209	–	30
'War against Germany declared 3 September'						
1939/40	154	66	118	116	–	38
'A very cold hard winter. Very little shooting owing to war. Fully occupied with food production. BSB [Basil Stanlake Brooke] as Minister of Agriculture.'						
1940/41	76	8	93	145	–	45
1944/45	–	2	6	7	1,071	6
1946/47	–	5	82	160	17	32
1947/48	43	–	47	71	210	64
1949/50	50	–	32	190	441	42
1950/51	47	2	68	134	244	11
1952/53	46	1	73	139	130	8
1953/54	–	1	30	186	175	4
'Many Grouse drowned in heavy rainstorm in June. No wc [Woodcock] until February. Open winter on continent.'						
1955/56	–	–	3	144	473	–
1957/58	–	1	1	169	86	–

Family members and relations continued to play a strong part in the shooting throughout this period. Sir Basil's brother-in-law Sir Henry Mullholland was one of the most regular Guns.

Sir Henry George Hill Mulholland, 1st Baronet PC (1888-1971)

The third son of Henry Lyle Mulholland, 2nd Baron Dunleath, and Norah Louisa Fanny Ward. He was a good cricketer at Cambridge University and also played a first-class match for Ireland against Scotland in 1911.

He was a member of the House of Commons of Northern Ireland for Down and was Assistant Parliamentary Secretary at the Ministry of Finance and assistant whip from 1925 until 1929, after which he served as Speaker of the House. He was admitted to the Privy Council of Northern Ireland in 1930 and in 1945 he was created Baronet of Ballyscullion Park in the County of Londonderry. He married Sheelah Brooke, daughter of Sir Arthur Brooke, 4th Baronet, and sister of Basil Brooke, 1st Viscount Brookeborough, Prime Minister of Northern Ireland. He died in March 1971, aged eighty-two, and was succeeded in the baronetcy by his son Michael, who in 1993 succeeded his cousin as 5th Baron Dunleath.

Two of Lord Brookeborough's sons, John Warden and Lt Henry Alan Brooke, were also about shooting in the early 1940s, as was Sir Basil's uncle, Alan Francis Brooke, 1st Viscount Alanbrooke, KG, GCB, OM, GCVO, DSO and Bar (1883-1963). He was the Chief of the Imperial General Staff during the Second World War and was promoted to Field Marshal in 1944. As chairman of the Chiefs of Staff Committee, Brooke was the foremost military advisor to Prime Minister Winston Churchill, and in the role of co-ordinator of the British military efforts was an important but not always well-known contributor to the Allies' victory in 1945. After retiring from the army, Alanbrooke (as he then was) served as Lord High Constable of England during the coronation of Queen Elizabeth II in 1953. His war diaries attracted attention for their criticism of Churchill and for Brooke's forthright views on other leading figures of the war.

There are numerous other landed families members of which are to be found shooting at Colebrooke during and after the Second World War. Amongst those most frequently present

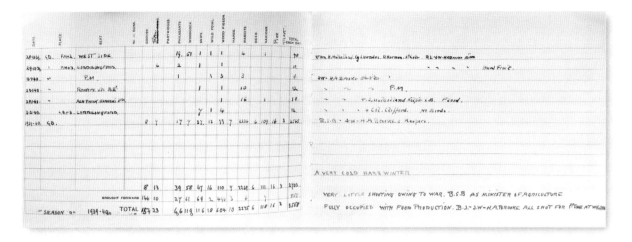

70 **Page from 1939/40 season of the Game Book of Sir Basil Brooke.**

was Col. Gerald Hugh Grosvenor, 4th Duke of Westminster, DSO, PC (1907-1967), who was the son of Capt. Lord Hugh William Grosvenor and Lady Mabel Crichton, and a grandson of Hugh Grosvenor, 1st Duke of Westminster. He was commissioned into the 9th Lancers from Sandhurst in 1926 and commanded his regiment in the Second World War as a lieutenant-colonel. He married Sally Perry on 11 April 1945. He inherited the dukedom on the death of his cousin the 3rd Duke in 1963. He died in 1967, aged sixty, and his titles passed to his brother Robert Grosvenor.

Daniel Stewart Thomas Bingham Dixon, 4th Baronet and 2nd Baron Glentoran (1912-1995)

Another frequent guest was Daniel Stewart Thomas Bingham Dixon, who was the last of that family to have been heavily involved in politics. When Belfast became a city with a Lord Mayor instead of a Mayor, the first to hold that office, in 1893, was his grandfather Daniel Dixon. Starting as a builders merchant, he imported timber, acquired his own shipping line and, in the days when the city was expanding explosively, both in the inner wards and the suburbs, built himself the considerable Dixon fortune. He was responsible for the creation, in 1906, of Belfast's magnificent City Hall.

Daniel Dixon was elder son of Herbert Dixon, 1st Baron Glentoran. After Eton and Sandhurst, he served with the Grenadier Guards in France, North Africa, Sicily, Italy and, after the Second World War, in Palestine. He was mentioned in despatches, and finished with the rank of lieutenant-colonel. From 1953 until 1961, he was Minister of Commerce, where he took charge of the new industries drive with a large degree of success. Glentoran was considered to be unassuming and courteous, never aggressive or abrasive, and he had the easiest of relationships with political opponents. In 1933, he married Lady Diana Wellesley, a descendant of the Duke of Wellington, who predeceased him in 1984. They had two sons and a daughter.

The Hon. Richard Blackett Beaumont (1926-2010)

Another notable Gun from beyond the local shores was the Hon. Richard Blackett Beaumont. Beaumont owned the London gun and rifle maker James Purdey & Sons from 1949 until 1994, and was its chairman from 1971. He was the second son of the 2nd Viscount Allendale and his childhood was spent between family's Northumberland Estate and their home in Mayfair. Beaumont left Eton in 1943, aged seventeen, to join the Royal Naval Volunteer Reserve. He finished his service in Hong Kong in 1947 with the rank of sub-lieutenant. He returned home via India, where he spent a year as personal assistant to Sir Walter Monckton. Back in London in 1948, he took a job as a shipping clerk in Billingsgate. In 1949, he was telephoned by his father, Lord Allendale, who said, 'Uncle Hughie [his mother's brother Sir Hugh Seely] has given you Purdey.'

'What's Purdey?' was his response.

'It's a well-known gun shop,' his father replied. 'Uncle Hughie thought it might be rather fun, but you don't have to go into it if you don't want to.'

Soon after this exchange, Beaumont met Tom Purdey, the managing director, who had sold the company to Sir Hugh and his brother Sir Victor Seely in 1946. In his book *Purdey's: The Guns and the Family* (1984), Beaumont described his first visit to the Long Room:

> Tom was charming. He told me about the firm, the families who made the guns, and his own family, and introduced me to Harry Lawrence, the factory manager. It all sounded so wonderful I decided that this was what I wanted to do, which is how I came to be associated with the great firm of James Purdey & Sons and entered a career so entirely different from that which I had planned.

Before doing so, however, Beaumont served for two years, until 1955, as *aide-de-camp* to the last British High Commissioner of Malaysia, Sir Donald MacGillivray. He then joined the company, taking over from Tom Purdey in 1956, with Sir Hugh Seely (Lord Sherwood) as chairman.

Over the next forty years, Beaumont demonstrated an astute business brain and a fierce determination to maintain traditional gun-making skills. These kept Purdey afloat throughout the difficult business climate of the 1970s, coping with high inflation, the loss of skilled craftsmen, unacceptably long delivery times and having to persuade customers to pay prices far higher than those quoted when they had placed their orders. Any of these problems could have brought the firm down, but it was saved by Beaumont's tenacity and the loyalty and affection in which he was held by his craftsmen and staff.

For twenty-three years he was ably supported by his wife Lavinia, whom he married in 1971. She managed the clothing and accessories side of Purdey, transforming it from a sideline to a significantly successful part of the business. Beaumont retired after a heart attack, having sold Purdey to the Geneva-based luxury goods group Richemont. His family connection with Purdey continues through his cousin Nigel Beaumont, the company's chairman, whom he had brought in as a trainee gun maker in 1977.[203]

Today the shooting tradition at Colebrooke Park continues in the hands of Alan Henry Brooke, 3rd Viscount Brookeborough, Baronet (b. 30 June 1952), a Northern Irish peer and landowner. It remains focused on Woodcock and Snipe and is open to shooting parties. He was educated at Harrow School, Millfield, and the Royal Agricultural College, Cirencester. He joined the British Army in 1971, being commissioned into the 17th/21st Lancers. In 1977, he transferred to the Ulster Defence Regiment, which was to become the Royal Irish Regiment in 1992. He was promoted to lieutenant-colonel in 1993 and became Honorary Colonel of the 4th/5th Battalion, Royal Irish Rangers, in 1997.

Lord Brookeborough married Janet Elizabeth Cooke (daughter of J.P. Cooke of Doagh), now Viscountess Brookeborough, in 1980, and he has been a Lord-in-Waiting to the Queen since 1997. He is President of the County Fermanagh Unionist Association, was appointed as an independent member of the Northern Ireland Policing Board in 2001, and is one of ninety-two hereditary peers to remain in the House of Lords for life.

5

THE WEST AND SOUTH-WEST

CASTLEGAR, AHASCRAGH, COUNTY GALWAY

Ahascragh had two Anglo-Irish seats of residence, located at Castlegar and Clonbrock, with respective period houses.

Castlegar was the home of the Mahon family, who were eminently respect-

71 Returning to Clonbrock House after a morning's Grouse shooting.

able members of the nineteenth-century elite and were related to the Mahons (subsequently Pakenham-Mahons) of Strokestown, County Roscommon. One member of the family, John Ross Mahon, land agent, was a founding partner of the banking firm Guinness & Mahon. Their successive generations survived through prudent estate management, successive marriage alliances with leading members of the established elite, the attainment of patronage from powerful

noble families, and 'an uncharacteristic hard-headed detachment from the intrigues, excesses and idiosyncrasies attributable to so many of their peers in County Galway … The Mahons were, foremost of all, survivors, and were able to successfully adapt at crucial historical junctures when others of their class were disposed, marginalised or bankrupted.'[204]

They inter-married on a number of occasions with members of the Browne family of Westport and with the Dillons of Clonbrock. In the 1870s, the Castlegar Estate amounted to over 8,000 acres in County Galway, as well as over 800 acres in the parish of Termonbarry, Barony of Ballintober North, County Roscommon, which provided very good Grouse shooting. In 1906, Sir William Mahon held over 1,200 acres of untenanted land in the Ahascragh area.

There were two Big Houses on the Castlegar Estate: Castlegar House, the principal seat of the Mahon family, and Weston House. Like a number of other prominent Galway families, the Mahons planted a large demesne at the centre of their estate, with both native and foreign woodlands, which provided the base for much of the shooting. The extended family lived at Weston House, including unmarried brothers and sisters, with Sir Mahon and his family living a short distance away at Castlegar, and game records were kept for both. Most of the estate was sold to the Land Commission in 1977[205] and in 1979 the house was sold by the Mahons to John Horan, who advertised the house for sale again in 1988. There is still a house at this site.

In the early part of the nineteenth century, there was considerable agrarian and Ribbon disturbances in the Ahascragh district, and in east Galway generally. Sir Ross Mahon was absent from Castlegar from the early 1820s until his death in 1835, during which time he lived in Booterstown, County Dublin. The Mahon title then passed to the second Sir Ross Mahon (1811-1842), and then to Sir James FitzGerald Ross Mahon (1812-1852), both of whom died without issue. Sir William Vesey Ross Mahon (1813-1893), son of the first Sir Mahon, succeeded to the title in 1852, whilst he was rector at Rawmarsh church, near Rotherham, Yorkshire. Sir William remained at Rawmarsh, ministering to his parishioners, and the estate remained in the hands of a succession of land agents.

By now, the extended family had married into a broad network of similar families with strong connections to the Church of Ireland elite: in 1857 Thomas Adair Hunt, son of the Bishop of Elphin, married Caroline Mahon, younger sister of the 4th Baronet; the Revd William John Purdon, Rector of Carlow, married another sister.

During this period, there was renewed trouble on the estate, with a bomb exploding in Weston House at the height of the Land War in 1882. Three years previously, in October 1879, William Mahon, who acted as gamekeeper on the estate, was murdered and his body found in the River Suck.

Following the death of his father, Sir William Henry Mahon (1856-1926) returned to live at Castlegar in 1902, following his service in the second Boer War as lieutenant-colonel, 4th West Yorkshire Rifles. A resolute Conservative and active Unionist, Sir W.H. Mahon took an active part in the anti-Home Rule cause in County Galway, as well as organising the Galway Pro-War Fund Association in 1914.

The family's status amongst the Conservative, Protestant landowning elite in the west of Ireland was confirmed when he later married Lady Edith Augusta Dillon, his near neighbour and daughter of Lord Clonbrock in 1905. He died on 13 August 1926 and his wife outlived him by several decades, passing away at Castlegar on 24 April 1964.

The shooting record below is mainly that of Sir William, relating to the period 1886-1920. In the early years of this record, the pattern of shooting over the season commenced with Grouse in August on the Roscommon bogs and bogs around east Galway. Six to twelve days' shooting by three or so Guns yielded 86 to 140 Grouse per season. September and October saw Partridge shooting take place around Ahascragh. The Partridge shooting appears more consistent than on many estates for which records have been examined. Partridge bags of up to 117 were recorded, although more typically they averaged between 60 and 70. These were shot in the course of a dozen or so mixed-Pheasant days. From late November, in most years, the Pheasant-covert shooting also yielded bags of Woodcock of fifty to sixty birds.

The Guns in question, aside from Sir William, included: Frederick Adair, presumed to be a cousin and son of his aunt, Caroline, who was married to Thomas Adair Hunt, son of the Bishop of Elphin; members of the family of Edward Crofton, 2nd Baron Crofton of Mote Park; sons of Robert Dillon, 3rd Baron Clonbrock, and, later, sons of Gerald Luke Dillon, 4th Baron. It was not unusual for Sir William to spend several days shooting alone, or in the company of gamekeeper Christopher Bracken, a member of that well-known family of gamekeepers. Thus, in 1886, he is to be found alone shooting on 4 November (two Pheasants, eleven Snipe and a hare), 6 November (one Pheasant, six Snipe and a hare), 11 November (two Pheasants, two Partridges, three Woodcock, ten Snipe and a hare), 12 November (thirteen Snipe), 13 November (five Snipe), and 15 November (four Pheasants, one Grouse and five Snipe).

This was followed by three days of more formal shooting, from 16 to 18 November, at Weston Coverts (218 Pheasants, 1 Partridge, 5 Woodcock), Castlegar Coverts (90 Pheasants, 1 Partridge, 3 Snipe and 11 Woodcock), and Wellpark Bog and Weston Coverts (64 Pheasants, 5 Snipe, 3 Grouse and 14 Woodcock). The party included Sir William Henry's brothers, the Hon. Edward (1862-1937) and the Hon. John FitGerald (1858-1942), who married Lady Alice Evelyn Browne, daughter of the 5th Marquess of Sligo in 1898, thereby continuing an association between the Mahons and the Browne family that went back to 1786, when Sir Ross Mahon (1763-1835) married Lady Elizabeth Browne, daughter of Peter Browne, 2nd Earl Altamont. He inherited the Guinness Mahon fortune, which was eventually passed on to his only child, Sir Denis Mahon (1910-2011), the renowned art historian and collector who specialised in Italian art.

Next there was 'The Hon. Mr Dillon', which doesn't allow a precise identification, but the likelihood is that it was Luke Gerald Dillon (1834-1917), who would succeed his father Sir Robert on his death in 1893 as 4th Baron Clonbrock. He had a closer association with Castlegar than his younger brother (Robert Villiers) and in subsequent years his name appears frequently in William Henry Mahon's Game Books, both shooting at Castlegar and hosting the Mahons at Clonbrock shoots. His daughter the Hon. Edith Augusta was to become Sir William Henry's wife in 1905. He was deeply attached to Clonbrock. In the 1870s the Clonbrock Estate in County Galway amounted to over 28,000 acres. Lands, house and the demesne at Cahir, Barony of Clonmacnowen, owned by James Dillon, were offered for sale in the Encumbered Estates Court in July 1854. In 1906, Lord Clonbrock held over 2,000 acres of untenanted land and the mansion house at Clonbrock. Furthermore, as noted by Terence Dooley:

> Unlike most of his fellow landlords, who as a result of sweeping socio-economic and political changes from the early 1880s had come to accept that the sale of their estates was inevitable, the 3rd and 4th Barons refused to sell any part of their property under the early Land Acts. Indeed, Luke Dillon, 4th Baron, was reluctant to sell under the terms of the 1903 Land Act, despite the generous incentive that it offered in the form of a 12 per cent cash bonus to vendors. It was, however, this very reluctance to sell that eventually strained the relationship the 4th Baron had with his tenants. If he had been reluctant to sell under the 1903 Land Act, they had been just as reluc-

tant to purchase during the 1880s and 1890s simply because the early Land Acts had provided few incentives for them to do so. However, when the 1903 Land Act guaranteed that purchase annuities repayable to the government would be less than annual rents payable to the landlord, his tenants called upon Lord Clonbrock to sell. When he refused, the United Irish League began a concerted campaign of agitation on the estate. From 1903 to 1907, the estate was subjected to extreme agitation. Demands for rent reductions were accompanied by frequent cattle drives as smallholders and the landless demanded the breakup of large grazing farms on the estate. By 1907, rental income on the estate had fallen by around 15 per cent as a result of strikes and fair rent fixing, while arrears had risen at an unprecedented rate from £4,362 in 1902 (twice the level they had been even in 1882) to £6,370 in 1907. With expenditure remaining consistent, the estate was now running at a loss. In 1907, Lord Clonbrock, once hailed as the most benevolent landlord in the west by one particular newspaper editor, was now being castigated by the same editor as 'a fossilised bigot' for refusing to sell his lands. By 1909, Lord Clonbrock had no alternative but to sell. By 1914, he had sold the majority of his tenanted lands for which he received £250,000, in today's terms roughly £15 million. As he was largely unencumbered he was able to invest the bulk of this capital. He invested globally in stocks and shares from Argentina to Australia, from Canada to South Africa and from Britain to Russia. Until around 1917, life at Clonbrock continued in relative splendour. Possibly, the family were better off than they had been for generations, having shed the myriad of estate expenses that had been part and parcel of the annual running of an estate. Then in 1917, the 4th Baron, Luke Dillon, died and was succeeded by his only son, Robert (who was to die prematurely and unmarried in 1925 when the title became extinct).[206]

Another of the party is entered as 'The Hon. Mr Crofton'. Again, precise identification is not possible with certainty but the most likely person would seem to be Charles St George Crofton (1836-1895), second son of Edward Crofton, 2nd Baron Crofton of Mote, and Lady Georgina Paget, and a brother

72 Shooting party hosted by Dillons of Clonbrock.

of the wife of Luke Gerald Dillon, the Hon. Augusta Caroline Crofton. His older brother, Edward Henry Churchill, had become 3rd Baron Crofton some years earlier in 1869, one of his younger brothers, the Hon. Alfred Henry had died in 1881, and his youngest brother, Captain, the Hon. Francis George (1838-1900), was referred to as such when he did make appearances at Castlegar.

Charles St George married Theresa Augusta Bunbury-Tighe, daughter of Daniel Bunbury-Tighe and the Hon. Frances Crofton, in 1864. They continued a long association with the Mahon family; in 1929, their grandson Arthur Marcus Lother Crofton (1898-1962) married the Hon. Ursula Augusta Jane Mahon (b. 1906), eldest child of Sir William Henry Mahon and Edith Augusta Dillon.[207]

Henry Sandford Pakenham-Mahon (1823-1893)

Henry Sandford Pakenham-Mahon was another Gun present at this shoot. He was a son of the Very Revd the Hon. Henry Pakenham (1787-1863), Dean of St Patrick's Cathedral, Dublin, and Eliza Catherine Sandford, and he was married to Grace Catherine Mahon (d. 1913), only daughter of Maj. Denis Mahon of Strokestown Park.

Major Denis Mahon inherited Strokestown on the death of his cousin Maurice Mahon, 3rd Baron Hartland, who was declared insane and died without issue in 1845. The estate had been mismanaged for years. Denis appointed another cousin, John Ross Mahon, a land agent and founding partner of the merchant bank Guinness Mahon, as his agent. However, the estate became notorious during the years of the Famine, and Maj. Denis was assassinated by several local men, including Ciaran Feeney, in an incident that became infamous across Ireland and England at the time. The killing was motivated by the removal of starving tenant farmers from the estate lands. The killing of Denis Mahon did not halt the evictions, and in all over 11,000 tenants were removed from the Mahon Estate during that period, a story told by Peter Duffy in *The Killing of Major Denis Mahon: A Mystery of Old Ireland* (2007).

Henry's wife, Grace, never returned to Strokestown after her father's murder. However, her son Henry Pakenham-Mahon (d. 1922), who married a great beauty, the only daughter of Col. Sidney Burrard, did, and he spent about half the year there.[208] Their daughter Olive inherited her mother's good looks but she too was to experience tragedy and heartbreak at Strokestown.

Thomas George Wills-Sandford (1815-1887)

Another related Gun on this shoot was 'Wills-Sandford'. It is presumed this was Thomas George Wills-Sandford, who in the 1870s was recorded as the owner of 24,410 acres in County Roscommon and a further 949 acres in County Dublin.[209]

Edward Willoughby Fowler (1831-1900)

Yet another noteworthy member of the party was Edward Willoughby Fowler. He was the son of Revd Luke Fowler and Elizabeth Wynne, and theirs was a distinguished Anglo-Irish family which was to become well known on the cricket field, not so much for Edward's somewhat unspectacular deeds, but for those of his second cousin Bob Fowler, the hero of 'Fowler's Match' – the Eton v. Harrow game of 1910. Edward's club cricket was for Leinster. Having had several homes in their formative years, the Rathmines men were at Emor Ville, opposite Portobello Gardens on the South Circular Road, when Edward first appeared for them. Observatory Lane was acquired in 1865. His only appearance for Ireland was the MCC match of 1862, Ireland's second visit to Lord's and their second win.

Later, Edward became a land agent and a JP in County Galway. He was, for example, the agent on the Clancarty Estate. (Clancarty was the landlord of Ballinasloe.) He appears to have been a very active and regarded agent.

He married Kate Mary Barrett Jones, daughter of Michael Obins Seely Jones, in 1871. He lived at Cleaghmore, Ballinasloe County Galway, and died on 17 January 1900, aged sixty-eight.

Finally, two Brownes completed the party. These were 'Captain Browne' and 'G. Browne'. It is considered that both were sons of Henry Ulick Browne (1831-1913), 5th Marquess of Sligo, and his wife Catherine Henrietta Dicken. The former was either Capt. Herbert Richard Browne (1858-1890), who was unmarried and treacherously killed by Lushais, or Capt. Alfred Eden Browne (1878-1918), killed in action. The latter was George Ulick Browne (1856-1935), 6th Marquess of Sligo, who married Agatha Stewart Hodgson in 1887. He gained the title of 6th Marquess of Sligo. The son of Henry Ulick Browne, 5th Marquess of Sligo, and Catherine Henrietta Dicken, he succeeded to the title of 4th Earl of Clanricarde, County Galway, on 12 April 1916.

A summary of the bag returns from Castlegar for the period 1886-1892 is shown below:

	Pheasants	Partridges	Grouse	Woodcock	Snipe
1886	605	44	94	59	246
1887	493	19	148	65	91
1888	519	32	120	37	23
1889	239	101	129	31	111
1890/91	681	33	117	60	45
1891/92	568	19	64	33	79
1892	493	10	34	25	49

Five years later, in 1891/92, the pattern of shooting remains similar. Sir William spent fifteen days between 11 August 1891 and 15 October, and it appears that he was shooting alone. He accounted for sixty-four Grouse, eleven Partridges, twenty-five Snipe and twenty-three Pheasants (the Pheasants in five days in October). Then on 8 and 9 December, there was a 'First Shoot of the Weston Coverts', which resulted in an overall bag of 328 Pheasants and 12 Woodcock. This was followed by a 'Second Shooting of Weston' on 19, 20 and 23 January 1892. On that occasion the bag was modest enough: 185 Pheasants and 15 Woodcock.

The party comprised some of the same names mentioned earlier and also some new ones. 'G.R.W.S.' is presumed to be G.R. Wills Sandford, who resided at Castlereagh House in 1894, the principal residence of the Sandford Estate.[210] Edward Willoughby Fowler was there for all of the days, as was the Hon. Luke Gerald Dillon, whose brother Col. Robert Villiers Dillon was also present on for a few days.

Another prominent shoot participant was Frederick Oliver Trench, 3rd Baron Ashtown (1868-1946), a County Galway landlord who had many dealings with both the Mahon and Dillon families. He was the eldest son of Frederick Sydney Charles Trench (heir apparent to the 2nd Lord Ashtown) and Anne Le Poer Trench (eldest daughter of the 3rd Earl of Clancarty of Garbally). At the age of twelve, he became the 3rd Baron Ashtown, inheriting a vast estate and reputedly over £1 million.

The family was responsible for laying out the town of Ballinasloe and their principal seat was at Woodlawn, about twelve miles from Ballinasloe, County Galway. In 1894, he married Violet Grace Cosby, the youngest daughter of Col. Robert Ashworth Godolphin Cosby of Stradbally Hall, Queen's County. Ashtown was a hard-line Unionist; from 1906 to 1910 he edited a monthly publication, *Grievances from Ireland*, which denounced all political expressions of Irish nationalism as treasonable, and *The New York Times* of 14 August 1907 reported on an attempt to bomb him, as follows:

73 **Beaters at Castlegar.**

Clonmel, Ireland, August 14 – Lord Ashtown, one of the landlords whose activity in the cattle-grazing war has aroused the most bitter animosity, narrowly escaped death this morning from the explosion of a bomb, which partly destroyed the hunting lodge in which he was sleeping.

Lord Ashtown has large estates in the west of Ireland, where the grazing troubles have occurred. He arrived at his lodge at Glenahiry, in the country near here, last Monday, coming direct from his western estates. He was awakened at 2 o'clock this morning by a crashing explosion. He rushed from his bedroom into the hall just in time to escape a falling mass of timber and glass. Meeting a gamekeeper, he exclaimed: 'They missed me this time!' The exterior on one side off the house was shattered by the force of the explosion and part of the interior is a heap of debris.

The attempt upon the life of Lord Ashtown was most determined. In addition to the bomb, which Lord Ashtown describes as consisting of about seven pounds of blasting powder placed in an iron pot with three fuses, all of which were fired, there were found the remains of a number of quart bottles, smelling of petroleum, which had been thrown into the drawing room after the explosion, and had set the carpet and curtains on fire. Had it not been for the prompt action of Lord Ashtown and the members of his household the hunting lodge must certainly have been burned to the ground.

Lord Ashtown believes that the explosion was the work of peasants from the west of Ireland. He has been under police protection for some time on account of threats against his life, but the perpetrators of the attempt of this morning took advantage of the absence of the constabulary usually guarding the premises, who had been sent to Belfast.

There has been considerable feeling against Lord Ashtown arising from a remark he made in the course of a speech on the cattle-grazing war. This remark was: 'I would rather have bullocks on my estate than Catholic labourers.'

Justice of the Peace Kelly was recently tried at the Galway Assizes on the charge of inciting to the murder of Lord Ashtown. He was accused of saying in a political speech that if Lord Ashtown's acts had occurred in his town he would have been carried home on a stretcher. Kelly was acquitted.

Ambrose Congreve (1832-1901)

It is presumed that the 'Congreve' referred to at this shoot is Ambrose Congreve. The Congreves were inter-related with the Dillons over several generations. Ambrose was the son of John Congreve (1801-1863) and the Hon. Louisa Harriet Dillon, daughter of Luke Dillon, 2nd Baron Clonbrock. He married his cousin the Hon. Alice Elizabeth Dillon, daughter of Robert Dillon, 3rd Baron Clonbrock, and sister of Luke Gerald, 4th Baron Clonbrock. However, it is also possible that the reference is to a son of Ambrose and Alice, of which there were three: John (b. 1872), Ambrose (b. 1875) and Leopold (b. 1877). Jack [John] Congreve is recorded shooting the Weston Coverts in January 1894. The Congreve seat is Mount Congreve, near Kilmeadon, County Waterford.

Howard St George

Howard St George (and H.B. St George, presumably the same person) is referred to at this shoot and indeed many others in subsequent years, but precise identification of the person is difficult. According to one source:

> Richard St George was a member of a Cambridgeshire family which came to Ireland in the seventeenth century and was appointed Governor of the town of Athlone. His grandson Richard St George of Carrick-on-Shannon, County Leitrim, had two natural children, Richard St George, founder of the Hatley Manor, County Leitrim branch of the family, and Mary St George, who married James Mansergh and they were the parents of Colonel Richard Mansergh St George (c. 1750-1798) of Headford, County Galway.[211]

It seems likely that the man referred to is from the Headford Castle branch of the family but there can be no certainty on this point. Mansergh St George was an active, local magistrate who was appalled by the poverty that he found on his estates in County Cork and County Galway. His response to this was an *Account of the State of Affairs in and About Headford, County Galway*, which laments the condition of the Irish peasantry, and whilst considering establishing a linen industry to improve matters, he doubts the willingness or the ability of his tenants to make the enterprise work. Mansergh St George's wife had died in 1791, leaving her husband a widower with two infant children. During the Rebellion of 1798 he was murdered along with his servant with a rusty scythe by a party of marauders from North Cork and South Tipperary.

Frank Shawe-Taylor (1869-1920)

The final Guns making up this shooting party were the Shawe-Taylors. Frank Shawe-Taylor was a land agent who was murdered as result of a land dispute in County Galway during the War of Independence, which led to a series of further deaths and tragedies. Shawe-Taylor was a member of the Taylor family of Castle Taylor, Ardrahan. He was related to Lady Gregory and was married with a family, living at Moorpark House, Coshla, Athenry. Frank had served as High Sheriff of County Galway in 1915. While he was a land agent to a local landlord, he was himself a tenant. Early in January 1920, a group of local men approached Shawe-Taylor on behalf of people who were requesting a road to travel to Mass. While Shawe-Taylor himself was amenable to their demands, his landlord refused them outright and made this known via Shawe-Taylor. On

3 March 1920, Shawe-Taylor and his driver, Barrett, were making their way to Galway to attend the fair. At 6 a.m., the coach reached Egan's Pub, Coshla, where they found the road blocked. The donkey cart of a local, Johnny Kelly, had been stolen and placed across the road.

From behind the wall, at least two shooters fired at Barrett and Shawe-Taylor, wounding the former and killing the latter. This resulted in a huge security presence in the area, which in turn led to more unrest. This increased with the arrival of the Black and Tans. Moorpark House was placed under Royal Irish Constabulary protection out of fear of further killings. Others who subsequently died as a result of the unrest in Galway included: Ellen Quinn (1 November 1920), a pregnant mother of six and a tenant of Lady Gregory; Fr Michael Griffin (14 November 1920); Tom Egan and Patrick and Harry Loughnane (brothers). In addition, there were numerous incidents of violence, many of which were recorded with horror in the journal of Lady Gregory, who remarked that 'the country has gone wild since the killing of Frank Shawe-Taylor'. His sons were the music critic Desmond Shawe-Taylor (1907-1995) and British racing driver Brian Shawe-Taylor (1915-1999), and his grandson Desmond Shawe-Taylor has been Surveyor of the Queen's Pictures since 2005.

Moving forward another five years to 1896/97, there is continuity and change in the Guns assembled for shooting at Castlegar and Weston. Luke Gerald was present, as was his son the Hon. Robert Edward Dillon (1869-1926), who became the 5th (and final) Baron Clonbrock on his father's death.

Other participants were brothers Bernard Arthur William Patrick Hastings Forbes, 8th Earl of Granard (1874-1948), and Capt. the Hon. Reginald George Forbes (1877-1908), who were sons of George Arthur Hastings Forbes, 7th Earl of Granard, and his second wife, the Hon. Frances Mary Petre (1846-1920).

Their brother-in-law Sir Henry Christopher Grattan-Bellew, 3rd Baronet (1860-1942), was there also. He was married to their half-sister Lady Sophia Maria Elizabeth Forbes, daughter of the 7th Earl by his first wife, Jane Colclough Morgan (d. 1872) (see Illustration 106, p. 264). The son of Thomas Arthur Grattan-Bellew and Pauline Grattan, he succeeded to the title of 3rd Baronet Bellew of Mount Bellew, County Galway, in 1867. He gained the rank of lieutenant in the service of the 5th Dragoon Guards and he held the office of High Sheriff of County Galway in 1884. He achieved the rank of lieutenant-colonel in the service of the 4th Battalion Connaught Rangers, and held the office of Deputy Lieutenant of County Galway in 1922.

He lived at Mount Bellew, County Galway. A branch of the Bellew family of Williamstown, County Louth, in the 1870s the Bellews owned over 10,000 acres in County Galway and almost 1,895 acres in County Roscommon. The Bellews retained this acreage until the early twentieth century. By March 1916, the Bellews had accepted an offer from the Congested Districts Board for over 1,000 acres of their estate. The estate was taken over by the Land Commission in 1937.[212]

It may be through the Bellew connection that Lord Grey de Ruthyn became a guest at this shoot. Bellew's Grove, County Galway, was his seat in Ireland. However, he appears at other Castlegar shoots from 1894. The person involved was either Rawdon George Grey Clifden (1858-1912), 23rd Baron Grey de Ruthyn, or Cecil Talbot Clifden (1862-1934), the 24th Baron.

As to the shoots themselves, on 17 November 1896, Castlegar produced two hundred and fifty Pheasants and sixteen Woodcock. The next day, Weston accounted for two hundred and thirty-nine Pheasants and three Woodcock, with the comment 'many birds missed both days', and the following day, in the Well Park Covers, there were five Pheasants, seven Woodcock and two Grouse (on 19 November!). Then, on 20 December, Castlegar produced one hundred and two Pheasants and twelve Woodcock, while Weston, the next day, yielded sixty-seven Pheasants and four Woodcock. A summary of the bags for the seasons 1893/4-1903/4 is shown below:

	Pheasants	Partridges	Grouse	Woodcock	Snipe
1893/94	79	–	16	10	4
1894/95	124	5	58	66	35
1895/96	96	21	84	18	27
1896/97	801	51	141	49	30
1897/98	871	71	82	40	83
1898/99	1,322	76	157	55	129
1899/00	1,207	57	161	43	109
1900/01	791	76	130	26	111
1901/02	1,472	61	148	57	195
1902/03	1,418	117	160	68	166
1903/04	1,230	90	174	49	249

It is noticeable that from 1896/67, the Pheasant bag increased on average by a factor of at least two. There is not any specific remark as regards the bag in the Game Books, and the shooting effort remained the same in terms of number of days shooting and number of Guns. Clearly, more birds were put down and it is also noticeable that the bag of wild game was also greater. A change of keepers and keepering policies may well be the explanation.

For whatever reason, the shooting was very good around the turn of the century and continued to be enjoyed by much the same 'set' as in previous years. For example, in November 1902, shooting at Castlegar on both 25 and 26 November, the bag comprised 383 Pheasants and 9 Woodcock on the first day and 350 Pheasants and 12 Woodcock the next day.

The party was much the same as in earlier years, with Sir William Henry Mahon hosting his neighbour Lord Clonbrock, his son the Hon. Robert Edward Dillon, Capt. Crofton (considered to be Capt. the Hon. Francis George Crofton (1838-1910), brother of Edward, 3rd Baron Crofton), Ernest Browne, of the Sligo family, Lord Ashtown and Lord Clancarty.

The last of these is William Frederick Le Poer Trench, 5th Earl of Clancarty (1868-1929). He was born at Fort Eyre, County Galway. He first married Maude Penrice Bilton, daughter of John George Bilton, in 1889, and later Mary Gwatkin Ellis, daughter of William F. Ross-Lewin Ellis, in 1908.

He was the son of Richard Somerset Le Poer Trench, 4th Earl of Clancarty, and Lady Adeliza Georgiana Hervey. Styled as Viscount Dunlo between 1872 and 1891, he was educated between 1883 and 1887 at Eton and succeeded to the title of 5th Earl of Clancarty, County Cork, in 1891. In 1907, he was bankrupted in Ireland and in 1910 he was bankrupted in England.

For the next ten years, the pattern continued as before, though during the years of the First World War the number of Guns shooting diminished, as did the bags. Lord Clonbrock, who died in 1917, was shooting until 1915, by which time he was over eighty years of age. Sir William Henry continued each season, following the pattern of a lifetime, out many days alone or in the company of a keeper, right up to 1920, by which time he was seventy-six years old.

There are no further shooting records after this date and there was no record of either of William Henry's surviving sons – George Edward (1911-1987), who succeeded him as 6th Baronet, or Luke Bryan Arthur (b. 1917) – participating at shoots during his lifetime. The shooting tradition which William Henry inspired and chased may simply have died with him.

Lough Cutra Castle, Gort, County Galway

Lough Cutra Castle and Estate has a long and varied history. It is presently the home of Susan Gwynn Jones, whose family acquired the property in 1972. The current Pheasant and duck shooting that takes place there was established by Dromoland Game Sports in 2001, which runs a very successful shoot at the Dromoland Castle Estate. On an average day the bag includes Pheasant, Woodcock, duck, Partridge and Snipe.

Many of the woodlands at Lough Cutra were planted in the late 1700s and 1800s, specifically with the sport of shooting in mind. At the end of the nineteenth century, Lough Cutra was famous throughout Ireland for the quality and number of Woodcock presented. However, it has had a stormy history, and for much of the twentieth century it lay idle.

The early history of Lough Cutra is documented thoroughly by Robert Sangster Rait in his book *The Story of an Irish Property* (1908). For his role in the preservation of William of Orange on the throne of England, the Gort lands – which comprised nearly 13,000 acres, including the town of Gort and 2,000 acres around Lough Cutra and the lake itself, comprising 1,000 acres – were seized and presented to Sir Thomas Prendergast, who came to Ireland on King Williams's death in 1701 and lived in Monaghan. There was confusion regarding the titles of the land, and the issue was in the process of being resolved when, in 1709, Sir Thomas was killed during the Spanish Wars. His widow, Lady Penelope, let the lands around the lake and the islands. On these islands, large numbers of apple, pear and cherry trees were planted, and some still survive today. The O'Shaughnessys, the previous landowners, still tried to lay claim to the lands that had been taken from them by King William. In 1742, the government confirmed the Prendergast title, but

74 **Lough Cutra Castle, County Galway.**

it was not until 1753 that Roebuck O'Shaughnessy accepted a sum of money in return for giving up the claim.

Following Sir Thomas's death, John Prendergast Smyth inherited the Gort Estate. It was John who created the roads and planted trees, particularly around the Punchbowl, where the Gort River disappears on its way to Gort and Coole. When John died in 1797, he was succeeded by his nephew, Col. Charles Vereker, who in 1816 became Viscount Gort. The estate at this time was around 12,000 acres. Vereker decided to employ the renowned architect John Nash to design the Gothic-style building known as Lough Cutra Castle. Colonel Vereker had visited Nash's East Cowes Castle on the Isle of Wight and was so taken with it that he commissioned the construction of a similar building on his lands on the shore of Lough Cutra. The Viscount Gort was forced to sell the castle and estate through the Encumbered Estates Court in 1852, having been bankrupted as a result of famine relief efforts.

The estate was purchased by Gen. Sir Hugh Gough, 1st Viscount Gough (1779-1869), in 1854 and his family was to retain ownership (although not occupancy) for the next hundred years or so. The Goughs set about refurbishing the castle to their own taste and undertook further construction work, adding large extensions to the original building, including a clock tower and servant quarters. Great attention was paid to the planting of trees, the location of the deer park, and creation of new avenues. An American garden was created to the south-west of the castle and the entire building operations were completed between 1858 and 1859. However, once the building operations at the castle were completed, Lord and Lady Gough decided they were too old to undertake the task of managing the castle and estate, and retired to St Helen's in Booterstown, County Dublin, although they continued to visit Lough Cutra. The first reference to shooting relates to about this time, when it is noted in 1861 that Malachy Comyns was employed to look after Pheasants.[213]

Further development of the estate is attributed to George Stephens, 2nd Viscount Gough (1815-1895), who succeeded in 1869. A further extension, known as the Library Wing, was built by Gough's grandson Hugh, 3rd Viscount (1849-1919) – who was married to Lady Georgina Pakenham (1863-1943), elder daughter of the Earl of Longford – at the end of the nineteenth century to house the war spoils of Gen. Sir Hugh Gough.[214]

Shooting was the favourite pastime of the Goughs. Pheasants were reared on the estate, corn was fed to them, and they were later released into the woods. Four shooting parties were held every year: a rabbit shoot, a deer shoot and two days' Pheasant shooting. Deer were kept in the deer park which covered approximately 300 acres in area. The deer were fed during the winter and those who escaped to the adjoining woods were shot and sent by rail to Dublin butchers. The guests at the shooting parties were titled people as well as retired British army officers. During the 1920s the estate was constantly being trespassed and poached to the extent that the Free State army had to move in to protect the Gough family and the estate. Timber was constantly being cut and stolen and on one occasion the saw-mill was broken into and all the removable pieces of machinery taken. Cattle were driven onto the land at night and taken away in the mornings with the 'Free Staters' having to enforce the 'pounding' of the trespassing cattle. At one stage there were 100 Free State troops at Lough Cutra.[215]

The shooting record that is available for Lough Cutra is not in the form of a Game Book but unusually is laid out in a matrix (see illustration) and is described as an 'Analysis of Lough Cutra's shooting' – somewhat ahead of its time. However, a lot of information is packed into this

75 Deer jumping through the Gun line.

one table, which appears to comprise the complete shooting record from 1896 to 1903. The main points, to judge from this, is that at most, *two* (the quoted commentary above suggests four) shoots per season took place, each of three (consecutive) days' duration. These took place in December and January respectively, in common with practice on many shoots where Woodcock were a feature. With only one exception, there were seven Guns in each shooting party; in January 1897 there were six. The only piece of information not available is who precisely the Guns were.

The record speaks for itself. There were evidently a lot of Pheasants, especially in 'Home Coverts', but good bags were obtained also in 'Nut Scrubs' and to a lesser degree in Gorlecarnarnt Wood. However, it is clearly the case that Woodcock was the main strength and attraction of the shoot. On Gen. Gough's shoot in January 1902, 189 Woodcock were taken on one day by seven Guns. In addition, they shot 451 Pheasants and a lot of ground game. It is unclear who the Gen. Gough referred to here is. General Sir Hugh Gough died in 1869. The most likely candidates are his grandnephews Gen. Sir Charles Stanley Gough (1832-1912) or Gen. Sir Hugh Henry Gough (1833-1909), cousins of Hugh, 3rd Viscount Gough. This was the best shoot in the record, but in six of the eleven shoots recorded, the Woodcock bag exceeded 100 for the three days. The worst was forty-four in December 1899, when the shooting took place over 'three wet days'.

However, Lough Cutra, like many other estates was to become an unhappy place:

In November 1921 the Gough family, suffering under the strain of 'the Troubles' were forced to put the castle and grounds up for sale and auction the furniture and contents of the castle. The furniture was auctioned successfully but no buyer was found for the castle itself. During the Civil War the Free Staters left Lough Cutra and the Republicans then took possession of the castle. In July 1922, Robert Houston, the Goughs' gamekeeper told Lady Gregory that the Irregulars had gone to Lough Cutra, throwing down the wall along a part of the road and then went to the castle where the Free State army were stationed and fired about twenty shots at the windows of the castle, shattering them. Mr Robert Clarke, Lord Gough's steward, stated that there had been a raid on the castle in 1922 and stabling removed. Iron and other gates had been removed, trees cut down and removed. A clock tower and other articles at the castle had also been damaged. Stables at the castle had been burned and a rick of turf for the use of the household had received the same treatment. The fences were broken down and cattle and other stock trespassed on the lands. Two years later, in February, Hugh Viscount Gough received £1,000 in compensation at Gort Quarter Sessions for the damage done to the castle during the raid.[216]

Analysis of Lough Cutra Shootings.

	1st Day - Gortlecarnane Wood.							2nd Day Home Coverts							3rd Day Nut Scrubs.						
	No. of Guns	Woodcocks	Pheasants	Rabbits	Hares	Sundries	Observations	No. of Guns	Woodcocks	Pheasants	Rabbits	Hares	Sundries	Observations	No. of Guns	Woodcocks	Pheasants	Rabbits	Hares	Sundries	Observations
1896 end Dec	7	30	57	4	1	2		2nd Feb 7	3	410	6	0	1		4th Dec 7	16	124	531	0	1	Total in 3 days Pheasants — 594 Woodcock — 49 Rabbits — 541
1897 5th Jan	6	17	16	1	3	0		6th Jan 5	145	4	0	0			7th Jan 7	34	50	30	0	0	Total in 3 day Pheasants — 211 Woodcock — 56 Rabbits — 35
1897 Dec	7	34	47	2	1	2		7	8	312	4	0	0		7	40	28	481	0	1	Total in 3 days Pheasants — 387 Woodcock — 103 Rabbits — 487
1898. 7th Dec	7	47	56	3	1	3		1898 7	6	293	3	0	2		1898 Dec 7	30	46	506	0	1	Total in 3 day Pheasants — 395 Woodcock — 83 Rabbits — 512
1899 19—	7	16	33	569	0	0	Gortlecarnane and Pollagh	7	29	46	1	0	0	Home Cov Dec 21st 3 2nd day	7	5	348	2	0	0	Total in 3 day Pheasants 427 Woodcock — 44 Rabbit — 572
1900 Jan 29th Pollagh and Deer Park	7	17	79	160	0	0	Nut Scrubs Jan 30th	7	47	28	14	0	0	Home Coverts Jan 31st 3 days large mondays wood not shot	7	6	192	16	0	0	Total in 3 day Pheasants 299 Woodcock — 70 Rabbits 190
1900 Dec.																					
1901 Dec 18th Pollagh and Gortlecarnane	7	50	32	1	3	3		7	19	319	1	0	0		7	52	48	26	0		Total in 3 day Pheasants 399 Woodcock 124 Rabbit 26 Sundries 8
2nd Shooting 1902 Jan 14	7	32	11	0	2			7 Jan 4th	22	167	0	0	4		7 Jan 15th	28	56	11	0		Total in 3 day Pheasants 174 Woodcock 82 Sundries 19
1902 Dec	7	189	417	438		31		General Gought Shoot											Total Pheasant 417 Woodcock 189 Rabbit 438 Various 31
1903 Dec 18th	7	79	31	6	0			Dec 16th 7	15	301	3	0		Nut Scrubs Dec 17th 7	14	19	40			Total 3 days Pheasant 351 Woodcock 108 Rabbit 43 3 Deer
2nd Shooting 1904	7	34	11	3	2	2		Jan 27th 7 Guns	9	70	6		3		Jan 28th 7 Guns	18	8	26	3		Total in 3 days Pheasant 89 Woodcock 61 Rabbit 35 Various 8

76 Analysis of Lough Cutra shootings, 1896-1903.

By 1929, the Goughs had moved out of the castle and it was left unoccupied until Standish Robert Vereker, the 7th Viscount Gort, managed to regain possession in 1954.[217] However, restoration was not undertaken by the trustees until the tenure of his grand-niece in 1966. The family of the present owner bought the estate in 1972 and has pursued an on-going programme of redevelopment and restoration, which saw the re-establishment of a successful driven Pheasant and duck shoot from 2001.

EDEN VALE, ENNIS, COUNTY CLARE

Eden Vale is an ancestral home of the Stacpoole family of County Clare. William Stacpoole (1743-1796) moved from Annagh to Eden Vale in 1776 and this house continued to be the main Stacpoole residence until it was sold to the Clare Board of Health in the 1920s. William Stacpoole, MP (1840-1879), of Ballyalla, Ennis, is listed in 1870 as being the owner of 7,441 acres in that county, although it is unclear whether this includes Eden Vale.[218] The house was a tuberculosis sanatorium in the 1940s. Kohl, a German traveller staying at Eden Vale in the early 1840s, found that:

> Eden Vale is one of the prettiest country-seats in the county of Clare; and its proprietor is an influential Protestant landowner, from whom I received, and accepted with pleasure, an invitation to spend some days in his Eden. The British, including the Irish, understand better than any other people how to select a site for a country house, and how to encircle it with a little Eden: perhaps, therefore, this will be a sufficient inducement to my readers to accompany me thither, especially when I add that Eden Vale has attained some celebrity in Ireland for its charming situation. The house is situated upon the steep slope of a little glen, and is approached by a slight ascent from the Ennis road. In the bosom of the glen is a small oblong lake, in which its leafy shores are mirrored. I found my hospitable host in his garden, busied with his trees and flowers, and immediately set out with him to inspect his charming property.
>
> The glen at Eden Vale has two declivities or sides: the one is rugged, the other gently sloping to the lake. The former has been allowed to retain its original character, except that it is closely planted with the most beautiful forest trees, above which project steep cliffs, partly covered with the thickest ivy. Footpaths lead along the lake and over the rocks: and on a projecting cliff which juts out into the lake, is a little wooden hermitage. This wild part, as opposed to the garden, is called *par excellence* 'the Glen'. A portion of the Glen, which affords good pasture, is set apart for the deer; and on another the cattle graze. In a third is the rabbit-warren, which no English park is without. As on *terra firma* the deer mingle with the cows, even so on the waters of the lake, amid the graceful, slow, tame swans, swim wild ducks and other waterfowl, which have not yet been induced to breed in the neighbourhood of our dwellings nor even in our pleasure grounds.
>
> Such is the wild side of the valley. Opposite to it lies the cultivated side. First, the pretty dwelling-house, with its 'pleasure grounds', as the English term those which immediately surround the mansion, the beautifully kept grass plot, and the 'shrubberies', through which serpentine walks meander. Further on, the gardens, properly so called, are seen – fruit, vegetable and flower gardens – the latter displaying the most beautiful profusion of flowers on its several terraces, which run down close to the lake, while its many-coloured tints form a charming contrast with the simple green of the opposite side …
>
> The most remarkable thing I saw in this charming glen was an obscuration of the sun, towards evening, caused by an immense flock of rooks. Never, at any time of my life, have I seen

so many birds collected together. It seemed as if all the twenty thousand ruins of Ireland had at once assembled and sent forth their troops of feathered inmates. The air appeared to be literally filled with them up to the stars. The cawing of these myriads occasioned an uproar in the lately so quiet glen, beyond any I had ever heard, and their droppings rained down like a shower of hail. Their number was beyond computation. At first I thought, as I have said, of the many castles of the old chieftains and of the Danes … My friends at Eden Vale assured me that this phenomenon was quite common, and that the glen was one of their chief gathering places …

The English make of these birds the well-known rook-pies, which we do not envy them. The Irish do not eat them, and when the numerous flocks are seen, will deridingly say to the foreigner, 'The English soldiers here shoot them and make pies of them.' … In England, where servants are always kept in a proper distance, they seldom display that impertinent familiarity which is so often met with in Ireland, and of which the coachman of my friend, a well-fed, good-humoured-looking fellow, who attended us through the stables and farm buildings, was a striking instance. Although his master was present during the whole time, the servant never ceased talking, and he even preceded his master, who followed silently and modestly behind us. 'This stable *we* finished only last year,' said the coachman to me. 'It has given *us* a deal of trouble, for *we* had first to blow away the whole of that great rock. May it please your honour to remark how much *we* had to blast there. But we shall have a beautiful view when those trees there are felled. Look down there, your honour, all that are his dominions,' continued he, pointing to his master. 'In two months we will have finished the new building he has begun' … On my return to Eden Vale I visited some of the splendid mansions in its neighbourhood. They appeared to me no less spectral than that fairy-ground, for not a human being was to be found in them. The white window-blinds were drawn down, and all was still and silent as the grave. Their proprietors were 'absentees' in England, where they spend their Irish revenues. Such spectral deserted palaces are, alas!, like the fairy-grounds and ruins, but too often seen in Ireland. The wealthy Protestant proprietors have a hundred reasons for not finding themselves at home among their poor Roman Catholic tenants. The wild and uncultivated country, which is not so easily remedied – the barbarism of the people, who sometimes make attempts on the lives of their landlords – the greater attractions of English society – the unfortunate division of the Irish community into a number of hostile parties – and perhaps a certain feeling of shame and remorse for the injustice of the legalised tyranny which the rich Irish landlords exercise over the poor – all this may have driven many wealthy persons from the country, and produced the evil called 'absenteeism'. There are many families, also, who possess estates both in Ireland and England; and all these prefer residing in the latter. The more to be praised, therefore, are those landlords who remain at home, live on good terms with their tenantry, and, by ruling them in person, heal many of their wounds. There are many who make themselves, in a certain degree, voluntary martyrs; and as my hospitable host of Eden Vale was one of these, I returned to his house with stronger feelings of esteem for his character, and unwillingly took leave of him on the following day.[219]

From 1909 to 1925, there are records to show that it was a very fine Woodcock shoot. It was a shoot in earlier years too. 'The coverts were put in proper order in 1900. Before that year the bag was from twenty to thirty first-time over.'[220] But firstly, what of the family behind the estate?

The Stacpooles have a long, colourful and genealogically complex history. One amongst many examples of these is that before William Stacpoole's (1743-1796) first marriage and after the death of his first wife, and before his second marriage, he maintained a liaison with Bridget Lynch, who, in those two periods, bore eight children: six boys and two girls.[221] By his first marriage to Dorothea Burton (d. 1775) in 1773, he had a son, George William (1774-1822), who died unmarried, and with his second wife, Honoria (d. 1820), daughter of William Stamer and widow of Temple French, who he married in 1788, he had a son, Richard John Delazouche (1793-1866), and a daughter, Georgina Maria. Georgina went on to marry Andrew Stacpoole (b. 1776) of Ballyalla, son of George Hogan Stacpoole (1745-1812), as his second wife and with whom there was no issue. Andrew's first wife was Bridget Comyn, with whom he had two children: George (who died as an infant) and Jane. As Jane married Richard John Delazouche, her first cousin Andrew's second wife (Georgina) was his daughter Jane's sister-in-law and his own first cousin! Andrew's third wife, Diana Finucane, had as issue, William (1840-1879) of Ballyalla, Ennis, the owner of 7,441 acres in 1870, noted above. Genealogy is seldom more complicated!

Richard John Dalazouche Stacpoole (1793-1866)

Stacpoole inherited Eden Vale in 1822 following the demise of his half-brother George William, who died unmarried. With his wife Jane (daughter of Andrew Stacpoole of Ballyalla and his own first cousin) he had seven children: three boys, William (1827-1867), Richard (1828-1891), and George William (1852-1894), and four girls, Georgina Maria (1826-1905), Honoria (1829-1843), Jane (1834-1859), and Elizabeth (1837-1857). His eldest son William commenced an army career but soon ran into financial difficulties. His debts were cleared by his father in 1848, on condition of the breaking of the entail of the estates, and this arrangement saw his second son Richard eventually inheriting Eden Vale.[222] Richard's death was marked with an obituary of his achievements, 'there were few landlords who excelled Richard John Stacpoole: in kindness, in simplicity, in honesty he stood unequalled. His tenantry looked on him more as a friend than a landlord'.[223]

His son Richard is the first of the family, in respect of whom there is evidence, of a keen interest in field sports, 'In the early 1860s he kept a pack of harriers near Limerick. These were taken to Eden Vale after his marriage, and hunted as a subscription pack under the name of the Clare harriers.'[224] He married Alice Julia Westropp (d. 1907), daughter of John Westropp of Attyfin, and his second cousin through her mother Georgina Stamer. She too had an interest in hounds. However, they were not to have such a happy relationship with tenants as Richard's late father. Matters began to deteriorate with the poisoning of twelve harriers at Eden Vale in 1874 and escalated thereafter with Richard being boycotted and all labour being withdrawn from his estates.[225] Richard was placed under constant police protection and went nowhere without a revolver.[226] Richard's sister-in-law, Alice Julia's sister Mary Johnson Westropp, and her husband Col. John O'Callaghan of Maryfort were under boycott too, after he served a number of processes on non-paying tenants.

His son Richard died in June 1891, following a year's illness. His eldest son, Richard John Stacpoole (1870-1959), had already taken over the management of the estates and came into full possession on the death of his mother in 1907. He was made High Sherriff for County Clare in 1894, a JP in 1922 and a Deputy Lieutenant in 1923. In 1894, he married Geraldine Norah Crowe, only daughter of Robert Hume Crowe, JP, of Toonagh, County Clare, and formerly

77 A dapper Richard John Stacpoole (1870-1959).

of Dromore. Whether it was Richard who commenced shooting at Eden Vale is debatable, but the records discussed below start with him in 1909, along with his only brother, George William Robert Stacpoole (1872-1939), members of the Crowe family (his in-laws), family members of Charles Randal Armstrong-MacDonnell, who was second husband of his older sister Mary Eva Louisa (1869-1921), and others, who are introduced below.

His tenure at Eden Vale, however, was short and at times troubled, as will be seen from the interruptions in the records below in the early 1920s. During some of his time there he acted as agent for Clare landowners living abroad. He sold Eden Vale in 1926 and moved to Cheltenham, and with that the shooting record ceases.

Writing to Acland-Hood, Richard Stacpoole states:

Woodcocks do not breed in County Clare in any number. I have heard of occasional nests being found and have seen one or two couples in the woods here on April and May but not sufficient to warrant my saying that they are nesting here is at all common.

The flights arrive generally with the full moon in October and November. I have been told that sometimes when the birds have first arrived they have been killed with sticks on the seashore, being so tired that they were quite unable to rise. Where these flights come from seems very doubtful; if they come by sea, what brings them round to the west of Ireland, when they could easily land on another part of the coast without reaching the state of exhaustion which they are in when they arrive? I have heard it said that they fly across Ireland and are only stopped by the Atlantic. If this is so, one would think that in the case of very tired birds (as they undoubtedly are at times), that they would settle on the east coast instead. The fact remains, however, that the great majority of the flights arrive on the west coast and spread inland from there. I have seen new arrivals, tired birds, as early as the first week in October. My Woodcock coverts consist of hazel and blackthorn bushes with occasional trees of oak and ash; these grow among limestone rocks where, with the exception of occasional grass patches, there is hardly any earth, except in the fissures of the rock. I have noticed hazel leaves freshly turned over during the daytime, but except for what they can find among these the 'cock have no feeding in the coverts and we generally find them in the bare patches of rock. That they like absolute quiet is certain. In one of my coverts I allowed the rabbits to increase with the result that for a couple of seasons I had hardly any 'cock in it. When I killed down the rabbits they returned to it again. When the under covert gets too high and bare underneath, Woodcocks will not stay in it. Since 1902, my coverts have been regularly cut; this makes the hazel break low and grow bushy, with the result that the bags have considerably increased as the following list will show:

Year	Beat	Fist Time	Season
1903	Eden Vale	54	102
1904		56	102
1905		67	110
1906		73	135
1907		52	84
1908		43	111
1909		82	142
1910		67	112
1911		46	46*

* The worst year we have had the weather being so mild.

As the summary record table below shows, the broad pattern of the early years above was maintained subsequently until about 1919, after which there were interruptions and a reduction in shooting effort before the end in 1925.

Date	Beat	No. Guns	Pheasants	Woodcock
1909, 21 Oct.	Barloughra	4	18	–
7 Dec.	Home Coverts	8	276	7
8 Dec.	'Cock Coverts	8	89	82
22 Dec.	Ballybeg	4	4	8
1910, 11 Jan	Home Coverts	8	92	4
12 Jan.	'Cock Coverts	8	25	30
20 Jan.	Ballybeg Limetrap	4	17	4
13 Oct.	Barloughra	3	16	–
22 Nov.	Home Coverts	8	360	5
7 Dec.	Ballybeg	4	4	2
13 Dec.	'Cock Coverts	7	105	67
14 Dec.	Home Coverts	7	118	5
1911, 24 Jan.	'Cock Coverts	8	18	23
25 Jan.	Home Coverts	6	45	2
2 Feb.	Ballybeg	3	2	2
12 Oct.	Barloughra and Curragh	4	15	–
24 Nov.	Home Coverts	7	361	2
7 Dec.	'Cock Coverts	8	122	46
8 Dec.	Home Coverts	8	122	6
20 Dec.	Ballybeg	2	6	4
27 Dec.	Barloughra, New Hall, The Glen	6	49	3
1912, 16 Jan.	'Cock Coverts Knockshine	6	13	18
20 Nov.	Home Coverts	8	201	2
26 Nov.	Barloughra and New Hall	5	13	1
4 Dec.	'Cock Coverts	8	86	82
5 Dec.	Home Coverts	8	70	2
30 Dec.	Barloughra, New Hall and the Glen	4	37	1
1913, 15 Jan.	'Cock Coverts and Knockshine	8	21	23
7 Nov.	Home Coverts	6	100	1
5 Dec.	'Cock Coverts	8	22	50
1914, 13 Jan.	'Cock Coverts and Knockshine	6	9	46
5 Feb.	'Cock Coverts and knockshine	4	–	19
20 Nov.	Home Coverts	6	160	1
8 Dec.	'Cock Coverts	8	65	54
18 Dec.	Home Coverts	5	43	11
1915, 5 Jan.	'Cock Coverts and Knockshine	6	10	33
8 Dec.	'Cock Coverts	8	8	53
13 Dec.	Ballybeg and Rockmount	3	9	2
1916, 12 Jan.	'Cock Coverts Glen and Knockshine	6	33	31
20 Nov.	Glen and Knockshine	6	43	1
13 Dec.	'Cock Coverts and Knockshine	8	23	67
15 Dec.	Ballybeg and Rockmount	3	7	3
1917, 3 Jan.	'Cock Coverts and Knockshine	6	4	30
12 Dec.	'Cock Coverts	8	15	39

Date	Beat	No. Guns	Pheasants	Woodcock
1918, 16 Jan.	Glen and Knockshine	4	16	8
13 Feb.	'Cock Coverts and Knockshine	7	–	23
11 Dec.	'Cock Coverts	9	4	49
1919, 16 Jan.	Glen, Knockshine and 'Cock Coverts	6	21	24
19 Nov.	Home Coverts	5	11	2
10 Dec.	'Cock Coverts	8	18	48
1920, 21 Jan.	'Cock Coverts and Knockshine	7	4	33
1920/21	NO SHOOTING			
1921/22	Various	–	25	11
1922/23	NO SHOOTING			
1923, 20 Dec.	'Cock Coverts	6	4	66
27 Dec.	Glen and Knockshine	6	38	22
1924, 3 Jan.	'Cock Coverts	6	5	18
8 Dec.	'Cock Coverts	8	7	40
1925, 15 Jan.	'Cock Coverts and Glen	6	6	20

The most striking feature of the records in this table is the consistency of the shooting on the 'first-time-through 'Cock Coverts', which occurred every year between 4 and 13 December. In 1914, the season's bag was 131, as good almost as 1909, which was the best year in the record at 134. On 4 December 1912, the bag was eighty-two on the first time trough, ''Cock Coverts', with an eight-Gun line. This was identical to 8 December 1909.

It is evident that this was a well-managed shoot and organised to optimise the return. Typically, there was six days' shooting over a season – usually three days before Christmas and the balance after – which took place between November and January, with occasional days in October or early February. The usual Gun line was six to eight, with three on occasion – usually on the day following a 'first-day-through', so probably reduced expectations and/or aching muscles accounted for attrition!

Another feature is the concentrated nature of the Woodcock returns; about 90 per cent came from the aptly named 'Cock Coverts, which was shot only twice in the season and where good management played a role, as outlined above by Stacpoole in his letter to Hood. However, the consistency also points to a unique, naturally advantageous habitat situation, much like Ballykine on the Ashford shoot. It is likely the ground was a Woodcock oasis, surrounded by otherwise inhospitable day roosting habitat.

Up to 1916, there was evidently a policy of having a couple of 'good' Pheasant days, so the pattern overall was a strong Pheasant day (200-300 birds) in November followed by a good Woodcock (and Pheasant) day in December, and then another crack at Woodcock sometime after Christmas. It's a nice formula. There seems also to have been a few days (undated) each season in February devoted to Snipe, where a bag of twenty to thirty was usual, along with rabbits and hares, which appear on all days' shooting. After 1916, there is a marked reduction in the Pheasant bag; probably the result of reduced gamekeeping during the First World War. Indeed, the Pheasant end of the shoot seems to have been allowed to drift off around this time.

The shooting parties comprised mainly members of the Stacpoole family; aside from Richard John, there was his son George Hassard, his brother George William, his in-laws the Crowes of Dromore and MacDonnells of Newhall, the neighbouring estate of Eden Vale. In addition, there were members of other families of landed gentry, notably Bloods, Studderts and Macnamaras. A brief profile of each follows.

78 A shooting party at Edenvale, 1909. Top picture rear: G.W.R. Stacpoole, Mary Macdonnell, Bryan Mahon. Middle row: Edward O'Brien, Fred Studdert, – Croker, Captain White. Seated: Mrs R.J. Stacpoole and Unknown.

George William Robert Stacpoole (1872-1939)

Richard John's only brother, he was a frequent member of the shooting parties. He was distinguished both as a soldier and a horseman. He never married. With his brother, he had been schooled at St Columba's and Cheltenham Colleges, and was then commissioned, again with his brother, in the Clare Artillery Militia before transferring to the South Staffordshire Regiment in 1892. He was in South Africa during the Boer War, as adjutant of the Mounted Infantry and second in command of Montmorency's Scouts, and was made a Companion of the Distinguished Service Order. He retired as captain (temporary major) in 1907 but was recalled in 1914, and he retired finally as lieutenant-colonel in 1919. For his services in the First World War as a Deputy Provost Marshal, he was awarded the Belgian *Croix de guerre* and the Order of Leopold. He had made fortunate investments in insurance shares and was able to retire to a house called Abbeyville, near Croom in County Limerick, where he died in September 1939. He was a member of the Limerick Hunt, a member of the National Hunt Committee (at the same time as the Duke de Stacpoole) and a successful amateur rider. He first began to ride races in Egypt in 1899. He won the Gold Cup and the Grand Military Cup at Sandown in 1905, the National Hunt Cup at Punchestown in 1906 and the Louth Hunt Cup in 1905 and 1909, besides point-to-points with his father's Clare Harriers and others. He kept a few race horses, had a share in a moor in Scotland and made a big-game hunting expedition to India and Burma.

Richard Hassard Stacpoole (1896-1973)

Only son of Richard John, Richard Hassard Stacpoole was another family member who was involved in the shoot and whose autograph appears on the Game Book when he wasn't away at war. Richard Hassard – known almost always as Hassard – was educated at Cheam School and Cheltenham College, and went on to the Royal Military College at Woolwich. He served as a sub-altern with the Royal Artillery, embarking for France in May 1915 and saw action at Ypres and on the Somme. He was gassed at Passchendaele and spent almost nine months in hospital. By 1917, he had been awarded the Military Cross.

After the war, Hassard was in Palestine with the Field Artillery from August 1919 to May 1921, and in India from December 1925 until January 1932. In 1939, he landed in France, less than three weeks after the declaration of war, and he took part in the evacuation of Dunkirk. Promoted lieutenant-colonel, he had assumed command of the 3rd Medium Regiment Royal Artillery on 9 March 1940. When he retired from the army in March 1949, he decided to return to Ireland, and soon afterwards he bought an eighteenth-century house on several acres on the east bank of the Shannon at Castleconnel. It was known as The Grange. Hassard had met his wife in India and they were married at St Mary's church, Warwick, in July 1929. She was Helen Muriel Clare, daughter of Richard Lionel Morphy of Blennerville, Tralee. Her mother was an American, from Virginia, but her father's father was a Church of Ireland parson and his father a captain in the 3rd Buffs, the East Kent Regiment. Their sons, Patrick Michael Richard and George Hassard, were born in 1930 and 1937.

Thomas and Algernon Crowe, Richard John's brothers-in-law, and their uncle Thomas of Dromore were regulars at Eden Vale. In the mid-nineteenth century, Thomas Crowe, grandfather of Richard's wife, Geraldine Norah Crowe, owned 6,121 acres in County Clare and the repre-sentatives of his brother Wainwright Crowe owned a further 3,126 acres. By 1909, Wainwright F. Crowe had agreed to sell over 1,600 acres to the Congested Districts Board. The mansion house of Dromore and almost 1,000 acres of untenanted land was still in the possession of the Crowes in 1906. Thomas Crowe's grandson, another Thomas Crowe, sold Dromore in 1936.

The MacDonnells of Newhall

Richard John's older sister, Mary Eva Louisa, was the second wife of Charles Randal Armstrong MacDonnell of Newhall, the neighbouring estate of Eden Vale. The Armstrongs of Mount Heaton, County Offaly, succeeded to the MacDonnell Estate, William Henry Armstrong having married a granddaughter of Charles MacDonnell in 1809. The second son of this marriage, William Edward Armstrong, succeeded his uncle John MacDonnell in 1850. He adopted the name MacDonnell in 1858 and by the 1870s, his estate amounted to 6,670 acres in County Clare. It is probably his grandson, W.H. MacDonnell, who graces the pages of the Eden Vale Game Book.

Fitzgerald Blood (1884-1950)

Fourth son of five of William and his wife Mary Alicia (née Whitton) of Lower Gardiner Street, Dublin. He was twin to Henry Bindon (who served in the First World War as Lieutenant E. Kent Regiment, and died unmarried in 1938) and had six sisters. The Blood family, a large and influ-ential one, became established in County Clare from the early seventeenth century. Edmund Blood of Kilnaboy Castle was the ancestor of the two main branches of the family of Cranagher and Ballykilty. Fitzgerald was a descendant of the Ballynakilty branch. One of his ancestors, Col. Thomas Blood, became well known for his attempt to carry out a theft of the British Crown Jewels.[227] His third son, who became a major-general, distinguished himself as Chief Engineer at the Siege of Venloo and commanded artillery at the battles of Blenheim and Ramillies under Malborough.[228] By the mid-eighteenth century, the senior branch of the family was living at

Roxton, and by the end of the century their main residence was Cranagher, inherited through William Blood's marriage to Elizabeth Bindon in 1772. In June 1858, Roxton and 452 acres were advertised for sale in the Encumbered Estate Court and by the 1870s, it was in the possession of James Darling Wilson.

Cranagher was sold by Gen. Sir Bindon Blood in 1905. In the 1870s William Bindon Blood owned 2,464 acres and his brother Bagot Blood owned 4,460 acres in County Clare. At the time of Griffith's Valuation, Neptune Blood of Applevale held three townlands in the parish of Rath and Frederick William Blood held land in the parishes of Rath and Killinaboy. In March 1879, part of the lands of Applevale (formerly Boharsallagh), including the house, the estate of Fanny Copleston and Margaret Augusta Biscoe (*née* Blood), was advertised for sale. In July 1911, 1,288 acres of tenanted land belonging to Neptune W. Blood was vested in the Congested Districts Board, and over 3,000 acres belonging to Capt. Bindon Blood was sold to the Board in June 1913.

The Bloods intermarried with the Studderts, an equally large and influential County Clare family.

Frederick Naunton Studdert, OBE (1886-1930)

Third son of Maj. George Studdert and Agnes (*née* Waller) of Moy House, Ennis, County Clare. He married Isabel Millar Ballingale, MBE (1920), and resided at Templemaley, Ennis, County Clare. The Naunton connection arose from his mother's side; her grandmother on her mother's side was Naunton. There are many 'Studdert' houses in Count Clare, the best known of which is Bunratty Castle.[229]

William James Macnamara (b. 1863)

Mcnamara, of Bushy Park, Ennis, was a member of the Doolin branch of this widespread County Clare family, which was established in north County Clare at the beginning of the eighteenth century by Bartholomew Macnamara (b. 1685). Bartholomew's eldest son, William Macnamara, settled at Doolin following his marriage to Catherine, daughter and heiress of Francis Sarsfield of Doolin. Later generations married members of the Stamer and Finucane families, so by the time of Griffith's Valuation, Capt. Francis Macnamara of Doolin had a large estate, including the town of Ennistymon. Ennistymon House became Macnamara property as a result of the marriage of William Nugent Macnamara and Susannah Finucane in 1798. Susannah was a daughter of Anne O'Brien of the Ennistymon family. In the 1870s, the estate of Henry Valentine and William James Macnamara, Francis's two sons, amounted to 15,246 acres, and their great-uncle Admiral Sir Burton Macnamara of Tromra House owned 732 acres in the county. Sir Burton's half-sister Louisa Macnamara was the second wife of Mathian Stacpoole (b. 1780). William James married Mary Sarita Keane, eldest daughter of Francis Burton Keane, JP, Hermitage, Ennis. The date of his death is unclear; however, he was shooting at Eden Vale at least up to 1917.

DROMOLAND, COUNTY CLARE

There is vibrant driven Pheasant shoot at Dromoland at present, comprising about twenty-eight drives which have been developed over the years, and thirty acres of cover crops are planted annually. The recorded ancestry of shooting at Dromoland dates back to at least 1830. As such, it is the shoot with the longest recorded history of any included in this book.

The O'Briens claim descent from the earliest kings of Ireland, and the family name was derived from the eleventh-century King Brian Boru, who died at the Battle of Clontarf in 1014. The ori-

79 Dromoland Castle, County Clare.

gins of the Dromoland Estate can be traced back to the will (26 June 1551) of Murrough O'Brien, 1st Earl of Thomond and 1st Baron Inchiquin (d. 1551).

The present Dromoland Castle was completed in about 1835 by Sir Edward, 4th Baronet (1773-1837). Like his predecessors, Sir Edward played a prominent role in local political life. He was returned for Ennis at the by-election occasioned by the death of his father, Sir Lucius, 3rd Baronet. He went on to vote against the Union in both 1799 and 1800. He was elected for County Clare in 1802 and took his seat in the Imperial Parliament, where he exhibited consistent support for Catholic claims for emancipation. He continued to represent Clare until the general election of 1826.

Like his father and grandfather before him, Sir Edward fathered a large family, nine children in all, including his eldest son and heir, Lucius, and his second son, William, later William Smith O'Brien (1803-1864), the well-known Young Irelander.

On his succession in 1795, Sir Edward, 4th Baronet, appeared to have been content to follow the successful administrative ways pursued by his father. To this end, his marriage to the wealthy heiress Charlotte Smith, who brought a dowry of £20,000, was vital, as it allowed Sir Edward to clear the debts his father had long struggled to pay. Anxious to avoid the recurrent indebtedness which had long bedevilled his family, Sir Edward also attempted to enforce stricter economies, not only on the estate, but also within the household. 'All expense must be cut down to the lowest level,' he told his wife, 'for myself,' he added, 'I shall mortify the flesh like an anchorite.' In spite of his incessant calls for budgeting, he later admitted that he was giving serious consideration to the idea of 'breaking up altogether the Dromoland establishment' and moving his family to Dublin. The Dromoland Estates, however, continued to yield a lucrative income for the O'Briens. In 1795, a year after Sir Edward had succeeded, his rental stood at £7,128. By 1806, this had risen to £8,155 14s 6d. In the second decade of the nineteenth century, the estates were yielding more than £14,000 per annum.

Additional revenue was secured from the Cahirmoyle Estate in County Limerick, part of which came into the possession of Lady Charlotte O'Brien following her father's death. This estate, which included the profitable lands of Mountplummer, Banemore, Kilscannel and Liscarroll, was jointly administered by Sir Edward and his wife, and by 1827 was generating a yearly rental income of £5,080. According to Edward Wakefield in his *Account of Ireland* (1812), Sir Edward usually let land for twenty-one years, and continued his predecessor's support for local industry, fostering plans to build a corn market on his property in Ennis 'in preference to letting it to paupers to build cabins,' and financing the building of a new school house in Newmarket-on-Fergus.

It is from this period of Edward, 4th Baronet, that the first reference to shooting at Dromoland is found in the shape of a verse entitled 'Directions for a Day's Shooting at Dromoland', written and illustrated by Sir Edward O'Brien (*c*.1830).[230] It is worth recounting in full, because, style of language apart, it could apply to any gathering at an organised shoot today, although delivered with a great deal more wit than many modern shoot briefings, as shooting readers will readily appreciate!

CANTO I

At half past seven be called, at eight awake,
To dress thee neat with sixty minutes take.
Thy heart 'gainst every ill full well prepare,
Thy body too, with clothes that will not tear.
Moleskin the dress should be, or velveteen,
Or corduroy, of black or bottled green.
Gaiters must sheathe thy legs, thy shoes will be
Both high and stout and goosegreased plentiously.
The bell will ring at nine, immediate run,
The important work of breakfast is begun.
Spare not, rude havoc make, 'twill nerve your arm
And clear your sight and the gay lifeblood warm.
What e'er there be, partake, or meat or eggs,
Or ham, or breast of fowl or turkey legs.
And should a pie of perigord be there,
Nor it, nor any other pasty share.
If steak appear, surrounded with chalottes,
Take, 'tis my advice, my friend and you lay in lots.
Then hunger sated, former feats recall.
Tell of the varied game that strewed the hall
In seasons past, tell how your trusty gun
At fifty yards has slaughtered many a one.
The lady of the house must then be prayed
A place for game when dinner shall be laid.
A hare shall grace the head, Woodcocks the foot.
Snipe shall a side dish make and Grouse be put
With Wigeon, duck and Teal in balance true,
To Partridges, and quails, and a curlew,
Turn to your brother sportsmen then and say,
'I hold a wager that I win the day.

But as I do not bet, this I promise,
Who e'er is last today his beaver throws
Into the air, a mark for all the rest
To practice on and try who'll hit it best.
'Tis time to be abroad if you are done
We'll not delay, I go to fetch my gun–.'
'This gun was made in Limerick, shew me yours.
''Tis neatly finished, safety too insures,
'But it must take a charge with such a bore
'Would load a cannon' – opening the hall door.
'Oh what a lovely morn, how bright the sun
'Beams through the frosty air, the fields upon
'The earth is strewed with glittering sparks of hoar
'A pearly whiteness shrouds the bushes o'er.

'How sharp but clear the breeze, the cheeks grow red
'And stiff with cold – is everything prepared?
'Are there the beaters? – pray whose son are you?'
'McGrath's your honor' – 'you look very blue
'Where is your stick?' – 'I'll get one please you Sir,
'At the first wood 'ere many yards we stir.'
'Here is a piece of bread, ''twill make you strong –
'I'm loaded now – come let us get along.'

The hill ascended – 'You will follow here,
'This is your place your brother will go there.
'Now hit the bushes well but do not call
'The birds are round too soon when beaters bawl.'
Bang! Bang! ''Tis well, we have slaughtered two.
'Touch them not beaters or my wrath you rue.
'And rest to charge, stir not a single foot,
'Till ready you shall hear from him who shot.'
'Mark, sir, outside.' Bang! 'Come here you, Sir, run,
'Under that wall he lies, his last flight done.
Bang! Bang! Bang! Bang! ''Tis down at last.
'The face of each is wiped, by whom it passed
'Poor bird you ran the gauntlet and well nigh
'Had escaped their fury but I stopped your fly.'
'Mark! Mark!' the hare – Bang! Bang! It runs away.
'That shot sir very nearly closed its day,
''Twas there it ran, the copse is very thick,
'I scare could see it, it was gone so quick.'
Bang! 'Who fired then? You almost shot my face.
'You were too forward, pray you keep your place.
'It is not possible to shoot the groves,
'Unless in order every shooter moves.

'Just keep the line, each bird that's flushed will then
'Be fired at and you will not shoot the men–'
'There, there again you will not keep the line–'
'Now all is right, the sight is very fine.
'See how we sweep the copse, nought can escape
'While thus our course in order due we shape–
'Look at this splendid cover, see what green
'Bramble I think excels the trees between.
'The Woodcocks love to shelter 'neath a bower,
'Where neither frost can reach nor storm can shower.
'Leaving the cover you must cross a wall
'The stones are slippery, take care not to fall.
'This is the deer park wood, for formerly
'They pastured here and that is Lebanlee,
'Look at the castle and the bird's eye view
'Of lake and river, wood and mountain blue,
'That is the Fergus with its hundred isles,
'And that Mount Callan drear where now a sunbeam shines.
'Here take my gun and fill my belt with shot
'And Paddy count how many birds we have got,
'Tell me a story while we cross the plain.'
'Tis fold and heard with pleasure – 'Each again
'Will take his place – this wood is rather bare,
'But oft beneath its shade there lies a hare.'
Bang! Bang! 'I told you so, you rolled him o'er,
'Like the spent wave that breaks upon the shore.'
Mark! Bang! 'That Woodcock lay in such a spot,
'I was not well prepared to fire a shot–'
'Well done, who fired? That bird was killed by you.'
'I'm glad to hear it for I have killed so few.'
'When you have passed the roads still keep the ranks
'But to the right diverge; by yonder banks
'You'll meet a rabbit; when you reach the wall
'I will the pivot be, and you shall all
'Beat round in order due'; this wood is great
For game so shots are fired at merry rate.
Bang! Bang! Bang! Bang! Each kills his bird while more
Fly here and there and o'er the shooters soar
And rabbits are beneath their feet and hares
A constant cannonade assails the ears.
Tis o'er at last, emerged from Larry's wood,
This is the spot where Larry's gateway stood,
Two lofty columns here arose in air,
And a park wall full high extended there,
A lodge was here with ivy overgrown,
The wall is levelled now, the gate o'erthrown.

In former times the house was closed around,
With walls and hedges now 'tis open ground,
In my mind fairer far, for I approve
The modern acts that old enclosures move.
'Again well beat this hedge in Lebanlee,
'Then cross the field to yonder large ash tree –
'Kilkeran wood is this, which while we beat
'Who walks below when we the river meet
'Will look about, a duck is sometimes seen
'Or diver floating on its placid stream–'
''Tis nobly done, we now will make for home,
''Tis luncheon time, I hope you will take some.'
'I never luncheon eat' – 'I hate the sight'
'I am not hungry' – 'I could shoot till night.'
'Well as you please, but I confess I feel …
'The pains of hunger on my senses steal–'
'And so do I,' cries one, another too
Yields to the soft delusion, which shall well be
told in canto number two –

CANTO II

'This is my room, your guns deposit here,
'I'll lock the door and there will be no fear
'Of false alarm from child or cautious dame,
'Least some one meddling cause disastrous flame,
'Now follow me – will you have chop or steak
'Or will you ham, or beef, or pasty take.
'Ten birds, I understand, were shot, five hares,
'A hare for each when split in equal shares,
'But someone must have missed, for you and I
'Two hares and Woodcocks four killed equally.
'Who is the haply wight, I think I know,
'Who failed today by that dark brow of woe
'Did you not slaughter one, I saw you fire
'Over and over till it made me tire.'
'I know not how, my gun was wrong today,
'Else why I missed so oft I cannot say,
'My aim was good, when luncheon shall be done
'I'll get some water warmed and wash my gun.'

The luncheon ended in the evening fair,
Again we sally forth with mirthful air,
The beaters too are rallied, who have all
Been well replenished in the servants' hall.
This is the Temple wood, which entered straight,

For lack of game you need not idle wait,
But some who shot full well erstwhile must now
Their want of certain skill unwilling show,
While those who in the former woods had failed,
Are now with plentious fall of game regaled,
This wood is well in front, there holly bowers
Are much beloved by birds in wintry hours,
And now the limekiln wood and cottage hill,
And then Ailue the tattling thunders fill.
The crag likewise is beat, both sides the road,
The young plantation too and entrance wood,
Now all is over I see the garden wall,
There where the birds arc laid when flushed they fall
On days of shooting but 'tis growing dark,
'I have a cigar case here, pray make a spark.
'Will you have one and you and you, it warms
'The heart and soul and every ill disarms–'
The spark is struck the perfumed gale ascends
And to each wight a cheerful aspect lends,
As when at midnight hour some noble dame
Leaves in sedan the rout, the torches flame,
So as along the road our train was led,
On night the blaze of the cigar is shed.

The mansion house, lit up, upon the lake looks down,
And there is seen like an illumined town,
The terrace reached, we fire a volley there,
The sound reverberates through all the air,
Rock, dale and hill and wood repeat the tale,
The echos open round the astonished vale,
Responded long, the warlike sounds endure,
Then die away upon the lake and distant moor.

(Opening the hall door.)

'How dazzling to the eyes the candle light,
'After the dark chill eve, it pains the sight.
'The bell has rung, the first, which bids prepare
'For dinner rime, least you be late beware,
'Go quickly dress, to stand in wet is wrong–'

Whereas Sir Edward, 4th Baronet, had mostly personal debts to deal with, his son and heir Sir Lucius (1800-1872), who became 5th Baronet in 1837 and was later made 13th Baron Inchiquin, faced difficulties of a far more grave nature. The Famine conditions which prevailed in the country for the four years from 1845 prompted not only a vast human catastrophe but also presaged a period of severe economic austerity for landlords.

Sir Lucius married twice, firstly in 1837 to Mary, daughter of William FitzGerald of Adelphi, County Clare, by whom he had one son and five daughters. Mary died on 26 May 1852 and Sir Lucius married secondly Louisa, daughter of Maj. James Finucane, by whom he had a further six children. Sir Lucius was educated at Harrow and at Trinity College, Cambridge, where he graduated BA in 1825 and MA in 1828. He enjoyed a distinguished political career, representing County Clare in Parliament from 1826 to 1830, and again in 1847, remaining an MP until the general election of 1852. He was appointed Lord Lieutenant and Custos Rotulorum of County Clare in June 1843, and he was elected a representative peer for Ireland on 20 October 1863.

Lucius died at Dromoland on 22 March 1872. An obituary in the *Clare Freeman* (30 March 1872), lamented his passing and remarked:

> … the tenantry … have lost a kind and generous landlord; the public an impartial and high-spirited ruler and magistrate who was, in every sense of the word, a nobleman. Though ever foremost in all works of charity and utility throughout the county, he did not forget those dependants immediately surrounding his magnificent residence, and many a cottage-home was the brighter for a ray from the castle …

He was succeeded by his eldest son, Edward Donough, from his first marriage to Mary FitzGerald.

According to De Burgh, Edward Donough, 14th Baron Inchiquin, possessed 20,321 acres in County Clare.[231] Shortly after succeeding to the title in 1872, he moved to pay off the encumbrances affecting the Dromoland Estate. His agent, Robert Vere O'Brien, and his legal advisors drew up an agreement with the Representative Body of the Church of Ireland to raise a mortgage loan for the required sum of a little over £85,000. The debts and encumbrances curtailed his ability to meet all his obligations and grant the kind of abatements demanded by tenants after 1879. His woes were further exacerbated by the establishment in 1881 of the Land Commission. Fixed charges, such as mortgage interest payments and tithe rent charges, not to mention mounting personal debts, continued to consume a large proportion of the dwindling annual rental income of the estate.

Edward Donough, 14th Baron Inchiquin (1839-1900)
Educated at St Columba's College, Dublin, and at Trinity College, Cambridge, where he graduated with an MA in 1860. Like his father, Edward Donough married twice, firstly in 1862 to the Hon. Emily Holmes à Court, daughter of William Holmes à Court, 2nd Baron Heytesbury of Heytesbury House, Wiltshire, by whom he had four children. Emily died in 1868 and so he later married the Hon. Ellen Harriet White, daughter of Luke White, 2nd Baron Annaly of Luttrelstown, County Dublin, in 1874, with whom he had a further ten children.

He was elected an Irish representative peer on 5 April 1873, but took only an occasional part in debates, most frequently when Irish affairs were discussed. He was appointed a Knight of the Most Illustrious Order of St Patrick on 5 August 1892. From a more local standpoint, he continued to assume the roles traditionally held by the heads of the Dromoland O'Briens, serving as magistrate, sheriff, chairman of the Ennis Board of Guardians and county lieutenant, as well as adopting a leading role on the board supervising the construction of the Ennis & West Clare Railway.

Edward Donough also took an interest in the activities of the Irish Landowners' Convention. After its formation in 1887, this organisation campaigned on behalf of Irish landowners seeking to secure concessions in respect of land reform. In response to agitation to secure better

THE WEST AND SOUTH-WEST

conditions for Irish tenant farmers, the British Government had introduced a number of legislative measures which heralded a revolution in land ownership in Ireland. The heavily mortgaged Dromoland Estate was not immune to such challenges, as Lord Inchiquin averred in the House of Lords in a wide-ranging speech on the land question on 25 May 1897. In seeking some form of redress 'for the injuries which had been inflicted' upon Irish landholders, he reminded the House that, 'what the landlords said [to government] was this: "You have reduced our rents, you have taken a large slice out of our property and handed it over to the occupying tenant, who is at liberty to go wherever he likes with the money. That was what Parliament had done."'

Edward Donough spent most of his later years at Dromoland, where he died on 9 April 1900.

Edward's financial difficulties do not appear to have hampered his shooting activities, to judge from his Game Book for November 1875 to June 1884. This commences with an entry for 16 November 1875, which reads, 'Robert O'Brien, who accompanied us, but did not shoot, was accidentally shot half an hour after lunch in Lanigan's Copse – severely wounded – no more shooting afterwards.' Up to lunchtime, the party had shot Barnhill Wood, Larry's Wood and Crag Lewis, and the bag for the eight Guns was eight Woodcock, one Snipe, fifty-nine Pheasants and twenty-seven hares. The party included Lord Ormonde, Lord Drogheda, Lord Annaly, Col. Aldworth and Lord Inchiquin himself. It seems likely that the Robert O'Brien referred to was Edward Donagh's uncle Robert O'Brien (1809-1890), who was married to an Eleanor de Vere.

Lord Ormonde, previously James Edward William Theobald Butler, 3rd Marquess of Ormonde, KP, PC (1844-1919)

Styled Earl of Ossory until 1854, James Edward was the son of John Butler, 2nd Marquess of Ormonde, and Frances Jane Paget. He was Vice-Admiral of Leinster and a member of the Privy Council of Ireland. He was awarded the Order of the Crown of Prussia (first class). He married Lady Elizabeth Harriet Grosvenor, daughter of Hugh Grosvenor, 1st Duke of Westminster, on 2 February 1876. They had two daughters: Beatrice Butler (1876-1952), who married Lt-Gen. Sir Reginald Pole-Carew, KCB, CVO, and Constance Mary Butler (1879-1949), who died unmarried.

Lord Annaly, previously Luke White, 2nd Baron Annaly, KP (1829-1888)

Son of Henry White, 1st Baron Annaly, and his wife Ellen (née Dempster). Educated at Eton, he later served in the British Army and achieved the rank of captain in the 13th Light Dragoons and lieutenant-colonel in the Longford Rifles.

In 1859, he was returned to Parliament for County Clare, a seat he held until 1860, and he then represented County Longford from 1861 to 1862 and Kidderminster from 1862 to 1865. Annaly served in the Liberal administrations of Lord Palmerston and Lord John Russell (the latter as a Junior Lord of the Treasury between 1862 and 1866). From 1868 to 1873, he was State Steward to the Lord Lieutenant of Ireland Earl Spencer. He also held the honorary positions of Sheriff of County Dublin (1861) and of County Longford (1871), and was Lord Lieutenant of County Longford from 1873 to 1874. In 1885, he was made a Knight of the Order of St Patrick.

Lord Annaly married Emily, daughter of James Stuart, in 1853. They had five sons and three daughters. All his sons had military careers, his third son, the Hon. Robert White, notably achieving the rank of brigadier-general in the 184th Infantry Brigade. Lord Annaly died in March 1888, aged fifty-eight, and was succeeded in the barony by his eldest son, Luke. Lady Annaly died in 1915. The family seat was Luttrellstown Castle, Clonsilla, County Dublin, which was acquired by bookseller turned lottery operator Luke White in 1800. He changed the name to Woodlands before the 3rd Baron Anally changed it back to Luttrellstown. Several of his sons, including the

Hon. Luke, who succeeded as 3ʳᵈ Baron, and the Hon. Robert, are to be found in the records from about 1878 onwards.

Lord Drogheda, previously Henry Francis Seymour Moore, 3ʳᵈ Marquess of Drogheda, KP, PC (I) (1825-1892)
Henry Francis Seymour Moore of Moore Abbey, Monastrevin, County Kildare, was styled Viscount Moore until 1837, becoming Marquess of Drogheda in 1837 on the death of Charles Moore, 2ⁿᵈ Marquess of Drogheda. He was appointed a Knight of the Order of St Patrick on 7 February 1868. As well as yachting, the 3ʳᵈ Marquess was involved in Irish hare coursing. He planted a special coursing arena in Boherbaun in the parish of Monasterevin. Up until 1903, the Boherbaun Cup was one of the most coveted prizes in Irish coursing. His greatest legacy, however, was to Irish horse racing. Henry Moore was one of the keenest and most influential supporters of horse racing in Ireland and England during the mid-1800s. As master of the Emo hunt, he encouraged race meeting on the Great Heath in County Laois, donating a silver cup for the winner. He was a steward at many of the great racecourses of the age. To his eternal credit in the county of Kildare, he founded the meeting at Punchestown, which today attracts thousands upon thousands to the racecourse.

He made one further contribution which has touched upon countless lives in Kildare and across Ireland: he founded a hospital for sick and injured jockeys at the edge of the Curragh. Today, the 'Jockey Hospital' – or more correctly, the Drogheda Memorial Hospital – is a hospice carrying on a tradition of care and compassion. The 3ʳᵈ Marquess died without issue in 1892 and the Marquessate of Drogheda ceased to exist. The Earldom of Drogheda passed to another branch of the family, the Ponsonby Moores. The entry for 18 November, two days after the shoot, reads, 'Party not recovered their nerves and spirits, lost three Guns – Robert going on well. Total head in three days':

Pheasants	Hares	Woodcock	Rabbits	Snipe	Total
135	115	33	13	3	298

Edward Donagh hosted shooting parties in November, December and January, and the usual format was three days' shooting, often spread over five days. The November shoot appears to have been reserved for fellow peers, and the list of visiting Guns amounts to a 'who's who' of peers of the realm. In that respect, Dromoland rivals the days of Ashford in Lord Ardilaun's time. For example, 8 and 9 November 1876 saw the Duke of St Albans, Lord Drogheda (again), Lord Kildare, his son Lord Maurice FitzGerald, Lord Carysfort and Lord Clarina shooting over the two days, with rather indifferent results. The comments for the first day are, 'wet in morning, cleared up later. Shooting not good – scarcely any Woodcock in covers'. In fact, there were only three in the bag on the first day and two on the second, when it is remarked, 'Lovely day – lots of Pheasants, few Woodcocks, frosty morning – powder might have been straighter.'

William Amelius Aubrey de Vere Beauclerk, 10ᵗʰ Duke of St Albans, PC (1840-1898)
The Duke of St Albans in question was William Amelius Aubrey de Vere Beauclerk, 10ᵗʰ Duke of St Albans, styled Earl of Burford until 1849, who was a British Liberal politician. The only son of William Beauclerk, 9ᵗʰ Duke of St Albans, and Elizabeth Catherine, daughter of Maj.-Gen. Joseph Gubbins, St Albans succeeded his father in the dukedom in 1849, aged nine. He later took his seat as a Liberal in the House of Lords and served as Captain of the Yeomen of the Guard from 1868 to 1874

in Gladstone's first administration. In 1869, he was sworn of the Privy Council and never returned to political office, but served as Lord Lieutenant of Nottinghamshire between 1880 and 1898.

St Albans was twice married, firstly to Lady Sybil Mary Grey (1848-1871), daughter of Lt-Gen. the Hon. Charles Grey and granddaughter of Charles Grey, 2nd Earl Grey, on 20 June 1867 in London. They had three children. After Sybil's early death, he married Grace Bernal-Osborne (d. 18 November 1926) on 3 January 1874 in County Tipperary. She was the granddaughter of the London Sephardic Jewish Shakespearian-actor-turned-parliamentarian, Ralph Bernal. Her father, Ralph Bernal Jr (later Ralph Bernal Osborne), was Secretary of the Admiralty and a parliamentarian. Grace's mother, was an Osborne. St Albans and Grace and they had five children and when William died in May 1898, aged fifty-eight, he was succeeded in the dukedom by his only son from his first marriage, Charles.

Lord Kildare, known until 1874 as the Marquess of Kildare, was Charles William FitzGerald, 4th Duke of Leinster (1819-1887), who was born in Dublin. Leinster was the son of Augustus FitzGerald, 3rd Duke of Leinster, and Lady Charlotte Augusta Stanhope. He was MP for Kildare from 1847 to 1852 and died at Carton House. He was married to Lady Caroline Sutherland-Leveson-Gower (1827-1887), daughter of George Granville Sutherland-Leveson-Gower, 2nd Duke of Sutherland, and Lady Harriet Elizabeth Georgiana Howard, on 12 or 13 October 1847, at Trentham, Staffordshire, England. They had fifteen children, including Lord Gerald FitzGerald, 5th Duke of Leinster (August 1851-December 1893) and Lord Maurice FitzGerald (1852-1901), who married Lady Adelaide Forbes (1860-1942) at Longford on 13 April 1880. He accompanied his father on this shoot and many others at Dromoland and elsewhere in Ireland.[232]

Lord Carysfort was William Proby, 5th Earl of Carysfort, KP (1836-1909), of Glenart Castle in County Wicklow. Known as William Proby until 1872, Carysfort was the fourth son and youngest child of Admiral Granville Proby, 3rd Earl of Carysfort, and his wife Isabella (née Howard), who died only four days after his birth. He was educated at Eton and Trinity College, Cambridge. He served as High Sheriff of Wicklow in 1866, as Lord Lieutenant of County Wicklow from 1890 to 1909, and was made a Knight of the Order of St Patrick in 1874. In 1872, he succeeded his elder brother to the earldom and entered the House of Lords. Lord Carysfort married Charlotte Mary, daughter of Revd Robert Boothby Heathcote, in 1860. The marriage was childless. He died in September 1909, aged seventy-three, when all his titles became extinct, and his wife, the Countess of Carysfort, died in 1918.

General Eyre Challoner Henry Massey, 4th Baron Clarina of Elm Park

Born on 29 April 1830 at Baker Street, Marylebone, London, the son of Eyre Massey, 3rd Baron Clarina of Elm Park, Limerick, and Susan Elizabeth Barton.

Educated at Eton between 1843 and 1844, he served in the British Army, where he had a very distinguished military career. He fought in the Siege of Sebastopol and was decorated with the award of Order of the Medjidie in 1856. He was promoted to the rank of major in 1857, in the service of the 95th Foot, and gained the rank of lieutenant-colonel in 1858. He fought in the Indian Mutiny and was decorated with the award of Knight, Legion of Honour. He gained the rank of brevet colonel in 1865 and the rank of major general in 1870. He succeeded to the title of 4th Baron Clarina of Elm Park, County Limerick, in 1872 and achieved the rank of lieutenant-colonel in 1873, while serving with the 97th Foot. He gained the rank of lieutenant-general in 1885 and was invested as a Companion, Order of the Bath (CB) in June 1887. He held the office of representative peer (Ireland) between 1888 and 1897. He gained the rank of general in 1891 and was Colonel of the Durham Light Infantry between 1895 and 1897.

He died on 16 December 1897, aged sixty-seven, at Albert Bridge Road, Battersea, London, from pneumonia, unmarried, and was buried on 20 December 1897 at Elm Park, Clarina, County Limerick.

There was considerable turnover in the visiting Guns each November. In 1877, the shooting was over three days, 14-16 November. On this occasion, the party included: the Duke of Marlborough, Lord Wicklow, Lord Powerscourt, Lord Cloncurry, Lord Annaly, and Lord Crichton, and conditions were not very favourable to begin with, according to comments in the Game Book, 'Raining all day, part of the time cats and dogs. [Numbers of] Hares killed down. In the spring bad breeding season owing to cold and wet. Consequently fewer Pheasants than last year – Shooting good.' The third day was: '[A] Very fine day – no Woodcocks in cover – only twelve Pheasants shot in Andrew's Wood. Total of three days':

Pheasants	Hares	Woodcock	Rabbits	Snipe	Total
252	64	14	181	1	512 head.

Indeed, over the decade 1875-1884, the most Woodcock shot over three days appears to be thirty-eight and on any one day eighteen. However, the guest list was not dissuaded by quality of shooting, with Lord Bandon coming back on numerous occasions, Lord Listowel, Lord Wallscourt and Lord Donaghmore making appearances, and English peers like Lord Coke (3rd Earl of Leicester and owner of the Holkham Estate in Norfolk)[233] and Lord Randolph Churchill (brother of the 8th Duke of Marlborough, who was shooting there in 1877, and father of Sir Winston Churchill) also making appearances during this time.

An interesting, untitled Gun, who 'makes the cut' for November shooting is William Barton, who was there from 13 to 15 November 1878, in the company of Lord Randolph Churchill, Lord Bandon and Lord Maurice FitzGerald. He is believed to be a member of the Barton dynasty. For five generations they owned both the estate at Straffan and a 37-hectare vineyard in St Julien, near the Gironde, north of Bordeaux, where they produced Château Léoville-Barton and Château Langoa-Barton. The Barton dynasty is believed to hold the record for the longest period of single-family ownership of any vineyard in Bordeaux.

The pattern of shooting remained constant until Edward Donagh's death in 1900, i.e. mainly peers in November with some other family members, and local gentry dominating more in December and January. The latter included, notably, Richard John Stacpoole and his in-laws, the Crowes of Dromore and MacDonnells of Newhall, neighbouring estate of Eden Vale. In addition, there were members of other families of landed gentry, notably Bloods, Studderts and Macnamaras. Three regulars at Dromoland were Lord Bandon, Sir Eustace Becher and the Hon. Edward O'Brien, all of whom are to be found at Ashford for Lord Ardilaun's record Woodcock shoot of 31 December 1910.

When Robin Vere O'Brien finally succeeded in resigning as agent, Edward stepped into his shoes and managed Dromoland.[234] He married Lady Beatrice Hare, younger daughter of the Earl of Listowel at Ballyhooley, County Cork, in 1899. They lived at Roslevin, a house on the Tulla side of Ennis. His father-in-law, Lord Listowel, was a frequent Gun at Dromoland around this time.

Edward Donagh was succeeded by his eldest son from his first marriage to Emily Holmes à Court, Lucius, 15th Baron Inchiquin (1864-1929), who was educated at Eton and served as a lieutenant in the 2nd Battalion Rifle Brigade (Prince Consort's Own). He was a regular shooter

Date 1915	Beat	Pheasants	Rabbits	Hares	Woodcock	Various	Total	Guns 1st Day	2nd two days
Nov 11th	Lake Beat	250	12	1	5	.	298	Ld Sligo	Sir E. Beecher
								Sir C. Barrington	W. R. Stacpoole
Nov 24th	Barn Hill Crag, Lewis Tarry's Wood, Old wood Taungha	620	41	2	17	Snipe 4	684	Sir E. Beecher	Lt W. MacDonnell
								W. Maxwell	Mr F. N. Studdert
Nov 25th	Hill and Lake Beat	252	18	3	25	3 1	302	Hon E. O'Brien	W. W. Ball
									The Hon E. O'Brien
TOTAL	...	1152	71	6	47	4 3 1	1284	Lord Inchiquin	Lord Inchiquin

REMARKS ... Only shot the morning of the 1st day. Rain Snow and gale from the N.E. the rest of the time. Shooting good. Fine weather the other two days. Shooting good. NB. Mr Studdert shot 2nd Day and Mr Ball the third.

80 **Dromoland Castle shoot card, 1915.**

from December 1880, as were his younger brothers Murrough O'Brien (1866-1934) and Edward Donagh (1867-1943).

Lucius was an unsuccessful Tory candidate in the parliamentary election for County Clare in 1885, but served as JP and Deputy Lieutenant, and was appointed High Sheriff in 1898. He married Ethel Jane Foster, elder daughter and co-heiress of the late Johnston Jonas Foster of Moor Park, Ludlow, Shropshire, and Cliffe Hall, Lightcliffe, Yorkshire, in 1896, with whom he had six children. His early years were spent in the army, during the course of which he served in India and Egypt, and, after retiring, he divided his time between his wife's estate of Moor Park and Dromoland.

Fully engaged by the maintenance of these estates, Lucius devoted little time to political life. Nevertheless, he was elected an Irish representative peer on 23 November 1900. With the outbreak of hostilities in 1914, the Inchiquins expended much effort in supporting various wartime charities, including the local Red Cross committee, the Belgian Refugee Fund and the Irish Counties' War Hospital.

With the onset of the dislocation caused by the revolutionary period, Lucius struggled to make ends meet. By 1921 he was involved in protracted negotiations regarding the terms of purchase by tenants of his properties on the Sixmilebridge Estate. Lucius was still in possession of 20,000 acres (3,000 of which remained in his own hands, the rest let to tenants) but he was mired in crippling debt. 'I have very big charges on my estate,' he conceded, 'including head, quit, tithe rents, drainage charges and a big mortgage [about £2,377 per annum] and other charges.' The estate rental in April 1921 stood at £7,868, but this figure was dwarfed by the arrears due, which amounted to over £12,000. He admitted that of the 850 tenants remaining on the estate, over 700 had not paid 'a single penny for over two years; and 400 of them have paid me nothing for over two years and a half'.[235] This, combined with the financial burden of maintaining a large residence and farm – £6,000 was paid in wages alone whilst Lady Inchiquin expended about £5,000 yearly in paying domestic bills – resulted in ever frequent defaults on paying off the mortgage interest. A £12,000 overdraft from the bank was the inevitable, if dispiriting, outcome of these difficulties, which presaged the transfer of the ownership of the estate into the hands of former tenants until Dromoland Castle remained as the only substantial property held by the Lords Inchiquin.

Throughout this tumultuous era, the Inchiquins lived in continuous fear of an assault on their property. In 1922, the family's motor cars were commandeered by Republicans, compensation for which was sought for by Lord Inchiquin in correspondence with W.T. Cosgrave, Minister of

Finance in the provisional government. In his correspondence, Lucius also referred to his wider difficulties, 'It is very hard to carry on as my gross income used to be six or eight years ago £8,000, last year it was only £3,700 … and I fear if this sort of thing goes on we shall have to close up this place.' He would go on to serve as one of the first members of the Senate, the upper house of the newly created Irish Free State legislature. He died on 9 December 1929.

Like his father before him, Lucius and his brothers (especially Edward Donagh) shot through their financial and other political troubles with a guest list that included the same local families recorded there in the previous twenty-five years. Local members of the gentry such as Sir Charles Barrington of Glenstal, itself a notable shoot at the time, Frederick and Hallam Studdert, Richard Stacpoole of Eden Vale, their in-laws the Crowes, John Blood of Ballykilty, County Clare, William Hawkins Ball of Fort Fergus and Ballinacally, and the other regular Guns found at Eden Vale all frequented the Dromoland shoots. In addition, the list of peers from both Ireland and overseas (like Acland-Hood and Neville Chamberlain) continued as before.

Moreover, there is a noticeable improvement in the Woodcock (and overall game) bag in the first two decades of the twentieth century. In the first three days of December 1903, six Guns accounted for 61 Woodcock and 1,730 Pheasants. The record includes the comment, 'saw a great many Woodcock, short of a Gun or would have shot more – fine day'. The Guns on this three-day shoot included the Earl of Arran. Arthur Jocelyn Charles Gore, 6th Earl of Arran, KP, PC (1868-1958), known as Viscount Sudley from 1884 to 1901, was an Anglo-Irish peer and soldier. He was the only son of Arthur Saunders Gore, 5th Earl of Arran, and Lady Edith Elizabeth Henrietta Jocelyn. He fought in the Second Boer War and in the First World War, and achieved the rank of lieutenant-colonel in the Royal Horse Guards. He was also a JP for Hertfordshire, County Louth and County Mayo, a Deputy Lieutenant of County Mayo and Essex, and served as Lord Lieutenant of County Donegal from 1917 to 1920. He was made a Knight of the Order of St Patrick in 1909 and admitted to the Irish Privy Council in 1917. Lord Arran first married Maud Jacqueline Marie Beauclerk van Kattendyke, daughter of Huyssen van Kattendyke, 3rd Baron van Kattendyke, in 1902. She died in 1927, and two years later he married Lilian Constance Quick, daughter of Joseph Quick. Lord Arran died in December 1958, aged ninety, and was succeeded in his titles by his eldest son, Arthur. Also shooting was Sir Frederick Bathurst (1870-1956) of the renowned cricketing dynasty.

Another good bag is recorded in November 1906, when seventy-two Woodcock were shot over three days (20-22 November) with fifty-seven on 21 November. In addition, there were 1,870 Pheasants and a good assortment of ground game to seven Guns. 'Beautiful day; more 'cock than I ever saw all on the Hill. Shooting excellent all round. Record in Pheasants,' reads the comment. The Guns included Lord Bandon (who has a knack for turning up on the best shoot days – or perhaps he causes them to be good), Lord Cairns and Lord Ennismore, each of whom were regular Guns at Dromoland. Ennismore was William Hare, 3rd Earl of Listowel, KP (1833-1924), known as Viscount Ennismore from 1837 to 1856, an Anglo-Irish peer and Liberal politician.

Listowel was the eldest son of William Hare, 2nd Earl of Listowel, and Maria Augusta Windham. He succeeded his father in the earldom in 1856 but as this was an Irish peerage it did not entitle him to a seat in the House of Lords. However, in 1869 he was created Baron Hare of Connamore in the County of Cork in the peerage of the United Kingdom, which gave him an automatic seat in the House of Lords. Lord Listowel later served as a Lord-in-Waiting from May to September 1880 in the second Liberal administration of William Ewart Gladstone. In 1873, he was made a Knight of the Order of St Patrick. Lord Listowel married Lady Ernestine Mary, daughter of Ernest Brudenell-Bruce, 3rd Marquess of Ailesbury, in 1865. He died in June 1924, aged ninety-

81 Donagh, 16th Baron Inchiquin (standing left of entrance) at field trials, Dromoland Castle, 1955.

one, and was succeeded by his eldest son, Richard. Two of his grandsons, William Hare, 5th Earl of Listowel, and John Hare, 1st Viscount Blakenham, became British government ministers.

Lucius's successor, in 1929, was his eldest son, Donough Edward Foster O'Brien, 16th Baron Inchiquin (1897-1968), who in 1962, burdened by the financial difficulties of maintaining such a large residence, sold Dromoland Castle and the surrounding 350 acres to an American developer, Bernard P. McDonough, who converted the family seat into a luxury hotel. McDonough owned Dromoland until 1987, when he sold it to a consortium of mainly Irish American investors who continue to operate it.

Lord Inchiquin subsequently built Thomond House on a hill overlooking Dromoland. He moved his family into this Georgian-style house in 1965 but he died in 1968. He was succeeded by his brother Phaedrig Lucius Ambrose O'Brien, 17th Baron Inchiquin (1900-1982), who lived at Thomond House until his death. He and his wife (Anne Molyneux Thesiger) had no children, and the title passed to his nephew Conor Myles John O'Brien (b. 1943), 18th and present Baron Inchiquin.

Donagh Edward's personal Game Book opens in 1926, with the remark:

Discovered through shooting at a hare going away from me in a dead straight line over wet grass why for years I have been shooting so badly. The reason is that I have been shooting with a straight stocked gun, whereas my left eye is the master eye and I should therefore have a cross-over stock.

He continues, in 1927:

> Sold my single gun to Stephen Grant (£65), who has built me a pair of cross-over stock guns. The result is that my shooting has improved by almost 100 per cent. This shows how important it is to have a gun properly fitted to one. Cost of pair of twelve bore guns and cases, etc., £250.

The book mainly records his shooting at English Partridge shoots and Scottish Grouse moors. He was only at Dromoland once before 1942, which was in 1930, when there was shooting on 8, 9 and 11 January, and in respect of the first day, he remarked:

> A small shoot held a month after my father's death. Guns: Major G. Studdert, Capt. F. Blood, Capt. R. Tottenham, Hon. E. O'Brien, Hon. F. O'Brien, Self. Cocks only. Shooting moderate. Only fine frosty morning in a month of wild stormy weather. Shot over whole demesne in the day, which was too much.

The bag was twenty-three Woodcock and forty-six Pheasants and ground game. The following day was 'cold and stormy weather' with only himself, his brother the Hon. Fionn Myles, and their uncle the Hon. Edward Donagh, and the same Guns were out the third day despite, 'heavy snow on ground and snow storms all day'. Eight Woodcock and thirty-one Pheasants was the bag for the two days.

A summary of the bag record for Dromoland over the period 1928-1935 is contained in the table below. There is clearly a falling-off in the bags recorded in these years compared with the pre-1914 period. The First World War, the Troubles, and the associated economic and social upheaval clearly took a toll on the shooting at Dromoland.

Summary Bag Record, Dromoland, 1928/29-1933/34:

Season	Pheasants	Woodcock	Snipe
1928/29	58	40	55
1929/30	110	34	29
1930/31	86	19	51
1931/32	50	30	71
1932/33	23	28	101
1933/34	22	32	120

Indeed there appears to have been rather little shooting until after the Second World War, and when it was recommenced in 1948, bags were poor: a couple of dozen Pheasants only but some reasonable Woodcock days, e.g. forty on 22 December 1948 to seven Guns.

In February 1951, a new head keeper, Christopher Shaw from Knockdrin, County Meath, was engaged. 'Reared 800 Pheasants this year. Head Keeper first rate. Dickie Adare and I share Dromoland syndicate shoot,' the Game Book notes.[236] The shooting steadily improved in the early 1950s and the 6th Earl and Countess of Dunraven and Mount Earl, of nearby Adare Manor, were frequently shooting there. Indeed, Nancy Yuille, wife of the 6th Earl is reputed to have taken a 'left and right' at Snipe on one occasion.[237]

Another new Gun in the syndicate was Hew Jellet, a stalwart from the North Slob in County Wexford. Other shooters at this time were Lord Kildare, Col. Howard Bury, Sir Cecil S-K-Harman, Stuart Pakenham-Mahon, Col. the Hon. Bertram Forbes, P. Dunne Cullinan, Col. Giles

Vandeleur, Capt. Alec Drought (author of *A Sportsman looks at Eire*), Maj. Dereck Morley, and Mr and Mrs A. Hutton Wilson (both shooting). However, there is evidence of frustration in some of the comments: 'Perfect day but Woodcock scarce'; 'shot all the best coverts with poor results'. And in 1956 comes the comment, 'Owing to general financial stringency in the country am unable to get sufficient Guns to complete syndicate for three shoots, am therefore reducing to one of 2 days, end of Nov., rent £20.' The first entry for 1957 reads, 'This spring I decided not to rear any Pheasants and to employ one keeper only, Martin Lowry. There was quite a good hatch of wild birds.' Shooting at Dromoland after this time seems to have fizzled out.

In 1984, Don Walshe was invited by Conor Inchiquin to manage the shooting rights, which were in his ownership, and with this initiative a process of renewal commenced. The shooting rights were bought by the hotel in 1987 and since then it has been developed to the broadly based driven Pheasant and duck shoot which is available today.

GLENSTAL ABBEY, COUNTY LIMERICK

> The Barrington family's Glenstal Abbey coverts in County Limerick were among the best in Victorian and Edwardian Ireland.
>
> Colin McKelvie, *The Book of the Woodcock* (1990).[238]

The Barringtons were a major landowning family with an estate of over 9,400 acres in Murroe, County Limerick, towards the end of the nineteenth century.[239] They had lived in Limerick since the seventeenth century, but it was not until 1818 that Sir Matthew Barrington, 2nd Baronet (1788-1861), acquired a lease of a substantial area of land, including Cappercullen, Garranbane, Glenstal, Meentolla, etc. Soon a new village – Murroe – was constructed on the estate, the castle was built, and Matthew took up residence in 1840. In the same year the freehold was bought out from the heirs of Lord Carbery.[240] Sir Matthew was a Crown Solicitor. However, this did not prevent him becoming friendly with Daniel O'Connell, with whom he corresponded.

Sir Croker Barrington, 4th Baronet (1817-1890) succeeded to the title in 1872 following the death of his older brother Sir William Hartigan Barrington, 3rd Baronet (1815-1872). He held the office of Deputy Lieutenant and like his forbearers he enjoyed generally good relations with his tenants. His son John Beatty Barrington (1859-1926), of Ashroe House, Murroe, became agent to Lord Cloncurry, in respect of the latter's neighbouring estate. Cloncurry's record of tenant relations was considerably less fortunate than Barrington's. In the early years of the twentieth century, following the passing of the Land Acts, the Barringtons sold much of their estate lands, but continued to live at Glenstal until the 1920s.

In 1895, Sir Charles Burton Barrington, 5th Baronet (1848-1943), eldest son of Sir Croker, married Mary Rose Bacon, daughter of Sir Henry Hickman Bacon, 10th Baronet (Redgrave), 11th Baronet (Mildenhall) (1820-1872), and Elizabeth Beckett. Sir Charles graduated from Trinity College Dublin with an MA and he held the office of High Sheriff of County Limerick in 1879 and became 5th Baronet Barrington of the City of Limerick in 1890. He gained the rank of honorary colonel in the service of the Limerick City Royal Filed Reserve Artillery, South Division, and was invested as a Member, Order of the British Empire (MBE) in 1919. He held the office of Deputy Lieutenant and JP for County Limerick.

Social life at Glenstal was generally vibrant:

> Entertainments were arranged on a grand scale, especially during the shooting season. A large number of people were employed both in the castle and in the grounds. All in all it is clear that Glenstal was the centre of considerable activity throughout the second half of the nineteenth century.[241]

82 **Glenstal Abbey, County Limerick.**

There was great rejoicing by the tenants at Sir Charles's wedding, which was a reflection of the esteem and warmth in which the Barringtons were held. Equally impressive celebrations occurred two years later, in 1902, with the birth of his heir, Charles Bacon Barrington(1902-1980).[242]

'As the Glenstal Estate was consolidated and landscaped the sport of shooting evolved and became formalised. The great Rhododendron plantations and woodland coverts grew to form the basis of the Glenstal Woodcock beats, where record bags at the turn of the twentieth century exceeded 200.'[243]

The family was involved in the development of the Irish Water Spaniel, specifically for hunting and retrieving Woodcock, and these were used exclusively on the shoot, for both Sir Croker and Sir Charles maintained that, 'the smaller land spaniels were of little use, having neither nose nor brain for Woodcock'.[244]

References to these dogs exist in the correspondence of Sir Matthew (1788-1861) and also in a journal of Sir William (1815-1872), from the early part of the nineteenth century:

> The dogs generally were bred and kept in the stable yard and some with the keepers at the back lodge. The dogs that the keeper O'Neill kept were generally called 'Paddy' and 'Duchess' and the later ones that the keeper Verrent had were generally called 'Punch' and 'Judy'.[245] When Mary Rose

Bacon married Sir Charles, then one or two of the dogs began to play a larger part in family life. 'Grouse' was a family favourite in the early 1900s; she was a great worker on the shoot but also travelled extensively with the family and the late Sir Charles Barrington regularly took her fishing with him for she was very clever at pointing and retrieving fish. My cousin, the late Miss Florence Barrington [d. 1968] with her great Annagh dogs, is a name that has become almost synonymous with the breed. Although the family always had the dogs, the first that Miss Barrington actually owned was 'Paddy' (No.1), who was bred in 1918 by Brian Day, the gamekeeper at Ballinagard, and went back in time to Sir Charles's 'Paddy' of 1883, and John [Beatty] Barrington's 'Tweedie' of 1906. Miss Barrington subsequently dedicated much of her life to the breed and at one time had as many as sixty-four dogs in the kennels at Clonshavoy [the home of Florence Barrington until her death in 1968. She was the last of the Barringtons to live in County Limerick]. Her brother, Capt. C.E. Barrington [Brigadier Croker Edward Barrington, 1897-1944] also had several Irish Water Spaniels; he married Miss G.M. Bligh [Gwendoleen Mary], who although known throughout the world with her Brittas German shepherds, is also very well known for her Brittas Irish water spaniels.[246]

The whereabouts of the Glenstal Game Book are not known, but there are several secondary references to the shooting (and shooters) that enable a good picture of shooting life at Glenstal to be assembled.

The earliest shooting records are for the years 1853 to 1868 and are contained in a copy of a manuscript ledger page which records the shooting party, place, bag details and observations and shoot dates for these years. The shooting parties were small, often comprising just Sir Croker Barrington and his older brother William and/or his brother-in-law William Richard Le Fanu (1816-1894), author of *Seventy years of Irish Life* (1893), who was married to Sir Croker's eldest sister, Victorine Barrington.[247] Others to appear at this time were 'Massy' and 'Speight' and 'J. Bayly'. During these fifteen years, shooting took place about four times during the season, usually in the month of December. The bag averaged between eighteen and twenty Woodcock a day, to two or three Guns, and the shooting seems to have been confined to 'Upper' and 'Lower Woods', presumably because many of the planted coverts were not yet sufficiently mature. In summary over the fifteen seasons, the bag was 898 Woodcock, 213 Pheasants, 578 hares and 54 Snipe.

Following on, from *The Field* of 2 January 1875, there is a report of the Christmas shooting party, which comprised Lord Clarina, his younger brother Col. Lionel Massey (1837-1922), who became 5th Baron Clarina in 1897, Sir Croker Barrington, his sons Charles Burton (1851-1926) and John Beatty, John Bayly (1830-1890) or his son John (1858-1912) of Debsborough Lodge, Neenagh, County Tipperary, and an E.D. Brickwood of London. Two daughters of John Bayly the elder (who himself was married to a Mary Anne Charlotte Barrington), Florence Jane and Catherine Charlotte, were married to brothers Croker and John Beatty Barrington respectively. It is unclear how many days' shooting were involved, however the overall bag comprised:

84 Sir Charles
Barrington
(1848-1943)
with his son
Charles Bacon
Barrington
(1902-1980)
at the Killaloe
Gate, Glenstal.

Pheasants	382
Hares	115
Woodcock	37
Rabbits	234
Snipe	30

Two years later, on 6 January 1877, *The Field* contained a report of shooting over two days in December 1876, when the bag was:

Pheasants	278
Woodcock	76
Hares	45

The party again comprised Lord Clarina and John Bayly, with Col. the Hon. John Massy, James Spright and H.S. Croker.

The John Massy was probably John Thomas William Massy, 6th Baron Massy (1835-1915), who was a cousin of Lord Clarina. John was a representative peer in the British House of Lords from 1876 to 1915. He succeeded to the title following the death of his older brother Hugh Hamon, the 5th Baron Massy, in 1874. He was one of Ireland's wealthiest landowners at the time, having large properties in Counties Leitrim, Dublin, Limerick and Tipperary. This included large country houses at Killakee in south County Dublin and Hermitage in Castleconnell, County Limerick. However, by the time of his death in 1915, his fortune had been reduced to almost nothing, and subsequently all his estates were sold by his successors, the 7th and 8th Barons Massy, or were repossessed by the banks. He was married to Lady Lucy Maria Butler (d. 1896), daughter of Somerset Richard Butler, 3rd Earl of Carrick, and his second wife, Lucy French.

Francis and James Spaight

This father and son were regulars at Glenstal (although they don't appear at either Dromoland or Eden Vale, in contrast with most of the others found here at Glenstal, who appeared regularly at these other shoots) and integral parts of Limerick life for the greater part of the nineteenth century.

Francis started a timber-importing business in Sarsfield Street. However, it is as a ship-owner that he is remembered, transporting emigrants through the port of Limerick in the aftermath of the Great Famine. Among his better-known ships – all of which were a couple of hundred ton each – was the *James Black*, the ill-fated *Derry Castle* and the *Francis Spaight*, which was lost at sea in 1835 while on a return journey to Limerick with a cargo of timber. It is reported that the captain and crew survived several weeks in the demisted vessel, without food or water, by devouring two of their fellows.[248]

Francis Spaight retired to a beautiful mansion on the shores of Lough Derg called Derry Castle and the business was carried on by his son James. James Spaight was MP for Limerick and elected High Sheriff in 1853. He lived at No.77 George's Street (O'Connell Street). While he was Mayor in 1856, he assisted in the ceremony of laying the foundation stone of St John's Cathedral. In 1867, he succeeded in influencing the Conservative Government to wipe out the debt on the harbour, which amounted to a staggering £175,000. Though the family has died out in the city, the name is well preserved close to the scene of their early activities.

Henry Stanley Monck Croker (1846-1897)

The second son of Edward Croker (1812-1869) and Lady Georgina Ellen Monck, sixth daughter of the 1st (and only) Earl of Rathdowne. He held the office of JP for County Limerick and also Deputy Lieutenant. He lived at Ballynaguarde, County Limerick. He died unmarried.

His younger brother, Courtney le Poer Trench Croker (b. 1853), also features at Glenstal, as he does at Eden Vale and Dromoland. He was auditor of the Local Government Board in 1882. He also held the office of JP for County Limerick as well as that of Deputy Lieutenant. He lived at Ballynaguarde and at Blackwater, County Limerick. He was married to Mary Hare, daughter of the Venerable Charles Hare, Archdeacon of Limerick. He died without issue.

Finally there was Charles de la Poer Beresford Croker (1856-1891), who was the youngest of this generation. He married an Edith Elizabeth Adams and had one child, Alfred Edward Beresford Croker, who was born in 1886. He was shooting during a ten-day shoot over Christmas 1881, along with Sir Charles Barrington, his sons, James Spaight and Mr Brickwood from London. The bag, reported in *The Field* (8 January 1881), was:

Pheasants	379
Hares	251
Woodcock	80
Various	68

However, it was noted that it was 'a bad season for Woodcock this year, this time last season 225 Woodcock shot'.

In December 1883, six Guns shooting over three days accounted for the following (*The Field*, 29 December 1883):

18 December: Upper Woods

Pheasants	4
Woodcock	61
Hares	22
Rabbits	3

19 December: Demesne

Pheasants	230
Woodcock	8
Rabbits	4

20 December: Castle Wood and Coolnaleila

Pheasants	251
Woodcock	15
Rabbits	185

The Guns comprised Lord Massy, Sir Charles Barrington and his son John Beatty, Charles Croker, James Spaight and Sir David Roche. The last of these was Sir David Vandeleur Roche, 2nd Baronet (1833-1908). He was married firstly to the Hon. Isabella Susannah Adelaide Massey, a sister of Eyre Challanor Henry Massey and Lionel Massey, the 4th and 5th Lord Clarina respectively. He married secondly, in 1872, Mary Anne Massy, daughter of Hugh Massey (1796-1881) and

Mary Anne Harding. His second wife, therefore, was a cousin of John Thomas William Massy, 6th Baron Massy. Sir David held the office of Vice-Lord Lieutenant of County Limerick in 1865. He succeeded to the title of 2nd Baronet Roche of Carass, County Limerick, on 8 April 1865.

In 1884, according to *The Field* (3 January 1885), Barringtons shot the Glenstal coverts on 17-19 December and the Cutlying Woods after Christmas. The overall bag was:

Pheasants	658
Hares	243
Woodcock	114

The guest list, just as previous years, comprised a mixture of Massys, Crokers, Sir David Roche and a Mr Bagwell-Purefoy – likely to have been a son of Edward Bagwell-Purefroy (1819-1883) of Greenfields, County Tipperary. His mother was Margaret Croker, an aunt of Henry Stanley, Courtney and Charles, who married the Very Revd Richard Bagwell.

Captain Edward Bagwell-Purefoy

Captain Edward Bagwell-Purefoy was baptised with the name of Edward Bagwell. He was educated at Harrow and gained the rank of captain in the service of the 3rd Dragoon Guards. His name was legally changed to Capt. Edward Bagwell-Purefoy by Royal Licence on 5 April 1847, after he succeeded to the estate of Col. Purefoy, who died in 1846. He married, firstly, Isabella Petronella Langley, daughter of Maj. Henry Langley, on 10 July 1854. Their union was to be childless. He secondly married Charlotte Wilkinson, daughter of John Green Wilkinson, on 20 July 1861.

He died on 2 July 1883 at the age of sixty-three years, having held the offices of JP and Vice-Lieutenant. He gained the rank of honorary colonel in the service of the County Tipperary Artillery Militia and lived at Greenfields, County Tipperary. His children included Lt Wilfred Bagwell-Purefoy (1862-1930), Capt. Henry John Bagwell-Purefoy (1864-1917) and Capt. Edward Bagwell-Purefoy (1868-1960).

The Barringtons' shoot was renowned for its Woodcock, and a bag record is contained in Acland-Hood's *The Gun at Home and Abroad, British Game Birds and Wildfowl*. In correspondence of 4 February 1912, Sir Charles Barrington informs Acland-Hood as follows:

> Woodcock begin to appear here in numbers at the end of October and the beginning of November, but all the same, a few come dribbling in from end September and I am unable to see here any difference between what are said to be foreign birds and our own that have bred here. In fact, there is no difference but when someone picks up and feels a bird that is thin, he says it is a foreigner. I think our home bred birds do not go away to any great distance but only just move about locally as the food supply varies – of course this only refers to Glenstal and not to other places further north. I have seen them feeding on the lawn here just at dusk, sometimes almost standing on their heads, with the bill right down in the ground, after a worm I suppose, but generally getting the worms with a side thrust; after every five or six efforts they take an easy and shake themselves up and settle their feathers and then at it again until successful. I could never see them get the worm they are so quick …
>
> I have seen two nests within a yard of each other and close to this house. I showed them to a friend who was staying here, four eggs in each nest, and they are very fertile, as I have only once seen a bad egg in all the nests I have seen. They breed again in July and I have often seen young

birds in August. I had nine young ones marked some years ago. Two were shot the same year here and one was found dead six years afterwards and brought to me. I stopped marking them as I think it does harm to the young birds and causes injury and death. The following are the bags made on my best beat, Flavin, since:

1891	99 Woodcock
1892	105 Woodcock
1894	89 Woodcock
1895	73 Woodcock
1896	74 Woodcock
1897	55 Woodcock
1898	109 Woodcock
1900	53 Woodcock
1901	58 Woodcock
1902	60 Woodcock
1903	60 Woodcock
1904	Not shot regularly
1905	56 Woodcock
1906	76 Woodcock
1907	85 Woodcock
1908	61 Woodcock
1909	87 Woodcock
1910	100 Woodcock

I have another beat, Bobermanshill, where we average about 50 per day.[249]

Doubtless, shooting continued on after the years above; however, within a decade tragedy was to strike the heart of the Barrington family, with the killing of Sir Charles's only daughter, Winifred, in an IRA ambush of a car driven by twenty-six-year-old Maj. Henry Biggs, District

85 Shoot at Eden Vale, 1902. The gentleman second right, with cap, is Sir Charles Burton Barrington. The lady in the centre with gloves to her waist and a fur stole is Mary-Rose Bacon, wife of Sir Charles.

Inspector of the Royal Irish Constabulary. Biggs' reputation was as notorious as Winifred's was one of kindness and popularity. On 15 May 1921, she paid the ultimate price, at the age of twenty-two, for sharing company and friendship with Biggs, as the two of them (along with her friend Miss Coverdale, a guest at Glenstal, Capt. Tamgouse, Oxfordshire and Buckinghamshire Light Infantry, and Mr William Gabbett of Mount Rivers, Newport, County Limerick), having taken tea at a house, drove back over Coolboreen Bridge. The car was ambushed, 'twenty-five to thirty shots rang out from both sides of the road on a level with the car,'[250] and the driver (Biggs) and front-seat passenger (Winifred) were shot dead. Biggs was to have left Ireland on Whit Sunday, 1921. Winifred was buried at Abingdon churchyard on 16 May 1921. Her tombstone bears the inscription, 'Here lies all that could die of Winifred Frances Barrington'.

Sir Charles Barrington offered Glenstal to the State but this was declined, and it was taken over by the Benedictine community in 1927, where they established a school that remains to this day. Sir Charles Barrington left Ireland and settled at Fairthorne Manor, Botley, Hampshire, where he lived until his death in 1943. In his final year, Sir Charles, then ninety-five, recalled an occasion when he was:

> … entertaining a house party of English peers and their wives at his 10,000 acre estate in County Limerick, when a sinister-looking Irish man asked to see him and told him that six men were going to blow up the castle.
>
> 'How do you know?' asked Sir Charles.
>
> 'Because I'm one of them,' retorted the caller.
>
> 'What explosives are you going to use?'
>
> 'I don't know but it looks for all the world like stick of liquorice.'
>
> Sir Charles asked the man to tell his friends not to disgrace their country in the eyes of his English guests. 'They'll be gone on Wednesday so put the attack off until Thursday night,' he advised and then proceeded to demonstrate his prowess with the rifle. On the Thursday night, Sir Charles, armed with gun and a bottle of tea, sat on guard in the bushes, but no one came.[251]

MUCKROSS ABBEY, KILLARNEY, COUNTY KERRY (INCLUDING THE ESTATE OF THE EARL OF KENMARE)

Muckross House is located on the small Muckross Peninsula between Muckross Lake and Lough Leane, two of the lakes of Killarney, about four miles from the town of Killarney in County Kerry. It was designed by the Scottish architect William Burn and was built in 1843 for Henry Arthur Herbert and his wife, the watercolourist Mary Balfour Herbert.

The Herbert family connection with Kerry began in 1656, when Thomas Herbert of Montgomery in Wales was appointed land agent for his cousin the 3rd Lord Castleisland. The Herbert family became very wealthy during the eighteenth century from the copper mines on the Muckross Peninsula. However, it was not until 1770 that the family became the actual owners of the lands at Muckross, following the death of a MacCarthy relation.

With sixty-five rooms, Muckross House was built in the Tudor style. In 1870, the estate extended to 47,238 acres.[252] Extensive improvements were undertaken in the 1850s, in preparation for the visit of Queen Victoria in 1861, and it is said that these improvements for the Queen's visit were a contributing factor in the financial difficulties suffered by the Herbert family which resulted in the sale of the estate in 1899, when it was bought by Arthur Guinness, 1st Baron Ardilaun. Lord

Ardilaun was related through marriage to the Herbert family. His wife Olivia was a daughter of Jane, Countess of Bantry. Jane was the youngest sister of Col. Henry Arthur Herbert (1815-1866). The Ardilauns spent very little time at Muckross and it was let out on an annual basis as a shooting and fishing lodge.

Muckross has an illustrious shooting history, dating from the mid-nineteenth century. However, there does not appear to be an Estate Game Book and it appears that the shooting was frequently let. The same is true also of the Kenmare Estate.[253] In a diary entry by Lord Cloncurry for 4 January 1887, he expressed his admiration at Lord Ardilaun's account of a famous shoot at Muckross in 1863. During the shoot, 800 Woodcock were shot in eight days by six Guns.[254] The story may have grown a little in the telling. Acland-Hood quotes as follows:

> Lord Ardilaun has kindly sent the following interesting extract from a letter of Lord Wemyss referring to a wonderful week he had at Muckross, Killarney, in January 1863:

> 'And now as to the "cack", as the Irish beater, the best in the world, pronounces the word. These were muzzle-loading days and I shot with two Boss twelve bores, my servant loading for me. In the course of the eight consecutive days, I bagged 245. My smallest day, the first, eighteen. The best, on Thomies Beat, fifty-three, and if I had worked as hard and as carefully after I had got fifty as I did before, I'm sure that I should have made up at least sixty. The total bag for five guns was 620.'[255]

86 **Muckross House, County Kerry.**

Whatever the true position, it is clear there were a lot of Woodcock in the Muckross coverts in 1863!

Payne-Gallwey makes reference to the same shoot at Muckross and more:

The year Lord Elcho resided at Muckross, Killarney, the party, averaging five Guns, shot in ten days 420 couple of Woodcock (840 birds). In that winter (1863/64) there were killed 1,250 Woodcock and Lord Elcho shot to his own gun in one day 25 couple. Since then, Mr C. Balfour and Mr A. Herbert shot in one day 37½ couple at the same place. In these covers another year, 38 couple were killed by the Duke of Roxborough in a day. There were shot on two consecutive days, a few years ago in Tomies and Glenflesk woods, Muckross, 116 couple (232 birds). I learn from Mr H. Herbert of Cahirnane that Woodcock now breed in considerable numbers around Killarney.[256]

Francis Richard Charteris, 10th Earl of Wemyss, GCVO (1818-1914)

Styled as Lord Elcho between 1853 and 1883, he was a British Whig politician and founder of the Liberty and Property Defence League. Lord Elcho was commanding officer of the London Scottish regiment for seventeen years, from its formation in 1859. He developed an interest in the alternative medical practice of homeopathy and was President of the London Homeopathic Hospital until his death. He married Lady Anne Frederica Anson. In addition to his five sons he was also father of Evelyn Charteris, who married the 4th Viscount de Vesci (Vesey) of Abbeyleix, Queen's County. Their only daughter, Mary Gertrude, was the second wife of Aubrey Herbert (second son of Henry Herbert, 4th Earl of Carnarvon), whose daughter Laura Herbert married the writer Evelyn Waugh, and was the mother of Auberon Waugh.

Another visiting Gun was Lord de Grey, who was there on 7 January 1875, when sixty-two Woodcock were shot by six Guns at Muckross, with de Grey accounting for twenty-six Woodcock himself.[257]

J.B. Drought, writing in the 1930s had this to say of Muckross:

> I can just remember hearing of the days when, prior to taking over Ashford, Lord Ardilaun owned that other lovely property – Muckross Abbey. This, if I recollect rightly, he bought back in the 'seventies from the trustees of its original owners the Herberts and in his charge the Muckross coverts gained much the same reputation as Ashford subsequently held. My father used to shoot there and although my first recollection of the place dates back less than forty years, I think, writing off the book, that the record annual bag made sometime in the 'eighties was around 1,200 Woodcock.[258]

It is possible that Drought simply has his dates confused. (Ashford was acquired by Sir Benjamin Lee Guinness, for his eldest son Arthur, subsequently Lord Ardilaun, from Lord Oranmore and Browne in 1852, and Ardilaun acquired Muckross in 1899 from the Standard Life Assurance Company to whom the estate had been forfeited the previous year.) However, in other details Drought is quite accurate. Therefore, a more plausible theory (for which, unfortunately, no documentary evidence has been found) may be that Lord Ardilaun actually had leased the shooting from the Herbert family, to whom he was related (see above). This would explain his connection to the shooting and the correspondence of Lord Elcho to him referred to by Acland-Hood.

One man who leased the shooting at Muckross, from 1878 to 1886, and whose Game Books have survived and been made available, was Capt. Edward Amphlett (1824-1887) of Ashwood House, Kingswinford, Staffordshire, England. He also leased the stalking and shooting at Lord Kenmare's Estate. He later had at least two residences – one in Cheltenham and one in London

– though he clearly spent many months away hunting, shooting and fishing. As a young man he was a captain in the Royal Scots Greys regiment. He died on 23 November 1887 whilst on a shooting holiday in Scotland. Little else is known of the man. He was married firstly, in 1851, to Lavinia Flora Henrietta Greenhill (1831-1871) of Somerset, and secondly, in 1873, to Margaret Louisa Maria Brewster. There were two children from the first marriage – a daughter, Helen Mary Flora ('Nell') (1852-1906) and son, Edward Greenhill ('Ned') (1853-1930) – and two daughters and a son from the second marriage. The latter three had no issue and Ned's three children died without issue. The family has survived to date through Helen's daughter Rosalind Flora Bridge (1884-1966), who married Edward Stainer (1869-1948) of Oxfordshire in 1907.

Probably referring to Amphlett's lease of that same year, in 1884 Alexander Innes Shand noted that:

> The deer-forest of 23,000 acres is rented by Mr Amphlett, besides the deer ground of Lord Kenmare and lands belonging to Mr Herbert of Cloghereen. For the actual shooting Mr Amphlett pays a rental of £2,000, which would certainly be considered very cheap in Scotland. He is limited to forty stags; and last year he killed stags up to his limit, besides fifteen hinds … last year he and his party had 1,150 Woodcock, nearly 200 brace of Grouse, 350 brace of Pheasants, and 300 hares. As for rabbits they are swarming on the hills.[259]

Amphlett's Game Book for 1878 to 1880 contains a brief description of the habitat and terrain at Muckross at the time:

> Muckross Abbey, 3½ miles from Killarney – about 50,000 acres of which about 5,000 are forest, about 5,000 covert, about 5,000 mountain, holding as few Grouse and hares as hills could hold – the rest bog, water and cultivated land – most of this lying distant from house 8, 12, 10 and 25 miles off, the property being much dispersed and separated by Lord Kenmare's and others. Snipe, Partridge, hares and rabbits very scarce … Lots of wildfowl but hard to get at … Deer heavy and good heads – but too much covert renders them difficult to see and kill. About 3 miles of salmon on the Leaune. This was formerly good, has of later years been back. Hard winter so far, very favourable for 'cock, but on occasion of party so much snow fell as to cover bushes so that beaters could not work right. Also frost prevented boats from getting to Tomies and driving to Glenflesk.

For around thirty-five days' shooting over 1878/9, Amphlett and his party (six Guns at most, though more usually three to four) had a staggering bag of 997, comprising:

Grouse	33
Pheasants	54
Partridge	5
Snipe	76
Wildfowl	86
Woodcock	693
Hares	25
Rabbits	10
Extras	15

As the records show, it was predominantly a Woodcock shoot. Shooting was quite intensive. In 1878 the Guns were out on nine days between 20 and 30 November; fourteen days during the month of December; nine days in January 1879, and three days (the first three) in February. For the most part, there were four Guns shooting, including Amphlett, who appears not to have missed a day! The Guns are noted as: 'Spencer, self and Ross'; 'Spencer, self and Gill'; 'Bennett, Spencer, self and Ross'.[260] Other names to appear are Bence, Sullivan, Farley, Leahy[261] and Col. Herbert. The 'Colonel' is more correctly Maj. Henry Arthur Herbert (1840-1901), who succeeded his father, Col. Henry Arthur Herbert (1815-1866), at Muckross. The Bence may be William Francis Bence Jones ('Immense Jones') (1856-1883) of Lisselane, County Cork, who died in a shooting accident on 20 November 1883.[262] The Bennett is likely to have been a keeper. Indeed, with all leased shooting situations, which were characterised by visiting (rather than resident) shooting parties, it is very difficult to pin-down with sufficient certainty who the participants were. One figure that can be identified with reasonable certainty is Charles K. Akroyd. In his published diaries, *A Veteran Sportsman's Diary* (Inverness, 1926), Akroyd writes that he was invited by Amphlett to shoot in Muckross in 1879, who, he states, 'never asked anyone who was not a good shot'.

However, regardless of who they were, they certainly enjoyed good shooting. The best of it was on 11-13 December 1878, when fifty-five Woodcock were taken on 11 December on 'Tomies Beat' by 'Sullivan, Bence Farley, Bennett and Amphlett', followed by forty-four the next day by the same Guns at 'West Glenflesk', when 'snow cost us ten couple', followed by thirty-eight on 13 December on the Pool Beat.

The following year, the party was more or less the same, with the addition of the names 'Taylor' and 'Sutherland'. There are references also to Millar Davidson and someone of the name O'Connell participating in various dates.[263] Amphlett notes that:

The summer of 1879 was very wet and cold and probably the worst game season that was ever known – from 1 Oct. to Xmas however, the weather was very fine – it was the worst 'cock year ever known at Muckross, notwithstanding there was an east wind throughout November with severe weather in the highlands and Sweden combined with very fine weather for shooting…

The bulk of the shooting took place in December – thirteen days – and there was an unspecified number of days' shooting up to the end of November, with a further five days in January. For a 'poor' season, the bag comprised an impressive 734 head, including:

	1879/80	1880/81
Grouse	87	95
Pheasants	42	101
Partridge	9	31
Woodcock	355	370
Snipe	100	142
Wildfowl	72	110
Golden Plover	20	–

The best shooting in terms of Woodcock was Glenfesk East (twenty-eight on 18 December and twenty-seven on 15 December) and the Pool Beat (twenty-five on 8 December and twenty-seven on 19 December). And as may be seen, the following season of 1880/81 was on a par with the pre-

109 Kenmore, Hubert & Cahirmane — 1883 – 1884

1884 Date	Grouse	Black Game	Ptarmigan	Pheasant	Partridge	Woodcock	Snipe	Wild Fowl	Brown Hare	Blue Hare	Rabbit	Roe	Extra	Total	Where

87 **Page from Game Book of Capt. Edward Amphlett (1824-1887).**

vious one. Again, the same names appear shooting, with the addition of 'Browne'. This is likely to have been Valentine Augustus Browne, 4th Earl of Kenmare, KP, PC (1825-1905), styled Viscount Castlerosse from 1853 to 1871, from whom Amphlett also leased shooting.

Browne was the son of Thomas Browne, 3rd Earl of Kenmare, by his wife Catherine O'Callaghan, daughter of Edmund O'Callaghan of Kilgory, County Clare. He became known by the courtesy title Viscount Castlerosse when his father succeeded in the Earldom of Kenmare in 1853. Lord Castlerosse was appointed High Sheriff of Kerry in 1851. The following year he was returned to parliament as one of two representatives for Kerry, and in 1856 he was appointed Comptroller of the Household under Lord Palmerston, a post he held until the government fell in 1858. He was sworn as a member of the Privy Council in February 1857. When Palmerston resumed office in 1859, Castlerosse became Vice-Chamberlain of the Household, which he remained until 1866, the last year under the premiership of Lord Russell. He once again became Vice-Chamberlain of the Household in 1868, in Gladstone's first administration.

In December 1871, Valentine Augustus Browne succeeded his father in the earldom and took his seat in the House of Lords. In February 1872, he was appointed a Lord-in-Waiting, and in June of that year he was made a Knight of the Order of St Patrick. The Liberal Government fell in 1874 and when Gladstone returned as Prime Minister in 1880, Lord Kenmare was appointed Lord Chamberlain of the Household. He held this office until 1885 and again briefly in Gladstone's third administration. Apart from his political career, he was also Lord Lieutenant of Kerry between 1866 and 1905.

Lord Kenmare married Gertrude Thynne, daughter of Revd Lord Charles Thynne, Canon of Canterbury, and granddaughter of Thomas Thynne, 2nd Marquess of Bath, on 28 April 1858. They had three children: Lady Margaret Theodora May Catherine Browne (d. 1940), who married G.C. Douglas in 1889, and died childless; Valentine Charles Browne, 5th Earl of Kenmare (1860-1941), and the Hon. Cecil Augustine Browne (1864-1887).

From 1883 to 1886, Amphlett's records incorporate shooting at the Earl of Kenmare's Estate and Cahirnane, another Herbert property which he had obviously leased in addition to Muckross during these years. He describes the Kenmare shooting in 1883 as follows:

> Lord Kenmare's shooting consisted of about 140,000 acres of which about 3,000 are wood, many of the coverts being very good for 'cock, Pheasants and other game – there is also good cock shooting on some of his mountains, notably under the Paps. Muckross consists of about 50,000 acres, more scattered and not so easily worked – the deer shooting is much superior to Lord Kenmare's, the 'cock shooting decidedly inferior this year, though perhaps as a rule about equal, but all other kinds of game and ground far inferior – Grouse did badly, young destroyed by rain, Snipe and Golden Plover scarce and wild owing to such stormy weather which lasted throughout the autumn and winter and after there was a good supply of 'cock in the county. They stayed chiefly on the mountains and did not collect in the coverts, so did not afford a big day – also could not work the ducks owing to the weather. Other kinds of game did fairly well, but the tenants have destroyed the hares all over the low grounds.

It is somewhat difficult to reconcile the commentary with the outcome of the 1883/84 and subsequent 1884/85 and 1885/86 seasons, which, in aggregate (for Muckross, Kenmare and Cahirnane), were as follows:

	1883/84	1884/85	1885/86
Grouse	233	500	393
Pheasant	344	369	214
Partridge	144	287	113
Woodcock	1,147	1,002	1,091
Snipe	311	500	198
Wildfowl	51	24	38 (of which 3 geese)
Hares	316	140	98
Rabbits	575	335	185
Golden Plover	20	20	13
Pigeon	50	22	30

Shooting took place over seventy-two days in 1883/84 (fourteen days from August to mid-November; three days in November after that; twenty-two days in December; twenty-one days in January and twelve days in February); seventy-nine days in 1884/85 (fifteen days from August to end October; twelve days in November; twenty-five days in December; nineteen days in January and eight days in February), and seventy-eight days in 1885/86 (fourteen days from August to end October; thirteen days in November; twenty days in December; twenty-one days in January and thirteen days in February). However, there were seldom more than four Guns out. Consistency of shooting a couple of dozen birds on average each day, over more than forty-five days, is what yielded the extraordinary Woodcock bag. Weather was, of course, also was an important factor.

Amphlett has this to say of 1884:

> The year eighty-four was a very good breeding season everywhere and was the finest summer
> and autumn known in Killarney for many a long year. Thus we had a better show of game but
> the fishing was thereby spoilt altogether. Deer were in very good condition – Woodcock not so
> plentiful as last season and they were lately and partial. Some of the beats that were usually the
> best proving the worst, and in some parts of the Kingdom they were very scarce, moreover all
> this winter was wet and spoilt the shoots and the same remark applies to Golden Plover, Snipe
> and wildfowl.

The estates of Lord Kenmare and Herbert's Muckross Estate were both in deep financial trouble
and heavily indebted to Standard Life Assurance. In addition, there was deep unrest, tension and
ill feeling between landlords and tenants.[264] Lord Kenmare left Killarney at the end of 1880, following a death threat attributed to the Land League. The earl announced he was quitting Ireland
and pursued a successful political career in England.

However, the shooting (and stalking) continued to be leased at both estates:

> Among those who leased the shootings of Lord Kenmare were Captain Sir Thomas Freake and
> his party, recorded as taking the Earl's preserves 'for a long period' … Lettings were made to
> Captain Wade, Colonel Jenkins and Captain Murrogh for the Bantry shootings … Muckross
> Estate and House was occupied by the Hon. A. Burke and family for the 1890/91 shooting season
> and the following year the letting was taken by Captain A Greville for twelve months [Greville
> was a guest at Glenstal in December 1884].[265]

In 1910, Muckross was let to a wealthy American, Mr William Bowers Bourn. He was owner of
the Empire Gold Mine and Spring Valley Water Company of northern California. A short time
after, Mr Bowers Bourn's only child, Maud, married Mr Arthur Rose Vincent of Summerhill,
Cloonlara, County Clare. Her father purchased the Muckross property as a wedding present for
them. Maud and her husband had two children, Elizabeth Rose (1915-1983) and Arthur William
Bourn (b. 1919). The family travelled extensively but Muckross was their home. During the
years of Bourn and Vincent ownership, and between 1911 and 1932, over £110,000 was spent on
improvements on the estate.

Prior to his marriage, Mr Vincent had served as a judge in the British Colonial Service.
Afterwards, he continued to play an active role in public life. He served as Deputy Lieutenant
of County Kerry in 1914 and was then appointed High Sheriff in 1915. In addition, he served as
a JP. During the War of Independence Mr Vincent appears to have served as an 'honest broker'
between the IRA and the British Government, and he was appointed to the Senate of the Irish
Free State in 1931, but resigned in 1934.

Maud had died of pneumonia in New York in February 1929. She had been on her way to visit
her parents in California. Her husband and children continued to live at Muckross for a further
three years.

In July 1932, Mr Vincent wrote to Mr Éamon de Valera, President of the Executive Council of
the State. He stated that it was his intention, in association with his parents-in-law, to present
Muckross to the Irish nation. With his parents-in-law, Mr Vincent had come to the conclusion
that sustaining Muckross was going to become too big an undertaking for any private individual.
The Bourn Vincent Memorial Park Bill was put before Dáil Éireann on 7 December 1932 and it

88 **Shooting party, 1907, Lord Kenmare's Game Book.**

took effect on 31 December. Under this Act, the Commissioners of Public Works were required to 'maintain and manage the Park as a National Park for the purpose of the recreation and enjoyment of the public'. Following its acquisition by the State, Muckross House remained closed until 1964. Despite this, the park and gardens were open to the public and were visited by large numbers of visitors every year.

Arthur Rose Vincent continued to retain a lively interest in Muckross until his death in 1956. Like Henry Arthur Herbert, he is buried in the nearby Killegy graveyard. Killarney National Park was formed principally from the donation of Muckross Estate and was substantially expanded by acquisition of land from the former Earl of Kenmare's Estate.

6

DRIVEN SHOOTING IN COUNTY WICKLOW: NEW WINE IN OLD BOTTLES

County Wicklow as a shooting destination is remarkable for the fact that it is the modern 'home' of syndicated driven game shooting in Ireland. There are a number of well-established driven Pheasant shoots outside of County Wicklow, like Slane Castle, the home of Lord Henry Mount Charles in County Meath, and the Curraghmore Estate of Lord Waterford. However, there are six such shoots in County Wicklow, at the time of writing, comprising: Ballinacor, Ballyarthur, Castle Howard, Coollattin, Kilruddery, and Shelton Abbey.

Of course in times past, there were, in common with most other counties in Ireland, many more organised shoots than is the case now but what is striking is the revival (mainly from the 1960s) of driven shooting in its modern syndicated form at some of the former County Wicklow estates which hosted some very fine shooting in days gone by. Another feature of County Wicklow, with its close proximity to Dublin City, was the abundance of quality Grouse shooting which lasted until the 1930s or thereabouts, but of which, sadly, there is nothing left today.

This chapter describes the old and the new, and looks at the characters that in the past fifty years or so have forged a revival of estate-based driven game shooting in Ireland.

THE NATURAL HISTORY OF DRIVEN GAME SPECIES

The Pheasant[266]

The Pheasant of today is the result of much selective cross-breeding of various varieties of Pheasant aimed at providing birds of high flying quality while maintaining their quality as a table bird. The original bird introduced into Britain, and probably Ireland, was the Old English Blackneck. The next was the Chinese or Ring-necked Pheasant, probably around the 1740s. There was another introduction, about 1840, of the Japanese or Versicolour Pheasant, a gift from the King of Italy to the Earl of Derby becoming the foundation of this stock. Another strain which had a powerful influence on the bird's evolution has been the Mongolian, introduced in the early years of the twentieth century. More recently, the influence of American breeding has been quite noticeable with the Michigan Blue-backed Pheasant. This cross was developed by Kenneth MacFarlane of Wisconsin, who gave his name to the game farm business he founded 1928, which exists to the present day. A cross between the Manchurian and Chinese Ring-necked, this bird is much favoured for its strong flying ability but requires experienced keepering because of its

89 *The Pheasant*, Philip Rickman.

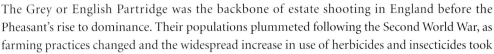

tendency to wander. Whatever the variety, the Pheasant is a beautiful game bird, and the bread and butter of most modern game shoots.

The Grey Partridge

90 The Grey Partridge, Archibald Thorburn.

The Grey or English Partridge was the backbone of estate shooting in England before the Pheasant's rise to dominance. Their populations plummeted following the Second World War, as farming practices changed and the widespread increase in use of herbicides and insecticides took its toll. However, even before this, it does appear that overshooting also played a role in their decline. In Ireland, even at the turn of the twentieth century, the position was that 'Partridges have long been said to be diminishing … Two causes can easily be assigned to this: the discontinuance of wheat growing and the use of breech-loaders combined with poaching.'[267]

In fact, Grey Partridges in Ireland seem to have been distributed quite locally, and were concentrated in Counties Tipperary, Offaly, Laois, Kildare and Meath. The Game Book records which are drawn upon in this book all point to Grey Partridge numbers being in decline by the final quarter of the nineteenth century. Indeed, up to recent years, Ireland's naturally occurring population of Grey Partridge was in serious danger of extinction, with only twenty-two birds nationally, in a single location at Boora Bog in County Offaly. On an encouraging note, October 2011 saw the release of a first batch of native Grey Partridges on a farm near Oldtown in north County Dublin. The Grey Partridge Release Programme is part of the first year of a five-year project aimed at re-establishing a viable population of Irish Grey Partridge in north County Dublin.[268]

While there has been some rearing and releasing of the more resilient red-legged or French Partridges in Ireland, these have been the exceptions, with the result that Pheasants are far and away the most dominant reared game bird in Ireland.

GLENART, WOODENBRIDGE

The Glenart Estate near Avoca, County Wicklow (on the south side of the River Avoca), was the Irish seat of the Proby family, which held the Carysfort Earldom until it became extinct on the death of the 5th Earl, William Proby (1836-1909). At that time, the estate extended to over 16,500 acres.[269] The Probys were related to the Howard family, Earls of Wicklow, of Shelton Abbey (on the north side of the River Avoca).[270]

The shooting at Glenart seems to have taken place only about twice a season. However, on those few occasions annually, truly enormous bags were shot, usually over four days' shooting. There is not a surviving estate Game Book. However, the Game Book of Lord Maurice FitzGerald (1852-1901) of Johnstown Castle, County Wexford, who was a regular guest there, provides a record for the twenty years from 1876.[271] The shooting 'set' at this estate comprised a core of regulars, including Lords Inchiquin of Dromoland, Lord Drogheda of Moore Abbey, several of the Bartons of both Straffan and Glendalough, and of course the host, William Proby, 5th Earl Carysfort (see Dromoland, where all of these are encountered shooting). Captain Edward Symes Bayly (1807-18884) of Ballyarthur, a near neighbour, was there also in most years. More occasional guests were Lord Clarina, Lt-Col. Robert Howard Brooke of Castle Howard, County Wicklow, Capt. Henry Monck, of Charleville, County Wicklow, and Lords Cloncurry and Powerscourt.

A summary of the shooting at Glenart as it is contained in Lord Maurice FitzGerald's records is shown below:

Four days' shooting in November	Pheasants	Hares	Woodcock	Comments
1876	519	136	70	'Cock not in second year of Pheasants.
1877	411	113	174	Beautiful weather hit off a flight of Woodcock.
1878	135	17	58	No Woodcock and very few Pheasants.
1880	675	28	89	Fine show of Pheasant.
1881	505	22	47	One wet day. Pretty shooting.
1882	621	3	45	
1883	492	–	52	
1884	1,321	5	42	
1885	559	–	55	
1886	774	–	94	Second shoot.
1888	2,138	–	46	HH Prince Edward of Saxe-Weimar.
1890	2,127	–	53	Second shoot.
1892	3,145	–	21	
1895	280	–	–	Pheasants failed.
1897	478	–	12	No Woodcock hardly this season – very mild.

The comment 'second year of Pheasants' in respect of 1876 would seem to suggest that prior to 1875 Pheasants were not put down. However, there was clearly a taste for big Pheasant bags thereafter, with some exceeding a thousand, two thousand and even three thousand being recorded for four days' shooting to eight or nine Guns. No other shoot in Ireland known to the author ever produced bags of this magnitude.

Prince Edward of Saxe-Weimar
It is worth noting also that in 1886 there was a record in a diary of Lord Cloncurry relating to a shoot at Glenart on 9-12 of November attended by Prince Edward of Saxe-Weimar, the Marquess of Drogheda, the Earl of Bandon, the Earl of Carysfort, Lord Powerscourt and Lord Inchiquin, at which the bag was 1,687 Pheasants, 68 Woodcock and a few hares.[272] Lord Maurice FitzGerald attended the 'second shoot' there, less than a month later, from 30 November to 3 December, along with eight other Guns, and shot a further 774 Pheasants and 94 Woodcock.

His Highness Prince Edward of Saxe-Weimer (1823-1902) obviously liked what he got. He was back two years later in November 1888, along with the Marquess of Drogheda, the Earl of Bandon, the Earl of Carysfort, Lord Powerscourt, Capt. Henry Monck and Lord Maurice FitzGerald, with devastating results! Moreover, at a 'second shoot' in 1890 a similar bag of over 2,125 Pheasants was shot.

Prince Edward was a British military officer who in 1851 married Augusta Katherine Gordon-Lennox, a daughter of Charles Lennox, 5th Duke of Richmond (a match deemed to be beneath him). She was created Countess of Dornburg by the Grand Duke of Saxe-Weimar the day before the wedding. Edward's royal connections ensured that he proceeded quickly through the ranks, becoming colonel in the Grenadier Guards. In 1870, he was appointed major general commanding the Brigade of Guards and General Officer Commanding, Home District, and in 1878 he became General Officer Commanding, Southern District. In 1885, he became Commander-in-Chief, Ireland, thereby becoming a member of the Irish Privy Council. He was promoted to Field Marshal in 1897 and died in 1902 at Portland Place, London.

The shoot of 8-10 November 1892, when 3,145 Pheasants were shot over just three days by nine Guns, was attended by the Earl of Mayo, Viscount Wolesley, the Earl of Bandon, Mervyn Wingfield (7th Viscount Powerscourt), Lord Annesley, Lord Maurice FitzGerald and the host, the Earl of Carysfort.

The Earl of Mayo at the time was Dermot Robert Wyndham Bourke, 7th Earl of Mayo, KP, PC (1851-1927), styled Lord Naas from 1867 to 1872. He succeeded as Earl of Mayo on the death of his father, Richard Bourke, 6th Earl of Mayo, in 1872, who was murdered while visiting a convict settlement at Port Blair in the Andaman Islands. His mother was Blanche Julia, daughter of George Wyndham, 1st Baron Leconfield. He married Geraldine Sarah Ponsonby, daughter of the Hon. Gerald Henry Brabazon Ponsonby and Lady Maria Emma Catherine Coventry, in 1885. He was one of the four landlord representatives during the 1902 Land Conference. Between 1921 and 1922 he served in the Senate of Southern Ireland and he was nominated by W.T. Cosgrave to the Seanad of the Irish Free State on its formation in 1922. He was nominated for twelve years and served until his death in 1927.

Field Marshal Garnet Joseph Wolseley, 1st Viscount Wolseley, KP, GCB, OM, GCMG, VD, PC (1833-1913) was an Anglo-Irish officer in the British Army. He served in Burma, the Crimean War, India, China, Canada, and widely throughout Africa, including his Ashanti campaign (1873-1874) and the Nile Expedition against Mahdist Sudan in 1884-85. His reputation for efficiency led to the late-nineteenth-century English phrase 'everything's all Sir Garnet', meaning 'all is in order'.

Hugh Annesley, 5th Earl Annesley (1831-1908)

British military officer and MP for County Cavan from 1857 to 1874. He was the second son of William Richard Annesley, 3rd Earl Annesley. He became a professional soldier and served in the Kaffir Wars in South Africa (1851-1853). He was wounded in this war and in the Crimean War his jaw was shattered at the Battle of the Alma (1854). He became Colonel of the Scots Fusilier Guards in 1860. In 1874, his brother William Richard Annesley, 4th Earl Annesley, died unmarried, and Hugh succeeded as 5th Earl Annesley. In 1877, he was elected as a representative peer, serving until his death.

He was a pioneering amateur photographer. Thirty-five albums of his photographs are in the Public Record Office of Northern Ireland. They include pictures taken during the wars in South Africa and the Crimea, and during a visit to Japan, as well as photographs of his home, Castlewellan, County Down, and the surrounding area. He married, first, Mabel Wilhelmina Frances Markham on 4 July 1877. He was forty-six years and she was nineteen. They had a daughter, Lady Mabel Annesley (1881-1959), who became well known as a watercolour painter and wood engraver, and a son, Francis (b. 1884). Francis became 6ᵗʰ Earl Annesley, but was killed in November 1914 in the First World War. Countess Mabel Annesley died at Castlewellan on 17 April 1891 (within three weeks of the death of Hugh's mother, the Dowager Countess Annesley, wife of the 3ʳᵈ Earl, on 29 March 1891). He went on to marry his first cousin Priscilla Cecilia Armytage Moore (1870-1941) on 2 July 1892. He was sixty-one and she was twenty-two.

The last year Lord Maurice FitzGerald shot at Glenart was 1897 and indeed his shooting records after that date are very few. He died in 1901. As noted earlier, Carysfort died in 1909 and, with no direct heirs, his title became extinct. The estate by that time had already been reduced under earlier Land Acts. The residual estate passed initially to his nephew Col. Douglas James Proby, a son of the 5ᵗʰ Earl's sister Emma Elizabeth and her husband Lord Claud Hamilton (1813-1884), of the Abercorn family, which changed its name in 1904 to Proby by Royal Licence. In 1921, there was a devastating fire at Glenart Castle and the estate was diminished further. In 1931 it passed to Col. Douglas's fourth son, Jocelyn, and in 1947 it was sold to the Vincentian Order.

Shooting was taken up on about 1,600 acres of the former Glenart Estate by Mr Jimmy Hamilton (1893-1982) of Falls Road, Shankill, County Dublin, under lease from the Land Commission. This was during the 1950s, when a syndicate under his management engaged in walked-up shooting there. Jim was born in Gorey, County Wexford, and was, by the accounts of some who remember him, a strong character who knew what he wanted and how to get it. He was an entrepreneur with a successful millinery business, which included Pym's Department Store of South Great George's Street in Dublin. He became an early member of the Woodenbridge Syndicate, the forerunner of the Ballyarthur Estate Syndicate of today, when it was first established in November 1967. Jim was still shooting well into his eighties, using a gun built by William Kavanagh & Son of Dame Street, which he purchased for £25 from a Dublin dentist in the early 1940s.

BALLINACOR, RATHDRUM

Ballinacor Estate, a premier shooting estate with a distinguished sporting history dating back to about 1864, was in the ownership of the Kemmis family from 1805 until 1965. After that, it was owned by a cousin of Capt. William Kemmis, namely Col. Richard Lomer, until 1983, when it was acquired over a number of years by the Earl of Meath, Jack Ardee, who completed the acquisition in 1986. Since 2001, it has been in the ownership of Col. Sir Robert and Lady Sheelagh Goff, who have continued to run the estate as perhaps the finest driven Pheasant shooting estate in Ireland.

Thomas Kemmis (1753-1823) acquired the estate from the Rt Hon. Francis Rawdon Hastings. In 1802, Thomas and his son William Kemmis (1777-1864) were made Crown Solicitors for the Leinster circuit and for the County and City of Dublin.

William married Ellen Mansergh, County Tipperary, in 1805. He was regarded by Daniel O'Connell as 'high orange' and was condemned by Lord Clarendon as overly impartial for his failure to exclude repealers from the jury empanelled for the first trial of William Smith O'Brien in 1848. Kemmis had an address at 45 Kildare Street, Dublin, and a country estate at Ballinacor, Rathdown, County Wicklow. In 1876, the Ballinacor Estate consisted of 8,100 acres. After William Kemmis, the estate passed to his eldest son, William Gilbert (1806-1881), who died unmarried. It then passed to his nephew Col. William Kemmis (1836-1900), eldest son of Revd George Kemmis (1808-1880) and his wife Caroline Olphert.

The shooting record begins in 1864 with the personal Game Book of Col. William. In 1862, he married Ellen Gertrude de Horne Steinman. Their eldest son William Henry Olphert Kemmis (1864-1939), born in Canada, succeeded him, and his son Capt. William Daryl Olphert Kemmis (1892-1965), of the Enniskilling Dragoons, was the last in the Kemmis line to own the estate. He was married to Rosalie Armstrong (d. 1923), daughter of Capt. Marcus Beresford Armstrong of Castle Moyaliffe, County Tipperary, and Rosalie Cornelia Maude, a sister of Capt. Anthony Fritz Maude of Belgard Castle. It appears he spent a significant part of his time at Moyaliffe Stud, where he trained horses.[273] Kemmis's shooting records do not extend beyond 1925, although shooting was almost certainly was taking place after this date.

During the Kemmises' tenure, the shooting comprised Grouse mainly in August and September, and Woodcock from November onwards, into February. The Kemmises were a large family and the shooting was dominated by family members. In addition, there were guest appearances from other prominent County Wicklow families and some from further afield. Charles Stuart Parnell (1846-1891) of Avondale House, Rathdrum, landowner, nationalist political leader, land reform agitator, and the founder and leader of the Irish Parliamentary Party, was there in 1864. He was one of the most important figures in nineteenth-century Ireland and Great Britain, and was described by Prime Minister William Gladstone as the most remarkable person he had ever met. John Dudley Oliver (1809-1870) of Cherrymount (now Tigroney), Avoca, County Wicklow, who was involved in copper mining, was a more frequent visitor. Another neighbour to appear frequently was Col. Robert Howard Brooke (1840-1902) of Castle Howard, Avoca, County Wicklow, along with his uncle Sir Victor Brooke. Captain Charles Pennefather (1846-1904) of Rathsallagh House, County Wicklow, was there during several Grouse-shooting seasons in the company of D.T. Tynte, who is presumed to be of Tynte Park, County Kildare. Sir Robert Adair Hodson, 4th Baronet (1853-1921), of Hollybrook, Bray, County Wicklow, and his neighbour Henry Darley (1801-1883) of Wingfield, Bray, County Wicklow and Dr Leeper were the other main local families who were regular visitors to Ballinacor in the last thirty or so years of the nineteenth century.

It isn't any wonder Ballinacor attracted a lot of visitors. The shooting records, which are presented in summary below, demonstrate the consistent strength of the estate for both Grouse and Woodcock in these early years.

	No. of Days	No. of Guns	Grouse	Woodcock
1864/65	10	5	85	–
	35	2	–	96
1865/66	6	2/3	62	–
	24	1	–	50
1866/67	6	3	76	–
	–	1/2	–	74
1867/68	8	3/5	95	–
	8	1/2	–	32
1868/69	6	3	74	–
1969/70	4	1/3	48	–
GAP				
1881/82	17	1	73	–
	8	2	–	42

1882/83	10	1	32	—
	10	1	—	17
1883/84	8	3	58	—
	4	1/2	—	36
1884/85	13	2	213	—
	12	1	—	81
1885/86	10	4	248	—
	14	2/3	—	65
1886/87	8	3	111	—
	7	1/2	—	30
1887/88	14	4	216	—
	13	3	—	97
1888/89	10	3	254	—
	8	3	—	72
1889/90	14	3/5	235	—
	10	3/4	—	112
1890/91	n/a	n/a	49	—
	n/a	n/a	—	70
1891/92	n/a	n/a	258	—
	n/a	n/a	—	93

It is evident that there was a considerable amount of coming and going by the Kemmises at Ballinacor, and in many of the instances where only one Gun was shooting it was a keeper. There were three of these over the thirty-year period summarised above: Donald Sutherland (b. 1846), Elliott Hope (b. 1856) and F.W. Bagnall (b. 1840).[274] In addition, there are several individuals described as 'trappers', which were for rabbits, of which there were great numbers.

Somewhat unusually, from about 1890 it is clear that the shooting, or perhaps part of it, was leased. The estate Game Book records the lessees by season but more often than not there are members of the Kemmis family shooting at the same time. William Bolton Nunn (1843-1905) of Castlebridge, County Wexford (grandfather of Joshua Nunn, who controlled shooting on the North Slob, County Wexford, for most of the first half of the twentieth century) was one such lessee, taking shooting in from 1892 to 1894. This was followed by annual leases to a Mr Edward Kavanagh (1895), a Capt. Caulfield (1896) and an E. White (1897). The Hon. Ernest Guinness was a lessee in 1899-1901 and 1905-1909, and from 1909 to 1914 the lessee was a Mr Archer. It is difficult to interpret what precisely the arrangements were. For example, the Hon. Ernest Guinness, described as a lessee, was shooting with three friends from 16 to 19 August 1899 and on 6 to 8 September 1899, during which dates they shot 178 Grouse, while on 10, 11 and 29 October, Lewis, Edward and Capt. Christy Kemmis shot 117 Grouse. So evidently the arrangements could entail quite short lettings, an unusual feature at the time, and regardless of the duration of the lease some members of the Kemmis family were at least occasional shooters during these periods.

There are also some unusual features in the shoot record during the first quarter of the twentieth century, which is summarised below:

	Grouse	Pheasant	Woodcock	Snipe	Partridge	Hares
1900/01	283	14	100	28	8	22
1901/02	77	–	16	11	14	3
1902/03	63	27	12	16	25	1
1903/04	163	333	68	22	1	47
1904/05	79	771	143	17	5	9
1905/06	158	193	120	37	15	44
1906/07	118	62	64	36	8	6
1907/08	73	57	131	17	5	79
1908/09	200	37	169	126	16	23
1909/10	129	933	167	30	–	4
1910/11	185	903	211	54	–	50
1911/12	189	891	147	18	–	12
1912/13	193	2,021	186	56	–	10
1913/14	192	–	96	4	–	17
1914/15	72	1	74	12	–	4
1915/16	129	24	116	27	–	8
1918/19	99	–	3	7	–	7
1919/20	61	26	50	23	–	5
1920/21	83	2	13	16	–	4
1921/22	106	20	10	–	2	3
1922/23	81	13	24	–	–	6
1923/24	115	20	102	52	5	14
1924/25	33	6	16	35	–	2

Most noticeably, there is a sporadic appearance, from 1903/4, of significant numbers of Pheasants, commencing in 1903 when 333 were shot and peaking a decade later at 2,021, although some very mediocre returns of Pheasants are recorded in the interim. A new gamekeeper arrived in 1902, namely Frederick W. Bagnall (b. 1876), who the previous year is recorded as being employed at Curraghmore, County Waterford. He may have been joined a few years later by Robert James Bracken (b. 1874).[275] It would appear that they were charged with rearing and releasing significant numbers of Pheasants, presumably to enhance the value of the shooting leases.

A number of game cards have survived from the years 1903 to 1905 (see Illustration 91 p. 232). However, it is remarkable that, given the number of birds being reared, the estate did not have customised game cards printed, relying instead on promotional cards of Gilbertson & Page Ltd, game food providers. The intervention of the First World War probably put paid to whatever commercial strategy was being pursued about the development of the shoot, for although shooting continued during these years, it was at a lesser pace than earlier and the records are uninformative as to who the participants were.

After the war, the shooting record is that of Capt. William Kemmis, along with one or two others, but either records ceased to be taken after 1925 or they have not survived. After Capt. William Kemmis's demise, the estate passed in 1965 to his cousin Col. Richard Godfrey Lomer, MC (1907-1997), who had a solicitor's practice in London.

Pheasant shooting began at Ballinacor in 1966, shortly into Lomer's time, and instigated by Lomer's agent Michael Twist (1919-2006).[276] Twist was also agent to the Duke of Westminster with respect to his interests in Ireland. He was a keen all-round country sportsman and raconteur, and his books, *Irish Sporting Memories* and *The Glory Days*, are collections of his reminiscences.[277]

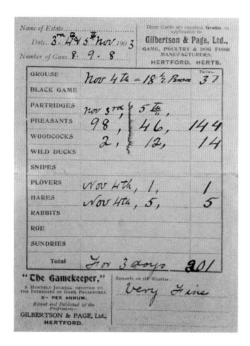

91 Ballinacor game card, 1903.

92 (right) Michael Branigan, Gamekeeper, Powerscourt, Charles Gray, RHA (1808-1892). An isolated record in the Game Book of Lord Maurice FitzGerald records that for the three days 24-26 September 1890, at a shoot in Powerscourt, the bag was 750 Grouse to eight Guns.

However, Michael Twist's tenure was short. He returned to England in 1970, where he established kennels, when Col. Lomer came to live in Ballinacor in that year. Other founding members of the syndicate were Lt-Col. W.B.P. Bradish of County Wexford, who played a prominent role in the shoot on the North Slob, County Wicklow; James and Billy McCormick; Maurice O'Rorke of Broadlough House, County Wicklow (a significant wildfowl shoot in its own right at the time), who was Shoot Captain, and Dr William Thomas Irwin ('Willie') (b. 1927).[278]

Willie was born at Grouse Lodge, Drumkerrin, County Leitrim, the only son of Archibald and Jenny Irwin. He took his medical qualifications at Trinity College Dublin in 1952 and since 1955 has been a general practitioner in Drogheda, County Louth. He commenced shooting at the age of thirteen with his father on his family farm and surrounding areas, where he shot Grouse, Snipe, Woodcock and duck. In addition to Ballinacor, he was a founding member of the syndicates at Dowth and Mountainstown, County Meath, and a member at Carton, County Kildare, Mellifont, County Louth, and Shelton Abbey, County Wicklow, where he remains active to the present day. Bradish and the McCormicks had been shooting at Coollattin.

In the first year of its existence, the shoot acquired its birds from Carton House, where the owner since 1949, Arthur Ronald Nall Nall-Cain, 2nd Baron Brocket (1904-1967), had died.[279] The first keeper was McClean, who had a short tenure owing to falling foul of the IRA and he left in 1970. He was succeeded by Albert Davison. Then, in 1976, at the instigation of Ian Morrison, the shoot employed Keith Wooldridge (b. 1939) as head keeper.[280] Keith's skill and dedication have undoubtedly contributed greatly to the deserved reputation of shooting at Ballinacor. He was employed previously at Birr Castle, home of the Earls of Rosse, where Morrison, along with Robert Ganley, held the stalking, and was first employed at Broadlands in Hampshire.

Another ingredient in the success of Ballinacor was the increasing involvement of a number of titans of Irish business at the time. These were the new aristocracy, whose credentials were not gained through family inheritance but rather entrepreneurship in an Ireland that had begun to embrace outward-looking economic policies. Ballinacor had attracted a cluster of them, including Ian Morrison, Don Carroll and Joe McGrath.[281] Their commitment to developing Ballinacor was reinforced after Jack Ardee, 15th Earl of Meath (b. 1941) finally secured the estate in 1986. To Jack Ardee's immense credit, it was an alliance which achieved greatness. Ian Morrison brought superlative marketing skills, Don Carroll provided financial backing, Bill Bradish gave good advice with respect to planting, and Keith Wooldridge was a gifted and dedicated gamekeeper.

Ian Morrison (1929-2004)

Chief executive of the Bank of Ireland Group for seventeen years, up to 1983. For most of that period, he was a key member of a small group that could justifiably claim to be the most powerful people in Irish business. Stern and forbidding to those with an occasional business acquaintance, Ian Morrison was the very model of a traditional accountant. When he accepted the invitation of Don Carroll, another member of Ballinacor, to take up the chief executive position (which required him to give up his accountancy practice), the bank was emerging from a regime where its very independence was questionable. The entire capital of the bank as late as the mid-1960s was on deposit with the British Treasury, earning 2 per cent per annum. Ireland had no international banks in place. None of the Central Bank controls that were needed for a modern economy were present either. Carroll described his friend's role as chief executive as 'quite remarkably successful'. When he retired from the bank, handing over to another banking 'outsider', Mark Hely Hutchinson, Ian Morrison pursued a long career in business serving on many boards. He married June Nesbitt in 1953 and was widowed in 1982. He married Sheila Higginbotham in 1986. He had two children from his first marriage.

Don Carroll (1927-2000)

A major, influential figure in Irish industry and banking for the best part of half a century, he was born in Cork, he was educated at Glenstal Abbey and Trinity College Dublin, and qualified as a chartered accountant in 1952. In the same year, he joined the family firm, P.J. Carroll. By 1961, he was chairman and managing director. By this time he had also become a director of the Bank of Ireland and of John Jameson & Son. The following year he became deputy governor of Bank of Ireland and two years later began his first of many terms as governor. He received an Honorary Doctorate in Law from his *alma mater* in 1969. During the 1960s, he reorganised Carroll Industries, forming an alliance with Carreras and, in time, taking half the Irish market. In the 1970s, major diversification plans failed but in the 1980s, the group engaged in a variety of other activities, including fish farming, marketing and venture capital. He was survived by his wife Monica and their two children.

Joe McGrath

Joe McGrath was the youngest of the three sons of Joe McGrath (1887-1966), founder of the Irish Hospital Sweepstakes in 1930, which was the basis for the family's fortune. His older brother Paddy McGrath (1927-2001) succeeded his father at the Sweepstakes and developed the family's business and investment interests; Seamus McGrath (1923-2005), the eldest and last surviving, was principally occupied by horse-racing interests (as indeed was Joe) from his home, Brownstown Stud, in County Kildare, where he also farmed. All three brothers took a keen interest in shooting and in addition to their involvement with Ballinacor, they were members at Ballyarthur and Shelton Abbey, as well as taking shooting leases at Carton House, County Kildare, and Luggala, County Wicklow.

In the first decade or so, the average bag was fewer than 100 head of Pheasant. Indeed up until about 1980 it was fewer than 200 head. On 21 November 1981, the bag reached 330 head.

An interesting connection of Ballinacor has been with the Swedish Royal Family, members of which – including the King of Sweden – have been shooting guests. This relationship came about originally through Ian Morrison's connections with Vera Axison Johnson, a member of the family which owns Axel Johnson and Nordstjernan Shipping, both of Sweden. The first record of a 'Swedish Party' referred to in the personal Game Book of Lt-Col. Bill Bradish was 14-15 November 1986. The total bag for the two days was 1,137. He remarks, 'a great success with charming people shooting sportingly and safely … *extremely* well managed by Keith'. So it has continued to the present.

KILRUDDERY, BRAY

The title Earl of Meath was created in 1627 and is held by the head of the Brabazon family. This family descends from Sir Edward Brabazon, who represented County Wicklow in the Irish House of Commons and served as High Sheriff of Staffordshire in 1606. Since the creation of the title, the Earls have owned an estate in Bray, County Wicklow, called Kilruddery House, which extended to over 18,315 acres at the close of the nineteenth century.[282]

The present holder of the title is John Anthony Brabazon ('Jack'), 15th Earl of Meath (b. 1941). He is married to Xenia Goudime-Levkovitsch, daughter of Paul Goudime-Levkovitsch and Sheila Violet McNeill. He is the son of Maj. Anthony Windham Normand Brabazon (1910-1998), 14th Earl of Meath, and Elizabeth Mary Bowlby.

From the mid-1980s until his succession in 1998, Jack and his family lived at Ballinacor, a handsome Georgian retreat in the midst of the Wicklow Mountains, where he oversaw the development of one of the finest shooting estates in the country. There is a long history of shooting in his family, extending back at least to the tenure of his great grandfather Reginald Brabazon, 12th Earl of Meath, KP, GCVO, GBE, PC (Ire.) (1841-1929), who was a British politician and philanthropist.

He was born in London, second son of Lord Brabazon, and educated at Eton. In 1863 he joined the Foreign Office as a clerk and later became a diplomat. In 1868 he married Lady Mary Jane Maitland, daughter of Thomas Maitland, 11th Earl of Lauderdale. On the insistence of his in-laws, Brabazon refused to accept a posting to Athens (which they considered too remote) in 1873 and was effectively suspended without pay, finally resigning from the Diplomatic Service in 1877. He and his wife decided to devote their considerable energies to 'the consideration of social problems and the relief of human suffering'. Both were subsequently involved in many charitable organisations.

In May 1887, Brabazon succeeded his father as 12th Earl of Meath. Lord Meath was also a prominent Conservative politician in the House of Lords and an ardent imperialist. He was a member of the London County Council, the Privy Council of Ireland and the Senate of Ireland, and was also Chief Scout Commissioner for Ireland.

Up until the First World War, his shooting was conducted principally on the 15,000 or so acres of heather moorland around the area of Glenmalure, where the Meath Estate bordered that of Kemmis of Ballinacor. The townlands offering the best Grouse shooting were Ballinfuinshogue,

Ballyboy, Ballinagoneen, Culintra Park and Ballybraid, many of which today are forestry planta-tions owned by Coillte Teo. His shooting companions at that time were his younger brothers, Capt. the Hon. Ernest Brabazon (1884-1915) and the Hon. Claud Brabazon, and Dr Richard Leeper, Medical Director of St Patrick's Hospital from 1899 to 1941. Their best day's shooting was ninety-six brace on a driven day (about once a decade all moors would be driven). More usually, the style of shooting was walked-up over setters and pointers with about six Guns, and the bag was usually thirty to forty brace. The moors were shot for three or four days only. There were three keepers managing the moors. After the war, the moorland slowly became the freehold of tenants, and in the early years of the Free State some was sold to the emerging Forestry Service.

During the tenure of the Maj. Anthony Windham Normand Brabazon, 14th Earl of Meath (1910-1998), Grouse shooting took place up until the late 1930s around Knockgrass Hills in the company of Henry Cornelius O'Callaghan Prittie, 5th Baron Dunalley of Kilboy (1877-1948) and Walter Stuart Tighe (1861-1925) of Rossana, Ashford, County Wicklow. However, by then num-bers had dwindled and bags averaged five to six brace a day.

For the past thirty-five years or so, there has been a syndicate shooting driven Pheasants over about 1,000 acres near Kilruddery, which has been managed by the Hon. David Brabazon (b. 1948) and John Goor. Angus Lee is the keeper.

Lough Bray, Glencree and Luggala, Roundwood

Lough Bray House was built as a shooting lodge for the Powerscourt Estate towards the end of the nineteenth century. It was subsequently bought by the Guinness family and in the last fifty years it has changed hands several times as a private residence. Sited on the south-facing shore of Lower Lough Bray, it can only be seen from the opposite side, from the ridge-top path that leads to the Eagle's Crag. There was the lodge itself, the gamekeeper's house, and, out at the roadside, a gate lodge, believed to be the highest inhabited house in Ireland.

Luggala Lodge was built in 1787 and extended in 1805 by the La Touche family, Dublin bankers of Huguenot origin. In 1937, Ernest Guinness bought Luggala and gave it as a wedding present to his daughter Oonagh on her marriage to Lord Oranmore and Browne, although he held the shooting rights there as part of the acquisition of Lough Bray. It became a noted gathering place for Dublin's intelligentsia, as well as artists and musicians from around the world. Luggala passed to their son, Dr the Hon. Garech Browne, who continued this tradition to the present day.

The Lough Bray Game Book of Ernest Guinness covers the years 1912 to 1933, during which time the shooting took place over Lough Bray itself, Luggala, Kippure, Liffey Head, Camp Hill and Maulin. Shooting was mainly in August, September and early October, when the focus was on Grouse, with Woodcock in later months. The pattern of shooting and a summary of the bag by season are shown below. In both 1912 and 1913, over half the annual bag was taken in three days' shooting by ten Guns towards the end of October. It is presumed that these were driven days. The rest of the shooting during those years, and in all other years, consisted of one (usu-ally Ernest Guinness himself), two or three Guns (usually Ernest and a guest or two), and this is presumed to have been walked-up work. There was no shooting between 1920 and 1924. From about 1931, the shooting seems to be under the management of gamekeeper George McLaren. It is understood that he was a Scot who came to work at Ashford Castle and from there came to Lough Bray.[283] This was about the time the Guinness family sold Ashford Castle, which may explain the gamekeeper's transfer to County Wicklow.

	No. of Shooting Days	Grouse	Woodcock	Snipe	Hares
1912	18	634	5	5	296
1913	26	514	14	–	292
1914	37	344	35	2,626	222
1915	55	939	52	3,535	198
1916	38	544	20	80	63
1917	35	488	10	10	100
1918	58	497	22	14	288
1919	34	317	7	6	287
1920	14	148	1	2	130

Ernest Guinness was out most days during this time and his most frequent shooting companion was Raymond Brooke. Indeed on some days Brooke was there shooting alone.

Raymond Frederick Brooke (1885-1964) was a cousin of Basil Brooke, 1st Viscount Brookeborough, Prime Minister of Northern Ireland from 1943 to 1963, and was related also to Field Marshal Alan Brooke, 1st Viscount Alanbrooke. A forefather had moved to Dublin, established himself at Summerton, Castleknock, and founded a very successful business under the style of George F. Brooke & Son, wine merchants. The Brooke Baronetcy of Summerton, Castleknock, was created in 1903 for George Brooke, who was then head of George F. Brooke & Son and a Director and Governor of the Bank of Ireland. He was also father of Raymond.

Raymond, the fourth son of Sir George Frederick Brooke, was one of a family of ten. He was educated at Winchester and he worked for a time with the Norwich Union Insurance Company in Dublin before entering the family wine business, of which he became a director, in 1906. In 1922, when George F. Brooke & Son were taken over by Thompson D'Olier, Raymond joined this company and later became its managing director. He retired in 1955.

Raymond Brooke became Master of the Meridian Lodge in 1914, holding various sub-offices in the Grand Masonic Lodge before his election as Deputy Grand Master on 27 December 1930, a position he held for some eighteen years until his appointment as Grand Master in 1948. He was Grand Master for sixteen years, until his death in 1964. He was an authority on the history of the Kildare Street Club and in 1930 he published a book on the subject entitled, *Daly's Club and Kildare Street Club, Dublin*. In 1961, he had another book published entitled, *The Brimming River (A History of the Family of Brooke of Summerton)*. This set out the history of the Brooke family from the Plantation time in Donegal, as well as recalling his young days and characters of older Dublin. He did not marry.

Andrew and Frank Jameson

Other frequent guests were two members of the Irish whiskey distiller family the Jamesons. Both Andrew and Frank Jameson make their first appearance at the driven days in October 1912 and 1913, and subsequently appear as individual guests of Ernest on many days. Andrew Jameson (1855-1941) was a Scottish-born Irish public servant, politician and businessman. Jameson was born in Alloa, Clacmannanshire, Scotland, the second son of Andrew Jameson (1812-1872) and Margaret Cochrane. His brothers John Alloa Jameson (1853-1942) and James Sligo Jameson (1856-1888) were noted big-game hunters.

Andrew was educated at London International College, Trinity College, Cambridge and Trinity College Dublin. He was a director of the Bank of Ireland 1887-1941 and its governor 1896-98. In 1902, he was High Sheriff of County Dublin. He was also chairman of the Irish Lights Commission and chairman and managing director of John Jameson & Son from 1905 to 1941. He was appointed to the Privy Council of Ireland in the 1921 New Year Honours, entitling him to the style 'The Right Honourable'.

From 1922 to 1936, Jameson served as a Senator of the Irish Free State. As a member of the Memorial Committee set up to further the process of the Irish National War Memorial Gardens, in December 1930 he advised W.T. Cosgrave, then president, who was very interested in bringing the memorial to fruition, on the suitability of the site running along the south bank of the River Liffey; this site was eventually decided upon by Cosgrave and agreed by the committee. In 1877, he married Grace Elizabeth Burke of Baggot Street, Dublin. They resided at Sutton House, County Dublin, and had three daughters and a son, who died aged one year. Francis Bellingham Jameson (1859-1942) of Glencormack House, Bray, County Wicklow, was a cousin of Andrew's.[284] He was the son of James Jameson (b. 1806) and Lucy Cairnes (1819-1907).

Archibald Darley

Darley, of Wingfield, Bray, County Wicklow, was member of a family which was intermarried with the Guinnesses in several generations. For example, his grandfather Frederick Darley was married to Elizabeth Guinness, daughter of Arthur Guinness and Olivia Whitmore, and his uncle Revd John Darley was married to Susan Guinness. His older brother Frederick Matthew Darley became the 6th Chief Justice of New South Wales. These are just some of the marital connections between the Darleys and the Guinnesses.

Sir William Ireland de Courcy Wheeler, MD, FRCSI (1879-1943)

Consulting Surgeon to the Royal Navy in Scotland at the time of his death, it was in Dublin that Sir William forged his reputation as a surgeon – a reputation that was just as firmly established in Great Britain. He was the son of William Ireland de Courcy Wheeler, who, like his son, reached the presidency of the Royal College of Surgeons in Ireland. William the son was known as a writer of one or two textbooks and of many monographs on surgical subjects.

William was educated at Trinity College Dublin, where in 1899 he took honours in anatomy, natural science and experimental science. He completed his education at the University of Berne and qualified in Dublin in 1902. He was appointed demonstrator and assistant to the professor of anatomy at Trinity College. Choosing surgery as his field, he became FRCSI at just twenty-six years of age. It was at this time, in his twenties, that an unfortunate accident befell him, as the result of which he lost an eye. He overcame this disability and although he was prevented from taking up golf, other people at least were not conscious that he suffered from any handicap in his professional work. In 1904, he joined the staff of Mercer's Hospital, a famous Dublin charitable foundation to which he was attached for twenty-eight years, and he was senior surgeon when he retired.

Sir William's work in the war of 1914-8 brought him into close association with his British colleagues, having served in France with the rank of lieutenant-colonel, been mentioned twice in despatches and then knighted at the war's end.

He left Ireland for London – already over fifty years of age – when the 2nd Earl of Iveagh, Rupert Guinness, Ernest's older brother, gave him nearly £200,000 towards making a new hospital at Southend-on-Sea. The resulting hospital was one of the finest for its size in the country. The surgical block comprised the newest type of operating theatres and accessories, and Lord Iveagh persuaded Sir William to accept a position on the visiting staff. With his appointment at Southend, Sir William combined an appointment at All Saints' Hospital for Genitourinary Diseases, London, for although he was a general surgeon, he cultivated urology as what he called a 'sideline'.

In 1909, Sir William married the eldest daughter of the first Baron Craigmyle, better known as Lord Shaw of Dunfermline, a Lord of Appeal. They had a son and daughter, and the son went on to serve as an officer in the Gordon Highlanders.

When shooting resumed in 1924, after a three-year lapse, there was a noticeable reduction in the numbers of Grouse, even allowing for the fact that the shooting effort was less intense than earlier years, at least initially. It would appear that there was perhaps a reduction in, or suspension of, the keeping effort during these troubled years. However, by the 1930s, good numbers were evident again, as can be seen from the summary below. In 1932, of the thirty-one days' shooting that took place, twenty-seven were accounted for by George McLauren, the gamekeeper.

	No of Days Shooting	Grouse	Woodcock	Snipe	Hare
1924	17	44	1	5	25
1925	17	72	4	6	15
1926	23	117	3	8	30
1927	24	88	4	6	36
1928	14	85	1	2	9
1929	13	114	–	–	12
1930	18	266	1	7	15
1931	23	222	2	8	22
1932	31	204	4	5	9
1933	28	228	2	7	19

Captain Anthony Fritz Maude (1862-1933)

Many of the guests of earlier years continued shooting with Ernest after the revival of shooting and some new names also appeared, notably those of his future sons-in-law. One frequent guest was Capt. Anthony Fritz Maude of Belgard Castle, Clondalkin, County Dublin. He was the son of Maurice Cely Maude and Marie Elise Wehren, a well-known Anglo-Irish family. He was a grandson of Revd John Charles Maude, rector of Enniskillen, and cousin of Gen. Sir Frederick Stanley Maude (1864-1917), a British commander most famous for his efforts in Mesopotamia during the First World War and for conquering Baghdad in 1917, shortly after which he died of cholera.

Anthony Maude married Eva Emily Bereford, daughter of Maj. Henry Marcus Beresford and Julia Ellen Maunsell, in 1895. He was JP for Counties Fermanagh, Down and Dublin, High Sheriff of County Dublin, and secretary of the Representative Body of the Church of Ireland. He is commemorated by the Anthony Maude Perpetual Challenge Cup, which was presented to the Royal Dublin Society by his widow and third son Hugh A.C. Maude in 1939.[285]

Family members were prominent amongst Ernest's guests, remembering that on most occasions the shooting parties comprised just Ernest and one other. One of these was Sir George Michael Russell, 7th Baronet (1908-1993), a nephew of Clothilde Russell, Ernest Guinness's wife, who visited first as a young man of just sixteen years. Another was his son-in-law the Hon. Philip Leyland Kindersley (1907-1967), the son of Robert Molesworth Kindersley, 1st Baron Kindersley, and Gladys Margaret Beadle. He married Oonagh Guinness, daughter of Ernest Guinness and Marie Clothilde Russell, in 1929, and they were divorced in 1935. In 1936, he married Violet Valerie French, daughter of Maj. the Hon. Edward Gerald Fleming French and Leila King. He was there quite regularly from 1928.

Flight Lieutenant the Hon. Brindsley Sheridan Bushe Plunket (1903-1941)

A more frequent guest was Ft Lt the Hon. Brindsley Sheridan Bushe Plunket. He married Aileen Sibell Mary, eldest daughter of Ernest and Clothilde Russell, on 16 November 1927. He was often shooting and alone accounted for most of the shooting in 1931. He and Aileen were divorced in 1940. The son of William Lee Plunket, 5th Baron of Newton, and Lady Victoria Alexandrina Hamilton-

Temple-Blackwood, he died in November 1941 aged thirty-eight, while on active service. He gained the rank of flight lieutenant in the service of the Royal Air Force Volunteer Reserve.

Rupert Edward Cecil Lee Guinness, 2nd Earl of Iveagh (1874-1967)

Eldest son of Edward Guinness, 1st Earl of Iveagh, and Ernest Guinness's older brother, he served as the twentieth Chancellor of the University of Dublin from 1927 to 1963, succeeding his father, who was Chancellor between 1908 and 1927.

Rupert was educated at Eton and Trinity College, Cambridge. In 1900, he served in the Boer War with the Irish Hospital Corps. He was the Unionist MP for the East End constituency of Haggerston from 1908 to 1910 and for Southend from 1912 to 1927. He served as a captain in the Royal Naval Volunteer Reserve and was Commanding Officer of HMS *President* (London Division RNVR) from 1903 until 1920. In 1927, he succeeded his father as Earl of Iveagh and chairman of the family brewing business in Dublin, and for thirty-five years directed its consolidation at home and its expansion abroad with the establishment of breweries in London and in Nigeria and Malaya. A keen agriculturist, he transformed the barren shooting estate at Elveden in Suffolk into a productive farm.

He donated generously to Dublin hospitals and in 1939 presented to the government his Dublin residence, Iveagh House (80 St Stephen's Green), now the Department of Foreign Affairs, and gave the gardens to UCD. His only son, Arthur Onslow Edward Guinness, Viscount Elveden, who was shooting at Lough Bray on the last shoot recorded there in October 1933, was killed in action in Belgium in 1945, being an unlucky victim of a V-2 rocket strike.

It was during Rupert's management that the Guinness World Records started. The brewery was always on the look-out for good promotional ideas to bring the Guinness name to the public's attention. One of these ideas came about when Sir Hugh Beaver, then the managing director, went on a shooting party to the North Slob in County Wexford in 1951 as a guest of Joshua Nunn.

Rupert became a Knight of the Garter KG in 1955. He retired from Guinness in 1962, in favour of his grandson, Lord Elveden, and was elected FRS in March 1964, at ninety, for his services to science and agriculture. Lord Iveagh died in his sleep at his house in Woking, Surrey, on 14 September 1967. He was married to Gwendolen Onslow (daughter of the 4th Earl of Onslow), who succeeded him as MP for Southend-on-Sea.

The last shoot recorded took place on 7 October 1933 and involved eight Guns, which accounted for sixty-seven Grouse on the day. The Guns included Ernest Guinness, his nephew Viscount Elveden, his sons-in-law Philip Kindersley and the Hon. Brindsley Plunket, Capt. Anthony Maude and Mervyn Wingfield, 7th Viscount Powerscourt.

In 1985, there was a revival of shooting at Luggala when Ken Rohan of Charleville, County Wicklow, formed a syndicate to shoot driven Pheasants. The original members were Lord Holmpatrick, James O'Dwyer, John Carroll, Hugh O'Donnell, Eamon McEnry, George Fasenfeld and Paul Smithwick. The Kruger Family from Canada and Headford, County Meath, were members for some time. Robert Clothworthy ran the shoot, which operated successfully for a number of years. The tenancy concluded in 1988.

GLENASMOLE LODGE AND GLENCULLEN

Glenasmole Lodge, also known as Cobbe's Lodge, was part of the estate of the Cobbe family of Newbridge House, Donabate, County Dublin. Newbridge House was built by Archbishop

Cobbe between 1747 and 1752, and when his descendant Charles Cobbe, whose shooting records survive, died in 1886, leaving no male issue, his estate passed to his wife for her lifetime. Prior to her death, she persuaded Thomas Maherby Cobbe, a grandnephew of her late husband, to return to Newbridge from America to take over the estate. He died young in 1914, leaving two infant children, namely Thomas and Francis, the latter dying in 1949. Thomas did not marry and on his death in 1985 was succeeded by Francis's family, Hugh, Alec and Mary. While the property has now been acquired by the County Council, the Cobbe family will continue to reside at Newbridge House from time to time, due to a unique arrangement which had been entered into between the family and the council.

Thomas Cobbe (d. 1985) was a keen shooter and friend of Robert Jobson (1916-1999) (see 'Punt Gunning in Wexford Harbour'). The two punt gunned together at Rogerstown estuary, near Donabate, County Dublin, and it appears that for a time Robert Jobson managed the shooting at Glenasmole Lodge on behalf of the Cobbes. The estate there comprised about 8,000 acres of Grouse moorland. There are surviving shoot records in relation to Glenasmole dating from 1846, the time of Charles Cobbe. There are also some most interesting returns for the area – which is within thirty miles of the centre of Dublin city – in the Game Book records of James Joseph Smithwick (1869-1932) of Kilcreene Lodge, County Kilkenny, for the closing years of the nineteenth century.[286] James Smithwick, known as 'Mr James', was the second son of John Smithwick (1833-1894) and Christina ('Nina'), daughter of Nicholas Devereaux of Bishopswater, Wexford. The family were the founders and developers of the now famous Kilkenny brewing company, which bears the family name to the present day.

His shooting companions were also involved in the drinks business: distilling rather than brewing. These were Andrew and Frank Jameson and several of the Power family of County Wexford, who also lent their name to a well-known brand of Irish whiskey, namely Sir John Power, 3rd Bt (1845-1901) of Edermine, County Wexford, and his brothers Sir James Talbot Power, 5th Bt (1851-1916) of Leopardstown Park, County Dublin, and Sir Thomas Talbot Power 6th Bt (1863-1932) of Thornhill, Stillorgan, Dublin. Sir John Power had only one son, James Douglas, who was killed in action in 1914, hence the baronetcy moved to his younger brothers in succession. Sir Thomas Talbot Power was married to Margaret, daughter of Thomas Martin of Beaufield House, Stillorgan, and he also is to be found shooting with this party at Glenasmole. Thomas and Margaret had no children, so the wealth of the Powers passed to the O'Reilly family (Joseph Richard O'Reilly of Sans Soucci, Botterstown, County Dublin, being the husband of Frances Mary Power, Sir John's older sister) and the Ryan family (Sir John's eldest sister Gwendaline Anna having married Maj.-Gen. Thaddeus Richard Ryan of Scarteen, County Limerick). These two men were also members of the shooting parties at Glenasmole.

A summary of the shooting at Glenasmole and Glencullen taken from the Smithwick Game Book is shown below.

Year	No. of days shooting	Grouse	Woodcock	Snipe	Hares
1894	6	221	–	5	104
1895	6	322	1	6	79
1896	7	659	1	2	68
1897	5	276	2	28	108
1898	1	64	–	2	9

It is not known why Smithwick and his companions ceased shooting at Glenasmole after 1898. As noted above, shooting took place there during Robert Jobson's life. However short the record available is, it is intriguing that such good Grouse shooting was available at such a short remove, even by the standards of the time, from Dublin city.

BALLYARTHUR, WOODENBRIDGE

Ballyarthur has been the family home of the Bayly family since at least the middle of the eighteenth century, when it was occupied by the Revd Edward Bayly (1743-1825) and Elizabeth Symes (1749-1781). The estate extended to almost 3,000 acres at the end of the nineteenth century.[287] The current occupant's grandfather Lt-Col. Edward Richard Bayly (1845-1907), who was married to Adelaide Alicia Tottenham, daughter of Lt-Col. John Tottenham and the Hon. Isabella Maude, was a regular Gun at Glenart during William Proby's tenure.[288]

The present Edward Archibald Richard Bayly ('Ned') (b. 1922), is the son of Edward Archibald Theodore Bayly (1877-1959) and Ileene Caroline Ethel Otway Inglefield (d. 1960). He married Rosemarie Evelyn Gisela Steins Minkley, daughter of Paul Heinrich Johann Minkley, in 1964. The son of Edward Archibald Theodore Bayly and Ileene Caroline Ethel Otway Inglefield, he was educated at St Columba's College, St Albans, Hertfordshire, and later Trinity College Dublin and Trinity College, Oxford. He has two daughters and a son, Edward Alexander Christian Lambart Bayly ('Alex') (b. 1967), who now manages the shooting at Ballyarthur.[289]

93 Edward ('Ned') Bayly (b. 1922) of Ballyarthur, County Wicklow.

Edward's father fought in the Boer War between 1899 and 1902, where he was seriously wounded, and won two medals and seven clasps. He fought in the Sudan Campaigns of 1908 and 1910, between them winning two medals and four clasps. He fought in the First World War, where he was mentioned in despatches. He was decorated with the award of Companion, Distinguished Service Order (DSO) in 1917 and he was also decorated with the award of Commander, Order of the Crown of Italy. He was decorated with the award of Order of the Nile (3rd class) and gained the rank of major in the service of the Royal Welsh Fusiliers. In addition, he held the office of Governor of the Western Desert Province Frontier Administration, Egypt between 1924 and 1930.

From an early age, Edward was introduced to shooting by his father, who he accompanied shooting around Wicklow and beyond. Edward became passionate about shooting and has devoted a large part of his life to the establishment and development of driven Pheasant shooting at his beloved Ballyarthur – indeed for many, the author included, Edward Bayly stands as the figure at the forefront of the revival of estate shooting based on the syndicate approach in Ireland.[290]

In the 1960s, when game stocks in Ireland were at an especially low ebb (see Chapter 1), Edward Bayly, along with several other committed and equally frustrated shooters, decided that 'something needed to be done'. A meeting took place at Hoyne's Hotel in Arklow in 1967, attended by Edward, his neighbour Thomas (Tommy) Fenton Crammond (1907-1998) of Mine View, Avoca, who was born in Ramelton, County Donegal, Henry Horsman (b. 1927), a sheep farmer around the Arklow area who had returned from Cawnpore, India, after the Second World War, where his father Albert and mother Ursula (*née* Dixon) owned a Cotton Mill, and Charlie Hernon, who was a veterinary surgeon of Jubilee Hall, Bray, County Wicklow. They decided that to revive shooting it would be necessary to make a significant investment in rearing and releasing Pheasants, and in order to do this a gamekeeper would have to be employed. With that, the Woodenbridge Syndicate was born, which was renamed the Ballyarthur Gun Club in 1977. The first gamekeeper was Albert Hillditch, who was recruited from the Clandeboye Estate in County Down, home to the Marquess of Dufferin and Ava. Other founder members were: Jim Hamilton of Falls Road, Shankill, who had leased part of the Glenart Estate; James Edward Robert Emmet (1926-1990), a gentleman farmer of Altidore Castle, near Newtownmountkennedy, County Wicklow; Thomas Henry Ivory (d. 1984) of Dartry, Dublin, and Ballycooge in County Wicklow, who was a self-made-man who owned the Olympia Ballroom in Dublin, and John Fogarty of Arklow, County Wicklow.

In the first year, the syndicate reared and released 1,200 Pheasants, a fact recorded in its first Game Book, which is inscribed, 'To Woodenbridge Syndicate with my best wishes for many successful days and rewarding "Red Letter" Bags, from Jim Emmet, 1st November 1967.' The bag for the day was seven Pheasants and a Snipe! From this humble beginning, the shoot was been developed over the years and today is one of the most consistent driven shoots in Ireland. The syndicate shoots regularly during the season. Many of its members have been associated with Ballyarthur – or their families have been connected – from its inception. The steep wooded contours of the Ballyarthur Estate are ideal for the presentation of quality birds and the pre-shoot meeting at 'the house', presided over by Ned Bayly and son Alex, is unique.

SHELTON ABBEY, AVOCA

Until 1951, Shelton Abbey was home to the Howard family, Earls of Wicklow. They were related through marriage to the Probys of nearby Glenart[291] and the Abercorns of Baronscourt.[292] Shelton Abbey was built for William Howard, the 4th Earl (1788-1860), as a gothic revival exercise under the design of Thomas Morrison. However, the shooting records commence in the next generation, with the nephews of William, the 4th Earl (who died without male issue), namely Charles Francis Arnold, 5th Earl (1839-1881), and Cecil Ralph, 6th Earl (1842-1891).

The diaries of their younger sister Lady Alice Howard (b. 1846), who lived at Shelton Abbey, 'in the Vale of Avoca, among woods full of birds waiting to be shot,' provide an insight into the opulent social life of Shelton and elsewhere during the last quarter of the nineteenth century, including their attendance at various shoots.[293] Robert James Bracken was the gamekeeper at that time. However, in County Wicklow, where the shooting took place, the estate was not large, comprising about 1,100 acres in 1880, the bulk of the estate lands, which in total amounted to 28,000 acres, being in Counties Carlow and Donegal.[294]

The first shooting record comes from the Game Book of Lord Maurice FitzGerald of Johnstown Castle and relates to 1884, when he shot Shelton in the company of Cecil Ralph Howard, 6th Earl of Wicklow (1842-1891), Lord Drogheda, Maj. Randal Charles Skeffington Smyth (b. 1863) of Mount Henry, Portarlington, County Offaly, who was son of Col. Edward Skeffington Randal Smyth (d. 1887) and his wife Letitia (although it could have been the father himself who was there), and Maj. James Lenox Naper (1825-1901), a son of James Lenox William Naper (1788-1868) of Lough Crew, near Oldcastle, County Meath, which estate once extended to 180,000 acres. The same Guns were there the following year, with the addition of the Earl of Bandon (who seems to have been at every worthwhile shoot in the country), Lord Clarina and Capt. Henry Monck of the Charleville Moncks in County Wicklow. A summary of the shooting at Shelton recorded by Lord Maurice FitzGerald is contained below:

Three Days' Shooting in November	Pheasants	Woodcock	Hares
1884	485	27	52
1885	396	26	80
1889	312	30	–

It is not known how the shooting continued in the time after these dates. However, like neighbouring Glenart, the estate was broken up and the family's circumstances were reduced. By 1940, the remaining estate was facing bankruptcy and the property was opened as a hotel by the 8th Earl of Wicklow, William Howard (1902-1978). In 1950, it was finally closed, the contents auctioned off. The buildings and land were acquired by the government and used as a national forestry college. Subsequently, in 1974 it was transferred to the Department of Justice and became an open prison, in which use it remains today.

Shooting recommenced in the late 1950s or early 1960s when it is understood Dr John Dunne (1899-1991), first occupant of the Chair of Psychiatry at University College Dublin and for most of his career Chief Medical Superintendent of St Brendan's Psychiatric Hospital, Grangegorman, Dublin, held a shooting tenancy, in a way similar to Jim Hamilton's position at Glenart around the same time. Shooting was confined mostly to the fields and marshes between Shelton Abbey and the Dublin to Arklow Road. About 500 Pheasants were released and at the end of a day's shooting the Guns retired to Jack White's, where the bag was displayed. In addition to John Dunne, that group included Reginald Armstrong, the motorcycle racing driver who was killed tragically in 1979, at the age of fifty-two, following a road accident while returning home from a shoot in Shelton. Others included Noel O'Callaghan (now the longest-serving member of the North Slob shooting syndicate), Tim Murray, Paul Murray, John Hanlon and the late Michael Phelan.[295]

In the 1970s, when a rent increase had to be faced, it was Michael Phelan who suggested that an attempt should be made to return shooting at Shelton to its former glory and the outcome was the establishment, in 1974, of the Shelton Shooting Syndicate, with Michael Phelan as shoot manager and John Wright as the first keeper.[296]

Since its inception, Shelton has developed along similar lines to Ballyarthur. Its 'social home' since 1976 has been the Woodenbridge Hotel and over the years there has been some crossover in its membership with that of Ballyarthur. Like Ballyarthur, Shelton now provides consistent shooting of quality driven Pheasants.[297] In 2002, under the present Shoot Captain, Harry Nash (b. 1963), Shelton Syndicate leased additional land from Coillte Teo in the steeply wooded Ballycooge valley, a part of the former Glenart Estate. In effect, this allowed the potential to develop a significant number of new drives, in addition to its signature Oaks drives around Shelton Abbey.

CASTLE HOWARD, AVOCA

At Castle Howard, another estate situated in the Vale of Avoca, shooting commenced about a decade ago, under the stewardship of Ivor and Susan Fitzpatrick, who acquired the estate as a residence in 1991. In the short period since, the shoot has developed and is now on a par with other, much longer-established shoots in the county.

The estate and castle have a long history which is closely related with the Earls of Wicklow. The estate was given to the Hon. Hugh Howard (1761-1840) by his older brother Robert Howard, 1st Earl of Wicklow, in a family settlement and as a place in which to develop a suitable residence for a member of the gentry. The house was designed by architect Sir Richard Morrison. However, Hugh lost interest in the place and for no apparent reason took up residence at Bushy Park near Bray, leaving his son Ralph living at Castle Howard. Following Hugh's death in 1840, the estate was acquired by the Brooke family of County Fermanagh through a marriage settlement and it became the residence for several generations of the Howard-Brookes. However, there is no indication that the estate, which comprised only 358 acres in the 1870s, was ever used to host shooting or shoot parties.

The shooting at Castle Howard is the result of the commitment and dedication of its present owners, who have invested in drive development and on facilities: the dedicated shoot room is purpose built, with all the comforts befitting the heart of a serious shoot. Like its peers, Ballyarthur and Shelton, Castle Howard takes full advantage of the wooded contours of the Vale of Avoca, to produce high-quality driven Pheasants over the season, from November to January.

COOLLATTIN, SHILLELAGH

The Coollattin Estate once comprised 88,000 acres, had 20,000 tenants and occupied almost a quarter of County Wicklow. The owners of the estate, the Fitzwilliam family, lived in nearby Coollattin House, although the family's principal seat was at Wentworth Woodhouse in Yorkshire, England. The Fitzwilliams were passionate about hunting and this had some interesting influences on the manner in which shooting on the estate was managed.[298] Unfortunately, only fragmentary shooting records remain from the beginning of the twentieth century, but undoubtedly there was a serious commitment to shooting at this estate from much earlier.

	Pheasants	Grouse	Woodcock	Snipe	Partridge
1901	627	68	94	172	89
1902	945	23	112	148	35
1903	1,189	56	163	200	27
1904	1,819	31	106	162	46
1905	2,202	36	176	172	36

However, even with only fragmentary statistical records, it is possible to gauge something of the wealth of shooting which the estate provided. Moreover, its vast extent meant that every kind of habitat was available, from heather moorland at Ballybeg, which provided Grouse, to extensive deciduous woodlands, which supported large quantities of Pheasants and Woodcock, to wet areas that supported Snipe and other wildfowl.

The host at the shoots in the years above was William ('Billy') Charles de Meuron Wentworth-Fitzwilliam, 7th Earl Fitzwilliam (1872-1943), who came to Ireland mainly to partake in hunting and shooting. He was born in Pointe de Meuron, Canada, and died at Wentworth Woodhouse. He inherited the title Earl Fitzwilliam in 1902 on the death of his grandfather William Wentworth-Fitzwilliam, 6th Earl Fitzwilliam, as his father William Fitzwilliam, Viscount Milton (1839-1877), had pre-deceased him, at the young age of thirty-seven. On his succession, he became one of the richest men in Britain, inheriting an estate of significant land and industrial and mineral-right holdings worth £3.3 billion in current terms.

The unusual circumstances of his birth, in a remote part of Canada's frontier lands, were later to cause major controversy within the family. The accusation was that he was a changeling: an unrelated baby inserted into the family to purge the bloodline of the epilepsy from which his ostensible forebears had suffered, and to provide that arm of the family with a male heir to inherit the earldom.[299]

On 24 June 1896, he married Lady Maud Frederica Elizabeth Dundas (b. 1877), the daughter of Lawrence Dundas, 1st Marquess of Zetland. They had five children and the youngest was a son, namely William Henry Lawrence Peter Wentworth-Fitzwilliam, 8th Earl Fitzwilliam (1910-1948). His life ended tragically when he died in an aircraft accident over Saint-Bauzile, Ardèche, France. In 1933, he had married Olive ('Obby') Dorothea Plunket (d. 1975) – the daughter of Benjamin Plunket, Bishop of Ormonde, and thereby granddaughter of the 4th Baron Plunket, Archbishop of Dublin – with whom he had one daughter: Lady Anne Juliet Dorothea Maud Wentworth-Fitzwilliam (b. 1935). The marriage to Obby was strained and there was talk of divorce, with her living at Coollattin while he spent most of his time at Wentworth Woodhouse, returning to shoot but with increasing infrequency. He was linked romantically with the widowed Kathleen Cavendish, Marchioness of Hartington, sister of future US President John F. Kennedy. She was killed with Fitzwilliam in the crash.

As mentioned above, the Fitzwilliams were passionate about hounds. Not only were foxes preserved, they were actually reared and released to artificially constructed dens, which were even landscaped specially to encourage them. The potential conflict with Pheasant shooting on a large scale was overcome by artificially enclosing more than 150 acres with wire fencing, called 'Brow Wood', to which the annual release of many thousands of young Pheasants was made each year. The birds were driven from Brow Wood on shoot days and attracted back afterwards. In this way, the potential issue of fox predation was averted.

As was usual, the shooting parties comprised several members of the extended family. In particular, the 7th Earl's cousins – Dermot Henry Doyne (1871-1942) of Arden, Shillelagh, County Wicklow, and St Austin's Abbey, Tullow, County Carlow, and his brother Maj. Robert Wentworth Doyne (1868-1942) of Wells, County Wexford – are mentioned frequently in the shoot records of the first five years of the twentieth century. These were the sons of Charles Mervyn Doyne (1839-1924) and Frances Mary Fitzwilliam (1842-1903), daughter of the 6th Earl of Fitzwilliam of Wells, County Wexford.[300] Dermot Henry Doyne was married to Alice Gertrude Brooke (d. 1964), daughter of Rt Hon. Francis Theophilius Brooke (1851-1920) of Ardeen, County Wicklow.[301] He and his two sons, Lt-Col. George Francis Brooke (1878-1966) and Henry Hastings Brooke (1882-1920), were also very frequent members of Coollattin shooting parties at this time.

From outside the family there were other members of landed-gentry families. One of these was Robert Westley Hall-Dare (1866-1939) of Newtownbarry House, County Wexford.[302] His family had come to County Wexford from Temple House in County Sligo in 1861, following a scandal in which Hall-Dare's grandfather was the culprit (see Temple House). Another whose name figures prominently in the early records is Maj. Arthur William Mordaunt Richards (1860-1931) of Ardamine, Gorey, County Wicklow. Ardamine was burned down on 9 July 1921, after which Richards left and returned to England.

Also from this neighbourhood, and appearing regularly at Coollattin shooting parties, was James Walter Milles Stopford, 6th Earl of Courtown (1853-1933),[303] who was styled as Viscount Stopford between 1858 and 1914. He married, firstly, the Hon. Catherine Elizabeth Neville, daughter of Richard Cornwallis Neville, 4th Lord Braybrooke, Baron of Braybrooke, and Lady Charlotte Sarah Graham-Toler, in 1876. He married, secondly, Gertrude Mills, daughter of Gen. Charles James Conway Mills and Gertrude Whitbread, in 1886. The son of James George Henry Stopford, 5th Earl of Courtown, and the Hon. Elizabeth Frances Milles, he was educated at Trinity College, Cambridge. He held the office of Sheriff of County Wexford in 1877 and of County Carlow in 1878. He was *aide-de-camp* to the Lord Lieutenant of Ireland, Earl of Carnarvon, and he assumed the office of Lord Lieutenant of County Wexford on 27 July 1901.

There are no formal records to provide a guide about what happened for much of the first half of the twentieth century, but recollections of former gamekeeping staff recall that no birds were being put down for much of the time after the 1920s. The game department remained intact, but its principal task was to provide game to the house, which was home to Obby and her daughter. In the 1950s, shooting was undertaken by members of the estate staff, notably Maj. Francis Mervyn Doyne (b. 1909), son of Dermot Henry Doyne (1871-1942), who was the estate manager, and William Robertson, who was the farm manager. On occasions the house would 'send out for Snipe' and Willie Robertson and his son would head off to procure them, holding a competition between them as to 'who would be the first to *miss* a left and right on Snipe' – clearly, both men were extremely good shots. Brigadier John Roberts Booth (b. 1901) of Rainsford Lodge, Bunclody, County Wexford, who was the son of James Erskine Wise Booth (1862-1931) and Hilda Mary Hall-Dare (a sister of Westley Richard Hall-Dare), of Laragh House, Stratford, County Wicklow, was shooting Coollattin in the late 1950s and into the 1960s. Lt-Col. Bill Bradish became involved in a syndicate there from 1962, according to his personal Game Book records. However, his energies became devoted to Ballinacor, when a syndicate was formed there in 1966, and his shooting at Coollattin becomes increasingly infrequent after that date.

From 1968, the shooting at Coollattin came into the hands of Maj. Victor McCalmont (1919-1993) of Mount Juilliet, County Kilkenny, a race-horse owner and breeder, who was married to Beryl Sutton (d. 1987), daughter of Lt-Col. Francis Henry Sutton and Aileen Gosling. McCalmont had already taken the shooting at the Lisnavagh Estate, which is outside the village of Rathvilly, County Carlow, the family seat of the Bunbury family, Barons Rathdonnell. McCalmont shot Lisnavagh on Tuesdays and Coollattin on Saturdays. A Maj. R.L. Weaver, of Milford, County Carlow, ran the shooting syndicate on his behalf. Other members of the syndicate were Dermot Richard Claud Chichester, 7th Marquess of Donegall, LVO (1916-2007), the second son of Arthur Chichester, 4th Baron Templemore, whom he succeeded in the barony and who lived at the family home of Dunbrody Park, County Wexford, and Robert Mortimer, Victor McCalmont's son-in-law. By all accounts, the shoot was a well-run affair. However, the tenure of the shoot came to an end when the Coollattin Estate was sold in 1977. There followed a somewhat turbulent period for the estate, involving the sale of its house, the destruction of much of its woodland and the breaking-up of its land. There were a number of efforts to revive the shooting but these came to naught, until the Dowling family of Kiltegan, County Wicklow, took a shooting lease from about 1997.

In the past decade or so, shooting at Coollattin under the diligent management of Fiach Dowling and his family, has gone from strength to strength. Today it is one of the very few successful commercial shoots in Ireland, specialising in driven Pheasants and duck, over fifty or more days a season, and offering a range of walked-up options as well, in what is a scenically beautiful part of the country: County Wicklow, the 'Garden of Ireland'.

THE WILDFOWL OF WEXFORD HARBOUR AND SLOBLANDS

The Wexford Sloblands are of international importance as a wintering habitat for migratory wildfowl. The North Sloblands is winter quarters for half the world's population of Greenland White-fronted Geese and an important habitat for many wildfowl species like Wigeon, Teal, Pintail, Golden Plover and the like. Shooting and other conservation interests have been at one to secure these important habitats for the future, and although not always at one as regards how this aim should be achieved, together they have succeeded in securing the rare wetlands habitat for the benefit of the birds which flock to it. The Slobs contain over a century of shooting history, through to the present day.

The Slobs themselves are the outcome of man's reclamation efforts in Wexford Harbour in the nineteenth century, a story of engineering achievement, economic failure and the creation of about 5,000 acres of fertile, agricultural land, which have been, at different times, a source of economic activity, of frequent complex disputes surrounding land ownership, transfer, and shooting rights, of interpersonal rivalries, misunderstandings, and intrigues of one kind or another; but always a place of stunning natural beauty and a wildlife wonderland.

THE NATURAL HISTORY OF SELECTED MIGRATORY WILDFOWL OF WEXFORD

The Greylag Goose

This goose has been the subject of widespread changes in distribution in Ireland. In 1882, Payne-Gallwey records that, 'I have seen but few in a season and seldom on the coast. The only records I have of their capture (and they are not many) are nearly all from inland localities.'[304] However, the pattern changed soon afterwards. Kennedy, Ruttledge and Scroope, writing in 1953 said:

> The Wexford Slobs were until 1949 the great resort of this [Greylag] goose in Ireland. Three to five thousand frequented the North Slob and about that number were found on the South Slob. This is remarkable when one realises that Ussher had no record of this goose in Co. Wexford. The Slobs were reclaimed about 1845 and Mr J.L. Nunn has been told that that the 'bean goose' was the first to frequent the area. The Greylag first came in 1898, then, from 1900 it did so increasingly. Whether the dates given to Mr Nunn are exact or not may be doubted, as Barrett-

Hamilton, who lived in Co. Wexford, did not notice the Greylag in the county until 1912. Nunn states that the Greylag is rapidly being superseded by the White-fronted goose and in 1951 only 200 were present, in 1951 less.[305]

The pattern described above is confirmed in the shoot returns, which are discussed below. Greylags are found on the Slob in very small numbers in most years.

It is uncertain why Greylags have behaved as they did, arriving on the Slob at the end of the nineteenth century in small numbers to overwinter, building rapidly in strength to an overwintering population of several thousand and then disappearing, more or less, half a century later.

Theories abound about the Slobs' creation offering a suitable wintering habitat – a vacuum simply filled by nature – their demise here the result of an increased supply of food in the western Isles of Scotland in the form of potatoes sown during the Second World War; that the effects of drainage and clearance work on the Slobs made the habitat less suitable to Greylags and more suitable to Greenland White-fronts. Alas, mystery remains and that is part of the wonderment of the Slobs and the wintering wildfowl to which they play host.

According to a recent report, each winter Ireland supports over 5,000 Greylag geese, most of which migrate from breeding areas in Iceland and the remainder of which are resident feral birds descended from birds released during the twentieth century. Largest numbers are at the Lough Swilly/ River Foyle/ Lough Foyle complex during both the winter and autumn. Other relatively large flocks were recorded at Loughs Neagh and Beg, Dundalk Bay and Strangford Lough during the winter, and at Greaghans, Lady's Island Lake, the Mullet Peninsula and Belfast Lough during the autumn.[306]

The Greenland White-fronted Goose

This was *the* goose of Ireland. Its stronghold has always been the North Slob, where it started to increase from about 1925, when it was considered scarce, according to Mr Fintan O'Connor.[307] By about 1950, there were 3,000-5,000 on the North Slob, fewer on the South.

94
Unapproachable Geese, Archibald Thorburn.

From the third week of October, numbers build and the birds settle into a pattern of grazing by day on the wide fields of the Slob and roosting by night on sandbanks and islands in Wexford Harbour. As dawn breaks each morning, the entire wintering population arrives back on the Slob in gaggling skeins to spend the day once more grazing the grassland pastures. Thus passes the winter, until early May, when they make their return to Greenland.

Systematic counts of Greenland White-fronts have been undertaken since the late 1960s by the National Parks and Wildlife Service, and since 1983, these have been carried out consistently in the spring of each year, when numbers are at a peak, before the return migration commences. In that latter year, it was estimated that the global population was about 16,500. There were 6,350 on the Slobs and a further 2,900 or so in the rest of Ireland. Thus, Ireland accounted for approximately half the global population. Over the next decade, the spring population on the Slobs rose to a peak of nearly 10,500 in 1994. In addition, there were about 4,200 in the rest of Ireland at the same time, bringing the total in Ireland to almost 15,000. In the same year, the global population was estimated at about 29,500. Thus, Ireland continued to account for about half the expanded global population. Since then, numbers have tended to fall. By spring 2009, the global population was back down to just over 23,000. Numbers on the Slobs were at 8,000 and in the rest of Ireland there were an estimated 2,600.

Habitat destruction seems to be the main cause of the declines that have taken place in the rest of Ireland over the past decade. In addition, the geese no longer use the South Slob to any significant extent. As a result, the North Slob has become relatively more important, now holding almost 8,000 at peak-season levels. The Greenland White-fronted goose ceased to be on the Open Seasons Order from 1982 and consequently there has been no shooting of them since.

Widgeon

If the White-fronted Goose is the heart of the Slob, the Wigeon is its soul. No doubt there has been a considerable decrease in numbers compared with former times, due partly to the dis-

95 *Wigeon from Slob*, Robert Jobson (1916-1999).

appearance of *Zostera*, the favourite plant food of this bird, from Wexford Harbour and other estuaries. However, they are still to be found in strong numbers throughout the winter on many Irish wetlands. The piping whistle made by flocks of Wigeon is usually the first sound a shooter hears in the black dark before the dawn of a winter's morning on the Slob. Daylight brings sight of these flocks – from a dozen to several hundred at a time – wheeling and swooping down from steel grey skies to feed, rest and preen on wintery channels, buffeted by morning gales. Or at other times they float, drakes vivid in winter sunshine on glassy water, crystal clear in frosty air, their whistle seemingly more piercing through the cold. Several thousand Wigeon use the Slob and the adjacent Wexford Harbour as a wintering quarter.

Teal

Teal is the smallest and prettiest of wildfowl – and the most sporting. They begin to arrive in August from Eastern Europe and Russia. On the Slob, they are usually abundant through the winter, with several thousand populating the narrow back channels and small splashes which have been created especially to provide a suitable habitat for them. However, they have a habit of coming and going, and they are not as predictable or stable as, for example, Wigeon. Rainfall and water levels (and, as winter progresses, availability of food) are the factors which most influence their comings and goings.

In dry autumns especially, Teal tend to hold well on the Slob, with flocks of between fifty and several hundred collecting on the smaller flashes of water to rest and feed. Widgeon prefer larger, more open expanses of water, like that provided by the main channel of the Slob. Following

96 Wigeon and Teal, Archibald Thorburn.

heavy rain they usually disperse off the Slob in order to frequent marl holes and temporary splashes which have been formed by rain. Frosty conditions usually see a return of birds to the Slob, as the brackish character of the water in the channels there can mean that open water is available when it is frozen elsewhere.

In addition, an active grain feeding regime in recent years has encouraged larger numbers of Teal to frequent the Slob than in former years. Indeed, bag returns indicate that Teal are more abundant in the past ten to fifteen years than was the case in times gone by. Of course, a qualification should be added that shooters may not have bothered to shoot Teal in earlier times, preferring instead to pursue geese. However, from a sporting point of view, it is difficult to beat Teal, especially in windy conditions, when they require extra speed, agility and accuracy from shooters.

Shooting on the Slobs today continues to be based on managing the habitat to encourage and sustain the maximum numbers of wild, migratory species of duck and to facilitate the provision of secure environment for the Greenland White-fronted goose. The story of their creation is a fascinating, frustrating and engaging one, which is explored in greater detail later in this chapter.

Golden Plover

> The flocks of Golden Plover which winter in this country are enormous ... In western Connacht the flocks are at their greatest strength in spring and again in early winter ... In Dublin Bay ... on at least two occasions, 16 February 1929 and 27 December 1942 the birds were beyond count ... Ruttledge has seen thousands on the North Slob ...[308]

It is unsurprising that against this background, which prevailed as recently as 1953, that Golden Plover were a frequent quarry of game shooters. As with many wetland species which rely on moorland for breeding, there has been serious decline in numbers since that time. However, Wexford Harbour still plays host to a wintering flock which runs to thousands in most years.

97 Lapwing and Golden Plover 1903, Archibald Thorburn.

The Reclamation of Wexford Harbour [309]

Between 1845 and 1855, approximately 2,319 acres of the North Slobs in Wexford Harbour and 2,293 acres of the South Slobs were reclaimed.[310] These successful attempts were not the first; they followed a number of earlier attempts which were to end in failure or failure of execution. The first of these commenced as early as 1813, when a Maj. Boyd of Rosslare Manor House (on the site of what is now the clubhouse of Rosslare Golf Club) succeeded in reclaiming 240 acres from the harbour adjoining his demesne.[311] In the summer of 1847 – in the period of the Great Famine – oats were seen growing on part of this land, the straw from which was seven feet long. As a result, the area became known as 'Hopelands', a name which is used to describe it to this day, although it became inundated by the sea again following a breach in the barrier after a severe storm in 1935, since which time it has remained tidal.[312] Presumably influenced by Boyd's success, a more ambitious attempt at reclaiming 800 acres in the south-eastern portion of the harbour was made in 1814-16 by the Thomas brothers, but this failed shortly after completion, again due to inundation of the reclaimed area by the sea.

Next, in 1840, came what has come to be known as the 'Scottish' project. This was a most ambitious scheme, involving reclamation of both the north and south portions of the harbour,[313] but it ran into serious opposition from a range of individuals and groups, including adjoining landowners, shipping interests and merchants of Wexford Town. Opposition was based, in part, on technical engineering arguments surrounding the possible adverse effects on shipping of changes to the flows of water in the harbour. However, another strand related to the fact that the promoters were 'strangers'. It was considered that if successful, the rights and privileges they would accrue would be to the detriment of local interests. In the end, faced with opposition and hostility from all sides, the Scots abandoned their scheme.

Now it became the turn of John Edward Redmond MP (1806-1865) to become involved in Wexford Harbour reclamation schemes. He was the son of Walter Redmond Esq. of Newtown Lodge and afterwards Ballytrent House, County Wexford. Walter and his brother John Redmond (1770-1822) were well known in banking and shipping circles in Wexford, founding Redmond's Bank.

He stood for Parliament in 1859 unopposed, the two rival candidates (Mr Devereux and Sir Frederic Hughes, who we will read about later, in relation to punt gunning on Wexford Harbour) having retired in his favour, and he held the seat until his death in 1865. His memorial stands in Redmond Square near Wexford railway station, where these words are inscribed on the pedestal, 'My heart is with the city of Wexford. Nothing can extinguish that love but the cold soil of the grave.' John Redmond inherited Newtown Lodge, where he lived until his death, and his elder brother Patrick inherited Ballytrent House.

John Redmond was the first of an Irish political dynasty. His nephew, William Archer Redmond (1825-1880), sat for Wexford as a Home Rule Party MP from 1872 to 1880, and was the father of John E. Redmond (1856-1918), who succeeded Charles Stewart Parnell as the leader of the Irish Parliamentary Party.

John Edward already had successfully reclaimed land at the south end of Wexford Town (roughly the area from today's Paul Quay south to beyond the site of the present Talbot Hotel). He then took up the idea of reclaiming the north side of Wexford Harbour. He consorted with at least four others, including Sir Edward Grogan, 1st Baronet of Moyvore, County Westmeath (1802-1891), who was an Irish Conservative Party politician. He was elected as MP for Dublin City at the 1841 general election, and held the seat until 1865. He was a cousin of Cornelius Grogan (1738-1798) of Johnstown Castle, who was beheaded at Wexford Bridge for his part in the 1798

Rebellion. In the 1800s, the Grogan family were the largest untitled landowners in Ireland, with estates of around 20,000 acres.[314] Others consulted by John Edward were: Mr George, former MP for Wexford County; M.R. Maher, a former MP, and Mr William Dargan, a railway engineer who laid out the Irish rail network, amassing a considerable fortune in the process and who designed the Dublin Crystal Palace, as well as 'other gentlemen possessing capital and enterprising spirit'.[315]

These promoters overcame considerable opposition and saw the passing of a Wexford Harbour Improvement Act 1846, which established a Wexford Harbour Improvement Company.[316] The company was given certain rights and privileges under the Act, and crucially, 'the Estate, Right and Interest of Her Majesty to and over the lands so embanked and reclaimed have been duly granted and conveyed to the said Wexford Harbour Improvement Company'.

This company first began operations in 1847. The work of embanking and enclosing the North Slob, from the Raven Point to the strand at Ardcavan, and enclosing the three islands – Begerin, Big and Breast – continued for three long years, during which time 'the perseverance manifested by the workers and directors of the project in conquering apparently insurmountable natural impediments was extraordinary,'[317] and the project was completed in 1849. In 1850 and 1851, the entire enclosed area was ploughed into ridges and laid out in parallelograms of from 50 to 100 acres in size by canals and drains from nine to twelve feet wide. These conducted the water to the principal outlet, where sluices and a pumping engine periodically discharged it. The new ground hardened and settled, and in the second, third and fourth years, wheat and oats were cultivated, making the project a success.

In 1854, work was commenced to reclaim the South Slob.[318] Following the success of the North Slob and lessons learnt during that reclamation, it was anticipated there would be similar success with the South. This was not to be the case. When at last the work of constructing the canals, waterways and embankments was completed, it was found that inexplicably, the soil would not solidify, even though the same process had been applied as was used successfully on the North Slob.[319] Financial ruin followed for Redmond. On Thursday 12 July 1866, 1,189 acres of the South Slob in the ownership of Patrick Walter Redmond, representing his brother John who died the previous year, were put to auction in five lots in the Landed Estates Court before the Honourable Judge Dobbs.[320] The Redmond family suffered severe financial loss in consequence.

THE NORTH SLOB: A CENTURY OF WILDFOWL SHOOTING AND CONSERVATION

Land Ownership, Shooting Rights and Early Transfers

By Deed of Grant dated 19 March 1850, all the rights of the Queen over the reclaimed area of the North Slobs – 2,411 acres approximately (including 114 acres of water channels), statute measure, and consisting of two divisions, containing in the Eastern Division approximately 1,446 acres (including 41 acres of water channels), bounded on the eastern side by the Raven, on the south by the embankment, and the Western Division containing 964 acres (including 73 acres of water channels) and bounded on the eastern side by Big Island – were conveyed to the Wexford Harbour Embankment Company. Then, on 3 August 1860, there were four conveyances from the Wexford Harbour Embankment Company of these lands to John Edward Redmond (583 acres approximately and 130 acres approximately), Sir Edward Grogan (926 acres approximately) and William Dargan (657 acres approximately).

Significant changes took place to these initial ownership allocations of the North Slob. Most notably, by 1906, Redmond's and Dargan's holdings had been disposed of and the new owners were: Sir Edward Arthur Guinness, 1st Baron Ardilaun, then of St Anne's Clontarf, Dublin;[321] Albert Meldon of Vevay House, Bray, County Wicklow; Joseph Meldon of Coolarne, Athenry, County Galway, JP, Trustees of the estate of the late James D. Meldon which acquired the holding of William Dargan; Frederick A.B. Turner of Clonattin House, Gorey, County Wexford, land agent;[322] Robert MacNevin Bradshaw of Ballinascorney House, Brittas, County Dublin; Sir Edward I.B. Grogan of 9 Creffield Road, London, who had been a collaborator of John Edward Redmond from the outset in the project to reclaim the North Slob; Michael J. O'Connor of 2 George Street, Wexford, and William Hayes of Selskar Street, Wexford.[323]

By 1919, further significant changes had occurred and many of those listed in 1906 as owners were no longer so (see Appendix 1).[324] Notably, Ardilaun appears to have disposed of his holding. The ownership of the Prendergast Estate, which had acquired part of John Edward Redmond's original allocation, had in the main been sold to tenants, and M.J. O'Connor also had sold his ownership, although he retained the shooting rights (see Appendix 1).

The Meldon Estate

The Meldon Estate was founded by James Dillon Meldon (1803-1883), a Dublin lawyer, who bought part of the Glencorrib Estate of Arthur Dillon Browne, County Mayo, in 1851 from the sale of Lord Oranmore and Browne's estate in Claremorris. He also bought the Belmont Estate from the Blakes in 1853 and other properties near Tuam, County Galway, including some of the remaining estate of the Brownes of Coolarne in the parishes of Athenry and Lackagh, and the Blake Estate at Oranmore. In 1876, he owned 886 acres in County Mayo, 4,867 acres in County Galway and smaller acreages in Counties Dublin and Kildare.[325] Sir Albert Meldon (1845-1922) and Joseph M. Meldon (1855-1931) were sons of James Dillon.

Meldon acquired land from William Dargan (probably around 1866 and certainly by 1906) and sold three lots by conveyances of 1 April 1919 to: George Colloton, Garradreen, Taghmon, County Wexford (fifty-six acres); Margaret Hayes, Ballyla, Castlebridge, County Wexford (twenty-seven acres), and Robert Sinnott, Harveystown, Taghmon, County Wexford (twenty-six acres). In all cases, the shooting rights were withheld to the Meldons. The Meldons sold their holding on the North Slob (together with what they owned on the South Slob), including shooting rights, to Stafford Estates in 1951.

The Prendergast Estate

The Prendergast Estate can be traced back to Sir Thomas Prendergast, 2nd Baronet (d. 23 September 1760), who was the eldest son of Sir Thomas Prendergast, 1st Baronet, and succeeded his father to the baronetcy in 1709. It passed through the generations to John Prendergast Vereker, 3rd Viscount Gort (1 July 1790-20 October 1865), who was a British peer and politician. Gort was the son of Charles Vereker, 2nd Viscount Gort, and his first wife Jane, daughter of Ralph Westropp, and he was educated at Harrow. Gort succeeded his father as MP for Limerick in 1817 and held the seat until 1820. Between 1831 and 1832 he served as Mayor of Limerick. From June 1865 until his death in October of that year, he sat in the House of Lords as an Irish representative peer. Their seat was Lough Cutra Castle.

Michael J. O'Connor (1863-1937)

Michael J. O'Connor – or M.J., as he was known and always referred to – was the first to focus on the sporting potential of the Slobs (both North and South). He was married to Catherine Wickham (d. 1949), of a brewing family, and with her had three children: James (b. 1892), Joan (b.

1894) and Fintan Michael (1900-1979). He resided firstly at Glena Terrace, Wexford, and subsequently at Westlands, Wexford.

O'Connor was educated by the Jesuits at Tullabeg, County Offaly, and was trained as a potential student for the Indian Civil Service by Michael Cusack. However, although he had obtained a nomination through Lord Acton, he was advised that no Irish Catholic need apply following the murders of Burke and Cavendish in the Phoenix Park.[326] The result of this was that he became apprenticed to Marin Huggard, Wexford solicitor. After qualifying, in 1888, he established his own practice at George Street, Wexford, in premises reputed to have been the townhouse of Bagenal Harvey. He went on to open other offices in Arklow, Coolgreany and Gorey.

His main claim to fame, as a solicitor, came from his involvement in the Land Acts. On the enactment of Ashbourne Land Act in 1885, he negotiated on behalf of tenants the first purchases under that statute. M.J. was a close observer of the political and economic conditions of the country and could see the potential opportunities created by the Land Question. In particular, he observed the frustration of landlords who were unable to dispose of their estates because of the complications of substantial mortgages and other problems. He conceived of the idea of bonus payments to address this obstacle and wrote a number of newspaper articles under various pseudonyms on the subject. One series contained in the *Free Press*, written under the name 'B.L.', attracted the attention of Mr George Wyndham, then Chief Secretary for Ireland. In 1903, he introduced what was to become the Wyndham Land Act 1903, which contained some of M.J.'s propositions and recommendations as regards bonus payments. The Act facilitated the acceleration of estate disposals across the country, and M.J.'s name and reputation were enhanced

98 Map entitled, 'Mr M.J. O'Connor's Lands, North-West Slob, Wexford.'

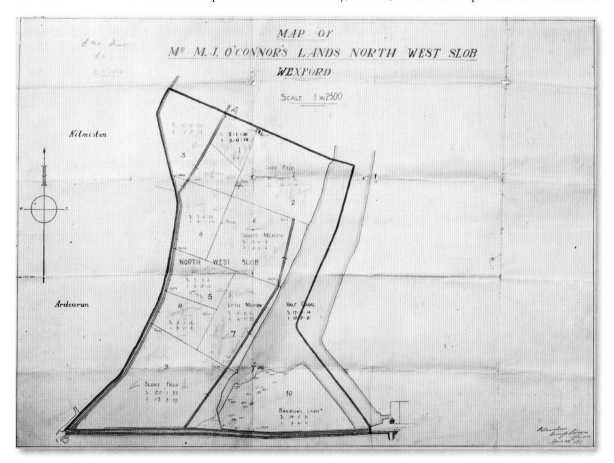

amongst the tenantry of Ireland. Indeed, one of his notable achievements was the completion of the sale of the estate of the late John E. Redmond.

M.J. had a broad interest in the North Slob. Firstly, he was an owner of approximately 104 acres known as North-West Slob, abutting the main channel, which were acquired from the Wexford Harbour Embankment Company. He was, along with his eldest son, James, a trustee to the Prendergast Estate, which acquired its interest on the North Slob from part of Redmond's original allocation. In the main, it was disposed of to tenant purchasers in 1919.

By 1885, it appears that there was a racecourse with a grandstand on the flat land of the North Slob.[327] M.J. was secretary of the North Slob Race Committee. For many years, numerous successful race meetings were organised and held there, until 1903, when a number of people travelling to the races by boat from Wexford Town were drowned.

M.J. was especially prescient when it came to foreseeing the recreational value of the wildfowl shooting on the Slobs, both North and South. Wexford Harbour had a strong tradition of punt gunning for wildfowl, but from the autumn of 1897, a flock of about fifty Greylag geese turned up on the Slob. None came in 1898 but from 1899, there were 'large' numbers and they increased steadily from then, as they returned each autumn. M.J. commenced preserving the shooting rights from 1903 and employed two 'gamekeepers' to enforce them.[328] In 1905, or thereabouts, he developed a Shooting Lodge opposite Begerin Island and constructed a bridge across the channel.

The North Slob abounded with hares. M.J. imported a large number of Belgian hares, and for many years these hares were caught and used to supply various coursing meetings around the country. The hares were very much sought after and before the First World War, they fetched from £1 to £2 each, depending on demand.[329]

M.J. was a gregarious individual – larger than life – and liked nothing better than entertaining his (many distinguished) guests to shooting on the North Slob. These included Sidney Galtrey, a

99 **Remains of Begerin Bridge, North Slob.**

100 M.J. O'Connor (1863-1937) in shooting gear with geese over his shoulder.

well-known racing journalist who wrote for many years for the *Daily Telegraph* under the pseudonym of 'Harry Hotspur'. He wrote an article on his experience in the *Badminton Magazine*.[330] Mr Steve Donoghue was also a frequent visitor and he too wrote an article on his experience of shooting there during the First World War, under the title 'Donoghue Up'.[331] On Sunday 9 November 1919, M.J. entertained the Prince Royal of Arabia (Faisal Iln Saud) and his suite to the Slob, including the party's interpreter Mr H.S. Philby, father of Mr Kim Philby, the 'third man' in the Philby, Burgess and McLean affair.

Other frequent visitors included John Redmond, his younger brother Maj. Willie Redmond (1861-1917), and his son Capt. Willie Redmond (1886-1932). Temptingly, it is said that 'the list of people who shot there during the time of Mr Michael J. O'Connor would fill many pages of any paper and would range from Peers to poachers'.[332] Unfortunately, that is as much as is revealed! Frequently, when M.J. found a poacher infringing his rights, he would invite him to take part in

101 The Saudi Arabian Royal Shooting Party on the North Slob, November 1919.

the following organised shoot and thus save a lot of trouble and unpleasantness. This might also have helped to reinforce M.J.'s property rights in relation to the shooting, since poachers would be regarded as guests of the owner instead of people posing a challenge to his ownership.

M.J. was instrumental in George Colloton (1864-1932), of Begerin House, purchasing some 1,500 acres of the North Slob in 1921, for £15,200.[333] George was the son of John Colloton[334] (1834-1916) of Ballyboggan, Castlebridge, and Begerin House, and Ann Hickey, of Mistern, whom he married on 14 February 1898. The vendor was the Grogan Estate. The balance of the area of the Slob, of approximately 800 acres, remained in the ownership of Meldons. In 1921 also, M.J. disposed of all his shooting rights to George for £2,000.[335]

It is not clear who exercised the shooting rights acquired by George in 1921, but he may have exercised them exclusively until he assigned them in 1931 to his son John Colloton (1898-1980) of Raven Gate, Colloton's Gap.[336] M.J. retired from shooting 'in the late 1920s',[337] so it is possible that he continued to exercise the rights for a number of years after he sold them through some lease arrangement with George Colloton. George disposed of about 500 acres of land between 1921 and 1931 to alleviate financial strain. He sold the 'Bridge Field' (thirty-four acres) and a portion of the 'Pound Field' (amounting to approximately twelve acres) on 30 July 1920, to William F. Scallan, thus retaining the remainder of about ten acres of the 'Pound Field'.[338] The bulk of the remainder was transferred to his son in 1931. He left Begerin and Big Islands to his daughter Nellie.[339] John Colloton leased the shooting rights to Joshua Nunn from 1931 until he sold them to him on 17 February 1950. However, it would appear that Nunn had some understanding, or perhaps a lease in relation to the shooting rights, since he was exercising them from 1924, according to the shoot records, which are available from that time.[340] Joshua employed 'Mosey' Nolan of Screen, County Wexford, as gamekeeper. Colloton sold approximately 500 acres (near the Raven) to auctioneer Harry Warren in 1954.

The Nunn[341]–Bradish Period, 1924-1967

This was a period of regular shooting each season on the North Slob and one for which there is a comprehensive record, as regards the numbers and species shot and the shoot participants, thanks to meticulous record-keeping, which has survived to date, and a copy of which is in the possession of the author.

Joshua Loftus Nunn (1889-1974)

Son of Joshua Loftus Nunn BA (Trinity), and Harriet Harvey, daughter of Henry Harvey Boxwell, MD. He had two brothers: John, who was older, was a major in the army, and Richard Narcissus, who was younger and rose to the rank of Brigadier, serving in two World Wars. He married his cousin Mabel F. Nunn ('May') (b. 1877), who was daughter of William Bolton Nunn (1832- *c*. 1905), who, by his marriage about 1870 to Barbara Breen, started the Nunn association with Castlebridge and the malting business. Joshua and May had one son, John Joshua, a lieutenant in the 1st Battalion Irish Guards who died in action in North Africa on Friday 30 April 1943, aged twenty-two.

Barbara Breen – a keen fox hunter and thought to be the best lady rider in the county at the time – was daughter of Patrick Breen Jr Breen – an excise officer – who had purchased Dixon's malting business when they went bankrupt in 1826. From then on, he carried out a successful business as sales malster, flour miller and grain merchant. By 1836, a relationship had commenced with Arthur Guinness breweries, which purchased 2,195 barrels, fetching £3,087, a significant sum of money at that time.[342] On taking over the business in 1875, William Bolton changed the name of the company to W.B. Nunn & Co. and embarked on an ambitious programme of expansion. Joshua Loftus, William Bolton's nephew, had joined the business about 1906, at the age of seventeen, and took over the business four years later in 1910, continuing the programme of expansion established by his uncle.[343]

102 **Joshua Loftus Nunn (1889-1974).**

Milling of corn was the main activity of the business until 1865, but malting of barley grew to become the principal business thereafter, with the supply of malting barley to Guinness becoming the core business; a position which continued until the firm closed in 1975. There was a close relationship between Guinness and Nunn, and a number of Guinness executives, as will be seen later, graced the Game Books of Castlebridge House, home of Joshua Loftus and May, and the North Slob.

This is an appropriate point to introduce the Bradish family, which was connected to the Nunn family through marriage and with whom there was a long and close association through the shoot at the North Slob. Capt. Gilbert Swan Bradish was son of James Bradish of Strandfield, Wexford, and Henrietta Harvey. They had six sons, 'Old Bill', Edward, George, Jack, Gilbert and Lyndon, and two daughters, Henrietta (known as Duchess) and Isobella. Bill and Edward emigrated to Canada to make their fortunes, and settled there and raised families. George married a French woman and lived in Paris for many years. Jack became a clergyman in Clonegal, County Carlow.

103 Gilbert Bradish with punt gun.

Captain Gilbert Bradish of Strandfield married Emily Violet Nunn, second daughter of William Bolton Nunn and sister of May, Joshua Loftus's wife.[344] He and Emily had one child, William Bolton Patrick Bradish (1916-1995). Gilbert originally went to Canada, where he became a champion weightlifter. He also had champion trotting ponies and won many prizes with them. However, there was no money in these activities, so he turned to India as a tea planter. However, most of his time was spent shooting, including various types of big game, again making little or no money. On returning to Ireland on leave, he married Emily in 1912. Together, they returned to India for a short time before returning to Wexford. Gilbert's principal interest in life was shooting: from big game in India, to ducks on the North Slob, and punt gunning in Wexford Harbour.[345] He died, having just shot a Snipe at a bog near Ferrycarrig, County Wexford, in the late 1940s.[346]

Lyndon Bradish served during the First World War in the Royal Army Medical Corp and returned to reside with his sisters at Strandfield, although for reasons unknown, he never practised medicine privately. 'He was a good tennis player and keen shot; a gentleman …'[347] He appears frequently with Gilbert as a shooting guest in the early days of Nunn's tenure of the North Slob.

William Bolton Patrick Bradish (1916-1996)

William Bolton Patrick Bradish was educated at St Edward's School, Oxford, before attending Sandhurst Military Academy. He was involved in the evacuation of Dunkirk, soon after which married Bridget Strutt (b. 1918). Immediately following his marriage, he was posted to Ringway Airport (now Manchester Airport) without any clear idea of the assignment. In fact, Winston Churchill had established a small staff to develop parachute training, which was then in its infancy and rather dangerous.

He retired and returned to join W.B. Nunn & Co. about 1949, taking up residence at Lonsdale House, Kyle, County Wexford. It would appear that Joshua was keen to secure a succession in the management of the business, what with his only son having been killed earlier in 1943, and he persuaded

104 Lt-Col. W.B.P. Bradish (1916-1996), *c.* 1985, Glensporen Estate, Angus, Scotland, carrying a Churchill 25. He had a pair, one of which was stolen while he was in Palestine in 1946. A copy was made to restore the pair.

'Bill' (as William was known) to return, which he reluctantly did. Bridget Bradish[348] recalls visiting Lonsdale on an extremely wet day, when Bill was returning from a day's hunting with the 'Islands'. It was in a terrible state of repair and they bought the house plus forty acres for £3,500 but had to spend the same again to make it tolerably comfortable.

Upon his return, Bill participated in managing the shoot on Joshua's behalf, although he found working at Nunn's frustrating, 'Uncle Joshua wouldn't modernise.' In 1957, Joshua conveyed his shooting rights to Bill Bradish.[349] Bill took over the running of Nunn's business about 1971, with the assistance of Michael and William Collopy. Joshua Nunn sold the business to Guinness in 1973, the year before he died. On Joshua Loftus's death, his land and shooting on the North Slob passed to Bill Bradish.

The Social Round of Shooting during the Nunn–Bradish Period

Life in Castlebridge House centred mainly round sporting activities indulged by family members and friends, including tennis, angling and fox hunting – but especially shooting.[350] During the shooting season, the house came to life, with many guests of note coming and going at regular intervals to make up the shooting parties, which took place about every two weeks.

During this period, extra staff were employed to assist with the lavish entertainment that was undertaken. However, only the prettiest and tallest girls were employed, making the house a focal point for the young men of Castlebridge and the surrounding area.[351] For example, three chefs, together with their required back-up were needed to prepare and serve the five-course dinners for which Castlebridge became renowned. Dinner was taken in black tie and the menu included local specialities such as Kilmore lobster, Snipe, duck, goose and beef, raised on their own farm. These, of course, were accompanied by the finest of wines from Joshua's cellar. Afterwards, the company retired to the Blue Sitting Room, for cigars and conversations.[352] Breakfast often comprised roasted Snipe or locally caught herrings. On a shoot day, Guns usually assembled at the farmyard at Begerin Bridge at about 11a.m. They spent the morning 'pottering around' before taking lunch from 1.30-3.30 p.m. at the farmyard. This, too, was a fine affair, sent down from Castlebridge House, along with a chef and staff to serve. Afterwards, Guns would take their positions for the evening flight, which in those years offered the strongest shooting.

Soon after Bill Bradish took over the running of the shoot in 1949, the shoot was changed to early mornings, as the flight pattern changed. When the shoot ended around midday, the Guns would return to Lonsdale for lunch.

Key Features of the Shoot Record, 1924-1967

The number of Guns varied but on average there were seven. The largest single bag was recorded on 4 November 1937: 292 birds, comprising 56 Golden Plover, 136 Teal, 35 Wigeon, 13 Mallard and 22 Greylags and a few others. The lowest bag was three on 7 September 1927 to seven Guns – and they were rabbits. That's wildfowling!

Some key features are noted here. The most significant perhaps is the preponderance of Greylag geese in the winters up to about 1941/42 and their virtual disappearance from 1945 onwards. It was not uncommon for bags of over a 100 to be obtained on suitable mornings during the months of November and December, although the last such record was on 13 November 1937, when 150 were taken.

It is generally thought that the decline of Greylag geese in Wexford coincided with an increase along the west coast of Scotland in the acreage planted with potatoes in support of the war effort. The result was easier pickings for the Greylags and a shorter flight to winter quarters. Generally,

105 Bag from a day's shooting at North Slob (Joshua & Mrs Nunn).

in this period, other geese species – Pink Feet, Bean, Snow, Barnacle and Greenland White-fronted – turned up in very small numbers in the bag. From the middle 1940s, White-fronts gradually replaced Greylags, although never in quite the same numbers in the bag as Greylags in former years. The highest number recorded was eighty-nine on 21 December 1954 but more typically between forty and fifty on a suitable winter's day.

Ussher and Warren, writing in 1900, state that, 'it [the Greylag] has been taken, in many cases repeatedly, in all quarters of the country except the south-eastern counties of Waterford, Kilkenny, Carlow and Wexford, from which I have no record of it'.[353] Kennedy, Ruttledge and Scroope, fifty-four years later state:

> Mr J.L. Nunn thinks that this goose is rapidly increasing there [the North Slob] and that it has certainly done so since 1935. Mr Fintan O'Connor believes that the increase commenced before that year but that up to 1925 this goose [the Greenland White-fronted goose] might be called scarce in comparison with the Greylag.[354]

When it comes to duck, the patterns are not very different from what they are today, Teal and Wigeon predominate, but as always with wildfowling, there is a wide variance, relating, of course, to weather conditions on the day. Another feature is the prominence of Golden Plover (which has some claim to fame arising from a shoot on the Slob on 10 November 1951), sometimes exceeding one hundred on a day, but more usually forty to sixty, especially in the seasons before the mid-1950s.

Participants, Guests and Notable Shoots

Those involved in the shoot fall into a number of broad categories. Firstly, there was Joshua, other Nunn family members, including Bradishes, Brigadier Richard Narcissus Nunn (b. 1896), Joshua's younger brother, and close friends like Hewett Barrington Jellett (1900-1992). Jellett turned up for the first time on 6 January 1927, was at most shoots throughout the period, and was there also when Bradish's records ceased on 31 January 1969. He was a true stalwart of the shoot and is worth recalling in greater detail.

Hewett Barrington Jellett (1900-1992)

Hewett Barrington Jellett was the only son of Matthew Barrington (1861-1925) and Belinda Granger, daughter of Charles Henry Granger. His grandmother on his father's side was Josephine, daughter of Sir Matthew Barrington, Baronet of Glenstal, County Limerick.

Hewett was educated at Wellington School in England and returned to Ireland, where he qualified as a solicitor and established a practice at 10 Ely Place under his own name. In January 1931, he married Iris Kathleen Crozier (1904-1993), daughter of Thomas Francis Crozier and his wife Georgina (*née* Robinson). Crozier was solicitor to Richard Berridge of Ballynahinch and his agent also. For some time, he resided at Fermoyle Lodge in County Galway, which was part of the Berridge Estate, and he was a regular visitor at Screebe House, also part of the Berridge Estate. So Hewett, solicitor and sportsman, married Iris, daughter of a solicitor and a sportsman! It appears Hewett was not keen on being a solicitor and enjoyed business and commerce to a greater extent (although not as much as shooting, fishing and hunting, which were his first loves).

Jellett became involved in what was Hughes Bros Dairies after that company experienced difficulties in the 1930s. He was solicitor to the company and together with Bill Freeman, who was accountant with the firm, they acquired the business. The business was subsequently sold to W.R. Grace & Co., a US industrial conglomerate, in 1964.[355] In addition, he had a shareholding in Minch Norton, malsters. It may have been through this connection that his association with Nunn came about, the basis of which otherwise is unclear. Hewett hunted with the Ward Union and fished the River Slaney at Hall-Dare's. In addition, he would spend the first two weeks of September on the Costelloe and Fermoyle fisheries.

As previously stated, his precise connection to the Nunns and the Slob is unclear. However, it is clear that he was involved deeply and from at least as early as 1925, until 1970, when the Nunns ceased. Indeed, he appears to have been manager of the racecourse there in the early 1920s.

He owned a pair of Henry Atkins (The Raleigh), which he bought from Watts Bros, Dublin, for £350, the case of which contains the inscription, 'Major T.C. Goff, Ballybrack'. Both guns had cast-off stocks. When this feature was pointed out to the gunsmith at Watts, he replied, 'we'll steam them straight again. I steamed them crooked in the first place.'[356] Both stocks broke within a year of each other. They were replaced by Holland & Holland in the late 1980s for £6,000.

One morning on the Slob, Hewett was shooting next to Lord Templemore.[357] After the shoot, he was heard to say, 'Don't put me with that man again. I only managed to get half-dozen birds and the other Guns got twenty to thirty.' In his opinion, 'Gerry Kildare [Gerald FitzGerald, 8th Duke of Leinster] was the finest wildfowl Shot he had ever seen.'

Hewett shot wherever he was invited and he received a lot of invitations. This included Jonny Pollock's shoot at Mountainstown, County Meath. Pollock was a cousin! Hew, according to his nephew Tom Crozier, was an outstanding shot and got invited everywhere. He was invited for many years to the Partridge shoot of Robert Grosvenor, 5th Duke of Westminster, in the south of Spain. He was probably the best Snipe shot in the country.

Hew told a story about a party arriving or leaving Dromoland via the West Clare Railway. Two of the engines were called the Lady Corduff and the Lady Inchiquin. The members of the group were playing cards, well oiled, when one of them noticed that they had stopped for even longer than was usual for the West Clare. They sent the guard up front to find out what was wrong. He duly returned to report, 'Ar shur, isn't it the Lady Inchiquin a lyin' on her back in the ditch a puffin and a' snarlin'.

Hewett shot his last – a Snipe – at a driven shoot in County Roscommon, aged eighty-seven years.

Business Associates of Nunn

Business associates of Nunn formed another prominent category of visitor. These included people engaged in malting and milling, such as Roches of Woodville, New Ross. Patrick Roche (d. 1905) established successful malting businesses in Ross and Enniscorthy, which was continued by his son of the same name, who was a regular shooter from 1924. Matt Minch of Minch Norton was an occasional visitor and Capt. Tom Fairhurst and Maurice Goodbody, directors of Ranks, were regulars for some years. The close relationship with Arthur Guinness was reflected in the frequent appearance of Sir Richard Levinge, assistant manager, who resided at Clohamon, County Wexford, and Sir Hugh Beaver (1890-1967), managing director of Guinness.

Military Associates of Lt-Col. Bill Bradish

Another group was military personnel, contacts and friends of Bill Bradish, including Gen. Sir Herbert John Mogg, Mungo Park, who was wounded during the D-Day landing, Maj.-Gen. Sir Charles Harvey, Maj. John O'Rourke, and Maj.-Gen. Doran of Ely House, Wexford.

Friends and Neighbours

Finally, there was a wide range of friends, many of whom were local to County Wexford or were neighbours. Johnstown Castle associations included members of the family of George Arthur Hastings Forbes, 7th Earl of Granard (who married Jane Colclough, daughter of Sir Thomas Esmonde and widow of Hamilton Knox Grogan-Morgan), including his nephew Capt. Ronald Ferdinande Forbes (1879-1960) of Kildavin Lodge.

Kildavin Lodge is said to have been built as a wedding present for Kathleen FitzGerald of Johnstown Castle on her marriage to Maj. Michael Lawrence Lakin (1881-1963) of Horetown House, County Wexford. Lakin was another frequent visitor to the Slob, especially in the early years.

Another association with Johnstown Castle was Gerald FitzGerald, 8th Duke of Leinster, who was godfather to Patrick Bradish (b. 1951), son of Bill Bradish. FitzGerald was a regular at the Slob between 1930 and the early 1950s. Patrick Bradish's other godfather was Sir Peter

106 Jane Colclough (d. 1872) was daughter of Hamilton Knox Grogan Morgan and Sophia Maria Rowe of Johnstown Castle, County Wexford. From 1858, she was wife of Arthur Hastings Forbes, 7th Earl of Granard (1833-1889). Captain Ronald Ferdinande Forbes (1879-1960) of Kildavin Lodge, a nephew, did not have a decent wall on which to hang the painting and so he gave it to Joshua Nunn of Castlebridge House.

107 Sir Peter Scott's personal pen-and-ink drawings contained in copies of his *Dawn Chorus* and *Morning Flight*, which were gifts to Patrick Bradish (b. 1951) on the occasion of Sir Peter standing as his godfather. His other godfather was Gerald FitzGerald, 8th Duke of Leinster.

Scott (1909-1989), who was a close friend of his father and also a regular on the Slob about that time.

Other prominent families whose names turn up with regularity are: Boyds of Kiltra, related to Maj. Boyd, who carried out an early reclamation of Wexford Harbour; Boyses of Bannow; Bruens of Oakpark, Carlow; Deane-Drakes of Landscape, New Ross; Hall-Dares of Newton Barry House, and Places of Rosemount, New Ross. The Leighs of Rosegarland were among the many other families who found themselves on the Slob, shooting as a guest of Joshua Nunn.

The Shoot of 1 November 1924

This is one the earliest shoots on the North Slob for which there are records. The day was hosted by Richard Joshua Nunn, then thirty-five years old, and six others (some of whom were associated through their membership of the Wexford Foxhounds).[358] The first was his brother-in-law Gilbert Bradish, followed by Maj. Charles Arthur Stephen Walker (1890-1928) of Tykillen House, Crossabeg, of the 1st Irish Guards. Thirdly, there was Capt. Patrick J. Roche (d. 1954) of Woodville, New Ross, whose father, of the same name, had died in 1905 and like Nunn was established in the malting business, in both New Ross and Enniscorthy. He married Gwendolene Kate Gallwey, daughter of William Joseph Gallwey in 1920, who was a member of the Place family of Rosemount House, New Ross. This Place family was related through marriage to the Roches.[359] Next there was John Bagenal Boyd (1855-1935) of Kiltra House, Wellingtonbridge, who married Dora Fletcher (1878-1956), the daughter of Revd John Knox Fletcher of County Wicklow, in 1904. Then there was Maj. Michael Lawrence Lakin DSO, MFH (1881-1965), of Horetown House, who in 1914 married the Hon. Kathleen FitzGerald (1892-1930) of Johnstown Castle, daughter of Lord Maurice FitzGerald (1852-1901) and Lady Adelaide Jane Frances Forbes (1860-1942). Finally there was Lady Adelaide's cousin Capt. Ronald Ferdinande Forbes (1879-1960). He was the fifth child of William Francis Forbes (1836-1899) and Phyllis Gabriella Rowe, daughter of John Rowe of Ballycross. He resided at Kildavin Lodge and was for some time the agent at Johnstown Castle. It

108 **Wigeon at Horse Field, North Slob, Robert Jobson (1916-1999).**

is said that Kildavin Lodge was a gift to Kathleen FitzGerald on the occasion of her marriage.[360]

At that time, shooting took place from mid-morning, with a long break for lunch at the lodge on the Slob. This was an elaborate affair, which involved the chefs (there were three employed) from Castlebridge House transporting the food and refreshments to the Slob. This was followed by evening shooting. The bag came to 127, which was the highest for that year and comprised 28 Greylag geese, 26 Wigeon, 12 Teal, 17 Pochard, twenty-one Golden Plover and several each of Pintail, Shoveler and Tufted duck.

The Scott Shackleton Shoot of 19 February 1949

A very interesting shoot was hosted on 19 February 1949 by Joshua Nunn and his brother Richard, who were accompanied by Lyndon Bradish, uncle of Bill Bradish, Hewett Jellett, Sir Peter Scott and Lord Edward Shackleton (sons of the famous explorers), Sir Charles Harvey and Gerald FitzGerald, 8th Duke of Leinster.

Sir Peter Markham Scott, CH, CBE, DSC and Bar, MID, FRS, FZS (1909-1989)

Sir Peter Scott was a wildfowler, conservationist, painter, naval officer, all-round nature enthusiast and close personal friend of Lt-Col. Bill Bradish. This is his first recorded visit to shoot the Slob but he returned on numerous occasions, including in December 1951, when he stood as godfather to Bill Bradish's only son Patrick (b. 1951).

He was born in London, the only child of Antarctic explorer Robert Falcon Scott and sculptor Kathleen Bruce. He was only two years old when his father died. Robert Scott, in a last letter to his wife, advised her to 'make the boy interested in natural history if you can; it is better than games'.[361] He was named after Sir Clements Markham, mentor of Scott's polar expeditions, and his godfather was J.M. Barrie, creator of *Peter Pan*. He was educated at Oundle School and Trinity College, Cambridge, initially reading Natural Sciences but graduating in History of Art in 1931. He was a founder of the World Wildlife Fund and several wetland bird sanctuaries in Britain, most notably at Slimbridge, Gloucestershire. Scott was knighted in 1973 for his contribution to the conservation of wild animals.

Edward Arthur Alexander Shackleton, Baron Shackleton, KG, AC, OBE, PC, FRS (1911-1994)[362]

British geographer and Labour Party politician. He was the younger son of Sir Ernest Shackleton, the Antarctic explorer who was part of Robert Falcon Scott's Antarctic expeditions. In 1950, he was elected MP for Preston South and he was re-elected in 1951. In 1955 he stood down and was made a life peer as Baron Shackleton of Burley in the County of Hampshire in 1958. In Harold Wilson's government, he served as Minister of Defence for the RAF (1964-7) and Minister without Portfolio (1967-8). He was Leader of the House of Lords from 1968 to 1970, and subsequently Opposition Leader of the House of Lords. From 1971, he was president of the Royal Geographical Society and in 1994 he became the Life President of the newly founded James Caird Society, named after the boat in which his explorer father and crew escaped Antarctica (itself, in turn, named for James Key Caird (1837-1916), jute baron and philanthropist).

Major-General Sir Charles Harvey CB, CVO, CBE, MC (1888-1969)

Officer in the British Indian Army during the the world wars and a friend of Bill Bradish. He was a frequent visitor to the Slob following his retirement from the army in 1946. He was appointed CVO in 1922, for performing the duties of Assistant Military Secretary to the Prince of Wales during His Royal Highness's Indian Tour, and knighted in 1946.

According to notes in Bradish's personal Game Book, the 'day steadily deteriorated, sending in mist and strong wind, should have shot more plover'. Bradish himself was at Barnes Lawn, where he had sixteen birds to his own Gun, thirteen Golden Plover, a goose, a Wigeon and a Teal. The overall bag was 146, of which there were sixty-three White-fronted Geese, fifty-three Golden Plover, nineteen Wigeon and seven Teal.

When Scott returned for the christening of Patrick Bradish, the shooting took place on 8 December 1951. The party comprised Joshua Nunn and his brother Richard, Hewett Jellett, Gerald FitzGerald, Maj. Sir Richard Levinge and Capt. (Henry) Arthur Bruen.

Major Sir Richard Vere Henry Levinge, 11th Baronet (1911-1984)[363]

The last to occupy the family seat of Knockdrin Castle, Mulligar, County Westmeath, which he left about 1946 when he leased Clohamon House, Bunclody, County Wexford from the

Sweetman family. He purchased the property in 1955. In 1935 he married Barbara Jardine Kidston of Hazelbury Manor, Wiltshire, and later, in 1976, he married Jane Rosemary Stacy. His association with shooting on the Slob dates from 1946, when he moved to Clohamon. However, he was also a director of Arthur Guinness & Co., so his connections with the Nunns may well have been multifaceted.

Captain Henry Arthur Bruen (1887-1954)[364]

A member of a distinguished and notable family in Counties Wexford and Carlow, Henry was the son of Henry Bruen and Agnes Mary MacMorrough Kavanagh of Oakpark and Coolbawn. He was born on 26 August 1887 and married Jane Catherine Gladys McClintock, daughter of Arthur George Florence McClintock of Leighlinbridge, in 1913. He was educated at Eton and he gained the rank of captain in the service of the 15th Hussars.

He lived at Oak Park, County Carlow, and had one daughter, Patricia, who was born in 1914 and in turn married Mervyn Anthony Boyse of Bannow House, County Wexford:

> Bruen strongly disapproved of the match and in his will he left his daughter the miserly sum of £6 per week for life. He cut his wife out of his will entirely as she had left him some years earlier for a Montenegran Prince, Milo Petrovic-Njegos, with whom she set up house in Roundstone, County Galway. His daughter contested the will and eventually received a share of the auction receipts. The bulk of his estate went to first cousin, Francis Bruen, then living in England.[365]

Bradish's personal Game Book notes that there was 'a fresh to strong westerly wind and a calm spell at noon. [He] shot with Scott. Good goose flight. Total 110.' This included forty-seven White-fronted geese, four Greylag geese, twenty-six Golden Plover, thirteen Wigeon and seven Teal. Bradish was in the Pound Field and accounted for thirty-two to his own Gun, comprising nineteen geese, twelve Golden Plover and a Wigeon.

The Shoot of 10 November 1951: Birth of the Guinness Book of Records

The shooting party on this occasion comprised the usual stalwarts of Joshua and Richard Nunn, Lt-Col. Bill Bradish, Hewett Jellett, Maj.-Gen. Sir Charles Harvey and Maj. Sir Richard Levinge, as well as Maj. John O'Rourke and Capt. Tom Fairhurst, a co-director with Bill Bradish on the board of Ranks (they also used to fish together at Delphi Lodge, County Mayo). Finally, there was Sir Hugh Beaver, who like Levinge, had been coming to the Slob since about 1946.

Sir Hugh Eyre Campbell Beaver, KBE (1890-1967)[366]

Born in South Africa, Sir Hugh was educated at Wellington College, Berkshire, after which he spent two years in the Indian police force from 1910. He worked as an engineer, principally with the firm of Sir Alexander Gibb & Partners, until he became a managing director of Guinness in 1946 and he stayed there until he retired in 1960. He was knighted in 1943 and awarded a KBE in 1956. He also received honorary degrees from the University of Cambridge, Trinity College Dublin, the National University of Ireland, and was made an honorary fellow of the London School of Economics in 1960. He also served as president of the Royal Statistical Society from 1959 to 1960.

Bradish's notes of the day state that there was 'A fair east breeze after a storm. There was a good showing of Wigeon, Teal and Golden Plover.' The total bag was 137, of which there were 29 White-fronted geese, 20 Golden Plover, 37 Wigeon and 49 Teal. Bill Bradish was on the 'Splashes' and accounted for seven geese, seventeen Golden Plover and a Wigeon.

Back at Castlebridge House after the shoot, Beaver became involved in an argument: which was the fastest game bird in Europe, the Golden Plover or the Grouse? When it was realised that it was not possible to confirm from a reference book whether or not the Golden Plover was Europe's fastest game bird, Beaver thought that there must be numerous other questions debated nightly in the 81,400 pubs in Britain and in Ireland which fell into the same category. He quickly came to the view that that a book supplying the answers to this sort of question might prove popular. His idea became reality when Guinness employee Christopher Chataway recommended university friends Norris and Ross McWhirter, who had been running a fact-finding agency in London. The brothers were commissioned to compile what became *The Guinness Book of Records* in August 1954. The rest is history.

The Shoot of 13 November 1965: Fiske's First Shoot with Bradish

Bill Bradish's notes sum up the situation on this day quite succinctly, 'First shoot in conjunction with Fiskes. All seemed to work excellently. Calmer day. Widgeon very good. Fair showing Wigeon and geese.' The bag was eighty-one, including twenty-four White-fronted geese, twelve Wigeon, twenty-eight Teal and a couple of Golden Plover. Bill Bradish was on 'Sandy Point', where he had four geese, five Teal and a Wigeon.

It was a quiet end to an era and the commencement of a new one.

The Fiske Era, 1965-2002

109 Bill Fiske (1939-2002) with terriers.

The Fiske era commenced as a father and son partnership between William Grant Fiske (1910-1982), a farmer and sportsman who shot, kept falcons and spaniels at his home farm of Debden

Hall Farm, Saffron Weldon, Essex, England, and his son William Grant (Bill) Fiske Jr (1937-2002). However, it was to be short-lived, and the period of Bill's tenure was to see heightened tensions in relation to shooting and other conservation interests.

Bill was the only child of William Grant and his wife Edna Romeril (1912-1983). He took a degree in agriculture from Cambridge in 1959, after which he travelled to Trinidad, where he spent a year practising tropical farming. In 1961, he travelled to Kenya, where a Cambridge class-mate, Mike Harries, was farming coffee and pineapples for Del Monte. In the same year, he arrived at the

Siriba Teacher Training College at Maseno, Kisumu, where the principal was Thomas William Sharrad (1915-1974), who was married to a Jessie Bowen (b. 1913). Their daughter Christine Elizabeth (b. 1939) had returned from Edinburgh, where she had studied science followed by teacher training at Murrayhouse and had a broken romance with Jim Beezley. Coincidently, Bill, too, was shortly after a break-up with a Maltese woman who had not met with his parents' approval. Before long, Bill and Christine struck up a relationship, which culminated in marriage on 25 July 1964, at Thika, Nairobi, Kenya. Soon after his marriage, Bill's parents William Grant and Edna parted.

William Grant had become aware of the North Slob and its wildfowl, and came over in February 1965, along with Bill, who left Christine teaching in Kenya while he made the exploratory trip with his father. The outcome was that William Grant decided he would seek to purchase a substantial holding, including sporting rights, in a partnership that would see Bill and Christine coming to Ireland to manage the venture, with William Grant making periodic visits in support of his son's management of the estate.

Negotiations took place with all landowners and during this time Christine returned to join Bill, the two of them living in a rented bungalow in Curracloe. It was at this time they met Redmond Gallagher and his son David and wife Margaret. They were of a similar age and stage of their lives, both contemplating adopting children. So there was much in common.

Colonel Bill Bradish was also very helpful to Bill at this time, recalls Christine. On 2 December 1965, with negotiations completed, about 2,000 acres of land and shooting rights over around 1,000 acres were acquired by Fiske in conveyances with Stafford Estates, John Colloton, Harry Warren and Col. Bill Bradish, with the balance of the shooting rights being retained by Bradish. The plan was that William Grant would reside in an apartment in Begerin House when he was over and he proceeded to remodel the house to this end. Miss Toole of Curracloe House then died, and so in 1969 Bill acquired that property (including eleven acres from the Toole Estate) for

110 **Bill and Christine Fiske celebrate their wedding on 25 July 1964 at Thika, Nairobi, Kenya.**

£40,000, which he then leased while he and Christine resided at Begerin House. They eventually moved to live at Curracloe House at Easter 1977.

Complications

In the event, circumstances changed and with them so did William Grant's plans. Firstly, Bill's mother moved to Ireland (and lived with Mary Hughes of Killinick, County Wexford).[367] This was not something he had reckoned on. Secondly, he became involved with Nina, daughter of his former wife's best friend, and was to marry her and have two children, who were born in 1971 and 1973.

Bill would have liked to purchase the estate, but couldn't raise the capital to do so. In addition, matters in relation to shooting rights were starting to become quite complicated. After the Fiske acquisition of the North Slob, progressive farming methods were employed, entailing grubbing of hedges and new drainage channels, which resulted in the 'prairie' appearance which visitors to the Slob see today.

These developments gave rise to concerns for the welfare of the Greenland White-fronted Goose. The Irish Wildbird Conservancy (IWC) instigated the involvement of the World Wildlife Fund (WWF), which donated money, along with Guinness and the Department of Lands. The outcome was the purchase of 250 acres from Fiske in 1968 and a licensing of a further 100 acres of land, for a twenty-year term from 17 April 1969, at an annual sum of £977, subject to conditions. Fiske refused to sell the 100 acres. The two sites were known as the Western and Eastern Refuges. However, no shooting rights passed in these transactions, which gave rise to taunting and ridicule of the department at the time.[368]

Around the same time, Col. Bill Bradish was experiencing some difficulties of his own, in respect of shooting rights.[369] In 1967, the Miss Bennets (who owned forty-three acres on the Slob) and Mr John Rossiter (who owned about thirty acres) preserved their land in 1967. Bradish made no response, nor did he make a response when they attempted to sell rights to him in 1968, which they alleged they had on these lands. However, the matter was brought to a head in a High Court case of 1970, which was taken by Bradish against Bennett, Rossiter and John Lacey, farmer of Ballyteigue, Kilmore, and Noel Whelan, farmer, of the same parish, and George Woodbyrne of Castlebridge. The case lasted four days and culminated in an agreement which accepted that Bradish had the rights, through a conveyance of October 1965, that there would be an injunction restraining the defendants, and that they would contribute £2,500 towards the costs of the plaintiffs.[370] However, a part of the agreement was that George Woodbyrne was granted shooting over an area of about five acres, with frontage onto the channel, known as the Swan's Nest.[371]

Sometime after this (but not necessarily influenced by the events), Col. Bradish decided that he wished to sell his shooting rights and proposed doing so to Fiske, with whom he had always had cordial relations.[372] Indeed, he entered into contracts for the sale of his rights to Fiske, dated 6 July 1970. However, such a transaction, involving as it would a non-national (Fiske), would require the consent of the Minister for Lands, which was not forthcoming. Discussions between the parties dragged on, with various alternatives being put forward, until in 1972 agreement was reached whereby the Minister for Lands would purchase the shooting rights of Bradish (coloured buff in Map 1: Shooting rights on lands controlled by Fiske and Bradish families acquired by the Minister for Lands, 1972), which were the subject of (a number of) contracts of sale to Fiske (with those in respect of the Western Refuge being then extinguished). In effect, the Minister took over the contract for the purchase of Bradish's rights at the sum agreed with Fiske, namely £19,000. In addition, he would acquire a selection of Fiske's shooting rights (coloured red and

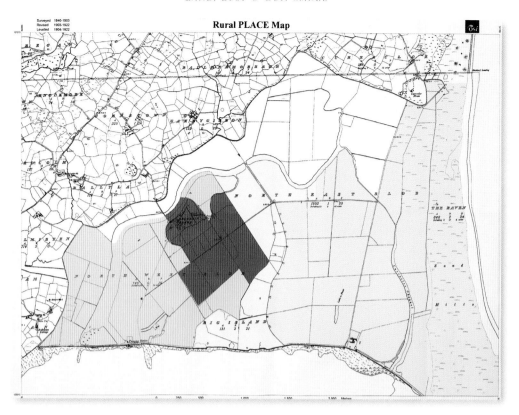

111 Map 1: Shooting rights acquired by the Minister for Lands from the Fiske and Bradish families, 1972.

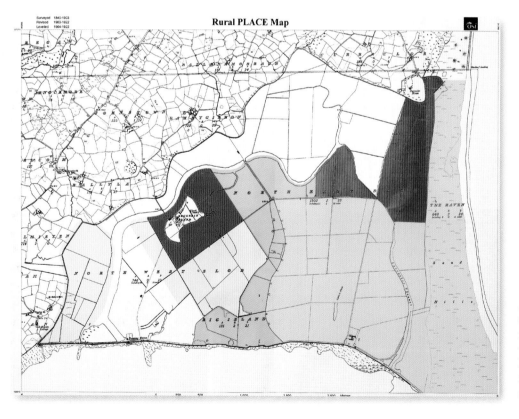

112 Map 2: Shooting rights controlled by the Fiske Family, 1972-1989 and subsequently.

green in Map 1) subject to conditions.[373] Fiske withheld certain shooting rights (coloured blue in Map 1), which he would not agree to include in the arrangements.

The Minister, in turn, agreed to sell back to Fiske a portion of the rights he acquired, amounting to 346 acres, for £2,500. (These comprised lands coloured red and pink in Map 2, Shooting rights controlled by Fiske family between 1972 and 1989 and subsequently.)

In addition, the Minister agreed to lease certain other shooting rights (shown in green and yellow on Map 2), for seventeen years, from 17 April 1972 to 16 April 1989, at an annual fixed rent of £675 per annum.[374] In effect, these rights comprised the balance of shooting rights sold by Fiske (coloured green) and those sold by Bradish (coloured yellow) (less those in respect of the Western Refuge, which had been extinguished). In agreeing to a lease with Bill, the department restricted the shooting over those areas owned by Fiske which were not transferred to the Minister (coloured blue on Map 2), in the same manner as would apply over the lands which were to be subject to the lease. The actual transfer of rights to the Minister took place by way of conveyance of 2 October 1973.

Essentially, the restrictions related to the number of shoots which could be held over the open season and the number of Guns who could shoot. The number of shoots permitted was not to exceed twelve, of which five goose shoots were to be confined within the period 1 November to 31 December.[375] The number of Guns was restricted to a maximum of sixteen for shoots prior to 25 October and twenty for shoots after that date.

These arrangements governed shooting on the Slob for the seventeen years until 16 April 1989. No renewal clause was provided for. Instead, it was stated that, 'it is a basic assumption to the entire arrangement that harmonious relations between the Minister and the lessee will continue and the Minister would not wish to introduce a third party into the arrangements'.[376] However, the lease referred to was not actually drawn up at the time.

So what had been achieved by this complicated set of arrangements? Fiske continued to own the shooting rights shown in blue on Map 2. Ownership of a further 346 acres was to be transferred back to him (coloured pink and red on Map 2) and he had a lease over those shown in green and yellow (Map 2). All of the shooting rights, whether leased or owned, were subject to a management agreement as regards how they could be exercised. A refuge of 250 acres – the Western Refuge – was secured for the geese, with a further 100 acres – the Eastern Refuge – under a management agreement until 17 April 1989, which restricted the land use to grazing and precluded any drainage work over the area. It was a compromise; it was very complicated but it worked.

A sale of land from Fiske to FBD Insurance took place in 1978. FBD acquired most of the Fiske lands and the family held on to about 210 acres and shooting rights over those. As part of this sale agreement with FBD, a lease was entered into on 30 May 1978 with respect to certain shooting rights. These were the rights which were withheld by Fiske from the conveyance to the Minister for Lands on 2 October 1973, but which were included with the sale of land to FBD (blue in Map 2). The term of the lease was 'for as long as Mr Fiske Junior will continue to reside on the North Slob or any land adjoining the North Slob' at a rent of £1 per annum, if demanded. In the event of the death of Bill Fiske, the leasehold interest in the shooting rights would revert to FBD or its successors. It was finally agreed that FBD or its nominees would have an entitlement to two Guns on any shoot day.

On their expiry in 1989, the lease arrangements with the State were renewed for a further ten years, to 31 January 1999. Thereafter, the term was reduced to five years, although the expiring lease referred explicitly to a 'further ten seasons' being considered. In addition, there was a reduction in the area leased; notably, the west side (i.e. Bennets') was excluded from Fiske and granted instead to another group of shooters. Bill protested about what was happening but to little avail.[377] It was shabby treatment of a man who had given so much to manage the shoot in a sustainable way.

Bill died, after a brief illness, in October 2002 on the day after his sixty-fifth birthday.

The Shooting Under Bill Fiske

It is important to point out that during Bill's tenure, shooting changed on the North Slob in a number of respects. In part, these changes resulted from the fact that Fiske undertook major drainage work and changed farm output significantly, both in terms of acreage under cereals and increasing milk output. With respect to shooting, nothing was done without careful consideration. He consulted with Charles Coles of the Eley Game Advisory Service in 1967, regarding the kind of grassland environment which would be most suitable for geese. He also sought advice about the design and potential benefits of developing duck ponds. In 1970, he commissioned the then Game Conservancy to advise on the potential for developing Pheasant and Partridge shooting. He corresponded frequently with Lt-Col. Bill Bradish on many aspects of the shoot management and he consulted with the Guns. There was a move to locate hides closer to the channels and away from field locations. This was in the interest of farming efficiency but there was some resistance to change and attrition of at least one Gun, who had a long history of shooting on the Slob.

A principal attraction of the Slob as shoot was the potential to bag a goose and, as may be seen from the table, the North Slob had a pretty consistent record over the years in this respect. However, Bill gradually supplemented the wild-bird bag with the introduction of hand-reared Mallard. His experiments with creating splashes and providing supplementary feeding also were successful. By the time goose shooting ceased in 1982, there was an adequate duck bag, comprising wild migratory species supplemented with hand-reared Mallard, to assure the North Slob's continued reputation as an outstanding wildfowl shoot (see table below).

Bill always followed a hands-on approach. He wasn't afraid to dirty his hands and he had the loyal assistance and support of Ger Foley (b. 1929), a guide who was there since the Nunn-Bradish years and who still serves with the present syndicate in 2011.

The management principals established by Bill Fiske have been upheld by the syndicate, which has continued the shoot together, with Tom Fiske, since Bill's demise. In the near decade now since his death, he would look with some pride at the return which has been achieved from their continued practice.

White-fronted Geese Bags, 1969/70-1989/90

Year	North Slob	South Slob	Total
1969/70	221	213	434
1970/71	257	121	378
1971/72	344	113	457
1972/73	113	42	155
1973/74	226	44	270
1974/75	211	43	254
1975/76	166	111	277
1976/77	124	91	215

1977/78	125	101	226
1978/79	127	170	297
1979/80	64	49	113
1980/81	151	44	195
1981/82	76	17	93
1985/86	196	98	294
1989/90	171	57	228

THE SOUTH SLOB

Land Ownership, Shooting Rights and Principal Transfers

The part of the South Slob owned by William Dargan, and amounting to 891 acres of land, was purchased by Meldons, probably in 1866, and presumably it was at this time that Meldons also acquired their holdings on the North Slob.[319] The Tynte Estate most likely acquired the balance (of about 1,165 acres), which was owned by the representatives of John Edward Redmond, when it was put for sale in the Landed Estates Court on 12 July 1866.

The Tyntes were a long-established family dating from 1667, when Henry Tynte was granted lands in Counties Limerick and Cork. The Tynte family's estate was near Dunlavin, County Wicklow, but they also held land in Counties Cork and Kilkenny, as well as in Leitrim. In the late 1850s, Joseph Tynte was leasing property near Tullaghan, County Leitrim, from the White estate, but he was also leasing lands to the Montgomery Estate. In the mid-nineteenth century, Joseph Pratt Tynte held land in the parish of Youghal, Barony of Imokilly, County Cork. In the 1870s, he was the owner of over 1,200 acres in County Cork, 2,532 acres in County Wicklow, 150 acres in County Kilkenny and 30 acres in County Leitrim.[379]

The shooting rights which they acquired on the South Slob may have been exercised by Lt-Col. Mervyn Challoner Tynte (1846-1910), eldest son of Joseph, and certainly were subsequently by his youngest daughter, the formidable Miss (Norah Ina) Violet Tynte (d. 1963), who succeeded her brother Maj. Mervyn Arthur Tynte at the family seat, Tynte Park, Dunlavin, County Kildare (built 1820), on his death in 1918.[380] Previously, she resided at Saunder's Grove, County Wicklow, and Tynte Lodge, County Leitrim. She was a fanatical horse woman, hunting with the Kildares, and as well as a keen shot, she was an excellent golfer and co-founder of the Royal Automobile Club of Ireland in 1901. In 1954, she presented a perpetual cup to the Cocker Spaniel Club of Ireland, on the occasion of the club's twenty-first championship show, for the best any-colour cocker, dog or bitch puppy, junior, maiden, novice or graduate class, bred by an exhibitor resident in Ireland.

Violet Tynte's interest in the South Slob was acquired by Maj. Beaumont, most likely between 1948 and about 1952. Major Michael Wentworth Beaumont (1903-1958) was a British soldier and Conservative politician. The son of Hubert George Beaumont and Elisa Mercedes Grace, he was the maternal grandson of Michael P. Grace and paternal grandson of the 1st Baron Allendale. He was educated at Eton, Oundle School, Northamptonshire, and the Royal Military Academy Sandhurst in Berkshire, later serving in the Coldstream Guards, reaching the rank of lieutenant.

In the service of the 90th Field Brigade, Buckinghamshire and Berkshire Yeomanry, Royal Artillery, he became major and received the Territorial Decoration. From 1927 to 1947, he was Justice of Peace for Buckinghamshire. He was elected MP for Aylesbury at the 1929 general election and held the seat until he resigned from the House of Commons on 2 May 1938. He was appointed Deputy Lieutenant of Buckinghamshire in 1938 and was Master of Foxhounds of Bicester and Warden Hill between 1945 and 1947, and of the Kildare Hunt between 1953 and 1959.

Beaumont married twice, firstly to Faith Pease, daughter of the 1st Baron Gainford, on 29 February 1924, and secondly to Doreen Christian Davis-Goff, daughter of Sir Herbert Davis-Goff, 2nd Baronet, on 30 December 1935.[381] He had one son, Timothy Beaumont, by his first wife. He resides at Harristown House, formerly home of the La Touche family.

Fintan M. O'Connor (1900-1979),[382] a son of M.J., was born on 10 July 1900 at Ballask Cottage, Carne, County Wexford, which was the family's summer retreat since his grandfather's day. He was educated at Mount St Benedict School, Gorey, County Wexford, and Clongowes Wood College, Dublin. He described moving from one school to the other as 'like moving from heaven into some sort of prison camp'. He then spent four years as a student of Trinity College Dublin, from November 1918, which he described as 'the happiest years of my life'. During his time there, he became active in the College Historical Society and on one occasion, in November 1920, he was asked to put up in his rooms Col. Cecil L'Estrange Malone, who was to be a guest speaker and for whom there was an arrest warrant outstanding. He did, but twenty minutes or so before the meeting the Provost arrived with two officers from Dublin Castle and arrested Malone in the Fellows Common Room over the college dining hall.

"LA SONNAMBULA"
– or how reputations are built up!

113 (above) Fintan O'Connor (1900-1979). This photograph shows him aged about thirty, at which time he became involved in the management of the shooting on the South Slob.

114 Fintan O'Connor's Christmas card, celebrating two of his passions: shooting and the Wexford Festival Opera.

From there, O'Connor joined the Officers' Training Corp, but four days later the Armistice was declared and he remarked, 'the Kaiser must have known Fintan O'Connor had joined up and that's why he threw his hand in four days later!' He went on to say:

> ... eventually in 1923 I qualified as a Solicitor. I didn't get any distinctions but I had the unique – I don't know what you would call it – achievement, I suppose, of getting my Bachelor of Arts, my Bachelor in both Laws and my Solicitor's final, within a month of each of the three of them. I don't believe that has ever been done before, and I can't think how on earth I ever did it.

He then joined his father's practice.

Fintan O' Connor was a most interesting and engaging character who lived life to the full.

Shooting During the Time of Fintan O'Connor

Fintan took over the shooting rights from the Meldon family about 1930, which covered about half the area of the Slob, while Miss Tynte retained the rights over her holding. His lease expired in 1965, at which point they reverted to Stafford Estates, which had purchased Meldon's in 1951. Both Stafford and Beaumont disposed of their interest to Gallagher in 1962 or thereabouts.

On the South Slob, on one occasion, Fintan placed three Guns on the Sea Wall: Maj. M.P. Leahy, who had only one leg (the other having been seriously mutilated during the war when he was with the Irish Guards); Capt. Cecil Cook, who had only one eye, and George Brown, who had only one arm. However, all three were excellent shots and produced a superb bag at the end of the day.

An interesting episode of poaching occurred on 4 December 1942. It was a Friday evening, at about 5 p.m., when Fintan O'Connor came upon a party in three black terraplanes, which drove to the Slob and decanted its occupants, who then went shooting. When challenged by Patsy Maguire, one of the gentlemen said that it was quite alright; that they would call to see O'Connor in the morning. They did not call, and Fintan O'Connor got his staff to work. He found that the party consisted of Lt-Gen. Daniel McKenna and six or eight others, including Brig. Woodhouse of the British Army, an American Officer, and their ADCs. These gentlemen were obviously working together – in spite of the alleged neutrality – inspecting the defences, drove onto the Slob and shot some birds, then drove away without leave or licence and without any apology.

Fintan O'Connor immediately had solicitor's letters sent to each one of them on 7 December and hot correspondence followed, including two special courtiers from the American Legislature Mr David Gray, who was then Minister, begging Mr O'Connor not to bring proceedings, as an international situation would have arisen which would have exposed the farce of neutrality and shown that the Irish Army, the British Army and American Army were all working together like mad to prevent an invasion, not by the Allies but by the Germans. Fintan, on receiving letters of apology from Gen. McKenna and from Brig. Woodhouse, did not proceed any further with the matter. But this was not O'Connor's only encounter with David Gray.

The next occasion was a Sunday in winter during the Second World War. It was the day upon which the English troops came into the war and landed in North Africa. Guests on that occasion were his Excellency David Gray, American Minister in Ireland, and Chief Justice Conor A. Maguire. At that time the general idea was that everyone should be on the Slob before dawn broke and placed in their different positions, including those who got into barrels and had wooden decoys placed around them.

David Gray had a very large American car and his driver's name was John Murphy, who for many years had driven the former American Minister John Cuddihy to the Slob and was therefore familiar with the area. The car drove down along a winding, rough, narrow lane and parked at the end of it but there was no sign of him getting out. Grey was listening to the radio. O'Connor urged that they should hurry on or they would be late. Gray replied that the news to which he was listening was most momentous and one of the great moments in history, namely that the American troops had a few hours earlier landed in North Africa, and O'Connor replied that the Americans would be there for a hell of a long time but the geese would be gone in a few minutes.

There was always significant overlap of shooters between the North and South Slobs. One of the great stalwarts of the two Slobs was Richard Michael John Hely Hutchinson, 8th Earl of Donoughmore (1927-2005), styled Viscount Suirdale from 1948 until 1981. He was the son of John Hely-Hutchinson, 7th Earl of Donoughmore, and he succeeded to his father's titles in 1981, sitting in the House of Lords under the Viscountcy of Hutchinson. Due to the House of Lords Act 1999, he lost his seat.

Donoughmore was educated at Winchester, Groton School (Massachusetts) and at New College, Oxford, graduating with a medical degree and later attaining the rank of captain in the service of the Royal Army Medical Corps. His home in Ireland was Knocklofty House, near Clonmel, County Tipperary, and he was a regular and frequent shooter on both the North and South Slobs for over thirty years from the 1950s. As may be seen (Illustration 115), he made a serious attempt at leasing the shooting rights on the South Slob at the end of the 1950s, when that Slob offered comparable quality shooting to that on the North Slob.

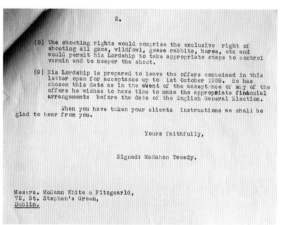

115 Letter dated 22 September 1959, re Earl of Donoughmore wishing to lease shooting on South Slob.

The Gallagher Family

The Gallagher family's association with the South Slob dates from their acquisition by Redmond Gallagher (1914-2006) in 1962. Redmond was the son of Harry Gallagher (1880-1975) and Eileen Cullen (1887-1976), daughter of John Baptist Cullen of New Ross, County Wexford. The family were the founders of Urney Chocolates and their story is told by Karen Nolan in *Sweet Memories, the Story of Urney Chocolates*. It was Redmond's mother, Eileen, who, at the end of the First World War, commenced making sweets – raspberry fudge – from the kitchen of her home in the village of Urney, near Strabane in County Tyrone, while Harry continued to practise law. In 1924, the

116 **Redmond and David Gallagher.**

family moved to Tallaght, to what was a disused RAF airbase (the family residing in the hospital building), and from there the business grew and grew.

In 1932, aged eighteen, Redmond Gallagher commenced his career at Urney Chocolates and he took over from his father as managing director in 1950. In the meantime, he had met, and in 1938 married, Audrey Kewley, a clergyman's daughter from Radnorshire in Wales, with whom he had two children, David and Sally.

With the passing of time, he became less interested in chocolate making, handing the managing directorship to Tommy Headon and taking the role of chairman from 1958. He was then more interested in farming, first at Ardtramon, a house on 600 acres in Castlebridge, County Wexford, acquired in 1960. Soon after, in 1962, he acquired the South Slob, buying out the holdings of both Staffords and Maj. Beaumont. His wife Audrey died in the early 1960s, and Ardtramon and its contents were sold in 1964, and Redmond moved to live in what was formerly the pumping station on the South Slob. A year earlier he had sold his interest in Urney Chocolates to US conglomerate W.R. Grace & Co.

However, tragedy was soon to follow. Tommy Headon died suddenly at the age of forty-eight in 1966. 'Redmond and Betty [Tommy Headon's widow], both grieving the loss of a spouse, were pushed together by mutual, well-meaning friends … the resulting marriage was a rash decision and an unsuitable union that several years on ended in separation.'[383] In 1977, Redmond retired to Spain and lived there with his third wife, Mairin McGrath, until his death in 2006, aged ninety-two years. His son David had been managing the shooting for many years.

Shooting During the Gallagher Era

Shooting on the South Slob followed a pattern similar to that on the North Slob for many years. Bill Fiske and David Gallagher frequently participated in the shooting on the other's Slob and, as noted earlier, there was a significant overlap of the membership of the two shoots. A comparative summary table below for the decade of the 1980s shows how the two Slobs performed during this time. The comparative strength of the South Slob was in diving duck species such as Pochard, Tufted, Scaup and Goldeneye, which preferred the significantly wider main channel which the South Slob had to offer. However, in the 1990s there was a virtual collapse in the diving duck population using Wexford Harbour, associated with increased mussel dredging. As a consequence, these species declined markedly and remain comparatively scarce.

Indeed, for reasons which are somewhat unclear, there was a deterioration of the South Slob as a wintering wildfowl habitat generally. The White-fronted Goose ceased using the South Slob with any regularity and there is a preponderance of hand-reared Mallard now in the bag. Differences in farm management practice or possibly consequences from the much more widespread afforestation that has occurred on the South Slob may hold the answers to these questions. However, in the past decade, the South Slob has not seen anything like the kind of diversity of shooting which it offered even as recently as in the 1980s.

	1981/82		1982/83		1983/84		1984/85	
	North	South	North	South	North	South	North	South
Mallard	524	209	478	271	341	512	352	608
Teal	142	54	154	106	150	113	46	77
Pochard	44	47	–	10	–	18	–	25
Pintail	4	24	–	18	–	25	7	72
Tufted	26	23	–	35	–	38	–	18
Widgeon	143	8	115	2	99	9	69	6
Shoveler	–	23	–	11	–	21	–	7
Scaup	–	1	–	–	–	1	–	7
Goldeneye	–	23	6	11	1	11	1	8
Gadwall	–	–	4	3	–	3	–	–

	1985/86		1986/87		1987/88		1988/89	
	North	South	North	South	North	South	North	South
Mallard	530	319	471	432	480	548	361	409
Teal	79	26	130	28	126	91	212	82
Pochard	7	72	9	75	2	64	17	67
Pintail	9	75	2	64	17	67	–	54
Tufted	20	46	10	70	4	35	3	46
Widgeon	115	8	128	17	245	21	271	52
Shoveler	–	1	2	24	1	1	–	6
Scaup	–	3	1	7	–	5	–	9
Goldeneye	–	17	4	59	–	19	–	18
Gadwall	1	5	–	12	–	14	–	1

THE PUNT GUNNERS: PROFESSIONAL WILDFOWLERS OF WEXFORD HARBOUR

Wexford Harbour has a rich tradition of punt gunning, going back at least to the middle of the nineteenth century. While other harbours and estuaries around the country also supported punt guns, the Wexford tradition has been immortalised by Sir Ralph Payne-Gallwey in *The Fowler in Ireland* (1882):

The fowlers of Wexford of whom there are seven or eight, nearly all live on the Point of Rosslare, a bar of sand hills three miles long that protects the harbour from the sea. From this 'coign of vantage' these men can spy the whole extent of ooze and water on which the birds are wont to alight. Their fowling is still very primitive, most of their big guns being limited by flint. The punts, or 'floats' as they are there called, are about fifteen feet long, and twenty-eight inches wide amidships. The sides are nearly upright with little flare, the stem, stern, and plank all round being nine to ten inches high. They have little or no spring in the bottom, so that they are bad boats in every way. These craft are also quite open and devoid of any deck, either fore or aft. Though built very light as regards wood and knees, the guns used in them are of fair size, and carry from a pound to a pound and a half of shot. These are made fast to a ring in the bow (for stem proper they have none) by light breeching ropes about two fingers in thickness. The barrel lies in a deep groove on the upper surface of the small bow piece that does duty for stem. The breech and short stock rest on a plain thwart, and between two pegs to keep it steady and fairly in the centre of the float; the muzzle projects a foot or more beyond the bow.

The shooter lies face downwards, and paddles over either side if the water be deep; but if shallow, he pushes with two short setting poles. He directs his craft as straight on the fowl as he can steer her, and pulls the trigger by hand when in shot, dropping at the same time his paddles or poles, which, as usual, are secured by strings to the gunwale. The elevation of the gun cannot be altered, and a flying shot is well-nigh impossible. The Wexford men, nevertheless, bag large numbers of fowl, mostly Widgeon and Brent geese, which latter, as usual, are misnamed 'Bernicle'. The vast extent of ooze inside the bar is seldom covered by more than two foot of tide, and, should the wind be strong, the long-weed lays the water smooth.

Were it not for the extreme safety of this harbour, such tiny toy shooting floats could not be used. When the birds gather on an island of slob or bank of weed at about half-tide, four or five floats will sometimes approach them together, drawn to the locality by the sight of the shot from various parts of the harbour. The oldest or most experienced fowler then fires first, and the others follow almost at the same moment. The spoil is afterwards fairly divided. Should two fowler 'set' by any chance to the same company of fowl, and there be an odd bird when all are

117 From *The Fowler in Ireland,* showing the punt gunners of Wexford setting out for a shot.

118 Larry Duggan Sr with the Hughes' punt gun.

picked up, the owner of it, or he who takes it, gives his companion a charge for his big gun to set matters straight between them. A. Bent, one of the oldest Wexford floatmen, once told me he remembered six shooters setting to Wigeon at the same time. They fired together, and picked up one hundred and fifty-four birds as the result of the general assault.

From three to four hundred birds apiece is a good season's work with these men, but they toil very hard for a bare existence thereby in winter. Dark or light nights, out they all go; if they cannot actually see the birds, they fire to the sound of their guzzling, so well do they know the creeks, and where to find their game. This leads, however, to great danger, and sometimes to a serious accident. A floatman one night in 1879 saw what he took to be in the gloom under the land two bunches of Wigeon, and fired at the half he thought the best. The supposed birds were alas! two float shooters lying low in their boats on the look-out for fowl that were piping all around. That winter's night the fowler in question towed astern of him a punt with a dead man in it, slowly threading his way in the dark through tortuous channels to the shore.[384]

Some Notable Guns

The Gun Involved in Two Fatal Accidents

The circumstances of the accident above are still recalled today by surviving float gunners. Larry Duggan (b. 1927), now eighty-four years old, recalls that it was traditional for the people of the 'Fort' at Rosslare to have a Ball on New Year's Eve, which would be attended by all able-bodied inhabitants of the area. So it was, on New Year's Eve 1879, when Pat Wickham, an eighteen-year-old man, 'borrowed' his father's punt gun to go fowling, on an evening he knew everyone would be otherwise occupied. A man by the name of O'Brien, from over towards Ely, on the opposite side of the harbour, put out about 9 p.m. for the Fort, also thinking there would be no one else out. Young Wickham had stalled, waiting for sufficient water to move in on a flock of Wigeon which was whistling ahead of him. O'Brien also heard the Wigeon and saw the vague outline of what he thought was the flock. He fired, killing young Pat Wickham. He is buried at the south-west corner of the church at Kieran, County Wexford.[385]

O'Brien left the gun at the Fort. It was used afterwards by Jim Wickham, brother of Pat, and his son, also Jim, used it in Bannow Bay until 1935. It was then sold to a Willie Hanrahan, County Engineer of Maudlintown, Wexford. One evening, he was cleaning the gun with his son, Young Willie, who he asked to blow into the muzzle of the gun to make sure there was no powder up it. He then lit the end, igniting some residue that was there which caused a blast, the fumes from which killed Young Willie. Thus, the gun had taken a second human life.

Frederic Hughes' Gun

Frederic (b. 1874) was son of Sir Frederic (1814-1895) of Ely House, Wexford, and the Fort at Rosslare, and his second wife, Theodosia James. They had five daughters and two sons. Frederic James Robert was the elder of the sons, the other being Walter Hastings Frederic, a cavalry officer in the Indian Army, who died unmarried.[386]

In 1902, Frederic James Robert married Anna Margaret (b. 1874), daughter of William Bolton, and with her had three daughters, none of whom married. He resided at Ballycross, Bridgetown, from 1905 to 1922. That house was originally owned by John Rowe, a landowner of some 8,000 acres. On his death, the house passed to his daughter, who was married to William Bolton, and presumably it was through that connection that Frederic Hughes came to live there. He also had a summer house at Rosslare Fort. It was there that he kept company with other punt gun-

119 The gun was built for Sir Frederic Hughes in 1864 for a 30ft launch and was mounted on a tripod. It carries a 9ft barrel, 2ft having been taken off the end of the barrel by 'Big' Billy Duggan, Larry Duggan's father, in order to fit the punt to which it was attached. It has a 13/4" bore and carries a 4oz charge to discharge 24oz of shot.

120 Partially collapsed summer house of the Hughes family, the Fort, Rosslare.

ners and fowled himself. Frederic left Ballycross because of threats. He passed his punt gun to Paddy Duggan, Larry Duggan's grandfather, in part payment for Duggan's deconstruction of his timber-framed summer house, following its partial collapse in 1925 after a storm. The gun has remained in the Duggan family, passing from one generation to the next. Larry Duggan's biggest shot, taken with this gun and at night, was 163 Golden Plover at seventy-five yards.

Sir Frederic wrote to Sir Ralph Payne-Gallwey on 14 November 1881 to state that:

> The small goose that used to frequent this harbour [Wexford] and coast in such prodigious numbers and even still shows abundantly during most winters is the Brent … The best shot I ever made at Brent geese was 23½ couple, 47 birds bagged, besides all that got away in the rough water, half a gale of wind blowing at the time.[387]

The Inchiquin Gun

Lord Inchiquin's gun came to Wexford in the mid-1940s, when it was purchased by Jimmy Allen of Wexford Town for £14.[388] Allen's son recalls how it was advertised in a national newspaper and that he and his father went by train to Limerick and from there by horse and cart to Dromoland. While it was originally thought that the gun had been made for Inchiquin, it wasn't the case. It had been bought over the counter in London in 1856. Jimmy Allen used the gun in Wexford Harbour before selling it for £16 in 1950 to a Jimmy Roche of John Street, Wexford. He was not really a shooting man, but acquired it because of its provenance. Thereafter, it passed through numerous hands, before being acquired by Larry Duggan. It has found a final home with the National Parks and Wildlife Services, and is on public display at the Pump House of the North Slob.

121 The Inchiquin Gun, with 2" bore and 9ft barrel.

The Families of Rosslare Fort and Peninsula

Many families at Rosslare Fort engaged in punt gunning. According to Larry Duggan, Ned and Jim Wickham, Jack and Jim Shiels and Bill ('Horse') Duggan accounted for three guns at the turn of the twentieth century. However, in November 1924, the peninsula was breached in two places by a strong south-easterly gale – the first or main breach being about a quarter of a mile from the northern tip and the second being about 600 yards further south. By mid-1925, the two breaches had widened to a dangerous degree. The inhabitants had no option but to abandon the settlement. [389]

Further south, the Bent family (Jim and Willie) referred to by Payne-Gallwey had four punt guns, which to this day are used occasionally. These comprised the 'Queen Anne', the breech-loader, Capt. Harvey's gun, and the Bell Barrel. The Duggan family (comprising 'Big' Billy, Larry, Bruno, Uncle Jim, Uncle Phil and Bill the lightship man) started with Hughes' Gun but finished up with five guns between them. Next were the Welshes (John and Jess), who had two guns, and Kevin Byrne, who also had a gun. Byrne's gun has passed to Philly Murphy, where it is still in use. Thus there were around a dozen punt guns in operation in Wexford Harbour, based at Rosslare peninsula.

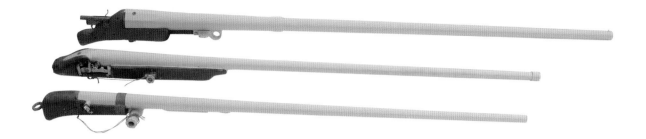

122 **Collection of Wexford Harbour punt guns: the breechloader Holland & Holland; Rigby Muzzle loader and probable Rigby muzzlel-oader.**

The bag in punt gunning, despite occasional large ones, was frequently quite small – fifteen for a shot would be regarded as quite good. However, it represented an important income supplement to fishing and subsistence farming. During the Second World War, prices were strong. Larry Duggan recalls:

Everybody lived out of it. It wouldn't pay you to go working when you could get 28/- for a pair of Greylag geese and 24/- for a brace of barnacle; 16/- for a brace of Mallard and 7/- for a brace of Wigeon. The prices were great. But when fowl pest came in 1949/50, the export of game from Ireland to England stopped and prices plummeted. In a relatively good day's shooting you could get sixty or seventy birds in a shot. It was a way of life and an awful lot of families down around the Burrow of Rosslare wouldn't have survived without the punt guns.[390]

The season lasted about five months, commencing with Golden Plover, which appeared in great numbers on Wexford Harbour and the Slobs. A yearly bag of 2,500 was not unusual.[391]

Other Gunners in Wexford Harbour

Mollie Neville

Mollie was a one-armed wildfowler who lived on Breast Island (enclosed by the reclamation), near the Raven Point, with her brother Tom. She could hold her own with any man and lived a hard life, wildfowling, fishing and cockling. The following piece says something of the woman:

Dr Boxwell, of the County Infirmary, performed the operation of amputating a hand which had been dangerously shattered a short time before by the bursting of a fowling piece. Strange to say the sufferer was a female and bore her affliction with the greatest heroism. Mary Neville, who has seen some sixty winters pass away, was born and lived on the Great Island in Wexford Harbour, now made *terra firma* by the successful efforts of the Wexford Harbour Embankment Company.

In the balmy days of years long gone by, when Wexford was celebrated for the abundance and cheapness of its wildfowl market, Mary was remarkable for the supplies she furnished to it by her own sharp eye and unerring fowling piece and was the envy of all he male competitors in the slaughter of barnacle and Wigeon. She was on the alert night and day, and winter and summer ministered nearly alike to her wants and avocation. The embankment of the Mudlands made a sad inroad to poor Mary's legitimate demesne, for where the barnacle swam and the Wigeon dived, grain crops now grow and cattle do pasture. Mary, however, still followed up her early and successful pursuits, and lithe of frame and buoyant in spirit, the gun was still dear to her, though time had laid its gnawing tooth on it and its owner; and the other day, it unfortunately betrayed the confidence so long fearlessly reposed in it and burst, frightfully shattering her hand. The amputation ably performed by Doctor Boxwell in the County Infirmary we hope will save poor Mary's life, but her occupation's gone, and no more shall she, with exulting voice and defiant look, as often she has done, challenge all male competitors in the Shooting Gallery, to send a rifle-bullet into the bull's eye of the target with her.[392]

Wexford Town Guns

The Lett family of Wexford Town were well-known punt gunners, and members of that family continue to use a punt gun to the present day. A gun was acquired by John Lett in the 1940s for £35 (probably from Col. Bradish), whose father Gilbert was an avid punt gunner. It was made by Holland & Holland and had a hexagonal breech. George Lett had a smaller gun. The Holland & Holland gun was subsequently bought by Robert Jobson, in 1954, for £150. This gun is believed to be now in the BASC Museum at Chester. According to Robert's son John, the gun was first taken by Duncan Wood, a grandson of Robert, to the Wildfowl and Wetlands Trust Reserve at Slimbridge in Gloucestershire, home of the late Sir Peter Scott, and from there it found its way to the BASC Museum.

Many guns were taken in by the Garda in 1932 when the licensing laws changed from 10s a gun to £2 per man, and many Wexford punt gunners decided to withdraw from shooting, at least temporarily. 'Pa' Breen was both a Garda and keen punt gunner at the time. As a result, he was able to add guns which were forfeited to his licence. He got the gun owned by John Colloton, who was the owner of much of the North Slob at the time.

Robert Jobson (1916-1999)
Robert Jobson was a great field-sports enthusiast – hunting shooting and fishing – an artist, especially of wildfowl scenes, a mine of information regarding antiques, and, for some time, a stockbroker with his father's Dublin firm of Jobson Brothers. It is worth recalling the life of this easy and relaxed sportsman, who devoted a life to shooting and sporting art.

He was born in Dublin in 1916, the son of Thomas Jobson and Kathleen Cusack (d. 1919) and the youngest of their three children, the other two being girls. Robert was fourteen years younger than his youngest sister. Following his mother's death, when he was three years old, he lived at Abbeville, Kinsealy, County Dublin, the family home of the Cusacks, where he was raised by his aunts. After preparatory school, he attended Wrekin College in Wellington, Shropshire. After school, about 1934, he joined the family stockbroking firm. By this time he had already commenced shooting with his father and a man known as 'Jack the Ranter' at Saggart, County Dublin, and he was both shoulder and punt gunning at Rogerstown Estuary, Malahide, and Baldoyle, County Dublin, with his close friend Tommy Cobbe of Newbridge House, Donabate, County Dublin.

In 1938 he married Cherry Lewis Crosby, daughter of Ernest Henry Cornwall Lewis Crosby, Dean of Christ Church Cathedral. They lived at Hollypark, Newtownpark Avenue, Blackrock, County Dublin, for the next ten years, during which time they had four children: one son and three daughters. There were forty acres with the house. Along with his father, Robert established a considerable market garden there. At this time also he was punt gunning at Banagher, County Offaly, on the shore of the River Shannon. There he had struck a friendship with Jack McGarry, who was a lock keeper on the Grand Canal, and there he kept his double punt. On one occasion he shot five geese with two guns loaded by Jack McGarry.[393] He had a Ford van and would use it to carry game back from Banagher, which he then brought to the Dublin market along with the produce from his garden at Hollypark, which he also sold directly to hotels and restaurants.

In addition, he painted all the time and he was able to educate his children from the proceeds of sales his paintings (see, for example, Illustrations 95 and 108 p. 249 and 266).

He came to Wexford about 1950 and by chance struck up a conversation with Larry Duggan's father on the Burrow at Rosslare. The encounter ended with Robert renting a cottage from Duggan for £1 per week. The cottage was known as Creeper Cottage and it was thatched with bennet grass from the nearby Burrow. They became great friends and Jobson would come down, mostly at weekends, to be joined by Duggan in the cottage. They roasted Snipe and herrings on an open fire, and consumed a glass or two! Larry Duggan bought a punt gun from Robert Jobson for £250 in 1960, which he still has. It is a 1¼ inch bore gun with a 7ft barrel.

Jobson was forced to sell Hollybrook after the stockbroking business got into difficulties in the late 1940s and he moved back to live in a wing of his parents-in-law's house for two years. However, he was irrepressible. He acquired the Glebe, Newcastle, Lyons, County Dublin, initially under lease from the Representative Church Body (RCB) in about 1950 and remained there for thirty years. From there, he ran a shoot for a syndicate. He also leased the Moorland Estate of the Cobbe family at Glen na Smol, where he ran a Grouse shoot. He was hunting with the Fingal Harriers and the Kildares, and was to be found shooting at Balinacor, County Wicklow, Ashford Castle, County Galway, Carton House, County Kildare, and at Abbeyleix. He was a great shot. His son John recalls how he shot five Woodcock out of six that rose from a spinney near Lough Arrow in County Sligo.[394] However, with the onset of respiratory illness when he reached his seventies, his shooting days became numbered and he was forced to retire from active field sports.

Sir Ralph Payne-Gallwey (d. 1916)

No account of fowling in Ireland would be complete without some remarks on the life and personality of one of its great Edwardian champions, Sir Ralph Payne-Gallwey. His particular love was wildfowling: in the period of spring 1891 to spring 1892, he covered over 7,725 miles in pursuit of it. The perseverance was typical of him, though he is most remembered today for the books on shooting which he wrote at the end of the last century. He collaborated with the late Lord Walsingham, writing a larger proportion in each of the two shooting volumes of the well-known *Badminton Series*. In later life, he wrote another outstanding book on shooting and ballistics, *High Pheasants in Theory and Practice*, but perhaps his most characteristic writings are the *Letters to Young Shooters* published in a series of three volumes between 1890 and 1896. In 1882, *The Fowler in Ireland* was published, containing so much information in respect of his times spent fowling in Ireland.

The *bon mot* came easily to him. He once occupied a railway carriage with a rather aloof middle-aged lady and all attempts at conversation having failed, both parties spent most of the journey dozing. When Sir Ralph alighted at his destination, he turned to the lady and said, 'We might not have had much conversation, but at least we can say that have slept together.' There is another story, too, about his visit to the oculist, when he observed the test card which he knew he would later have to read. He memorised all the letters and noticed in minute print, at the bottom of the right-hand corner of the card, the words 'McCorquodale & Sons, Printers'. Saying nothing, he waited until the test came, and having correctly identified all the letters, he turned to the oculist and said, 'Ah, but I think I can see more than that.' The oculist said that there was nothing else. Sir Ralph pretending to strain his eyes very hard in the direction of card, which was at the other end of the room, said, 'You are wrong. I can make out the words "McCorquodale & Sons, Printers" at the bottom right-hand corner.' The oculist thought it was a miracle!

In 1886, Sir Ralph moved to Thirkleby Hall near Thirsk. The hall and the surrounding estate were meticulously maintained and over the years he initiated a number of improvements, including an indoor riding stable, private golf links and an indoor rifle range. He entertained there on a regular basis and many of the shooting house parties were attended by the great social names of England. His natural eccentricity always shone through. He was skilled at the crossbow and held the British distance record for archery. He also invented a double-barrelled breech-loading punt gun, which was far ahead of its time and subsequently displayed at the Inventions Exhibition of 1885. His enthusiasm for the sport of shooting was immense. The shooting catalogues of the period bear testimony to his remarkable power of inventiveness: Payne-Gallwey shooting bags; Payne-Gallwey gaiters; Payne-Gallwey cleaning outfits.

He is laid to rest outside the main entrance of the chapel at Thirkleby, his grave inscribed with a short quote, 'He nothing common did, or mean.' It is a fitting epitaph.[395]

8

EPILOGUE

There are several aspects of this look-back in time that are worth setting in the context of today. The first and most striking feature is how prevalent and widespread the sport of game shooting was in former times compared with now, and how it was not only the exclusive preserve of the wealthy. However, game shooting as a means of *social networking* was the domain of the landed gentry. As such, it was a very important means of social contact, for winning desirable introductions, developing friendships and maintaining family alliances. It fulfilled a role whose place today has probably been taken by golf. It was a recreational activity and more. Indeed for some, it was a way of life.

Because of the pivotal social role it fulfilled, there was no shortage of cash for developing and maintaining a shoot. Ownership of a good shoot meant acceptance by desired guests of shooting invitations. It also resulted in good reciprocal invitations and the extended character of shoots – sometimes taking place over days – meant that the networking could actually bring about results, in terms of deeper understandings between neighbours, friends and relations, the forging of grand alliances, or the procurement of beneficial marriages. The apparently socially awkward Lord Ardilaun, who spent freely of his considerable newfound brewing wealth in order to achieve a reputation for owning the greatest Woodcock shoot in the world, is an iconic example. In achieving his goal, he found himself with royal guests orchestrating invitations to attend his shoots and stay at Ashford Castle.

Frequently, social historians and commentators have alluded disparagingly to the 'slaughter' of great numbers of birds at Edwardian shooting parties, inferring that nature paid a heavy price for the shenanigans of toffs. However, they miss a much more substantive point. Namely, enormous resources were expended on the creation and maintenance of suitable habitats to support game species such as Woodcock and Grouse. Coverts of rhododendron and laurel were planted and woods of deciduous hardwood trees were laid down for the *long-term* preservation of game species. Concerns about the viability of Woodcock numbers was in part addressed, at numerous estates, by the instigation of ringing schemes implemented by gamekeepers to learn about their migratory and breeding habits and their longevity. Grouse moors were managed through strip burning of heather that ensured a variety of different growths – some suitable for feeding, some for nesting cover, some for birds to stand and watch from. Careful assessments were made, using pointer dogs, of the breeding populations and their annual success, and on this basis the number of days' shooting which could be supported sustainably was estimated, thus allowing good sport not only for the forthcoming season but the ones beyond that.

Thus, the social *caché* of game shooting ensured that very considerable private investments were made in the development and maintenance of habitats suitable to wild game and its associated wildlife. Game shooting and conservation of fragile habitats such as native wood-land, moorland and wetlands went hand-in-hand, and this careful stewardship role exercised through private property owners was a benefit to most forms of wildlife. In a nutshell, the fashion of game shooting and its popularity amongst wealthy landowners resulted in very substantial investments being made in the preservation and conservation of habitats vital to game species like Woodcock, Snipe, migratory wildfowl species of duck and geese, and the native Irish Red Grouse.

Indeed, the collapse of the native Irish Red Grouse population on the island of Ireland during the twentieth century is probably the saddest conservation legacy of land reform in Ireland during that time. The destruction of woodland around the demesnes of old estates had a serious negative impact on Woodcock. However, a compensating factor in their case was the successive programmes of afforestation which have been undertaken, which have allowed Woodcock numbers to remain strong and probably more widespread than they were formerly. Indeed, it is possible that reduced densities of wintering Woodcock may act to the birds' advantage, compared with the situation where they were more densely packed into the sparse woodland covers of estate demesnes. But this may not be safely assumed either. For example, at Ashford and a small number of other estates where truly large bags of Woodcock were shot, the practice was to shoot only twice per season. Today, there is little or no restriction on the number of days' shooting or the number of shooters who can gain access to woodlands suitable for holding Woodcock. In truth, no one knows what numbers of Woodcock are shot because there is no owner of the shoot recording the numbers. It is quite possible there are more Woodcock being shot today than at the time of the large estates; there simply are not the bag records to judge. However, there is no argument about the status of native Red Grouse or of the causes of its decline. This species is extremely scarce now and destruction or mismanagement of its moorland habitat is the reason. To the present day, there are a small number of people who still strive to secure a halt to the decline of Red Grouse but they are lone voices facing a public policy bureaucracy with an agenda set more in terms of EU directives and framework agreements, which understands or cares little of the status of Irish Red Grouse.

These remarks are not to say that wildlife management was perfect in the time of the estates or that it is all wrong today. In some cases back then, there was widespread persecution of some predatory species in the interests of promoting game species, which no one could excuse. By contrast, in modern times, the initial attempts to revive Red Grouse numbers in the 1960s were undertaken by government at the behest of lobbying by farming interests, rather than those promoting game shooting. In the same vein, some initiatives to revive game stocks and promote game rearing and releasing, also in the 1960s, were sponsored by government, this time at the behest of tourism development interests. This was resisted by some vociferous shooting interests, who seem to have embraced a very narrow geography of the parish boundary which defined them. Similar initiatives by government to promote fishing and hunting as tourism products, it should be noted, were met also with local resistance.

Game shooting at present is frequently viewed unfavourably by a sceptical public, not only in Ireland, but also in Great Britain and elsewhere. It is a view which is born mostly of a lack of any understanding of the conservation benefits that can be associated with the pursuit of recreational game shooting, such as those that have been outlined above. However, in some part it is a view born out of prejudice: that wild birds should not be shot. It's cruel, unnecessary and *wrong*.

There would appear to be little doubt that this point of view is part of a much broader issue revolving round a widening disparity of understanding between the lives of urban and rural dwellers, and it seems that, increasingly, there are all kinds of judgements being made both ways in the debates that surround this issue. Taking the narrow focus of game shooting, there are some points that can be usefully made in this regard. Most notable is the fact that all game that was shot *was used as food and prized by consumers as food*. There is ample testimony, from the discussion of Game Book records, of gamekeepers shipping thousands of rabbits a year from estates to markets in cities in Ireland and England, which were destined for the human food chain. Similarly, there are many records which show that it was common practice to send parcels of seasonal game, like Grouse and Woodcock, by post to friends, relatives and others in cities, and there is evidence also of consumers in cities seeking out game in celebration of the season to hand – Grouse in August, Partridge in October, Woodcock in November and so on. This relationship has certainly been diluted and in most cases lost altogether. Despite its healthy provenance, and the seasonal and locally produced aspect, game is an insignificant component of the modern diet.

So, in times past, there was a chain with several reinforcing links that assured game shooting was the centre of a virtuous circle where not only was it socially acceptable, it was highly desirable. It resulted in very large private investments in conservation, with widespread benefits to wildlife species generally, and it provided a bountiful food resource which was seasonal, organic, locally produced and highly prized by consumers. These links are not in place today. Moreover, in Ireland there is an additional encumbrance, namely that game shooting – or anything else associated with the landed gentry of former estates – has been regarded with the same contempt that the landlord class in Ireland became the subject of, a sentiment that lives on today in some quarters.

If game shooting in Ireland is to have a thriving, long-term future, the issues which need to be confronted are: its role in the establishment, provision, development and maintenance of habitats which support game birds and benefit general wildlife; its role in promoting the re-establishment of game as a valued and prized part of a healthy diet; its role in contributing to and supporting the economic viability of rural communities. Collectively, if game shooters succeed in addressing these issues, the place of game shooting will have a secure future.

To be successful in the future, game shooting will have to have a resonance with those aspects which made it so popular in the past. However, this doesn't mean its success requires it to return slavishly to all the old ways. The importance being attached by consumers to food traceability, seasonal and local production characteristics, and the success of country markets in penetrating urban centres, all point to the potential of reviving game as an important component in a modern healthy diet. The move in EU agricultural policies away from production in favour of countryside stewardship and environmentally sustainable farming practice, offers a window through which to develop game shooting conservation policies. In addition, the scope for tourism shooting supporting rural communities in off-peak periods has been well demonstrated by the modern experience of the Yorkshire Dales and West Country Pheasant shoots. Of course, there is one obstacle to all of this that would need to be overcome first: the taking of entrenched positions, which risks preventing healthy debate on what is undoubtedly a deeply important part of our cultural heritage.

EVOLUTION OF LAND OWNERSHIP OF THE NORTH SLOB, 1850-1919

	Conveyance 19 March 1850 to	Conveyance 3 August 1860 to	Memorandum of Agreement, June 1906
	Wexford Harbour Embankment Company (2,311 Acres)	Sir Edward Grogan (926 Acres)	Sir Edward Grogan (926 Acres)
		John Edward Redmond (713 Acres)	Sir Albert Meldon, Vevay House, Bray, and
		William Dargan (657 Acres)	Joseph Meldon, Coolarne, County Galway, Trustees of the Estate of late James Dillon Meldon (546 Acres)
			Sir Arthur Edward Guinness, 1st Baron Ardilaun
			Frederick A.B. Turner, Land Agent, Clonattin House, Gorey
			Robert MacNevin Bradshaw, Brittas, County Dublin
			Michael J. O'Connor and William Hayes, Selskar Street, Wexford (121 Acres)

* Acquired from Michael J. O'Connor. See for example, Indenture 15 September, Michael J. O'Connor to William Lacey, Shooting rights, withheld to M.J.

Sources: *Memorandum of Agreement re North Slobs*, 2 June 1906, Meldon & Co. Solicitors, 14 Upper Ormonde Quay, Dublin. *Deed of Mutual Agreement, in reference to the Maintenance and Drainage of the North Slob Lands*, M.J. O'Connor & Co. Solicitors, 2 George Street, Wexford. 26 June 1919.

Deed of Mutual Agreement, June 1919
Lt-Col. George Meredyth Grogan, Clyde Road, Dublin, and Mark Oliver Hunter, Hatch End, Middlesex, Trustees of the Estate of Sir Edward Grogan (926 Acres, N.E. Slob)
Sir Albert Meldon, Vevay House, Bray and
Joseph Meldon, Coolarne, County Galway, Trustees of the Estate of late James Dillon Meldon (546 Acres, N.E. Slob)
Tenant Purchasers of the Estate of the Trustees (M.J. O'Connor and James O'Connor) of Prendergast (acquired from John Edward Redmond)
Ellen Neville, Begerin, Wexford (90 Acres, N.W. Slob)
John Colloton Jnr, Begerin, Wexford (61 Acres, N.W. Slob)
Lt John. J. Clancy, Silverspring, Ballycogley, County Wexford (172 Acres, N.W. Slob)
Peter Tiernan, Garrygibbon, Castlebridge, County Wexford (19 Acres, N.W. Slob)
Paul Murphy, North Slob, Wexford (33 Acres, N.W. Slob)
John A. Bennett, Johnstown, Castlebridge (45 Acres, N.W. Slob)
James Brien, Ballyvaloo, Blackwater, County Wexford (28 Acres, N.W. Slob)
James Kelly, Monck Street, Wexford (41 Acres, N.W. Slob)
John Rossiter, Johnstown, Castlebridge, County Wexford (30 Acres, N.W. Slob)
M.J. O'Connor and James O'Connor as Trustees of Prendergast Estate in respect of the tenancy of James Neville, who did not sign purchase agreements. (35 Acres, N.W. Slob)
George Colloton, Garradreen, Tagmon, County Wexford (56 Acres, N.E. Slob)
Margaret Hayes, Ballyla, Castlebridge, County Wexford (27 Acres, N.E. Slob)
Robert Sinnott, Harveystown, Taghmon, County Wexford (26 Acres, N.E. Slob)
William Lacey, Castle Ellis, Enniscorthy, County Wexford (19 Acres, N.W. Slob)*
Owen Doyle, Ardcolm, Wexford (3 Acres, N.W. Slob)*
William Murphy, Munroe, Screen, Wexford (17 Acres, N.W. Slob)*
Joseph Fortune, Knottown, Wexford (17 Acres, N.W. Slob)*
Richard Scallan, Ballyvaloo, Blackwater, County Wexford (39 Acres, N.W. Slob)*
Patrick Roche, Garrylough, Screen, County Wexford (22 Acres, N.W. Slob)*
John Monaghan, Killisk, The Ballagh, County Wexford (11 Acres, N.W. Slob)*

The Distribution of Gamekeepers by County in Ireland 1901

County	Number of Gamekeepers
Antrim	30
Armagh	6
Carlow	7
Cavan	6
Clare	17
Cork	30
Donegal	3
Down	29
Dublin	9
Fermanagh	19
Galway	33
Kerry	15
Kildare	22
Kilkenny	4
Laois (Queen's County)	21
Leitrim	9
Limerick	12
Londonderry	10
Longford	5
Louth	9
Mayo	22
Meath	24
Monaghan	10
Offaly (King's County)	13
Roscommon	16
Sligo	20
Tipperary	36
Tyrone	20
Waterford	18
Westmeath	11
Wexford	9
Wicklow	35

Source: National Archives of Ireland, Census of Population, 1901.

NOTES

Introduction

1 Jonathan Ruffer, *The Big Shots, Edwardian Shooting Parties*, with a foreword by HRH The Prince of Wales (London, 1998), p.7.

Chapter 1: The Ascendency & Subsequent Evolution of Shooting in Edwardian Ireland

2 W.H. Maxwell, *Wild Sports of the West* (1832), p.14.

3 *The Diary of Colonel Peter Hawker, 1802-1853* (London, 1893).

4 Jonathan Ruffer, *The Big Shots, Edwardian Shooting Parties* (London, 1998), p.19.

5 Charles Chenevix Trench, *The Poacher and the Squire: A History of Poaching and Game Preservation in England* (1967), p.172.

6 Terence Dooley, *The Decline of the Big House in Ireland* (Dublin, 2001), pp54-5.

7 Peter Somerville-Large, *The Irish Country House a Social History* (London, 1995), p.261.

8 *Ibid.*, pp297-8.

9 *Ibid.*, pp338-9.

10 Sir Ralph Payne-Gallwey, *The Fowler in Ireland* (London, 1882), pp347-8.

11 *Ibid.*, p.202.

12 National Archives of Ireland, Census of Population 1901 and 1911, occupational classification. The numbers cited are those for 'Gamekeeper' and include designations such as 'head gamekeeper', 'gamekeeper servant' or 'farmer gamekeeper'.

13 David S.D. Jones, *Gamekeeping Past and Present: An Illustrated History* (2009), p.10.

14 N. Virgoe & Susan Yaxley (eds), with an introduction by Lord Buxton, *The Banville Diaries: Journals of a Norfolk Gamekeeper* (London, 1986).

15 As the name implies, 'bog-watchers' were casually employed to keep an eye that bogs were not being poached. George Gossip recalls his father's comments about the minimum agricultural wage legislation and the resulting end of bog-watchers.

16 National Library of Ireland, *Mahon Papers*, MS 23,036 acc 357.

17 David S.D. Jones, *op. cit.*, p.59.

18 Harcourt was known as a sexual predator attracted to both sexes. He committed suicide at his London home before an impending scandal.

19 See D.H.L. Back, *Great Irish Gunmakers, Messrs Rigby 1760-1869* (1992).

20 Richard J. Garrett, *Irish Gunmakers* (Hong Kong, 2008).

21 Patrick Bowe, 'Irish Sporting Lodges', in *Irish Architectural and Decorative Studies: The Journal of the Irish Georgian Society*, Vol.VII, pp107-139.

22 Somerville-Large, *The Irish Country House* (1995), p.339.

23 Charles Mosley (ed.), *Burke's Peerage, Baronetage and Knightage, 107th edition*, Vol. 2 (Delaware, USA, 2003), p.2,325. Hereafter cited as *Burke's Peerage and Baronetage, 107th edition*.

24 P.B. Musche, *Gentlemen and Poachers: The English Game Laws, 1671-1831* (Cambridge, 1981), pp156-7.

25 Report of the Select Committee on Game Laws: together with the proceedings of the Committee,

Minutes of Evidence, Appendix and Index, Parliamentary Papers, (HC 1872 and 1873), 337 X.I. and 285 XIII.I.

Chapter 2: The Influence of Economics and Politics: the Irish Land Question

26 There was interest from Great Britain in shooting and fishing in Ireland. J.B. Drought's *A Sportsman Looks at Eire* contains reminiscences of shooting and fishing in Ireland in the 1930s.

27 A brief biography of Stanislaus Lynch is contained in Noel Mullins, *Horse Tales and Hunt Talk* (2006).

28 Terence Dooley, *The Decline of the Big House in Ireland* (Dublin, 2001), p.80.

29 *Ibid.*, pp81-94.

30 *Ibid.*, p.90.

31 *Ibid.*, p.101.

32 L.P. Curtis, 'Stopping the Hunt 1881-1882: An Aspect of the Irish Land War', in C.H.E. Philpin (ed.), *Nationalism and Popular Protest in Ireland* (Cambridge, 1987).

33 See, for example, Lyons, Mary Cecelia, *Illustrated Incumbered Estates, Ireland 1850-1905* (1993).

34 The Board had the power to purchase with a view to organising resettlement and had the ability to offer slightly better terms than the Land Commission. The Congested Districts Board was abolished under the Land Act 1923, which transferred its powers to the Land Commission and vested it with powers of compulsory acquisition.

35 See Dooley, *op. cit.*, p.13. '… the majority of the 100 sample landowners [on which his book is based] were still substantial landowners up to the 1920s and with the exception of two of them they had retained their big houses'.

Chapter 3: The Great Shoots of the North -est: Woodcock, Snipe and Grouse

36 Quoted from McKelvie, *op. cit.*, p.112.

37 'Roding' is the term used to describe the display flight performed at dusk and dawn before the breeding season by male Woodcock to attract females.

38 Colin Trotman, *Woodcock Fieldcraft and Quarry*, Chapter 3 provides a good synthesis of the current state of knowledge regarding Woodcock migration to the British Isles.

39 Trotman, *op. cit.*, p.17.

40 This organisation is affiliated to FANBPO, a European Federation of Woodcock Associations which has the aim to develop an understanding among enthusiasts, hunters and other interested parties, of the need for conservation of Woodcock and the preservation of their habitat, under a number of headings, including: to develop and take part in research that will advance knowledge of wintering Woodcock in Ireland; to develop a strategy that will manage Woodcock into the future, and to work in co-operation with National and European organisations.

41 National Woodcock Association of Ireland, *Annual Report 2007/8.*

42 National Woodcock Association of Ireland, *Annual Report 2008/9.*

43 National Woodcock Association of Ireland, *Annual Report 2009/10.*

44 National Woodcock Association of Ireland, *Annual Report 2010/11.*

45 P.G. Kennedy, Robert F. Ruttledge, & C.F. Scroope, *Birds of Ireland* (London, 1953), p.157.

46 Sir Ralph Payne-Gallwey, *The Fowler in Ireland* (London, 1882), p.207.

47 J. Moray Brown, *Snipe Shooting* in *A Year of Sport and Natural History*, ed. Oswald Crawfurd (London, 1895), p.18.

48 Hugh B.C. Pollard, *Game Birds* (London, 1929), p.121.

49 Research carried out in the 1960s suggests that grouse densities in Ireland are more probably limited by the productivity of heather rather than the chemical quality of the foliage. Productivity is related to the quality of drainage. See, for example, P.J. O'Hare, 'Irish Red Grouse – Position and Prospects' in F. O'Gorman and Edna Wymes, *The Future of Irish Wildlife – A Blueprint for Development* (1973).

50 See, for example, Adam Watson, *Research and Management of Red Grouse in West Scotland* (Nature Conservancy, Blackhall, Banchory, Kincardineshire, Scotland, December 1971).

51 According to Watson (Dec. 1971), 'The main reason for the decline of grouse is that moors are now burned less well. They tend to be overburned with too frequent fires and little or no heather, or under-burned with too much old heather. Excessively heavy grazing by sheep and cattle has also led to heather getting too short or being replaced by grass on many moors, with consequent declines in grouse.'

52 Canada Life Irish Red Grouse Conference (1993), Proceedings, p.69.

53 Nigel Everett, *Wild Gardens: The Lost Demesnes of Bantry Bay* (Kerry, 2000), p.57.

54 Peter Campbell, 'Driven Woodcock Shoots at Cong', *Irish Forestry*, Vol.41, No.1 (1984).

55 J.B. Drought, *A Sportsman Looks at Eire* (London, 1930s), p.110.

56 The figures contained in this table are extracted from the original shoot records for Ashford. Figures are contained for many of these dates in both Maurice Semple's *By the Corribside* (1984) and in A. Milais, Acland-Hood *et. al*, *The Gun at Home and Abroad* (1915). However, there are discrepancies in certain figures for certain years in these sources. It is considered that the primary source is the most accurate.

57 Acland-Hood, *op.cit.*, p.250-1.

58 Olda FitzGerald, *op. cit.*, p.118.

59 See also Maurice Semple, *By the Corribside* (1984), p.121, and *Reflections on Lough Corrib* (1989), p.175.

60 Quoted in McKelvie, *op. cit.*, p.125.

61 Contained in a black leather album inscribed on the cover, 'India 1905-06, Photographs taken by Sir Charles Cust, Bt., 1905-06', Janus Library, Cambridge, England.

62 *Bandon Historical Journal*, No.12 (1996).

63 Ann Morrow, *Picnic in a Foreign Land* (1989), p.241.

64 Charles Mosley (ed.), *Burke's Peerage and Baronetage, 107th edition*.

65 National Library of Ireland, *Clonbrock Papers*.

66 *Dillions of Clonbrock*, p.59.

67 Margaret Ferrier Young (ed.), *The Letters of a Noble Woman: Maria La Touche* (London, 1908).

68 The love story of Rose and John Ruskin has been well documented; see for example Young, *op. cit.*

69 Michael McGinley, *The La Touche Family in Ireland*, p.239.

70 Probably Lord Bandon, who is reported to have shot forty-four birds with any amount of 'rights and lefts'; P. Campbell in conversation to O. FitzGerald, p.121.

71 *Dillons of Clonbrock*, p.61.

72 See Campbell, *op. cit.*

73 Dorchester, *Sport: Foxhunting and Shooting* (1935), p.220.

74 Acland-Hood (1909), *op.cit.*, p.56.

75 Weather records collected privately at Markree Castle, County Sligo, and supplied by Met Éireann.

76 Olda FitzGerald, *op. cit.*, p.142.

77 Sir Edward (1839-1900) married his second wife Ellen White (1854-1913), with whom he had a further seven children, only one of whom was a boy, namely Donagh (1879-1953). See Grainne Weir, *op. cit.*

78 See Grainne Weir, *op. cit.*

79 The estates at Ashford, Cong, Strand Hill, Lisloughrey, Rosshill and Doon passed to his brother, in accordance with a codicil in his will dated 25 February 1902, 'absolutely believing him the best person to deal with them, as it would impose too much care on my darling wife', FitzGerald, *op. cit.*, p.135.

80 Charles Mosley (ed.), *Burke's Peerage, Baronetage & Knightage, 107th edition*.

81 It is unclear from when there were two shoots per season; it is possible that this was always the case.

82 Peter Campbell, *op.cit.*, p.33.

83 Charles Mosley (ed.), *Burke's Peerage and Baronetage, 107th edition*.

84 The older barony of Oranmore and Browne, in the Irish peerage, did not entitle its bearer to a seat in the Lords.

85 Hon. Garech Growne in communication.

86 Acland-Hood (1909), *op.cit.*, pp50-2.

87 De Burgh, *Landowners of Ireland* (1878), p.352.

88 Their first son and Charles William's older brother, was Arthur Brook Cooper (1814-1845). There were four daughters. McTernan, *op. cit.*

89 The Game Book was a Christmas gift from the Adamson family (Glenfairne Hall, County Leitrim) to Charles Kean O'Hara.

90 The surname Cooper was not retained in association with the subsequent ownership of Coopershill, except as a second Christian name.

91 Colonel J.G. Adamson owned almost 400 acres of untenanted land at Glenfarne, as well as the mansion house there. The estate timber was later bought by Edward Harland of the Harland and Wolff Shipyard in Belfast. Moore Institute, Database of Landed Irish Estates.

92 Wilfred and Florence Tempest are believed to be the parents of Flt-Lt Edmond Roger Tempest (1874-1921), a First World War flying ace credited with seventeen aerial victories.

93 The Conde and Condessa O'Brien represented the Spanish branch of the Inchiquin family at a gather-

ing of the Inchiquin family hosted by Lord and Lady Inchiquin at Upper Berkeley Street on St Patrick's Day, 17 March 1936. *Tatler*, 25 March 1936.

94 Less regularly there are records of shooting parties in early November at Glywood, Athlone, home of Mr Edward Quinn Longworth. The bag was Pheasants, with a bag of around 1,000 for 8/9 Guns over five days.

95 McTernan, *op. cit.*, Vol.II, p.114.

96 His father died in 1860 in a boating accident at the age of twenty-nine.

97 McTernan, *op. cit.*, Vol.II, p.113.

98 McTernan, *op. cit.*, Vol.II, p.191.

99 *Op. cit.*, p.74.

100 De Burgh, *op. cit.*, p.107.

101 She was daughter of John Mulholland's land agent, Capt. Somerset Ward, and granddaughter of Viscount Bangor of Castle Ward.

102 Mary Isabella Houston (b. 1793), daughter of John Holmes and Eliza Houston of Orangefield House, married Richard Bayly Blackiston. The two families joined names, leaving J. Blackiston-Houston in charge of the Orangefield Estate from 1857.

103 McTernan, *op. cit.*, Vol.II, p.305.

104 Sandy Perceval, personal communication, 18 April 2011.

105 PRONI, Introduction to the Templehouse Papers (MIC597), p.12.

106 Samuel Ashton sold the estates at Newtownbarry of 5,000 acres to Hall-Dare for £83,000. The lands had been conveyed to Ashton in 1854 by the Encumbered Estates Court. Prior to that, the estate had been in the Farnham-Maxwell family. Hall-Dare acquired a similar amount of land in County Carlow. See A. Kavanagh & Rory Murphy, *op. cit.*, Vol.I, p.115.

107 He died five years later in 1866.

108 McTernan, *op. cit.*, Vol.II, p.306.

109 Sandy and Roderick Perceval in conversation, 18 April 2011.

110 *Ibid.*

111 McTernan, *op. cit.*, Vol.II, p.308.

112 The Knox-Gore lineage goes back to Francis Knox (1736-1818) of Rappa Castle, County Mayo, who married Mary, daughter and heiress of Paul Annesley Gore of Belleek, County Mayo.

113 Mervyn Pratt (1809-1890) was the son of Col. Joseph Pratt of Cabra Castle, County Cavan, and Jemima Roberta Tynte of Tynte Park.

114 Additionally, Muriel Wynne's great-grandfather Owen (1755-1841) of Hazelwood and Graham's great-grandfather William P. (d. 1855) were brothers.

115 See McKelvie (1990), pp120-1. De Grey also shot with Lord Kenmare at Muckross. On one occasion (7 January 1875), sixty-two Woodcock were shot to six Guns, with De Grey accounting for twenty-one.

116 Wynnes owned a further 15,436 acres in Leitrim, see De Burgh, *Landowners of Ireland*, (Dublin, 1878).

117 McTernan, *op. cit.*, Vol.II, p.307.

118 See A. Landsborough Thomson, 'The Migration of British & Irish Woodcock: Results of the Marking Method', *British Birds*, Vol.XXIII (1929). In addition to the Hazelwood scheme, there were marking schemes developed at Classiebawn, Temple House and Lissadell (all in County Sligo), Cong (County Galway), Barons court (County Tyrone) and Brookeborough (County Fermanagh).

119 Philip D. Perceval, 'Observations on the Movements of Woodcock', *Irish Naturalist*, Vol.22, No.11 (November 1913).

120 McTernan, *op. cit.*, Vol.I, p.392.

121 Burke's Peerage Limited, *Burke's Irish Family Records* (London, 1976).

122 On 3 May 1981, five members of a group called the Sligo H-Block/Armagh Committee entered Tanrego House, Beltra, the home of Lt-Commander John Farr. The group, which included a County Councillor, unfurled a banner and displayed protest posters from an upstairs window. Twenty others picketed the entrance. By 11a.m., Gardaí, including a Chief Superintendent, a Superintendent and five Special Branch men armed with Uzi machine guns, demanded that the protestors leave. Proclaiming that John Farr should be refused entry to Ireland and his 400 acres be nationalised, the protestors left by 2p.m. They were not charged. *Sligo Journal*, 8 May 1981, quoted in Timothy Knatchbull, *From a Clear Blue Sky*, p.207.

123 Ann Morrow, *Picnic in a Foreign Land*, p.17.

124 Ann Morrow, *op. cit.*, p.20.

125 McTernan, *op. cit.*, Vol.1, p.281.

126 McTernan, *op. cit.*, p.124.

127 McTernan, *op. cit.*, p.125.

128 McTernan, *op. cit.*, p.125.

129 PRONI D4131/C/1/1-10.

130 Charles Mosley (ed.), *Burke's Peerage and Baronetage, 107th edition.*

131 Payne-Gallwey, *The Fowler in Ireland* (London, 1882), p.227.

132 Wood was Charles William Wood (b. 1857), McGee was William George McGee (b. 1871) and Cadden was Patrick W. Cadden (b. 1889), all of Drumcliff, County Sligo. National Archives of Ireland, *Census of Population, 1911.*

133 Colin McKelvie, *The Book of the Woodcock* (Swan Hill Press, 1990), p.121.

134 McTernan, *op. cit.*, p.127.

135 'Their maternal grandmothers Frances Charlotte and Henrietta Susan Savile Lumney being sisters; their brother was the 9th Earl of Scarborough. Jocelyn's mother was born at Tickhill Castle, the Yorkshire property of the Earl, while her father, the Revd Savile Richard L'Estrange Malone was a rector in Yorkshire and domestic Chaplin to his uncle, Marcus Gervaise Beresford, Archbishop of Armagh.' Dermot James, *The Gore-Booths of Lissadell* (Ireland, 2004), p.101.

136 A detailed account of the lives of Sir Jocelyn and Lady Gore-Booth's children can be found in Dermot James, *The Gore-Booths of Lissadell* (Ireland, 2004).

137 Dermot James, *op. cit.*, p.103.

138 Charles Mosley (ed.), *Burke's Peerage and Baronetage, 107th edition.*

139 Colin McKelvie, *The Book of the Woodcock* (London, 1990), p.120.

140 The relationship was sustained with the appointment of Gabrielle Booth (1918-1973), daughter of Sir Jocelyn, as agent at Classiebawn by Lord Mountbatten. After her death the position was assumed by Aideen Gore-Booth, Dermot James, *op. cit.*, p.317 and Timothy Knatchbull, *From a Clear Blue Sky: Surviving the Mountbatten Bomb.*

141 Dermot James, *op. cit.*, p.137.

142 Another link is the artist Sarah Purser, who completed portraits of Jane L'Estrange, Eva and Constance Gore-Booth and the Sturgis family. See Whyte Auctioneers web archive.

143 See, for example, Dermot James, *op. cit.*, for a detailed account of the issue of his title and the turbulent marriage to Constance.

144 Colonel Malone, *The Russian Republic* (British Socialist Party; London; 1920).

145 Charles Mosley (ed.), *Burke's Peerage and Baronetage, 107th edition.*

146 The 3rd Earl of Erne, John Crichton (1802-1885), changed the spelling of his surname from Creighton, which had been used up to that point.

147 McTernan, *op. cit.*, p.67.

148 See Dermot James, *op. cit.*, pp309-39.

149 Dermot James, *op. cit.*, p.125.

150 Ten thousand acres of land had come into the possession of Sir John Temple of East Sheen, Attorney General of Ireland, forbearer of the viscount, in 1694. Knatchbull, *op. cit.*

151 Charles Mosley (ed.), *Burke's Peerage and Baronetage, 107th edition.*

152 Jules was married with one daughter, Yvonne Smith, who survives to date. In addition, there was a bachelor, Watty Bracken, who was Jules's brother.

153 Colin McKelvie, *The Book of the Woodcock* (London, 1990), p.121.

154 PRONI D4131/C/1/1-10.

155 S.R. Douglas, 'An Experimental Investigation of the Migration of Woodcock Breeding in the West of Ireland', in *Proceedings of the Zoological Soc. of London* (1917), p.159. And 'Further Results of Col. Wilfred Ashley's Experiment on Marking Woodcock Breeding in the West of Ireland', in *Proceedings of the Zoological Soc. of London* (1929), p.271.

156 *Nature,* 8 February 1936.

157 S.R. Douglas, 'Further Results of Col. Wilfred Ashley's Experiment on Marking Woodcock Breeding in the West of Ireland', *Proceedings of the Zoological Soc. of London* (1929), p.271.

158 S.R. Douglas, 'An Experimental Investigation of the Migration of Woodcock Breeding in the West of Ireland', *Proceedings of the Zoological Soc. of London* (1917), pp159-160. The wood is there today and has much the same appearance as described in Douglas's article.

159 Joe MacGowan, *A Bitter Wind* (2009), p.168-70.

160 The Metternichs referred to are not direct descendants of the famous Klemens von Metternich, as his

son Richard, who died in the mid-1890s, had three daughters. They may well be related to Richard's half-brother who took the family title when Richard died.

161 Desmond Norton, 'Stewart and Kincaid, Irish Land Agents in the 1840s', Centre for Economic Research, Working Paper Series, WP02/08, University College Dublin (February, 2002).

162 Knathbull, *op. cit.*, p.40.

163 Charles Mosley (ed.), *Burke's Peerage and Baronetage, 107th edition.*

164 Thomas Troubridge Stubbs of London came to Ireland in the 1830s and settled at Ballyshannon, County Donegal.

165 Richard Wood-Martin in conversation with the author, July 2011.

166 A comprehensive account of the role played by Richard and Elizabeth Wood-Martin is contained in Knathbull, *op. cit.*

167 The lease agreement reached between Lord Mountbatten and Hugh Tunney allowed the Mountbattens to come for the month of August each year, while Tunney picked up the running costs outside this period and paid an annual rent of £3,000, Knatchbull, *op. cit.*, p.36.

168 Knatchbull, *op. cit.*, p.246.

169 Tim Robinson, *Connemara, Listening to the Wind*, p.349.

170 Robinson, *op. cit.*, p.350.

171 See Robinson, *op. cit.*, pp350-1.

172 Dominic Berridge in conversation with the author.

173 Landed Estates Database, Moore Institute, University College Galway (www.landedestates.ie).

174 Dominic Berridge.

175 Robinson, *op. cit.*, p.355.

176 *Ibid.*

177 Anne Chambers, *Ranji: Maharjah of Connemara.*

178 These records are in the possession of the management of the Ballynahinch Castle Hotel.

179 According to William Peard, writing in 1865, 'a new house has been built, which will be opened for the first of May. There are seven bedrooms besides dining and drawing rooms. It has been built expressly for the comfort of anglers.' *A Year of Liberty: Or Salmon Angling in Ireland, from February 1 to November* (London 1867 and 2010).

180 Charles Mosley (ed.), *Burke's Peerage and Baronetage, 107th edition.*

181 *The Times*, Monday 28 June 1920.

182 Catalogue in 2003.

183 Probably William Magee Crozier (1873-1916). He was a barrister working in Belfast. He joined the Royal Inniskilling Fusiliers and was killed on the first day of the Somme, when the Ulster Division was decimated.

184 Robinson, *op. cit.*, pp216-7.

185 Peter Divorty was born in 1881 and in 1901 was at Cahir in County Tipperary. In 1911, he was at Harristown, County Kildare. In both instances he was working as a gamekeeper. National Archives of Ireland, *Census of Population, 1901 and 1911.*

186 Maurice Semple, *Where the River Corrib Flows* (1988), pp105-6.

Chapter 4: Some Shooting Estates in Northern Counties

187 Of the subsidiary titles, Marquess of Hamilton is the courtesy title of the heir apparent, and Viscount Strabane that of his heir apparent. The Dukes of Abercorn also claim the French title of *Duc de Châtellerault*, as heirs male of the 2nd Earl of Arran, who was granted the title in 1548 by Henry II of France.

188 Terence Dooley, *The Decline of the Big House in Ireland* (Dublin, 2001), p.55.

189 Robert Taylor (b. 1877), gamekeeper, National Archives of Ireland, *Census of Population, 1901.*

190 W.R. Millais, Arthur Acland-Hood, J.G. Millais, *et al., The Gun at Home & Abroad, British Game Birds and Wildfowl* Vol.1 (London, 1915), p.253.

191 *Op. cit.*, pp252-3.

192 Charles Mosley (ed.), *Burke's Peerage and Baronetage, 107th edition.*

193 Dermot James, *John Hamilton of Donegal, 1800-1884* (Dublin, 1998), p.20.

194 Dermot James, *op. cit.*, p.1.

195 Dermot James, *op. cit.*, p.23.

196 Dermot James, *op. cit.*, p.247.

197 From Geoff Pocock, *Legion of Frontiersmen, Australian Division* (2002).

198 Reported in Capt. James Hamilton (1913-1987) Obituary, NARGC.

199 This Archdale family was also associated with another country house: Crocknacrieve, Enniskillen, County Fermanagh, a Georgian house built by Capt. John Johnston, whose widow married H.M. Richardson of Rossfad, who, when he inherited the latter estate and part of Rich Hill, handed Crocknacrieve over to his cousin Nicholas Archdale, who added a wing, said to have been built with stone from the old Folliott Castle in Ballinamallard. Sir Edward Archdale sold the property in 1901; in 1921 it was bought by S.C. Loane, whose wife (*née* Barton) was the granddaughter of H.M. Richardson. See Mark Bence-Jones, *A Guide to Irish Country Houses* (London, 1988).

200 At the end of the nineteenth century, the estate had approximately 25,000 acres, but these lands had to be sold, due to the Land Acts, before the First World War. The estate now has less than 1,000 acres of grass and woodland.

201 PRONI, Introduction to Porter Papers (D1390/10, N/19, LR 1/178/1), p.10.

202 See J. & J. A. Venn, *Alumni Cantabrigienses*, Vol.II of X (Cambridge University Press, 1922-1958), p.415.

203 *The Times*, 15 January 2010, Obituary of Richard Blackett Beaumont (1926-2010).

Chapter 5: The West and South-West

204 National Library of Ireland, The Mahon Papers, Collection List 149, p.5.

205 Tadgh MacLochlann, *A Historical Summary of the Parish of Ahascragh, Caltra and Castleblakeny* (1979).

206 Terence Dooley, *Clonbrock: History of a Big House*. Ask About Ireland website, 'The Big House Experience'.

207 The Hon. Arthur Marcus Lowther Crofton (1898-1962) was the second son of Arthur Edward Lother Crofton, 4th Baron Crofton of Mote (1866-1942) and Jessie Castle Hewitson. Arthur Edward was the only son of Charles St George and Theresa Augusta Bunbury-Tighe.

208 See Ann Morrow, *Picnic in a Foreign Land: The Eccentric Lives of the Anglo-Irish* (1989), p.16.

209 Hussey U.H. De Burgh, *The Landowners of Ireland* (Dublin, 1878).

210 Landed Estates Database, Moore Institute, University College Galway.

211 St George Mark, Gordon. 'St George Family: Missing Names'. *Galway Roots: Journal of the Galway Family History Society*, III (1995), pp.117-118. Quoted in Landed Estates Database, Moore Institute, University College Galway.

212 Landed Estates Database, Moore Institute, University College Galway.

213 Excerpt from Workmen's Account Book for Saturday 13 August 1861, M. McNamara and Maura Madden (eds), 'Lords and Lore of Lough Cutra' in *Beagh: A History and Heritage*, p.89.

214 This was subsequently demolished in the 1950s and the cut stone taken to rebuild Bunratty Castle in County Clare. See M. McNamara and Maura Madden, *op. cit.*

215 *Ibid.*, p.90.

216 *Ibid.*, p.91.

217 The Gorts' fortunes were restored following John the 3rd Viscount's second marriage to Mrs Tudor, a wealthy widow who inherited London property and East Cowes Castle from her late husband.

218 De Burgh, *op. cit.*, p.423.

219 John Stacpoole, *Stacpoole: The Owners of a Name, A Family History*, pp95-7.

220 Acland-Hood, *The Gun At Home and Abroad*, p.255.

221 Bridget's children were, according to W.J. Westropp's account of the family, 'a source of great uneasiness, expense and distraction to the legitimate family and nearly procured the disinheritance of Richard Stacpoole by his [half-]brother George in 1822. Though left legacies conditionally on keeping the name Lynch, they took that of Stacpoole and had to be bought out of it'. See Stacpoole, *op. cit.*, pp86-7.

222 Eden Vale and attendant lands were left to Richard's widow. Stacpoole, *op. cit.*, pp102.

223 Obituary contained in the *Clare Journal* and quoted in Stacpoole, *op. cit.*, p.99.

224 Stacpoole, *op. cit.*, p.100.

225 Attacks against hunts became an organised form of agitation in Ireland around the 1800s. For an account, see L.P. Curtis, 'Stopping the Hunt' in C.H.E. Philpin (ed.), *Nationalism and Popular Protest in Ireland* (Cambridge, 1987), pp349-402.

226 See Bernard H. Becker, *Disturbed Ireland: Being the Letters Written during the Winter, 1880-81*.

227 Robert Hallam Studdert, *The Studdert Family: Notes and Records*, p.34.

228 *Ibid.*, p.35.

229 Bunratty was bought in 1725 by Thomas Studdert and it remained (though not as a residence after 1825) the principal seat of the family until 1939, when, on the death without issue of Thomas Studdert, the last direct male heir, it passed to his married sister Mrs Alicia Russell and her descendants. *Ibid.*, pp25-35.

230 The original manuscript of this wonderful and timeless piece, including illustrations, is contained in the Inchiquin Papers at the National Library of Ireland (MS 45,287/1).

231 De Burgh, *op. cit.*, p.230.

232 Lord Maurice Fitzgerald's Game Diary 1876-1900 is in the possession of the author. It records his days at Dromoland, Straffan, Moore Abbey, Glenart, Shelton, Carton, Castle Forbes and Adare.

233 Thomas William Coke (1848-1941) was married to the Hon. Alice White, daughter of Luke White, 2nd Baron Annaly, who was a regular guest at Dromoland. His half-brother, Maj. the Hon. Richard Coke was married to Doreen O'Brien, daughter of Edward, 14th Baron Inchiquin.

234 Robin Vere O'Brien (b. 1842) was second son of Robert O'Brien (1809-1880), who was seriously wounded while shooting on 16 November 1875.

235 MS 45,207/5.

236 'Dickie Adare' refers to Richard Southwell Windham Robert Wyndham-Quin, 6th Earl of Dunraven and Mount-Earl (1887-1965) of Adare Manor, Adare, County Limerick. He was son of Windham Wyndham-Quin, 5th Earl of Dunraven and Mount-Earl; he succeeded to the Earldom on the death of his father.

237 Personal recollection of Countess of Dunraven and Mount-Earl to the author.

238 Colin McKelvie, *The Book of the Woodcock* (1990), p.122.

239 De Burgh, *op. cit.*, p.21.

240 Donal Ryan, 'The Barringtons and Their Tenants', in *The Old Limerick Journal, Barrngtons' Edition*, p.63.

241 Dom Mark Tierney, *Murroe and Bothar*, quoted in Donal Ryan, *op. cit.*, p.66.

242 *Ibid.*, p.65.

243 Mary Rose Barrington-Manuel, 'The Barrington Dogs: Irish Water Spaniels', in *The Old Limerick Journal, Barrington's Edition*, p.120.

244 *Ibid.*, p.121.

245 Daniel O'Neill (1834-1921) was Head Gamekeeper at Glenstal for the last sixteen years of his life. Charles J. Verrent (b. 1862), from Donegal, was a gamekeeper at Kinitty, County Offaly in 1911. National Archives of Ireland, *Census of Population, 1911*.

246 *Ibid.*, p.121.

247 Revd Fletcher Sheridan Le Fanu (1860-1939), a son of William Richard Le Fanu (1816-1894) and Henrietta Victorine Barrington, aunt of Sir Charles Burton Barrington of Glenstal, was a regular Gun at Lissadell.

248 See 'Limerick Merchants of Note', *Limerick Chronicle*, 14 December 1993, pp8-9.

249 W.R. Millais, Arthur Acland-Hood, J.G. Millais, *et al.*, *The Gun at Home and Abroad, British Game Birds and Wildfowl*, Vol.1 (London, 1915), pp255-6.

250 Report of the Proceedings of the Military Inquiry into the Deaths, reported in *The Limerick Chronicle*, Thursday 19 May 1921 and quoted in Kevin Hannan, 'Tragedy at Coolboreen: The Death of Winifred Barrington', *The Old Limerick Journal, Barrington's Edition*, pp109-10.

251 *The Star*, Monday 15 February 1943, p.2.

252 De Burgh, *The Landowners of Ireland*, p.215.

253 PRONI D4151/P/1-9, Game Books of the Earl of Kenmare, County Kerry, 1844-1847. Contains a list of shooting available according to townland by area in acres and stating rental income, in respect of each townland.

254 Terence Dooley, *The Decline of the Big House in Ireland* (Dublin, 2001), p.55.

255 Acland-Hood, *The Gun At Home and Abroad*, p.256.

256 Ralph Payne-Gallwey, *The Fowler in Ireland* (London, 1882), p.228.

257 Colin McKelvie, *The Book of the Woodcock* (London, 1990), p.121.

258 J.B. Drought, *A Sportsman Looks at Eire* (London), pp110-11.

259 Alexander Innes Shand, *Letters from the West of Ireland, 1884* (Edinburgh & London, 1885), p.199. Quoted in Sean Ryan, *Deer Forests, Game Shooting and Landed Estates in the South-West of Ireland, 1840-*

1970 (PhD Thesis, UCC, 2001), p.98.

260 John Ross was Herbert's gamekeeper. See Sean Ryan, *Deer Forests, Game Shooting and Landed Estates in the South-West of Ireland, 1840-1970* (PhD Thesis, UCC, 2001), p.95.

261 Ryan, *op. cit.*, p.109, refers to a Johnny Leahy being a guest of Sir John Fermor Godfrey at a shoot in 1876. He therefore appears to have been a local man. There was also a Daniel Leahy of Scarteen, who was one of Lord Kenmare's bailiffs, who was murdered. Ryan, *op. cit.*, p.115.

262 This is the ancestral home of the author Mark Bence Jones (1930-2010).

263 Millar was probably James Millar, Head Gamekeeper at Muckross; Davidson was probably Thomas Davidson, a new Head Keeper of the Earl of Kenmare, who came from Blaydon on Tyne, County Durham, and O'Connell is likely to have been Sir Maurice O'Connell, a friend of Henry Herbert. See Ryan, *op. cit.*, pp55-107.

264 The problems of violence and disruption are described in some detail in Ryan, *op. cit.*

265 Ryan, *op. cit.*, pp129-33.

Chapter 6: Driven Shooting in County Wicklow: New Wine in Old Bottles

266 The information under this heading is taken principally from Hugh B.C. Pollard, *Game Birds, Rearing Preserving and Shooting* (London, 1929).

267 Richard J. Ussher & Robert Warren, *The Birds of Ireland* (London, 1900), p.233.

268 The Irish Grey Partridge Conservation Trust and Fingal County Council are managing the grey partridge reintroduction project in Fingal.

269 De Burgh, *op. cit.*

270 Granville Proby (1782-1868), 3rd Earl Carysfort, was married to Isabella, daughter of the Hon. Hugh Howard (1761-1840).

271 Lord Maurice FitzGerald's Game Diaries show that he did a regular annual circuit, usually incorporating all or a selection of Dromoland (Inchiquin); Glenart (Carysfort); Moore Abbey, Straffan (Barton's); Lough Cutra (Gough); Carton (Leinster, of which family he was a part); Castle Forbes (Earl of Granard, from which family his wife came); Shelton Abbey (Earl of Wicklow); Moore Abbey (Lord Drogheda), and Emo Court (Portarlington).

272 Terence Dooley, *The Decline of the Big House in Ireland* (Dublin, 2001), p.55.

273 Armstrong of Moyaliff, Estate and Family Papers, Eighteenth-Twentieth Centuries, University of Limerick: Special Collections and Information Services, Glucksman Library. An account of Ballinacor House and the estate given by Capt. William Kemmis a month before his death in 1965 is contained in an article entitled, 'Memoir of an Irish Past', *House and Garden*, May 1965.

274 Keepers' surnames are contained in the shoot records. These have been matched to Census of Population, 1901, information for gamekeepers. In the case of each surname there was only one keeper of that surname recorded in the census. With respect to Bagnall, the only entry is for a Sarah Bagnall, who is described in the census as a retired gamekeeper. She may be the widow of F.W. Bagnall.

275 *Census of Population, 1901*, National Archive of Ireland. Gamekeepers whose names appeared in earlier years in the Ballinacor records are recorded elsewhere in that year. Thus, Donald Sutherland is employed at Prospect, County Wexford, and Elliott Hope (b. 1856) is at Castlecrine in County Clare. Robert James Bracken (b. 1874), who appears at Ballinacor in 1907/1908, was employed at Shelton Abbey in 1901. Finally, there was a Sarah Bagnall (b. 1840) recorded in 1901 as a retired gamekeeper living in Castleblaney, County Monaghan, who, it is presumed, may be the mother of Frederick.

276 An obituary of Michael Twist is carried in the *Shooting Gazette* of August 2006.

277 *Irish Sporting Memories* was published posthumously in 2008.

278 Maurice O'Rorke was a long-standing shooter at the North Slob, extending back to Joshua Nunn's tenure.

279 The shooting at Carton was leased to the McGrath family. On Lord Brockett's death it appears the McGraths moved their shooting interest to Ballinacor.

280 Up until that time, the daily bags were in the range thirty-five to seventy-five Pheasants (and exceptionally above or below that range), judging from the Game Book returns of Lt-Col. W.B.P. Bradish.

281 Ian Morrison was a member of the Bill Fiske's North Slob Shooting Syndicate at this time also. The connection may have been through Bill Bradish.

282 De Burgh, *op. cit.*

283 He lived for a time at the gate lodge of Jubilee Hall in Bray, the home of Mr Charlie Hernon, a founder member of the Ballyarthur Syndicate.

284 Glencormack is the present-day site of Avoca Handweavers Ltd.

285 The cup is presented at the Annual Horse Show of the RDS for the champion three year old.

286 The Game Book covers the years 1894 to 1931 and relates to various locations around Counties Kilkenny, Wicklow, and Wexford. There is a more modern record dating from the early 1980s recording the shooting activities of Mr Paul Smithwick, a grandson of James Joseph.

287 De Burgh, *op. cit.*

288 The present Edward Bayly (b. 1922) recalls being told by his grandfather that he was responsible for installing the drains at Glenart.

289 Charles Mosley (ed.), *Burke's Peerage and Baronetage, 107th edition.*

290 The author's first encounter with driven shooting occurred in 1978, when as a guest of the redoubtable Martin Clancy he attended a shoot at Ballyarthur. The rest is history!

291 Isabella Howard (1783-1836), daughter of the Hon. Hugh Howard (1761-1840), was married to Granville Proby, 3rd Earl of Carysfort (1782-1868).

292 William Howard, 4th Earl of Wicklow (1788-1860) was married to Frances Hamilton, daughter of James, 1st Earl of Abercorn, and Ralph Francis Howard, 7th Earl of Wicklow (1877-1946), was married to Gladys Mary Hamilton, daughter of the 2nd Duke of Abercorn.

293 Diaries of Lady Alice Howard, commencing 1874, National Library of Ireland, MS 3,600.

294 De Burgh, *op. cit.*

295 Both Tim Murray and Michael Phelan were regulars on the North Slob around this time.

296 John's son Neill is the present keeper at Ballyarthur.

297 The record shoot on the Stafford Avenue drive was 750 Pheasants.

298 The family was associated with the island pack of hounds until 190. In addition, there was a private pack at Coollattin at that time which was known formerly as Lord Milton's (a subsidiary title of the Earls of Fitzwilliam), when they were kennelled at Carnew, County Wicklow.

299 The history of the Fitzwilliam family of Wentworth Woodhouse and Coollattin, County Wicklow, is compellingly told in Catherine Bailey's *Black Diamonds: The Rise and Fall of an English Dynasty* (London, 2007).

300 Charles Mervyn Doyne's mother was Sarah Emily Tynte-Pratt, being related to the Tynte's of Tynte Park, County Kildare (this family became involved in the South Slob and its shoot in County Wexford) and the Pratt family, a branch of which resided at Enniscoe House, County Mayo, where there is an organised Woodcock shoot to the present day.

301 Rt Hon. Francis Theophilius Brooke (1851-1920) was related to the Brookes of County Fermanagh.

302 His grandmother on his mother's side was Elizabeth Jane Doyne (d. 1849).

303 Charles Mosley (ed.), *Burke's Peerage and Baronetage, 107th edition.*

Chapter 7: The Wildfowl of Wexford Harbour and Sloblands

304 Sir Ralph Payne-Gallwey, *The Fowler in Ireland* (London, 1882), p.153.

305 P.G. Kennedy, R.F. Ruttledge & C.P. Scroope, *Birds of Ireland* (London, 1954), p.76.

306 Helen Boland & Olivia Crowe, 'An assessment of the distribution range of Greylag (Icelandic-breeding and feral populations) in Ireland', Final Report to the National Parks and Wildlife Service and the Northern Ireland Environment Agency, December 2008.

307 P.G. Kennedy, R.F. Ruttledge & C.P. Scroope, *Birds of Ireland* (London, 1954), p.70.

308 *Ibid.*, p.149.

309 For an account, see Nicholas Furlong, 'A History of Land Reclamation in Wexford Harbour', *Journal of the Old Wexford Society*, Vol.2 (1969). A condensed version is contained in D. Rowe & Christopher J. Wilson (eds), *High Skies and Low Lands, an Anthology of the Wexford Slobs and Harbour* (Wexford, 1996).

310 The reclamation resulted in a 50 per cent decrease in the inter-tidal area in the harbour and a 10 per cent reduction in the tidal volume. This change in tidal volume of the estuary resulted in changes in the flow and hence the pattern of sediment deposition at the entrance to the harbour. This resulted in the failure and recession of 3.5km of the spit, with accompanying large-scale recession of the shoreline at the northern end of the Strand. 'Rosslare, Wexford County (Ireland), Eurosian Case Study', Paul Sistermans, Odelinde Nieuwenhuiss, DHV Group, the Netherlands.

311 Descendants of Boyd are to be found shooting on the North Slob during Joshua Nunn's tenure of the shooting rights there.

312 D. Rowe & Christopher Wilson, *op. cit.*, p.97.

313 It appears the Scottish-led syndicate proposing the undertaking envisaged not only the reclamation of Wexford Harbour but also Lady's Island Lake, Tachumshane Lake, Ballyteige, Bannow, and the strands of Dunbrody, as well as places in County Waterford. The impetus to such a grand design appears to be an earlier Act of Parliament, which provided government aid for reclamation of wasteland in Ireland.

314 D. Rowe & Eithne Scallan, *op. cit.*, p.572.

315 D. Rowe & Christopher Wilson, *op. cit.*, p.86.

316 The 1846 Act was repealed by the Wexford Harbour Embankment Act 1852, which replaced the Wexford Harbour Improvement Company with the Wexford Harbour Embankment Company. The latter recognised that 'the Powers and Duties given to or imposed upon the said Company by the said Act are in many respects vague and indefinite and by reason thereof great difficulty has been and is experienced in carrying into effect the provisions of the said Act … it is expedient that new arrangements should be made for effective and expeditious execution of the purposes of the said Act so far as the same have not been effected'.

317 Rowe & Wilson, *op. cit.*, p.86.

318 This project appears to have been undertaken by Redmond and Dargan. A map contained in the estate papers and correspondence of James Agg Gardner of Cheltenham in relation to the sale of Redmond's portion of the South Slob in the Landed Estates Court in 1866, shows the owners to be John Redmond (1,165 acres) and William Dargan (891 acres), with a balance of 198 acres comprising water and drains which is not attributed. See Gloucestershire Archives, D1950/E8 1845-1867, Prospectuses, Reports and Balance Sheets of Railway and Other Companies: (vii) Wexford Harbour Improvement Company including sales particulars, Act of Parliament, correspondence, etc., addressed to Thos Fortescue of Cheltenham, 1866-67 (14).

319 See Rowe & Wilson, *op. cit.*, p.88.

320 Landed Estates Court, Ireland, 'Rental, Maps and Particulars of a Valuable Fee Simple Estate, Sold by Auction in five lots', 12 July 1866. Estate Papers and correspondence of James Agg Gardner of Cheltenham, Gloucestershire Archives: D1950/E8 1845-1867, Prospectuses, Reports and Balance Sheets of Railway and Other Companies: (vii) Wexford Harbour Improvement Company including sales particulars, Act of Parliament, correspondence, etc., addressed to Thos Fortescue of Cheltenham, 1866-67 (14).

321 It is believed that Ardilaun acquired his holding from Richard Richards of Ardtramon (Jack Cullen, recollection).

322 Clonattin was owned by the Fitzwilliams of Coollattin Estate in County Wicklow, so possibly it was the Fitzwilliams who actually held the title.

323 Memorandum of Agreement re: North Slobs, 2 June 1906, Meldon & Co. Solicitors, 14 Upper Ormonde Quay, Dublin. It appears Grogan conveyed lands to Bradshaw on 3 May 1888 and vice versa on 15 August 1906. Grogan acquired the lands in a number of conveyances from the Wexford Harbour Improvement Company on 3 August 1860 and 21 June 1862 (Maylor Collotton, private papers).

324 Deed of Mutual Agreement, in reference to the Maintenance and Drainage of the North Slob Lands, M.J. O'Connor & Co. Solicitors, 2 George Street, Wexford, 26 June 1919.

325 Landed Estates Database, Moore Institute, NUI Galway.

326 'The Life and Times of Fintan M. O'Connor', transcript of an autobiographical tape, 19 March 1961.

327 There is a field still known as the racecourse field to this day.

328 In a case reported in *The Irish Times* of Wednesday 9 October 1889, 'Wexford Coursing Club v. Captain Balman and Lt C.O. Shipley', both of the Shropshire Regiment, stationed in Wexford at the time, there is mention of a gamekeeper on the North Slob by the name of Thomas Murphy. M.J. was acting for the plaintiffs.

329 Untitled manuscript, O'Connor family.

330 Referred to in untitled manuscript, O'Connor family.

331 *Ibid.*

332 *Ibid.*

333 Receipt from M.J. O'Connor, Solicitor, from George Colloton. (Private papers, Maylor Colloton.)

334 John acquired Begerin House in 1889, probably from the Hoey family. He died by the channel, close to Begerin House.

335 Maylor Colloton.

336 *Ibid.*

337 Referred to in untitled manuscript, O'Connor family.

338 Conveyance, dated 2 December 1965, between Stafford Estates Ltd, Paul Quay, Wexford, Mr Redmond Gallagher, South Sloblands, Wexford and William Grant Fiske (Junior), Barnahask, Curracloe, Wexford.

339 Jack Cullen to Dominic Berridge.

340 Lt-Col. W.B.P. Bradish, North Slob Shooting Log, 1924-1967.

341 See 'Nunn of St Margarets & Castlebridge', in A. Kavanagh & Rory Murphy, *The Wexford Gentry*, Vol.1 (Wexford, 1994).

342 Warren, Stanley, 'The Nunns of Castlebridge', *Castlebridge Magazine: The Bridge*, Vol.2, No.1 (Christmas 2006).

343 He took over J.B. Pettigrew's premises, known as 'the field'. He also purchased premises at Gibson Lane and the West Gate, in Wexford Town, to complete Nunn's Wexford Branch. (Warren, *op.cit.*)

344 William Bolton's third daughter, Alice Nunn, married William Toole of Curracloe House, which was to become home to the Fiske family in about 1969. The Tooles and John Colloton sold land at Curracloe for a forestation in 1937, which today is known as Curracloe Plantation. The area was afforested for protection against erosion, as concerns mounted following the loss of Rosslare Fort in 1925.

345 See pp 286-7.

346 Patrick Bradish, recollections.

347 Bridget Bradish, recollections.

348 Conversation with Bridget Bradish, 25 March 2011.

349 *The Irish Times*, Friday 17 July 1970, Report of Case.

350 Joshua was a keen salmon angler on the Slaney and to the west of Ireland. *The Echo*, in 1985, records that Joshua Nunn caught 156lb of salmon on the Slaney at Ballycarney. It goes on to say that he caught two salmon weighing 30lb on one day, while the smallest fish he caught was 15lb. His favourite pack of hounds seems to have been that which was kept at Hollymount House, near Galbally, nothing of which remains today. It was owned by Leslie Carthy, Master of the Screen Harriers. (Warren, *op. cit.*)

351 Indeed, during times when Nunns were absent, for instance on holiday, the beautiful girls would dress in May Nunn's latest eveningwear and play about the downstairs room, where the young men of the village would vie for places at windows that would enable them to gaze in wonder at the spectacle inside! (Warren, *op. cit.*)

352 Warren, *op.cit.*

353 Richard J. Ussher & Robert Warren, *op. cit.*, p.175.

354 Kennedy, Ruttledge & Scroope, *op. cit.*, p.79.

355 Interestingly, it was W.R. Grace & Co. that bought Urney Chocolates, the family owned business of the Gallagher family which owned the South Slob in County Wexford.

356 Story related to author, 22 March 2011, by Ben Jellett, surviving son of Hewett.

357 Arthur Claud Spencer Chichester, 4th Baron Templemore, KCVO, OBE, DSO (1880-1953), see Classiebawn.

358 See Art Kavanagh & Rory Murphy, *The Wexford Gentry, Vol.1* (1994), p.54, which contains a 1927 photograph taken at Wexford Foxhounds Point-to-Point and shows Lakin, Boyd and Roche together.

359 D. Rowe & Eithne Scallan, *House of Wexford* (2004), p.891.

360 *Ibid.*, p.591.

361 R.F. Scott, *Scott's Last Expedition: The Journals of Captain R.F. Scott.*

362 T.E. Jellicoe (1999). Lord Edward Arthur Alexander Shackleton. 15 July 1911-22 September 1994: Elected F.R.S., 1989. *Biographical Memoirs of Fellows of the Royal Society* 45: 485.

363 Art Kavanagh & Rory Murphy, *The Wexford Gentry, Vol.1* (1994), p.145.

364 Hugh Montgomery-Massingberd (ed.), *Burke's Irish Family Records* (London, 1976), p.178.

365 Art Kavanagh & Rory Murphy, *The Wexford Gentry, Vol.1* (1994), p.68.

366 Richard Cavendish, 'Publication of the Guinness Book of Records: August 27th, 1955', *History Today* (August 2005).

367 She was a granddaughter of Sir Frederic Hughes.

368 *The Irish Times*, 13 August 1968, p.14.

369 His shooting rights were held through a company called the Irish Wildfowl Conservation Company.

370 *The Irish Times*, 16-20 July 1970.

371 George Woodbyrne promptly sold his acquired right to a party of three comprising: Des McEvoy, principal at solicitors J.A. Sinnott, Enniscorthy, which had represented George; Tom Hassett, and Jack

Devereaux, two businessmen of Wexford Town. This consortium has exercised its rights to date.

372 In fact, a contract had been entered into between Fiske and the Irish Wildfowl Conservation Company (Bradish's vehicle). Letter, 13 Eanáir 1977, Department of Lands, Forest and Wildlife Service to Messrs M.J. O'Connor & Co. Solr.

373 The acquisition was principally by way of purchase. However, the area of Raven Plantation was held by Fiske under lease from the Minister for Lands, which was due to expire in 1974. The arrangement incorporated a renewal of the lease on these lands coterminous with the lease on other lands being offered to Fiske.

374 *The Irish Times*, Monday 6 March 1972.

375 Greenland White-fronted geese were removed from the Open Seasons Order in 1982 and there has been no shooting of them since then.

376 Shooting rights on the North Slob were the subject of two contracts dated 6 July 1970 between the Irish Wildfowl Conservation Company and Mr W.G. Fiske Senior, continued in the name of Mr W.G. Fiske, Junior, Begerin Isle Estate, Wexford. *Memorandum of the Department of Tourism, Fisheries and Forestry, Forest and Wildlife Service*, 30 September 1986.

377 There is a letter of 20 July 1999 from Fiske to the department stating he wasn't going to take their treatment of him sitting down.

378 Meldons were certainly owners on the North Slob in 1906. See *Memorandum of Agreement re North Slobs, 2 June 1906*, Meldon & Co. Solicitors, 14 Upper Ormonde Quay, Dublin. See also Appendix 1.

379 *Landed Estates Database*, Moore Institute, University College Galway.

380 In 1926, James M. Meldon and John Meldon bought Rowesmount House, Rowestowne, Drinagh (overlooking the South Slob), from Jim Hayes of Enniscorthy for £1,400. The owners are named also as the company of Meldons and Miss Tynt. See D. Rowe & Eithne Scallan, *op. cit.*, p.898.

381 She is aunt of Sir Robert William Davis Goff, 4th Baronet (b. 1955), owner of Balinacor Estate, Rathdrum, County Wicklow.

382 From *The Life and Times of Fintan M. O'Connor*; Transcript of an autobiographical tape, 19 March 1961.

383 Karen Nolan, *Sweet Memories – the Story of Urney Chocolates* (2010), p.19.

384 Payne-Gallwey, *The Fowler in Ireland* (London 1882), pp24-7.

385 Larry Duggan recalls that the grave was opened, many years later for a funeral of a Wickham. When the grave was opened three skulls were unearthed. That of Pat Wickham was easily identified for it was riddled with shot.

386 Kavanagh & Murphy, *op. cit.*, Vol. 2.

387 Payne-Gallwey, *The Fowler in Ireland* (London, 1882), p.159.

388 Jimmy Allen was a skilled carver of duck and goose decoys from solid wood. A number of examples of his work remain and are in the possession of John Jobson, son of Robert Jobson (1916-1999).

389 See Gerard Kehoe, 'Rosslare Fort and its People', *Journal of the Old Wexford Society*, Vol. 4, pp43-52, and Vol. 5, pp39-47.

390 David Rowe, 'Punt Gunning', in D. Rowe & Christopher Wilson, *op. cit.*, p.130.

391 A wintering flock of around 5,000 can be found most years on Wexford Harbour.

392 *Wexford Independent*, 9 November 1853.

393 John Jobson in conversation with the author.

394 The sixth bird was shot by the Hon. David Brabazon, brother of John Robson's wife, Lady Lavinia Brabazon.

395 Jonathan Ruffer, *The Big Shots: Edwardian Shooting Parties* (London 1998), p.47.

Bibliography

Manuscripts

Clare County Library, Local Studies Centre
Henn, Francis Robert, 'The Henn family of Paradise, County Clare, Ireland: Notes compiled by Francis Robert Henn' (2008).

Cork City and County Archive
Bennett Papers.

National Archives of Ireland
Census of Population, 1901 and 1911.

National Library of Ireland
Estate Papers: Bruen Papers; Clonbrock Papers; Crofton Papers; Headford Papers; Inchiquin Papers: Game Books of the Lords Inchiquin; Mahon of Castlegar Papers: Game Books of Henry Mahon; O'Hara of Annaghmore Papers.

National University of Ireland, Galway
Landed Estates Database, Moore Institute.

Gloucestershire Archives, Alvin Street, Gloucester
Estate Papers and Correspondence of James Agg Gardner of Cheltenham, D1950/E8, 1845-1867, Prospectuses, Reports and Balance Sheets of Railway and Other Companies: (vii) Wexford Harbour Improvement Company Including Sales Particulars, Act of Parliament, Correspondence, etc., Addressed to Thos Fortescue of Cheltenham, 1866-67. (14)

Public Records Office, Northern Ireland
Abercorn Papers; Lissadell Papers, Game Books of Sir Henry and Sir Jocelyn Gore-Booth; Kenmare Papers, Game Books of the Earls of Kenmare; Crom Castle Papers;
Brookeborough Papers, Game Books of Arthur Douglas Brooke and Sir Basil Brooke.

Game Books, Game Registers and Game Records in Private Collections (classified by reference to the estate of origin)
Adare Manor, Adare, County Limerick, Game Books.
Annaghmore Manor, Collooney, County Sligo, 1904 to date.
Ashford Castle, Cong, County Galway, Game Records, 1886-1932.
Ballinacor, County Wicklow, Game Books of William Kemmis, 1864-1891, and of the Estate of the Kemmis Family at Ballinacor, 1894-1916 and 1918-1927.
Ballyarthur, County Wicklow, Game Books of Edward Bayly, 1967 to date.
Brown Hall, Ballintra, County Donegal, Game Books of the Estate and Personal Game Books of Capt. James Montgomery Hamilton.
Classiebawn Castle, County Sligo, Game Book of Jules Bracken, 1912-1959.
Coollattin, County Wicklow, Game Register of the Fitzwilliam Estate, extract thereof relating to 1901-1905.
Eden Vale, County Clare, Game Book of Richard Stacpoole, 1909-1925.

Enniscoe House, Castlehill, Ballina, County Mayo, Game Book, 1955 to date.

Glenstal, County Limerick, Game Records of Sir Croker Barrington and of Sir Charles Barrington, 1853-1868 and 1882-1905 respectively.

Glenasmole, County Wicklow. *Game Book of Charles Cobbe (d. 1886)*, 1846 (Glenasmole) – 1885 and continued in *The Sportsman's Game Book* 1885 - 1906 (none from 1901 to 1905). Covers both Glenasmole and Newbridge House County Dublin. *Shooting record* kept by Tommy Cobbe for each season from November 1933/March 1934 - 1945/1946. Continued by in *Game Book, Fowling Record and Accounts*: for seasons from 1946-47 to 1983-84. From season 1967-68 details are kept just of dates and numbers of what shot, and where.

Greenpark, County Mayo, Game Register of Ernest Henry Knox, 1895-1919.

Hazelwood, County Sligo, Game Diary of the Hon. John A. Wynne, 1829-1833.

Johnstown Castle, Wexford, Game Diary of Sir Maurice FitzGerald, 1876-1900.

Kilcreene Lodge, County Kilkenny, Game Books of the Smithwick Family, 1895 to date.

Lisnabrucka Lodge, Ballynahinch, County Galway, Game Book of Arthur V. Wilcox, 1898-1904.

Lough Bray, County Wicklow, Game Book of the Honourable A.E. Guinness, 1912-1933.

Lough Cutra, County Clare, Game Record of Gen. Gough, 1890-1895.

Markree Castle, Collooney, County Sligo, Game Book of Brig.-Gen. Richard Joshua Cooper (1860-1938) and descendants to the present day.

Muckross Abbey, Killarney, County Kerry, Game Books of Edward Amphlett, 1878-1880; Jan.-Feb. 1883; Muckross and Kenmare, 1883-1886.

North Slob, Wexford, Personal Game Books of Lt-Col. W.B.P. Bradish, 1935-1993; Game Records, William Grant Fiske, 1968-2002.

Screebe House, Connemara, County Galway, Game Books, 1880-1928.

Temple House, Ballymote, County Sligo, Game Books, 1895 to date.

The Irish Fly Fishing and Game Shooting Museum, Attanagh, County Laois
Game Council of Ireland: minutes of meetings held in the 1960s along with associated reports, records and correspondence with the St Hubert Club of Ireland.

University of Limerick: Special Collections and Information Services, Glucksman Library
Armstrong of Moyaliff, Estate and Family Papers, Eighteenth to Twentieth Centuries.

Contemporary Published Works

Acland-Hood, Maj. Arthur, *Shooting: Notes on Shooting in the British Isles* (London, 1909).

Akroyd, Charles K., *A Veteran Sportsman's Diary* (Inverness, 1926).

Becker, Bernard H., *Disturbed Ireland: Being the Letters Written during the Winter 1880-81* (1881, reprint London, 2009).

Broomhall, W., *The Country Gentleman's Estate Book, 1922* (London, 1922).

Crawfurd Oswald (ed.), *A Year of Sport and Natural History* (London, 1895).

De Burgh, Hussey, U.H., *The Landowners of Ireland* (Dublin, 1878).

Dorchester, Lord, *Sport: Foxhunting and Shooting* (London, 1935).

Drought, J.B., *A Sportsman Looks at Eire* (Hutchinson, London).

Gladstone, Hugh S., *Record Bags and Shooting Records* (London, 1922 & 1930).

Le Fanu, T.P., *Seventy Years of Irish Life* (London, 1893).

Lewis, Samuel, *Topographical Dictionary of Ireland* (1837).

Maxwell, W.H., *Wild Sports of the West* (London, 1832).

Millais, W.R., Arthur Acland-Hood, J.G. Millais, *et al.*, *The Gun at Home and Abroad, British Game Birds and Wildfowl*, Volume 1 (London, 1915).

O'Brien, Sir Edward, *Directions for a Day's Shooting at Dromoland* (*c.* 1830, reprint 1986).

Payne-Gallwey, Ralph, *The Fowler in Ireland* (London, 1882).

Peard, William, *A Year of Liberty: Or Salmon Angling in Ireland, from February 1 to November* (London, 1867 & 2010).

Pollard, Hugh, B.C., *Game Birds, Rearing Preserving and Shooting* (London, 1929).

Rait, R.S., *The Story of an Irish Property* (Oxford, 1908).

Scott, Peter, *Morning Flight: A Book of Wildfowl* (London, 1935).

Scott, Peter, *Wild Chorus* (London, 1938).

Shand, Alexander Innes, *Letters from the West of Ireland, 1884* (Edinburgh & London, 1885).

Thompson, William, *Natural History of Ireland* (1845).

Thom's Directory, *Dublin Street Directory* (1862).

Thornhill, Richard Badham, *Sporting Directory* (London, 1804).

Ussher, Richard J., & Robert Warren, *The Birds of Ireland* (London, 1900).

Ussher, Richard J., 'Snipe and Woodcock in Ireland', in De Visme Shaw, L.H., *Snipe and Woodcock: Fur, Feather and Fin Series* (London, 1904).

Walford's County Families of the United Kingdom (London, 1909).

Journals, Periodicals and Newspapers

Alexander, W.B., *The Woodcock in the British Isles* (Reprinted from IBIS).

Amderson, William, 'On the Reclaimed Lands at Wexford Harbour and the Machinery Employed in Draining Them', Proceedings of the Institution of Civil Engineers of Ireland (10 December 1862).

Barrington Edition, *The Old Limerick Journal*, No.24 (Winter, 1988).

Bary, Valerie M., 'The Hunting Diaries (1863-1872) of Sir John Fermor Godfrey of Kilcoleman Abbey, County Kerry', *The Irish Anscestor*, Vol.XI, No.2 (1979).

Bary, Valerie M., 'The Hunting Diaries (1873-1881) of Sir John Fermor Godfrey of Kilcoleman Abbey, County Kerry', *The Irish Anscestor*, Vol.XII, Nos 1 & 2 (1980).

Bowe, Patrick, 'Irish Sporting Lodges', *Journal of the Irish Georgian Society, Irish Architectural and Decorative Studies*, Vol.VII (2004).

Campbell, Peter, 'Driven Woodcock Shoots at Cong', *Irish Forestry*, Vol.41, No.1 (1984).

Douglas, S.R., 'An Experimental Investigation of the Migration of Woodcock Breeding in the West of Ireland', *Proceedings of the Zoological Soc. of London* (1917), p.159.

Douglas S. R., 'Further Results of Col. Wilfred Ashley's Experiment on Marking Woodcock Breeding in the West of Ireland', *Proceedings of the Zoological Soc. of London* (1929), p.271.

Kehoe, Gerard, 'Rosslare Fort and its People', *Journal of the Old Wexford Society*, Vol.4, pp43-52 and Vol.5, pp39-47.

Malone, Col., *The Russian Republic* (British Socialist Party; London, 1920).

Moran, Gerard, 'Landlord and Tenant Relations in Ireland: Sir Arthur Guinness and His Estate at Ashford Castle, 1868-1882', *Cathar na Mart*, Vol.10, No.1 (1990).

Norton, Desmond, 'Stewart and Kincaid, Irish Land Agents in the 1840s', *Centre for Economic Research, Working Paper Series*, WP02/08 (University College Dublin, February 2002).

Old Limerick Journal: Barrington's Edition, Vol.24 (Winter, 1988).

Ryan, Sean, 'Deer Forests, Game Shooting and Landed Estates in the South-West of Ireland, 1840-1970', PhD Thesis, UCC (2001).

Perceval, Philip D., 'Observations on the Movements of Woodcock', in *Irish Naturalist*, Vol.22, No.11 (Nov. 1913).

Thomson, A. Landsbrough, 'The Migration of British and Irish Woodcock', *British Birds*, Vol.23 (1929).

Warren, Stanley, 'The Nunns of Castlebridge', *Castlebridge Magazine: The Bridge*, Vol.2, No.1 (Christmas 2006).

Westropp, Thomas Johnson, 'The Massy Family', *Journal of the Royal Society of Antiquaries of Ireland*, Ser.6 Vol.V., pp152-155 (1915).

Country Life
Court Circular
The Field
Irish Field
Madame
The Times
The Irish Times
Stream and Field
Tatler
Vanity Fair
Westminster Gazette

Secondary Sources

Back, D.H.L., *Great Irish Gunmakers: Messrs Rigby, 1760-1869* (Norwich, 1992).

Bailey, Catherine, *Black Diamonds: The Rise and Fall of an English Dynasty* (London, 2007).

Bence-Jones, Mark, *Twilight of the Ascendancy* (London, 1987).

Bence-Jones, Mark, *A Guide to Irish Country Houses* (London, 1988).

Bickerdyke, John, *Wild Sports in Ireland* (Ireland, 2007).

Burke's Peerage Ltd, *Burke's Irish Family Records* (London, 1976).

Chambers, Anne, *Ranji: Maharaja of Connemara* (Dublin, 2002).

Curtis, L.P., 'Stopping the Hunt' in C.H.E. Philpin (ed.), *Nationalism and popular protest in Ireland* (Cambridge, 1987), pp349-402.

Dakers, Caroline, *Clouds the Biography of a Country House* (New Haven & London, 1993).

Donohoe, Tony, *Addergoole: Its Land and People* (Mayo, 2000).

Dooley, Terence, *The Decline of the Big House in Ireland* (Dublin, 2001).

Duffy, Peter, *The Killing of Major Denis Mahon: A Mystery of Old Ireland* (2007).

Everett, Nigel, *Wild Gardens: The Lost Demesnes of Bantry Bay* (Hafod Press, 2000).

Everett, Nigel, *A Landlord's Garden: Derreen Demesne, County Kerry* (Kerry, 2001).

FitzGerald, Olda, *Ashford Castle: Through the Centuries* (Dublin, 2000).

Ffolliott, Rosemary, *The Pooles of Mayfield and Other Irish Families* (Dublin, 1958).

Garrett, Richard J., *Irish Gunmakers* (Hong Kong, 2008).

Hajba, Anna-Maria, *Houses of Cork*, Vol.I (Cork, 1986).

Hamilton, John Stewart, *My Times and Other Times* (Donegal, 1950).

Henn, T.R., *Five Arches with 'Philoctetes' and Other Poems* (Oxford, 1980).

Irish Guards, Members of, *Irish Guards, the First 100 Years* (London, 1999).

James, Dermot, *John Hamilton of Donegal, 1800-1884* (Dublin, 1998).

James, Dermot, *The Gore-Booths of Lissadell* (Ireland, 2004).

Kavanagh, A. & Rory Murphy, *The Wexford Gentry*, Vols 1 & 2 (Wexford, 1994).

Kennedy, P.G., Ruttledge, R.F., & Scroope C.F., *Birds of Ireland* (London, 1954).

Knight of Glin & Hugh W.L. Weir, *House of Clare* (Ireland, 1986).

Knatchbull, T., *From a Clear Blue Sky, Surviving the Mountbatten Bomb* (London, 2009).

MacGowan, Joe, *A Bitter Wind* (Aoelous Publications, 2009).

McGinley, Michael, *The La Touche Family in Ireland* (2004).

McKelvie, C.L., *The Book of the Woodcock* (London 1990).

McKelvie, C.L., *Snipe and Woodcock: Sport and Conservation* (London, 1996).

Lyons, Mary Cecelia, *Incumbered Estates* (Ireland, 1993).

McNamara, M. & Maura Madden (eds), 'Lords and Lore of Lough Cutra' in *Beagh: A History and Heritage* (1995).

McTernan, John C., *Sligo, The Light of Bygone Days*: Vol.1, *Houses of Sligo and Associated Families*; Vol.2, *Chronicles of Sixty Families Past and Present* (Sligo, 2009).

Marson, Peter, *Belmore: Lowry-Corry Families of Castle Coole, 1646-1913* (Belfast, 2007).

Martin, Brian P., *The Great Shoots, Britain's Best, Past and Present* (London, 1987).

Morrow, Ann, *Picnic in a Foreign Land: The Eccentric Lives of the Anglo Irish* (London, 1989).

Mullins, Noel, *Horse Tales and Hunt Talk* (2006).

Musche, P.B., *Gentlemen and Poachers: the English Game Laws, 1671-1831* (Cambridge, 1981).

Nolan, Karen, *Sweet Memories, the Story of Urney Chocolates* (2010).

Norton, Desmond, *Landlords, tenants, famine: the business of an Irish land agency in the 1840s* (Dublin, 2006).

O'Brien, Grainne R., *These My Friends and Forebears: The O'Briens of Dromoland, Whitegate, County Clare* (1991).

O'Dwyer, Raymond, *The Irish Red Setter, Its History Character and Training* (Cork, 2007).

O'Gorman, F. & Wymes, Edna (eds), *The Future of Irish Wildlife – A Blueprint for Development* (An Foras Taluntais (The Agricultural Institute), 1973).

O'Loughlin, Michael, *Families of County Clare* (1996).

Purser, Michael, *Jellett, O'Brien, Purser and Stokes: Seven Generations, Four Families* (Dublin, 2004).

Ruffer, Jonathan, *The Big Shots: Edwardian Shooting Parties* (London, 1998).

Rowe, D. & Wilson, Christopher J., *High Skies, Low Lands* (Wexford, 1996).

Rowe, David & Eithne Scallan, *Houses of Wexford* (2004).

Somerville-Large, Peter, *The Irish Country House: A Social History* (1995).

Robinson, Tim, *Connemara: Listening to the Wind* (Dublin, 2006).

Semple, Maurice, *Reflections on Lough Corrib* (Galway, 1973).

Semple, Maurice, *By The Corribside* (Galway, 1984).

Smith, Michael, *Captain Francis Crozier – Last Man Standing?* (2006).

Stacpoole, John, *Stacpoole: The Owners of a Name: A Family History* (Printed for Private Circulation, Aukland, 1991).

Studdert, Robert Hallam, *The Studdert Family: Notes and Records* (For Private Circulation, Three Candles, Dublin, 1960).

Trench, Charles Chenevix, *The Poacher and the Squire: A History of Poaching and Game Preservation in England* (1967).

Trotmann, Colin, *Woodcock: Fieldcraft and Quarry* (London, 2010).

Twist, Michael F., *Irish Sporting Memories* (Downpatrick, 2008).

Twist, Michael F., *The Glory Days* (London, 2001).

Westropp, George, *The Westropp Family, 1250-2000* (London, 2000).

West, Trevor, *Malting the Barley: John H. Bennett, The Man and His Firm – 200 Years of Malting Barley in Ballinacurra* (2006).

Index